THEORIES OF PROPERTY
Aristotle to the Present

Essays by

C. B. Macpherson
William Mathie
David Daube
Susan Treggiari
Anthony Parel
James Tully
John Pocock
James Moore

James MacAdam
Nannerl Keohane
Douglas Long
John Gray
E. K. Hunt
Tom Settle
Thomas Flanagan
Shadia Drury

Edited by

Anthony Parel and Thomas Flanagan

Published for
The Calgary Institute for the Humanities
by
Wilfrid Laurier University Press

Canadian Cataloguing in Publication Data

Main entry under title:

Theories of property

"The essays in this book began as contributions to a
Summer Workshop arranged by the Calgary Institute
for the Humanities, and held at the University of
Calgary from July 7 to 14, 1978."

Bibliography: p.
Includes index.
ISBN 0-88920-081-5 pa.

1. Property — Addresses, essays, lectures.
I. Macpherson, Crawford B., 1911-   II. Parel,
Anthony, 1926-   III. Flanagan, Thomas, 1944-
IV. Calgary Institute for the Humanities.

HB701.T54   323.4'6'08   C79-094344-1

TABLE OF CONTENTS

FOREWORD AND ACKNOWLEDGMENTS. v

ABOUT THE AUTHORS. vi

EDITORS' NOTE. viii

Property As Means Or End. 3
    C. B. Macpherson, University of Toronto

Property In The Political Science Of Aristotle. 13
    W. Mathie, Brock University

Fashions And Idiosyncracies In The Exposition Of The
Roman Law Of Property. 35
    D. Daube, University of California, Berkeley

Sentiment And Property: Some Roman Attitudes. 53
    S. Treggiari, University of Ottawa

Aquinas' Theory Of Property. 89
    A. Parel, University of Calgary

The Framework Of Natural Rights In Locke's Analysis Of Property:
A Contextual Reconstruction. 115
    J. Tully, McGill University

The Mobility Of Property And The Rise Of
Eighteenth-Century Sociology. 141
    J. G. A. Pocock, Johns Hopkins University

A Comment On Pocock. 167
    J. Moore, Concordia University

Rousseau: The Moral Dimensions Of Property. 181
    J. MacAdam, Trent University

Rousseau On Life, Liberty And Property: A Comment On MacAdam. . . 203
    N. O. Keohane, Stanford University

Bentham On Property. 221
    D. G. Long, University of Western Ontario

John Stuart Mill On The Theory Of Property. 257
    J. N. Gray, Jesus College, Oxford University

Marx's Theory Of Property And Alienation. 283
    E. K. Hunt, University of California, Riverside

The Ground Of Morals And The Propriety Of Property. 319
    T. Settle, University of Guelph

iv

F. A. Hayek On Property And Justice. 335
    T. E. Flanagan, University of Calgary

Robert Nozick And The Right To Property. 361
    S. B. Drury, University of Calgary

BIBLIOGRAPHY. 381

INDEX. 391

FOREWORD AND ACKNOWLEDGMENTS

The essays in this book began as contributions to a Summer Workshop arranged by the Calgary Institute for the Humanities, and held at the University of Calgary from July 7 to 14, 1978. The Institute, which was founded by the University in 1976 for the encouragement of humanistic studies, has held such conferences each summer as a part of its programme of research.

We wish to acknowledge with gratitude the organisational work of those who arranged the meetings: Egmont Lee, the Institute's Acting Director during the first six months of 1978; our two editors, who were also co-chairmen of the conference; and Mrs. Lil Slattery of the University's Conference Office, whose contributions were far too numerous to mention in detail.

We wish to express thanks to the Social Sciences and Humanities Research Council of Canada for a grant-in-aid towards the costs of the workshop; and to thank the Faculties of Continuing Education, Management, and Social Sciences for financial support.

We are grateful to the editors for their labours in assembling the text, and to Gerry Dyer for the heavy work of preparing the final manuscript from successive drafts.

Terence Penelhum,
Director

ABOUT THE AUTHORS

C. B. Macpherson received his Ph.D. in Political Science from the University of London in 1935. He has long been Professor of Political Science at the University of Toronto. Among his books, *The Political Theory of Possessive Individualism* (1962), *Democratic Theory* (1973), and *Property: Mainstream and Critical Positions* (1978) are particularly relevant to the subject of this volume. He is a Fellow of the Royal Society of Canada and of the Royal Historical Society of England.

William Mathie received his Ph.D. in Political Science from the University of Chicago in 1974. After teaching at Waterloo, Dalhousie, and the University of Alberta, he is now Associate Professor of Political Science at Brock University. He has published articles on Aristotle and Hobbes, and on George Grant.

David Daube obtained the degree of Dr. Jur. from the University of Göttingen in 1932 and a Ph.D. from Cambridge in 1936. After being Regius Professor of Civil Law and a Fellow of All Souls' College at Oxford, he is now Professor of Law at the University of California (Berkeley) and Honorary Professor of History at the University of Konstanz.

Susan Treggiari was educated at Oxford, receiving the B. Litt. in 1967. She is presently Associate Professor of Classical Studies at the University of Ottawa. She is the author of *Roman Freedmen during the Late Republic* (1969).

Anthony Parel was awarded a Ph.D. in Political Science from Harvard University in 1963. He is now Professor and Head of the Department of Political Science at the University of Calgary. He has edited *The Political Calculus: Essays on Machiavelli's Philosophy* (1972) and *Calgary Aquinas Studies* (1978), and is now writing a book on Machiavelli.

James Tully received a Ph.D. from Trinity College, Cambridge in 1977. His dissertation will be published soon by Cambridge University Press under the title of *A Discourse on Property: Locke in the Natural Law Tradition*. He is Assistant Professor of Political Science at McGill University.

John Pocock was educated in New Zealand and England, and received a Ph.D. at Cambridge in 1952. After various appointments in both History and Political Science at universities in New Zealand, England, and the United States, he is now Harry C. Black Professor of History at the Johns Hopkins University. His books include *The Ancient Constitution and the Feudal Law* (1957), *The Machiavellian Moment* (1975), and an edition of *The Political Works of James Harrington* (1977).

James Moore studied Political Science at the University of London. He
is Associate Professor of Political Science at Concordia University, Montreal. He is the author of several articles on Hume.

James MacAdam received a Ph.D. in Philosophy from the University of
London in 1958. He is now Professor of Philosophy at Trent University. He is writing a book on Rousseau, and has published
several articles on this topic.

Nannerl Keohane received her Ph.D. in Political Science from Yale.
She is Associate Professor of Political Science at Stanford University. She has written several articles on Rousseau and
eighteenth-century political thought in France. Her book *Power
and Participation in French Political Philosophy* is to be published by Princeton University Press.

Douglas Long received a Ph.D. from the University of London in 1973.
He is now Assistant Professor of Political Science at the University of Western Ontario. His book *Bentham on Liberty* was published by the University of Toronto Press in 1977. He is editing
a volume for *The Collected Works of Jeremy Bentham* now in progress.

John Gray received a D. Phil. in Political Science from Oxford in 1977.
He is now Official Fellow and Tutor in Politics, Jesus College,
Oxford. He has published articles on Karl Popper and J. S. Mill,
and is writing a book on Mill.

E. K. Hunt received a Ph.D. in Economics from the University of Utah
in 1968. He is now Associate Professor of Economics at the University of California (Riverside). He has published extensively
in the history of economic thought and in Marxist and radical economics. His books include *Property and Prophets* (1972) and *Social Harmony and Class Conflict* (forthcoming).

Tom Settle has undergraduate degrees in Physics and Theology. He received a Ph.D. in Philosophy from the University of Hong Kong in
1966. He is now Professor of Philosophy and Dean of Arts at the
University of Guelph. In addition to his many articles in the
philosophy of science, he has written *In Search of a Third Way:
Is a Morally Principled Political Economy Possible?* (1976).

Thomas Flanagan received his Ph.D. in Political Science from Duke University in 1970. He is currently Associate Professor of Political Science at the University of Calgary. He is author of *Louis
"David" Riel: "Prophet of the New World,"* which will be released
by the University of Toronto Press early in 1979.

Shadia Drury received a Ph.D. in Political Science from York University in 1977. She is Assistant Professor of Political Science at
the University of Calgary. Her interests include historial and
analytical political philosophy as well as the philosophy of law.

EDITORS' NOTE

The editors do not feel it is necessary to add a preface to this volume. The essays can stand on their own merits as contributions to the theory of property. We have added only a short summary at the front of each essay which may be of some assistance to the reader.

We would like to thank those whose efforts have made this book possible. The University of Calgary and the Calgary Institute for the Humanities supported the workshop on "Property in the Western Tradition" in July, 1978, and are further supporting the publication of this volume. Thanks are also due to Tamara Palmer, who helped edit the papers; and Allison Dube, who compiled the bibliography and index.

Anthony Parel
Thomas Flanagan
January, 1979

C. B. Macpherson argues that most theorists of property have viewed it as a means to some greater end such as human happiness. However some modern thinkers, such as Hobbes and above all Bentham, have virtually made the accumulation of property an end in itself by identifying wealth as the universal means of obtaining pleasure. This confusion still plagues liberal democratic theory, and no satisfactory theory of property will be possible until property is returned to its proper status of means to a more important end.

PROPERTY AS MEANS OR END

There are several possible ways of taking an overview of the
theory of property in the Western political tradition. One is to give
a straightforward historical account of the successive theories justifying or criticizing the various types and amounts of property that
have been of concern to the political theorists of different eras,
showing the changing grounds on which their cases were based.[1] Another is to make a logical classification of the grounds on which
property has been or may be justified, and to subject each to tests of
logical consistency and adequacy.[2] Another way is to start from observable changes in the very concept of property, that is, in the content put into the definition of property itself, in successive eras in
the Western tradition, and to relate those changes to changing requirements of dominant and rising classes, as I have done in my discussion of the several narrowings of the concept, from an ancient and
medieval concept which included common as well as private property,
through an early modern one which thought only of private individual
property but defined it so widely as to include the rights to life and
liberty as well as to material estate, then a narrowing which confined
property to a right to some use or benefit of some material thing or
revenue, then a further narrowing which confined it to the right to
alienate or dispose of as well as to use or enjoy material goods.[3]

These three ways of taking an overview of property do not exhaust
the possibilities. I want now to try out another way: to look for
any pattern that may be found in the Western tradition between treating property as a means to ethical ends or to ontological concepts of
man, on the one hand, and on the other hand to treating property as an
end in itself.

A search for any such pattern may seem a waste of time. For
surely, it may be said, property has never, by any theorist, been
treated as an end in itself, but always as a means to some other end -
the good life of the citizen (Aristotle), the fulfilment of the will
without which individuals are not fully human (Hegel, Green) - or as a
prerequisite of individual freedom seen as the human essence
(Rousseau, Jefferson, Friedman).

Similarly, the outstanding critics of private property (More, Winstanley, the Utopian socialists, Marx), and of unlimited private property (Rousseau), have denounced it as destructive of the human essence, a negative means in relation to an ontological end.

In all these cases property is treated as means, not as end. But it must be noticed that in the liberal utilitarian tradition, from Locke to Bentham, the *accumulation* of private property is treated as an end. For them, maximization of utilities is *the* end, and by Bentham the command of utilities is measured by material wealth. Thus maximization of material wealth (property) is indistinguishable from the ethical end: property is virtually an end in itself. And as early as Locke, the insistence that unlimited accumulation is a natural right of the individual comes close to making accumulation an end in itself.

We may then at least hypothesize a continuum from property as means to property as end, and see where this leads us. It will become evident that the means/end distinction is not symmetrical with the limited/unlimited right distinction. Aristotle and Aquinas, treating property as a means, concluded for a limited property right. Hegel and Green, also treating property as a means, concluded for an unlimited right. An explanation of this difference is required, and should be revealing. In the Utilitarian tradition there is more symmetry. From Locke to Bentham, accumulation of property, being treated as virtually an end, always meant a right of unlimited accumulation.

Before seeking a pattern in the treatment of property as means or end, it may be well to set out the limiting definition of property I shall be using. I confine myself here to private property, defined as a right, i.e. an enforceable claim, of an individual - a natural or artificial individual - to some use or benefit of some thing (land, capital, labour-power, or other commodities) or to some revenue from the position he holds in the political society, and the right to exclude others from that use or benefit. This is narrower than the perfectly intelligible and at one time prevalent definition of property embracing both private and common property - both the right to exclude others and the right not to be excluded by others. But it is broader than the narrowest definition mentioned above, which confines property to the right to dispose of as well as to use material things or revenues.

Now let us look at, or perhaps to avoid begging the question I
should say look for, shifts back and forth between treating property
as a means and as an end.

There will be little dispute that in the prevalent concepts of
property throughout the ancient and medieval eras of the Western tradition the institution of private property was justified as a means
to some ethical or ontological end. Whether the institution was seen
as natural (Aristotle), or God-given (Augustine), or both (Aquinas),
it was justified as a necessary means to the good life of the citizen
(Aristotle), or as necessary to counteract the avaricious nature of
fallen man (Augustine), or to provide for peaceable and orderly relations between individuals (Aquinas).

A change to seeing property as an end in itself is foreshadowed
by Hobbes and fully implicit in Bentham. Let us look first at Bentham, then show how it is foreshadowed by Hobbes: this should enable
us to trace the reasons for the change.

For Bentham the ultimate end to which all social arrangements
should be directed was the maximization of the aggregate utility
(pleasure minus pain) of the members of a society. And while he
listed many kinds of pleasures, including non-material ones, he held
that wealth - the possession of material goods - was so essential to
the attainment of all other pleasures that it could be taken as the
measure of pleasure or utility as such. "Each portion of wealth has
a corresponding portion of happiness."[4] Further: "Money is the instrument of measuring the quantity of pain and pleasure. Those who
are not satisfied with the accuracy of this instrument must find out
some other that shall be more accurate, or bid adieu to politics and
morals."[5] So, even without his further postulate that the highest
pleasure was not in having but in acquiring wealth, he was satisfied
that each individual should and would seek to maximize his own wealth
without limit. The most general end, maximization of each individual's utilities, thus became indistinguishable from the general end of
each individual's accumulation of material property. Property - not
the institution of property, but the accumulation of property - has
become an end in itself.

Moreover, Bentham recognized that wealth was indistinguishable
from power, that is, power over others. "Between wealth and power,
the connexion is most close and intimate: so intimate, indeed, that
the disentanglement of them, even in the imagination, is a matter of

no small difficulty. They are each of them respectively an instrument of production of the other."[6] And "human beings are the most
powerful instruments of production, and therefore everyone becomes
anxious to employ the services of his fellows in multiplying his own
comforts. Hence the intense and universal thirst for power; the
equally prevalent hatred of subjection."[7]

So for Bentham, accumulation of property and accumulation of
power over others are indistinguishable, and both are ends in themselves. It will now be apparent why I spoke of Hobbes as having foreshadowed Bentham's position. For it was Hobbes who from a somewhat
different basis concluded that the search for power over others was
the dominant end of man. I have argued elsewhere[8] that it is only
where capitalist relations of production prevail - or if you like,
only in a fully possessive market society - that this is the necessary
behaviour of all men. We are then, I think, entitled to conclude that
the shift from seeing the institution of property as a means to seeing
the accumulation of property as an end comes with the rise of capitalist relations of production. And it is not difficult to see that the
shift was initiated, even required, by that rise. For the essence of
the capitalist market society is that the decisions about what shall
be produced and how the whole product shall be allocated among those
who contributed to its production are left mainly to the market forces
which respond only to the calculations of the enterprisers how to increase their accumulations of capital. To justify that system of
productive and distributive relations one must hold that unlimited
accumulation is just. And in the Utilitarian tradition that required
showing that maximization of accumulation is indistinguishable from
maximization of utilities. Thus the shift to treating accumulation of
property as an end was required to legitimate capitalist relations.

For Hegel and the English Idealists, accumulation of property was
perhaps less clearly an end than a means. Yet both Hegel and Green
treated the right of unlimited accumulation as entailed in their ultimate moral end, the realization of the human will or the consciousness
of oneself as a moral purposive being. As Hegel put it, "The rationale of property is to be found not in the satisfaction of needs but
in the supersession of the pure objectivity of personality. In his
property a person exists for the first time as reason."[9] This is

surely tantamount to treating property as an end rather than as a
means. And the Idealists, like the Utilitarians, were driven to this
because they accepted capitalist society as *the* model of civil society.

A further change in the treatment of property is evident in 20th
century liberal-democratic theory, beginning indeed as early as John
Stuart Mill in mid-19th century. The move is back towards treating
property as a means, not an end. It was inaugurated by the liberals'
realization that their market society (which they generally failed to
identify with capitalist society) had produced a working-class which
would not much longer put up with the exploitation to which it was
subjected, or be persuaded by the Benthamist rationale of an unlimited
property right. Mill still held to a virtually unlimited right, but
his 20th century followers increasingly recognized that that was incompatible with the end they espoused, i.e., the equal opportunity of
individual self-development. So they moved towards property as a
right limited in various ways by the end: property tended to become
again a means rather than an end.

What of the future? Can we expect that property as a means will
entirely replace property as an end? Here we must emphasize one distinction already made and introduce an additional one.

(1) Property as an institution, a set of enforceable claims
(enforceable by the state or by a self-acting community), can be and
has been justified as a means to some end - orderly peaceful relations
between individuals, the good life of the citizen, the autonomy of the
individual, the development of personality, and so on. But the institution itself, whether it confers limited or unlimited rights in
things or revenues, has never been thought to be justifiable *as an*
end. What can be and has been justified as an end is not the institution of property but the *accumulation* of property, specifically the
accumulation of capital. Accumulation is the heart of capitalism, so
much so that, as I have argued, it became indistinguishable from maximization of utilities as an end.

(2) We have been looking so far at justificatory theories, theories offered as rationales of this or that kind of property institution, offered with a view to shaping or confirming a desired or existing structure of property by persuading those members of the society
whose opinion counted that the structure in question was just or legitimate. The theories were openly avowed: no concealment was

necessary as long as those whose opinion counted were, or saw themselves as, beneficiaries of the structure. So from Aristotle to say
Bentham, the successive prevalent theories were those which supported
the structure of property that was required by successive modes of
production - slave, feudal, nascent and expanding capitalist.

If this correspondence between theory and practice still held,
one would expect that now, with capitalism globally contracting and
under heavy pressure in its homelands, the theory of property accumulation as an end in itself, indistinguishable from the end of maximization of utility, would disappear. And indeed as an avowed theory
it has virtually disappeared. Yet as long as our Western societies
continue to rely on capitalist incentives as the motor of production,
they will have to sanction accumulation of capital as an end. The
predictable result is increasing obfuscation. For property theory
must then sanction accumulation as an end while concealing that it is
doing so.

I do not suppose deliberate falsification by the writers who do
and will touch on property theory. They may, especially if they start
from a position of ethical liberalism, be unaware of the constraint
imposed by the accumulation factor, or may conceal it from themselves.
A few will justify modern property simply on grounds of prescriptive
right. But most will justify some institution of property as a means
to some further end - justice, efficiency, freedom, consumers' sovereignty, or whatever - and will deduce the desirable types and limits
of property from that end. Such an exercise can be carried out hon-
estly and conscientiously without any clear awareness of the accumulation constraint: indeed, only with such unawareness could it be
done conscientiously. But the constraint is still there: although
property is treated as a means, accumulation as an end cannot be denied if capitalist property institutions, in however modified a form,
are to be supported. I suggest that the recent Western tradition,
from Mill or even Hegel through to Rawls and Milton Friedman, sustains
this analysis, and offers us a murky theoretical prospect.

FOOTNOTES

1 As in Richard Schlatter's *Private Property, the History of an Idea*
   (London: Allen & Unwin, 1951).

2 As in Lawrence C. Becker's *Property Rights, Philosophic Foundations*
   (Boston: Routledge & Kegan Paul, 1977).

3 As in "A Political Theory of Property," in my *Democratic Theory,*
   Essays in Retrieval (Oxford: Clarendon Press, 1973), and "Human
   Rights as Property Rights," *Dissent*, Winter, 1977.

4 *Principles of the Civil Code*, Part I, ch. 6.

5 *Jeremy Bentham's Economic Writings*, ed. W. Stark (London: Allen &
   Unwin, 1952), I, 117.

6 *Constitutional Code*, Book I, ch. 9, in *Works* (ed. Bowring) IX, 48.

7 Stark (ed.), III, 430.

8 *The Political Theory of Possessive Individualism* (Oxford: Clarendon Press, 1962), Ch. II, Sect. 3.

9 *Philosophy of Right*, sects. 235-6; cf. T. H. Green: *Lectures on*
   the Principles of Political Obligation, sect. 213.

William Mathie presents a close analysis of Aristotle's treatment of property in the first two books of the *Politics*. Special attention is paid to the role of property in the household and *polis*, the question of slavery, the difference between natural exchange and the unnatural art of money-making, and Aristotle's critique of Plato's communism. It is pointed out in conclusion that, while Aristotle was not an egalitarian in the modern sense, he conceived of property as ministerial to virtue, as means to the "good life," not as desirable in itself.

PROPERTY IN THE POLITICAL SCIENCE OF ARISTOTLE

According to the teaching of Aristotle's *Politics*, the polis "comes into being for the sake of life but is for the sake of living well" (1252b30).[1] The role of property in Aristotelian political science may be adumbrated in relation to the two parts of this utterance. The pursuit of self-sufficiency through household and village which obtains its end in the polis is a satisfaction of daily and more than daily needs by acquisition; those goods acquired in this way so as to satisfy the needs of life we might call property. Yet if life itself and the desire to live a life with others are natural objects of the polis, the most important good obtained through the polis is a share in living well or nobly (1278b18-23).[2] As the polis is the most comprehensive of human associations, the good towards which it is directed as human action must be a more comprehensive or final good than those sought by lesser or more partial associations; that greatest or most final good which is also the object of political science (*politikē*) is happiness or the most complete activity of that which is peculiarly human - the activity of the soul in accordance with its own greatest excellence or virtue (1252a1-7; *EN* 1094a27-b7, 1098a16-18). Property, or at least its constituents as ordinarily understood, is connected to this most important good for the sake of which the political community exists, as also to the concern with mere life; but the complex character of this connection and indeed the complex relation between the ends of life and living well render the role of property especially problematic.

Happiness as full activity of the soul in accordance with its greatest virtues surely requires equipment and this includes external goods and hence property, but the pursuit of property is itself no part of virtuous activity. Although a certain material prosperity may be a necessary condition for the activity of the moral virtues generally and, indeed, is entailed in the very exercise of certain virtues, these virtues are manifested in the use of, not the acquisition of, property These virtues, on Aristotle's account, may even be said to consist in a kind of indifference to property. The greater vice associated with liberality is not prodigality but parsimony; the prodigal or wasteful youth is more likely than the mean one to acquire the virtue of liberality even though prodigality may easily lead to a carelessness in getting as well as giving.[3] Only justice as the particular virtue of fairness or equality can be regarded as a virtue pertaining in part to acquiring as such, and this virtue may also be described as the least of those moral virtues Aristotle enumerates and examines.[4]

Though property may be a necessary condition of virtuous activity, it seems that the virtuous or serious man (*ho spoudaios*) is as such not very serious about the acquisition of property. Those who are "serious about life rather than living well, as their desire for life is without limit, also desire the things productive of life without limit" (1257b 41-1258a2). Even those who aim at living well often see this as a life of bodily enjoyments and, as this seems to consist in acquiring and possessing, devote all their efforts to acquiring money. Property is then a necessary condition of virtuous activity but its pursuit is not itself a virtuous activity nor perhaps even consistent with virtuous activity.

II

To arrive at a more precise understanding of Aristotle's teaching on property, we must consider two distinct discussions that occur in the text of the *Politics*. Property (*ktēsis*) and its acquisition, various modes of obtaining money (*chrēmatistikē*) or those needful and useful things "whose worth is measured by money," and economic activity in general are examined in the first book of the *Politics* in relation to the household and its management, while Aristotle's consideration of whether property and possessions are best owned and used separately or in common is set out in the second book. The latter question is considered as the natural starting point of the inquiry into the best political community "for those capable of living in accordance with what one would pray or wish for"; more exactly, Aristotle's case for a modified form of private ownership is chiefly developed through his critical examination of the "communism" of Plato's *Republic*.

Property and acquiring are discussed most generally in relation to household management. The household and the relations that belong to it, as also the question of whether and how the acquiring of property or wealth is related to household management, are considered within a part of Aristotle's political teaching apparently intended to show that the polis exists by nature and that political rule must be distinguished from kingly rule, the rule of the head of a household, and the rule of a master of slaves. Economic activity is examined as part of a

discussion intended to manifest the distinctness and accordance with
nature of the political. Further, as Aristotle initially seeks to show
that the city is by nature, so the entire discussion of Book One is
guided by the standard of nature; the discussion proceeds from the demonstration that the city is by nature through the question of whether
the master-slave relation may be by nature, to the effort to distinguish between forms of acquisition and exchange as these accord with,
or are contrary to nature.

In order to understand that part of Aristotle's account of property which belongs to this most general treatment of economic activity,
we must examine the relation between household and polis as this is set
out in the first book of the *Politics*.[5] This relation is important to
our understanding of the Aristotelian account of property not merely
because our word and, perhaps, concept of "economics" have developed
out of some specific modifications of the Greek and Aristotelian term
for the art of household management, *oikonomikē*, but also because Aristotle's account of property, wealth, acquisition and exchange is primarily developed in relation to household management. Aristotle's
claim that wealth has properly a limit and his attack upon the limitless pursuit of wealth are, in the first instance, a subordination of
what we would regard as economic activity not to the polis or political
but to the management of the household. Indeed, the Aristotelian argument for private property is inextricably linked to a defence of the
separate household.

The *Politics* begins with the argument that the political community
as the most comprehensive of human associations must aim at the most
authoritative of human goods. This statement is presented as a refutation of the claim that statesman, king, head of a household, and master
of slaves are the same; those who suppose the latter do "not speak nobly," for they speak as if there were no difference between a large
household and a small polis. Household and polis are distinguished, in
the first place, by the fact that the former seeks a partial, the latter the most authoritative human good. If the greatest good sought by
the polis is living well, or happiness, or the complete exercise of
what is specifically human in man, what is the partial good sought by
the household? In the passage that follows, as we watch the polis
"growing from its beginnings," we learn that the household is the community that is formed according to nature for the satisfaction of daily needs; the village is on the other hand made up of several households for the satisfaction of "more than daily needs," while the polis

obtains complete self-sufficiency.[6] Yet we cannot suppose that the
household continues to be for the satisfaction of the daily necessities
for which it comes into being any more than we may suppose that the
city continues to be defined by that same kind of self-sufficiency for
which it comes into being. When Aristotle says the polis is prior to
the household and to each individual, he surely indicates that the
household as it comes initially into being is not the same as the
household as it exists as a part or constituent of the polis.

As Aristotle's refutation of the conventionalist thesis affirms
the natural character of the city both as the result of a natural
growth from sexual union and master-slave relation to household, village, and polis, and as the community within which man's capacity for
reasoned speech and even for distinguishing the just and unjust finds
expression, so the household may be understood in two ways: either as
a community for the satisfaction of daily needs and the joint result of
the union of male and female for procreation and natural ruler and naturally ruled for security, or as a constituent of the polis   (125a26-
31; 1280b34). The household may be understood as a natural unit as it
is the product of two natural relations. On this understanding, the
polis is natural as it is the result of the coming together of many
such natural units. Yet the household so understood is not the perfected household of the perfected polis; the household in the latter
sense is a natural unit only because it is a necessary constituent of
the city which is itself by nature, not because it arises out of the
natural association of natural units but because it is the necessary
condition or sphere of a fully human life.[7]

Following the demonstration that the city is by nature as natural
growth and/or as condition of the fully human, Aristotle says we have
first to discuss household management since "every polis is comprised
of households;" it therefore becomes necessary to examine the relation
of master and slave, husband and wife, and father and children. The
art of obtaining wealth, or those things the value of which is expressed by money, must also belong to this discussion because some consider
this art as identical with household management, others as the greatest
part of it. The household and the relations that belong to it as well
as the acquiring of wealth must be examined "before going on to speak
of the *politeia*."[8]

Why the household, the relations that belong to it, and the acquiring of property should be discussed before turning to the regimes

is not immediately clear. It is, of course, true that John Locke examines the question of property, as also that of the family, before turning to the forms of the commonwealth; but this does not explain the perplexing character of Aristotle's procedure, for Locke, unlike Aristotle, seeks to indicate the priority of property to government i.e., to show that the latter is instituted for the sake of the former. Aristotelian political science, on the contrary, seems to argue the primacy of the political or the regime.[9] If we say with Barker that economics (*oikonomia*) or the management of the household stands in the same relation to the household (*oikos*) as politics (*politikē*) stands to the polis, we would not thereby see why the household and its management should be discussed before the polis and its governance; for it would seem that just as every polis is informed by some regime or other so the household as a partial association must obtain a form appropriate to the regime in which it exists.[10] In fact, it appears that the household cannot be fully examined apart from the regime - the relation of husband and wife or children and father must be considered "in our discussions concerning the regimes" (1260b9-13). Only the relation of master and slave and the general question of acquiring, or property, can be discussed before turning to the regimes. Though "the excellence of the part can only be understood in relation to the excellence of the whole" of which it is a part, this does not apparently preclude an adequate discussion of property or the master-slave relation.

Having introduced the money-making art which some identify with household management and others consider its greatest part, Aristotle turns to the question of master and slave, what the slave by nature is and whether such exists. It has been suggested that Aristotle examines this question before *chrēmatistikē*, or property in general, both because it is his initial aim to show that the master of slaves and statesman are different and because the slave is a part of property (*ktēsis*) and "the part should be studied before the whole."[11] It is true that Aristotle speaks of property in general in the context of the discussion of slavery, but his procedure suggests that the slave constitutes an especially important or revealing kind of property. Aristotle steers a course between those who see the rule of a master of slaves as based upon the same science of ruling exercised by household head, statesman, and king and those who suppose one man can be master of another only by convention. By developing the notion of the

slave by nature, his teaching at this point anticipates the notion of
a natural art of acquiring and exchange; indeed the ambiguities in the
teaching of natural slavery anticipate those that belong to the teaching on natural acquiring and exchange.

Like the teaching that the polis is by nature, the teaching that
the master and slave relation is or can be in accordance with nature
has two meanings. In one sense, the natural slave is a human being who
shares in reasoned speech so far as to apprehend it without having the
capacity for it, or who differs as much from one who is by nature fit
to be his master as the body differs from the soul, or again, who
so lacks the capacity for deliberate forethought as to require the sup-
plying of that deliberation by another (1254b23, 1254b16-17, 1260a13).
The natural slave so understood is, of course benefited by the rule of
one who is by nature capable of ruling him. This description of the
natural slave belongs to Aristotle's response to the question of whether anyone exists who is by nature a slave. Prior to taking up this
question, however, Aristotle has set out "the nature and capacity of
the slave." He has defined the slave as a certain kind of property and
in doing so has defined property as well. As the demonstration of the
existence of the natural slave constitutes a description of a certain
kind of being, it must be considered whether such a being could actually satisfy the necessity that emerges from the previous definition of
"the nature and capacity" of the slave.

Property (*ktēsis*) is, according to Aristotle, "a part of the
household and the art of acquiring property (*ktētikē*) is therefore a
part of household management, for without the necessary things living
and living well are impossible" (1253b23-25). Like the practitioners
of "the arts with specific ends," the head of the household must have
the use of appropriate tools in order to accomplish his specific
work.[12] An article of property, including the slave as one such article, is to be understood as a tool - a slave is a live (*empsychon*) article of property. Property is not, however, *any* multitude of tools or
instruments; it does not consist of instruments of production but of
instruments for living, or action. From tools or instruments of production we get products as a consequence of their use, while property
as a number of tools for living or activity furnishes nothing beyond
the actual use of these - we simply wear a garment and sleep in a bed.
An article of property is, according to Aristotle's conclusion, "a
separable instrument for action" (1254a18).[13]

As a definition of property this Aristotelian account has seemed
particularly narrow to many because it considers property only as a
part of the household.[14] As an examination of slavery the discussion
similarly confines the sphere of the slave to that of domestic service
by ruling out the use of slaves in production. The present account
thus precludes the use of slaves in farming, though the primary union
of slave and master for security described earlier suggested the employment of slaves in farming (1252a31).[15] These two restrictions seem
to be related. As property is exclusively a part of the household, the
employment of slaves as property must belong to the sphere of the
household and so to activity (*praxis*) rather than to production (*poiē-
sis*). As Barker notes, property is not seen as "capital for the production of commodities" but as a source of services consumed by its
owner in the "sustenance of life."[16]

The discussion of the nature and capacity of the slave is followed
by the demonstration that there are by nature those who would benefit
by being ruled as slaves. That demonstration, however, does not establish the ready existence of human beings capable of performing the services indicated by the preceding discussion. As Aristotle points out,
though nature "intends" to make the bodies of free men and slaves sufficiently different as to indicate their appropriate status, "the opposite often happens"; further, the more important differences of soul
are perceived with even greater difficulty (1254b28-38). Nature is
similarly unable to carry out its intention to see that those born of
"free" parents should be by nature freemen (1255b3). If Aristotle's
analysis serves as much to undermine the practice as to confirm the
principle of slavery by nature, it also renders questionable the assumption that nature supports an account of property that can completely distinguish activity from production and ignore the latter.[17]

From the discussion of the rule of the master of slaves Aristotle
turns to a consideration of property in general and of the art of
acquiring wealth, since the slave just discussed "is a certain part of
property" (1256a2). The problem to which Aristotle's discussion of
property and wealth-getting is addressed is a revised form of the question implicitly posed by those who consider wealth-making the same as,
or the greatest part of, household management (1253b13). It must be
considered whether the art of acquiring wealth (*chrēmatistikē*) is the
same as household management, or some part of it, or ministerial to it.
If wealth-making is ministerial to household management, should it be

understood to serve the governance of the household as the making of
shuttles serves weaving by the provision of tools, or as the casting of
bronze serves the statue-maker by the furnishing of material? Aristotle seems to reject at once the possibility that *chrēmatistikē* and
oikonomikē are the same, for the work of the former is to provide while
that of the latter is to use. But is *chrēmatistikē* a part of *oikonomikē* or ministerial to it? In any case, we should note that the examples Aristotle provides both of tool-making and material-making are
related to production rather than action. If *chrēmatistikē* is ministerial to *oikonomikē*, it must be considered whether it furnishes tools
or material for noble actions.

In the sections that follow, before returning to the relation between *chrēmatistikē* and *oikonomikē*, Aristotle is concerned to distinguish between an art of acquisition that is in accordance with nature
and another sort of acquisition "especially and justly called money-
making" (1257a1). The difference between the two might be understood
in relation to the primacy of *oikonomikē*; the notion of wealth as an
object of unlimited pursuit belongs to the acquisitive art that is contrary to nature, and we might reasonably suppose that it is precisely
this which makes that art contrary to nature. This is not, however,
the only, or even the chief sense in which Aristotle distinguishes natural and non-natural acquisition. The account of acquisition begins
with an enumeration of modes of obtaining food or nurture (*trophē*) and
corresponding ways of life which are natural since in such settings
food is not obtained from others by retail trade; these ways of life
"whose work or operation arises naturally by itself" are those of nomadic herdsmen, farmers, robbers or pirates, fishermen and hunters
(1256b1).[18]

These natural or independent ways of life are explicitly compared
with the variety of modes of nurture among animals, implying that the
lives of men differ in accordance with the food they seek just as the
solitary or herd-living propensities of various animal species differ
in accordance with the source of nurture set out for each by nature.
Those engaged in these ways of life seek and obtain self-sufficiency
without entering into retail exchange; if necessary such men combine
these pursuits. Aristotle's association of the natural with the primitive in this context suggests the complex relationship between modes of
acquiring and forms of life. If such lives are furthest removed from
the unlimited pursuit of wealth and retail exchange and are freest of

human interdependence by reason of a more direct dependence upon nature, these forms of life are especially defined or restricted by the pursuit of sustenance. If in some sense the nomadic life is most leisured (1256a31-32), it is perhaps also least human.[19]

One kind of property and form of acquisition may be understood on the basis of this account of natural modes of nurture and further consideration of the generous sustenance afforded men by nature. Such property as is obtained through each of these modes "seems to be rendered to all by nature itself" (1256b9). Aristotle further leads us to reflect that nature furnishes sustenance for many species from birth until the offspring of those species are able to provide for themselves while others that are viviparous have milk for their young. On the basis of such reflections Aristotle says "one ought to suppose" that nature provides generally for men through the plants and other animals.[20] Acquisition in accordance with this understanding of the natural provision for man's welfare is that form of acquisition which belongs to the household; to the extent that sufficient is not at hand, the *oikonomikos* should provide a supply of such goods as are "necessary for life, capable of being stored, and useful for the community of the household and city" (1256b29-30). True wealth consists in this sufficient supply afforded by nature with the help of *oikonomikē*. If this account of nature's generosity suggests a limit to property and its acquisition, the same is confirmed by the example of the arts; as the instrument of no art is infinite in amount or size, wealth too must be limited, for it constitutes a number of instruments for household management and politics.

In addition to this natural form of acquisition which is subordinate to the household (and polis) and entails a limited notion of wealth, there is a kind of acquisition which "men justly call money making *par excellence*."[21] The opinion that wealth and property have no limit results from the existence of this *chrēmatistikē par excellence* as also from the fact that the two forms of acquisition are sufficiently similar as to be often confused. This second kind of acquisition is not in accordance with nature because it has come into being through some sort of experience and art. To understand the origin and non-natural character of this art, recall that every item of property has two modes of being used. A shoe may be worn or exchanged.[22] In both cases, according to Aristotle, the shoe is used as a shoe; but where the shoe is exchanged it is used in a way other than that for which it was made - it is not used "according to its proper use (*oikeian chrē-sin*)" (1257a14). The possibility of exchange, and through exchange of an art and activity directed to the pursuit of wealth without limit, is grounded in the fact that every item of property may be used for exchange; but how or why is this possibility realized?

Although *chrēmatistikē par excellence* is contrary to nature, the exchange out of which it emerges is not itself contrary to nature. Rather, we learn now that nature's providence was less adequate than we had previously been required to suppose; it is also by nature that men have "more than enough of some things and less than enough of others" (1257a18). Barter, the first and most natural mode of exchange, emerged out of this imperfection of nature's provision only when the association of several households had come into being; there is no need for exchange within a single household where all things are shared. In any case, barter as such remains natural because items of property are still traded for other items of property strictly with a view to use. Such barter remains common among many barbarian races.[23] From this form of barter to replenish natural self-sufficiency which is "according to reason," the art of money-making *par excellence* arose through the invention of currency.

According to Aristotle the use of money resulted from the practice of trade with more foreign parts; money was devised because not every thing that is a necessity by nature is portable. At first a metal employed as something useful, money finally acquired a conventional value. With this development the obtaining of wealth through exchange became possible - "through experience money-making became more artful, discovering whence and how to make the greatest profit by exchange" (1257b5). Thus, out of barter which is itself natural and reasonable and through the more or less necessary invention of currency arose that form of money-making properly called such, which is itself contrary to nature and gives rise to the notion that property and wealth are unlimited.

Against the view that wealth is a multitude of tools for living and living well or a multitude of those things necessary for life and useful for household and polis, *chrēmatistikē par excellence* regards wealth as a quantity of money. The acquiring of wealth so understood becomes an activity without limit. Some apparently question this notion of wealth precisely because of the conventional character of currency and its inability to satisfy the needs connected with life directly. These critics of *chrēmatistikē* point out that one could, like Midas, starve while possessing great sums of gold and that those who have established the value of a currency may alter it.[24] The latter objection suggests the dependence of economics upon politics; but, as generally in this part of the discussion, Aristotle emphasizes the natural account of wealth and acquiring and the subordination of these to the management of the household (1257b20).

As a consequence of the invention of currency and subsequent discovery through experience of how one's wealth might be augmented most by exchange, an art of *chrēmatistikē* has come into existence. Like medicine, or any other art, the new art of *chrēmatistikē* is "concerned with its end without limit" (1257b26). Such an art becomes possible once wealth is defined no longer as a multitude of tools for living but as a quantity of money. *Chrēmatistikē* is unlike the other arts and uniquely problematic, however, both because there is a powerful propensity to the unlimited pursuit of this art's end in human nature and because of the comprehensive sphere within which it may be exercised. *Chrēmatistikē* is an art whose end is likely to be pursued without limit because of its similarity to that natural and necessary art of acquiring to complete nature's provision that belongs to and serves household management. Proceeding from a proper concern to supply the things necessary for life, men are likely to regard it as the work of household management "to preserve or augment without limit the substance of the household" (1257b40). Some take this view because they are "serious about life but not living well." Others devote themselves to the unlimited pursuit of wealth because they associate living well with an excess of bodily enjoyments. The comprehensiveness of the authority *chrēmatistikē* may claim results from the fact that *chrēmatistikē* is an art that may be practiced along with every other specific art like the wage-earning art of Plato's *Republic*; this possibility belongs to the practice of each art to the extent that the products of each art may be used or exchanged.[25] *Chrēmatistikē* may thus take the place of *politikē* as the art that orders all other arts because the end it seeks may be falsely regarded as the greatest good of human action. When this substitution occurs "each of the powers comes to be used contrary to nature." The various arts and even the virtues may be then regarded only as so many ways of acquiring wealth (1258a10).

We have seen that in the first book of the *Politics* Aristotle develops a notion of property and acquiring as natural in opposition to

that non-natural and unlimited mode of acquiring that emerges after the
development of currency. In large part Aristotle develops this standard, in the light of which unlimited wealth-seeking is seen as deplor-
able, through an appeal to the providence and generosity of the natural order. He barely alludes to the questionable aspects of this
standard by identifying piracy as the central natural mode of acquiring and noting that it is among the barbarians that the natural form of
exchange is still practiced. He also remarks on the failure of nature
to accomplish its intention with respect to natural slavery and acknowledges the basis in nature and reason of that very art of *chrēmatistikē* he deplores as against nature. The difficulty to which Aristotle's insistence upon a large and somewhat unwarranted supposition as
to nature's providence responds is perhaps that acquisitiveness and a
serious concern for mere life obstruct and distort concern for living
well and yet contribute to that situation within which a life of noble
activity becomes possible.[26]

We have also seen that the teaching on property and natural acquisition entails the subordination of economic activity to the management of the household; again Aristotle barely suggests that a concern for wealth and its acquisition might properly be of interest to
the statesman (1256b30, 1258a33, 1259a23-36). In general, the relations among acquisition, household, and polis are set out by the statement that nature should for the most part furnish wealth as necessary
for the householder to use as is fitting and that it no more belongs
to the householder to see to acquiring than it belongs to the statesman to make human beings; as the householder makes good use of what is
supplied by nature, the statesman is to make good use of the human beings supplied by the households (1258a19-26). But we cannot leave it
at this, for the character of the household is at least partly determined by the city or more precisely by the regime. Further, the habits
and education of those human beings created within and by the household, who are to become the citizens of the polis, are no matter of indifference to the statesman. It becomes necessary to consider the relation between household and polis as Aristotle does in the second
book of the *Politics*.

III

Aristotle's general aim in the second book of the *Politics* is to
acquit himself of the charge of having sought novelty for its own sake

in pursuing his inquiry as to the best political community. This he
hopes to accomplish by showing the faults of various regimes that are
reputed to be good. His specific theme is the extent of sharing or
community (*koinōnia*) that ought to occur in a polis. The faults of the
highly regarded actual and proposed regimes seem connected with this
question of sharing and property. In any case, the question of how
much of what things should be in common is, according to Aristotle, the
natural starting point for the inquiry concerning the best political
community.

The present discussion belongs to the treatment of the best political order and so goes beyond the limits of that account of the household presented in the previous book. At the same time the present discussion remains preliminary to the political science of regimes, the
presentation of which commences in the following book. The polis as a
political community is most importantly the having in common (*koinōnia*)
or sharing of a regime, i.e. the members of a polis are united in the
most important way by their sharing in a way of life and form of governance (1276b1-13). The present question concerns the identification
and delimitation of that sharing which is proper to the polis regardless of the regime by which it is informed. The kind and extent of
having in common that is appropriate to the polis is to be examined so
far as this question can be abstracted from the question of the regime.
Although we are chiefly interested in Aristotle's account of property,
we shall need to attend to his treatment of family and household as
well, for the teaching on property and acquiring seeks to subordinate
economics to the household.

Aristotle's own view of what should be in common and to what extent in the polis takes the form of a criticism of the Socratic proposal that the wives, children, and possessions of the guardians in the
city founded "in speech" in the *Republic* should be held in common. It
is not our present concern to consider the fairness or true meaning of
this criticism of Plato except to note that the Aristotelian teaching
on community and its proper extent, within which the justification of
private ownership occurs, is a response to the Socratic assumption or
hypothesis that "the best city in its entirety should as fully as possible be one" (1261a15).[27] Aristotle sets out his own teaching on the
proper nature and extent of the city's unity or oneness through a critical examination of Socrates' teaching that separate families should
be abolished and that property should be common.

Aristotle argues that the city is by nature "a certain kind of
many" (1261a18) and will therefore be destroyed if it becomes "one" excessively. As the household is in a sense "more one" than the city and
one man is more unitary than a household, so the city will be reduced
to one man if it is permitted to become altogether one. The city as
such consists of several men and of men who differ in kind. A city is
not, like a military alliance, strengthened directly by each addition
to its membership; it is rather a unity that is necessarily made up of
parts that differ in kind. "The city would not come into being from
those who are the same" (1261a24). Pointing out that reciprocal equality preserves the city, Aristotle explicitly recalls his discussion of
reciprocity and justice in the *Nicomachean Ethics*.[28] That the city depends for its existence upon the possibility of bringing the products
of shoemakers and carpenters into a relation of equality reflects the
fact that the city is based upon a diversity among its constituents.
For Aristotle, as for Socrates, it is advantageous that men be shoemakers or carpenters rather than that one man should be both. What is
true for the arts is also true for governing. Reciprocity between
ruler and ruled, like exchange between carpenter and shoemaker, supposes a difference between the partners to the exchange: a "ruler renders to the ruled the offices of a good ruler, and the ruled repay him
with the offices of good subjects."[29] Even the free and equal who
practice rotation in office imitate the situation in which rulers and
ruled differ in kind. The elimination of such differentiation is the
destruction of the city.

That the city should not become one beyond a certain point is also
suggested if we recall that the city came into being through the pursuit of self-sufficiency. The household was superior to the single man
and the city superior to the household because the subsequent unit in
each case furnished greater self-sufficiency. A city becomes "what it
intends to be" when it constitutes a self-sufficient community in number and kind (1261b13), and self-sufficiency is only obtained when
those come together who are able to furnish what others lack. But this
will only be possible so long as different capacities are preserved as
distinct. If unity is sought in such a way and to such an extent as to
eliminate these differences, it must be at the expense of the self-
sufficiency sought in the creation of the polis.

Aristotle's objection to the Socratic scheme is not confined to
the claim that Socrates seeks an excessive degree of unification; he

also argues that the unity of the polis properly understood would be
reduced or destroyed by the elimination of separate families. The Socratic proposal will not result in that friendship which is the greatest of goods for a polis; contrary to Socrates' intention, it will
rather diminish that kind of friendship which prevents the formation of
faction. Socrates had intended that the polis (or its ruling class)
should become a single family so that for the members of each generation the older generation would be regarded as parents, the younger as
children. Familial bonds of affection would become coextensive with
the polis and no private interest could ever arise against that of the
city. Aristotle argues that the Socratic scheme can only be adequately
evaluated if the bonds of affection generated by each member of each
generation viewing all members of the other generation as parent or
child are compared with the various bonds of affection generated among
and within private families as these exist in actual cities. To perform this calculation, one would have to recognize that the expression
"my father" as used by a child in a city made up of separate families
must express a different degree of affection than the same words used
by a child in the Socratic city; such words are vastly diluted when
city and family are merged. One must also note that all those more
complex relations expressed by such terms as cousin, nephew, or uncle
will cease to exist through the Socratic reform. If these points are
kept in mind, a calculation will show that the degree of unity through
affection obtained by the Socratic scheme will be less than is produced by the existing network of private families. In examining this
criticism we must note that Aristotle will only have demonstrated the
inferiority of the Socratic proposal to the "unreformed" situation, in
Socrates' own terms, if the bonds of affection generated within and
among separate families are understood to benefit the polis itself.[30]

Turning to the question of property as such, Aristotle argues
that the common ownership of possessions proposed by Socrates would be
inferior to the existing system of private ownership, especially since
the existing system might be modified by "good habituation and the regulation of correct laws" so as to promote the common use of such possessions. Thus modified, the present system would avoid the problems
generated where use and ownership are common, benefit from the fact
that men generally display greater care for what is their own, and
still obtain the advantages of common use. The thought that something
is one's own also contributes greatly to the pleasure that something

can yield and is based upon a love of self that is natural (1263a41-
b1). Further, the exercise of temperance and liberality as well as
the legitimate pleasure derived from benefiting others whether
friends, strangers, or fellow citizens require the separateness of
households and possessions (123b5-14). Finally, such a system is consistent with the way in which the polis is one and many. The city according to Aristotle's account should remain "a many" while being "made
common and one" in and through education, i.e. through "habits, philosophy, and laws" (1263b32-40).

The polis is "many" and must remain so if it is to continue to exist as a city and if virtuous activity is to remain possible for its
members. Separateness of households and property must continue as the
foundation of this "manyness." On the other hand, the polis can and
should become "one" in a certain sense through habits, philosophy, and
laws; the fostering of this "sharing in use" is, indeed, "the distinctive work of the legislator" (1263a40). "The "oneness" of the polis is
consistent with its "manyness" insofar as that "oneness" is constituted by the virtuous activity of the members of the polis and insofar
as a necessary condition of that virtuous activity is the continued
separateness of property and households.

IV

The preceding comments have dealt exclusively with Aristotle's
treatment of property and acquisition in the first book of the *Politics*
and his argument for the separateness of property (and households) in
the second. Though these together constitute the chief Aristotelian
account of property and provide a proper starting point for any analysis of this subject, they do not yield a complete account of the role
of property in Aristotle's political science. This is so because the
two discussions occur somewhat in abstraction from the regime, which is
the central concern of Aristotelian political science. Precisely in
light of this fact, we may conclude this discussion by reflecting
briefly upon the relation between property and acquisition and Aristotle's chief political question of regimes.

In the first place, government for Aristotle does not exist to
secure property, much less to secure men's unequal abilities to acquire
it. The proper aim of lawmaker and government is rather the promotion
of happiness through the possession and exercise of the moral virtues.
Though some measure of wealth may be necessary equipment for virtuous

activity so understood, Aristotle barely acknowledges any responsibility of the statesman to furnish such wealth. On the other hand, it is
for Aristotle an indictment of a certain case for the rule of the many
that it could authorize an expropriation of the possessions of the
wealthy (1281a15-22). Aristotle's account of distributive justice does
not authorize a redistribution of existing wealth. The separate and
probably unequal ownership of property is for Aristotle a necessary
condition of virtuous activity; in any case, he does not regard an
equalization of possessions as a proposal that would eliminate the major causes of injustice (1267a39).

In the second place, though the Aristotelian political science of
regimes acknowledges and even stresses the importance of that difference between rich and poor generated by the existence of property and
men's varying success in acquiring it, that political science continues
to assert the primacy of the political. The complex relation between
the property question and the question of regimes as well as the final
primacy of the political is suggested both by Aristotle's treatment of
wealth, freedom (poverty), and virtue as claims to rule and by his attempt to promote the cause of polity. Thus the claim of virtue permits
an otherwise unobtainable reconciliation of the claims of wealth and
poverty and erects a standard in terms of which the partisans of both
must begin to act. So too, polity must satisfy rich and poor with
their share in the regime but in doing so may also create an opportunity for virtuous activity.

FOOTNOTES

1 References to the *Politics* will be made thus in parentheses. References to the *Nicomachean Ethics* will be preceded by *EN*. Translations are my own.

2 Aristotle does not describe this "most important" object as natural though he does label it the common advantage.

3 The liberal man will, of course, be scrupulous about getting, though not because he regards this as a noble thing. *EN* 1121a30.

4 I have argued elsewhere that the enumeration of the moral virtues constitutes an ascent from courage and temperance to magnanimity and a descent from magnanimity to justice as a particular virtue. "Political and Distributive Justice," Paper presented to Canadian Political Science Association Meetings, June, 1977, p. 35 n. 54.

5 Thomas Lewis has noted the necessity, not satisfied by many interpreters, "to recognize the distinction between the household and the polis." "Acquisition and Anxiety: Aristotle's Case Against the Market," *Canadian Journal of Economics* XI, no. 1 (February, 1978), p. 72, note 6.

But it must also be noted that the household itself is dealt with in a specifically abstract manner in the first book of the *Politics*; it is treated in relation to the polis and not in relation to any regime or a variety of regimes. The fact that the polis is necessarily and decisively informed by some or other regime is here ignored.

6 Abram Shulsky has suggested that "the more than daily needs" may be those of military defence. See his very valuable study, "The 'Infrastructure' of Aristotle's *Politics* " (unpublished doctoral dissertation, Department of Political Science, University of Chicago, 1972), p. 13.

7 When Aristotle speaks of the perfected household (οἰκία τέλειος) at 1253b4 as made up of slaves and freemen, he refers not to the primitive household of 1252a26 where natural ruler and ruled, or master and slave, are joined for security but to a household whose character is established by the fact that it is a part of a polis. Hence the slave is now a tool for life rather than production and the common interest of master and slave is much more tenuous.

8 Newman suggests this understanding of πρῶτον in light of the reference back to "the first speeches in which the household and slavery were discussed" (1278b17) and the reference forward at 1260b12 to "the regimes." *Politics of Aristotle* (Oxford: Clarendon, 1887) II, p. 131, n. 2.

9 Mathie, "Justice and the Question of Regimes in Ancient and Modern
   Political Philosophy: Aristotle and Hobbes," *Canadian Journal of
   Political Science* IX, no. 3 (September, 1976).

10 Sir Ernest Barker, *The Political Thought of Plato and Aristotle*
   (New York: Dover, 1959) p. 357. Barker suggests that in "dealing
   with the household before the State, Aristotle is following Nature: he is taking first that which comes first, and dealing with
   the part before he describes the whole"; but as we have noted the
   household as it "comes first" and the household as "part" are not
   identical.

11 Newman, *Politics* II, p. 133 n. 14.

12 ταîς ὡρισμέναις τέχναις is here translated according to Newman's
   suggestion. *Politics* II, p. 136 n. 25.

13 The addition of separable, χωριστόν, to the definition of κτῆσις
   would seem to indicate the difference between a man's own body and
   those other tools, animate or inanimate, that he might employ in
   acting. See H. A. Rackham, *Aristotle's Politics* (London: Heine-
   mann, 1967) p. 19.

14 Newman, *Politics* II, p. 137 n. 31.

15 Shulsky, "Infrastructure," p. 40.

16 *Political Thought of Plato and Aristotle*, p. 362.

17 On the failure of "natural rhetoric" as a support of the present
   account of slavery as property and, generally, the complete subordination of acquiring to the household, see Shulsky, "Infrastructure," pp. 51-52.

18 Newman translates ὅσοι γε αντόφυτον εχονσι τὴν εργασίαν as "'lives
   whose work is self-wrought' and not achieved with the help, or at
   the expense, of others, like the life of ἀλλαγῆ καὶ καπηλεία,"
   Politics II, p. 171 n. 40.

19 Barker speaks of Aristotle's teaching here as "a reactionary ar-
   chaism, which abolishes all the economic machinery of civilization in favour of the self-supporting farm and a modicum of barter" and thinks it curious that Aristotle should "have adopted a
   tone so much unlike the rest of the Politics" by identifying the
   natural with the primitive in contradiction of his own general
   teaching. *Political Thought of Plato and Aristotle*, pp. 375-
   376. Newman remarks that "if Aristotle had consistently adhered
   to the view that the primitive is the natural, we might have found
   him denying the naturalness of the City-State in comparison with
   the household, and of the pursuit of good life in comparison with
   that of mere life." *Politics* I, p. 135. Mulgan notes that "it
   does not follow...from his own theory of nature, that what is natural in the sense of primitive or unaffected by human technology
   is therefore best for man." *Aristotle's Political Theory* (Oxford:
   Clarendon, 1977), p. 50.

20 Shulsky demonstrates the inconsistency of this "external teleology" with the account of nature set out in the *Physics*. "Infrastructure," pp. 61-65.

21 Shulsky, "Infrastructure," p. 15. n. 2.

22 Karl Marx, *Capital*, Volume I, Part I, Section I.

23 This might cause one to hesitate in supposing that Aristotle is concerned to promote such a form of exchange.

24 On these critics see Newman, *Politics* II, pp. 187-188, n. 11.

25 *Republic*, 345E - 347A.

26 Joseph Cropsey remarks that because Aristotle saw acquisition as "'natural',...deplorable, and...indispensable to civil peace" it became the "public or political function of political philosophy... to turn attention toward the meaning of nature as end and to divert attention from nature as the beginning; or to turn attention toward nature as provident and friendly to human excellence, and away from nature as polemic and divisive, which it is." "On the Relation of Political Science and Economics," *American Political Science Review*, LIV, No. 1 (March, 1960), p. 10.

27 For an exploration of the meaning of this disagreement see Shulsky, "Infrastructure," pp. 98-144.

28 1132b31-34. "It is the reciprocal rendering of an equivalent amount of dissimilar things, not the receipt of an equal amount of the same things that holds the State together," Newman paraphrases. *Politics* II, p. 223 n. 30.

29 Newman, *ibid.* Shulsky argues that the extreme disjunction of ruler and ruled in the city of the armed camp constitutes one of Aristotle's more serious objections to the Socratic scheme. "Infrastructure," pp. 110-111. As the success of that city requires a great deception of ruled by rulers, the ruled can never honour their rulers for their actual service, for "the two groups are so far apart that proportionate reciprocity cannot exist between them."

30 A similar argument as to the political importance of such bonds is an important basis of St. Augustine's justification of the rule against incest. *The City of God* (New York: Random House, 1950), p. 500.

David Daube expounds a number of problems in Roman Law. He demonstrates how scholars' solutions to these problems have varied both
with the fashions of the time and with the personal characteristics of
the researcher. Particular attention is paid to the anomaly in the
law of usufruct by which the child of a slave woman held in usufruct
belonged to the owner instead of the usufructuary; to the debate between the Proculians and Sabinians over who owned an object made of
some one's raw material without the owner's permission; and to the
problem of interpolations in Justinian's compilation.

FASHIONS AND IDIOSYNCRACIES IN THE EXPOSITION OF THE
ROMAN LAW OF PROPERTY

I

There is no scholarly effort independent of fashion - by which I understand a cultural trend - and idiosyncracy - by which I understand a personal bent. In focusing on this aspect, I am myself providing an illustration. Distrust in the objectivity of academia is definitely the mode - in fact, it extends to what used to be the exact sciences and to mathematics - and my resentment against the authoritarianism under which I was brought up furnishes a private incentive. Of course, fashion and idiosyncracy overlap: the former may owe much to the energy of an individual, the latter is usually coloured by prevalent conditions. I hasten to add that to be directed by these forces does not mean to go wrong. It may mean that, as may any route. But, say, a survivor of Auschwitz writing on existentialist ethics could come up with valuable ideas. Anyhow, the risk of error is presumably lessened by awareness of it.

II

Let me begin with idiosyncracy. A Roman usufructuary had the right to use and take the fruits of another's property. By way of exception, however, the offspring of a slave woman belonged, not to him, but to the owner. Quite a few explanations of this rule have been proposed, and I would here mention three.

1. When, in the late Republic, the institution of usufruct grew up, experts at husbandry confined the term "fruit" to produce regularly recurrent, capable of planned cultivation. "There is a sixfold division of seasons [says Varro[1]] connected in some way with sun and moon, since virtually every fruit comes to its final perfection in five stages - preparation, sowing, nourishing, harvesting, storing - to be brought into use at the sixth - marketing." The jurists followed this definition they found in a prominent science. Nor, in so doing, were they forgetful of the practical consequences: the constant yield of a thing might well be deemed to be a usufructuary's main concern. A distant echo of this consideration may be contained in the *Digest*: "slave women are not hastily procured for the purpose of breeding."[2]

This, then, is solution number one of the puzzle, sober, academic. Something like it is advanced in many textbooks.[3] I taught it in my more earnest moods at Oxford.

2. Solution number two relies on another passage from the *Digest* which, not surprisingly, also appears in Justinian's *Institutes*:[4] all fruits are furnished by nature for mankind's sake, hence a member of mankind cannot possibly be "fruit." Few modern Romanists believe that such moral or philosophical esteem of humanity really caused or even contributed to the rule in question; they consider it - rightly, I think - a piece of late, cheap cosmetics. Girard calls it puerile,[5] Buckland remarks that "it must have seemed somewhat ironical to a slave"[6] - incapable of owning anything, indeed, a chattel. What difference does it make to a slave-baby whether its neck can be wrung by the mother's usufructuary or by her owner? Actually, if we look closely at the practical implications of the rule, the high-minded reason for it turns out quite inappropriate. There is enormous cruelty to the mother: as the child belongs to her owner, it will be physically separated from her who is being held in usufruct.[7]

Yet despite all this, Alan Watson accepts this number two as the true, historical background.[8] He speaks of a "noble" concept, though admitting that it might be imperfectly translated into practice. I would set this down to his upbringing in a deeply committed, non-conformist Scottish milieu: he wants to find a spark of idealism in the celebrated jurists.

3. The third attempt takes note of the fact that usufruct grew up as marriage without *manus* became prevalent. The wife, while retaining her prospects in her original family, would not, as in marriage with *manus*, acquire a daughter's rights to her husband's estate. Hence the latter would provide for her by will, appointing his children to be his heirs but leaving her a usufruct. In course of time usufruct was extended to other situations, yet a number of rules which had been laid down at the initial stage, in connection with widowhood, continued to live on - the one here discussed among them.

A man dies. His son inherits, the widow has a usufruct. A slave woman who is part of the estate gives birth to a child. More often than not, it will be the son's child. That is why, though apples and the young of animals and the earnings from leases go to the usufructuary, the offspring of a slave woman belongs to the owner - the son.

In the usufruct of the classical era, no longer specially associated
with its original area of operation, the rule is an oddity.

The author of this explanation is John Kelly,[9] both a professor
and a politician. His works on Roman procedure stand out by looking
beyond the dry law into what actually went on. He has also, under a
pseudonym, published some lively fiction. Clearly, he knows where
it's at.

Nowadays my heart prompts me to go along with him. And my head
comes up with a helpful thought. If he is right, in the original
setup - son-heir and widow-usufructuary living under the same roof
(ordinarily) - mother and child stay together. This is distinctly consonant with sound economics and convenience.

Scholars will try to assess the relative plausibility of the
three accounts. Some will make a choice, some will prefer a combination, some will reject all of them. If the debate leaves us in the
dark about the subject-matter, at least it will shed light on the
character of the participants.

III

Turning to fashions, though generally my selection will be rather
arbitrary, I feel I must open by a glance at the exposition of that
central notion: ownership. In the popular mind, ownership as an individual's absolute legal power over an object is among the two or
three most striking characteristics of Roman law. For several decades,
however, Romanists have done their best to demonstrate first, that
things were very different at the archaic stage, i.e. they resembled
what we find in other ancient Indo-European cultures; secondly, that
even the mature Roman ownership must be interpreted against a background of all sorts of extra-legal restraints such as tradition, ethics, state interest.

One of the factors accounting for the movement is the adoption by
most civil law countries of modern codes which completely replace the
original sources. As a result, the latter can be subjected to historical inquiry unfettered by any fear of how what emerges might affect actual decisions of the courts. Another cause far from negligible is
this century's reaction against the last one's apotheosis of private
capitalism.

Up to very recently, it was agreed that classical law allowed an owner of land unlimited freedom to build: if his neighbour's light was totally cut off, it was just too bad. Alan Rodger now has made a strong case against this view. Indeed, he argues persuasively that, from the middle of the first century B.C., even a valuable pleasant view must not be blocked.[10]

At times, the current re-evaluation is perhaps overdone. One could imagine flickers of absolute ownership existing even in the epoch of *legis actio*, when litigation looks like having concentrated on the relatively better right of one of two pretenders. From what moment would a child begin to feel that certain objects are his, or somebody else's, versus any third party's interference?[11]

Too much can be made of the absence from early Latin - or Greek or Hebrew - of a term for "ownership."[12] A social phenomenon no less than one in nature may considerably antedate its final labelling by a noun. Table manners and extradition went on long before so named. This is not to deny that such naming is a significant step; it is merely to warn against too far-reaching conclusions.

We must not forget that, in a way, it is easier to become aware of minor rights over an object than of the all-embracing title. In the latter case, the thing itself stands in the light: in the absence of painstaking reflection, the owner is apt to think of having it rather than of having a legal relationship to it. There is no such block with regard to servitudes and usufruct, hence they will more readily appear as rights over the thing encroaching on the owner's position. (At least after that remote period when a rustic servitude made the owner of the dominant estate a sort of co-owner with his neighbour.)

The tangle here in question is equally common outside the law: a material datum engrossing the attention slows up recognition of the abstract, general one back of it. The Old Testament has no inclusive designation for "to commit suicide;" it sticks to the concrete "to fall upon one's sword," "to strangle oneself." One of the earliest passages in Jewish literature with the comprehensive notion has regard to a prospective action: the *Fourth Gospel* represents people as wondering whether Jesus proposes "to kill himself."[13] No actual, solid incident obstructs the view. A comparable case is furnished by the Greek word for time, *chronos*, first used with reference to the interval between events - battles, raids and the like; while they go on,

time is unnoticed. Just so, in the *Winter's Tale*, Shakespeare brings
Time on the stage to represent, summarize, the fifteen quiet years
separating the remarkable happenings of the first part and those of
the second. Even today, when I say that this morning I have no time
since lecturing but I shall have time in the evening, I am speaking of
time not covered over by some going-on. An illustration from the *XII
Tables* is *iniuria*, unlawfulness, denoting an assault that leaves no
permanent, visible damage: a slap in the face, for example. The same
section deals with *membrum ruptum*, a limb torn off, and *os fractum*, a
bone broken: here people concentrate on the visible horror and not on
the unlawfulness behind it. Gradually, of course, it is realized that
these cases no less than a slap involve unlawfulness.

How long-lasting the effects of this type of development can be
is shown by the fact that, even in Justinian, while servitudes and
usufruct are classed as incorporeal things, more specifically, things
existing in or by the law, ownership is still not so classed, being
evidently mixed up with the object, the corporeal thing; and it is
significant that by *iura praediorum*, rights of estates, is still meant
only the servitudes attaching to the dominant property; the term never
includes the owner's right.[14]

IV

If, not acting at your behest, I made a new thing - a chair, a
vessel - with your raw material - your wood, your gold - according to
the Sabinians, the thing was yours, according to the Proculians, mine.
Many authorities regard the Proculian standpoint as a refinement, in
one or both of the following respects: (1) it put the spiritual, the
form, above crude matter, (2) it opted for social progress, the right
of labour, a sort of proto-socialism.[15]

Whether correct or false, these characterisations obviously imply
not only heavy value judgments but also the conviction that mankind,
or at least ancient Roman jurisprudence, moves from lower values to
higher ones. It is also clear that the two postulates - the Proculians recognize form, the Proculians recognize labour - must have been
first elaborated in different eras and milieus.

How unlikely they are to have paid homage to the right of labour
may be seen from the fact that, even for them, if I worked at your behest - say, you commissioned a statue and supplied the gold - the

product belonged to you. I might be the greatest artist in the
world, it made no difference. The technical justification would be
that at no moment in the process were you divested of possession. I
never had more than "detention."

     A view rapidly gaining currency is much more plausible: it was
the Sabinians who innovated.[16] The original setting of the problem
was surely, not academic reflection, but litigation. Suppose I, not
acting under your orders, made a chair with your wood and you brought
a *vindicatio*. In primitive times, you could not declare: "this chair
is mine." All you could show was that you had owned the wood - which
was gone. This must lead to the Proculian result: you lost, I was
owner of the new object. The Sabinians got away from the rigid interpretation of "this chair." They allowed your material to live on in
the artifact. Having owned the wood, you were also entitled to say:
"this chair is mine." The new object was yours.

     The jurists seem to have enjoyed expanding on the respective mer-
its of the two solutions. Actually, yet a further one was added; and
the matter was not finally settled till Justinian plumped for the
third one. A major reason indecision could be tolerated so long is
that the consequences in actual life were minimal. (The same goes
for not a few of the drawn-out disputes between the schools.) As already remarked, if I used your material by agreement with you, no
question arose: it was never doubted by anyone that you owned the
omelette I made as your cook with your eggs, or the shoes I made as
your employee with your leather. If I stole your material, I was liable for a multiple of its value as thief; whether what I worked it
into belonged to you or me would not be terribly important. This
leaves mainly the case where I used your material in good faith - having *bona fide* possession. It could not have occurred too frequently,
and even when it did occur would mostly be disposed of amicably. No
doubt one may think up some other relevant situations; but, on the
whole, there was plainly no undue pressure to cut short pleasurable
controversy for action.

     The practical unimportance explains also why Justinian could pro-
nounce in favour of the third solution, the most awkward of the lot.
If I made cider from your apples, mistakenly believing them to be
mine, it belonged to me (since irreducible to the raw material); if
Cellini made candlesticks from your ingot, mistakenly believing it to
be his, they belonged to you (since reducible). Stupid, but harmless.

The restriction of the problem to independent work, not under the owner's orders, has not been lost on medieval and modern thinkers trying to find here help in shoring up private property. Pius XI's encyclical *Quadragesimo Anno* affirms: "The only form of labour, however, which gives the working man a title to its fruits is that which a man exercises as his own master." The German translation adds the adverb *natürlich*: "naturally" this is the only form entitling him.[17] A hint, I suppose, that the ultimate source of the doctrine is natural law.

V

In paragraph III I stressed linguistic aspects, and increased attention to this province is definitely one modern trend. I have participated in various ways - for example, by commenting on the action noun derived from a verb, expulsion from expel, termination from terminate.[18] For an action noun to be introduced, there must have been a good deal of reflection on the activity concerned. People sell and donate for a long time before sale and donation come in as a result of abstraction, systematization, classification. The doings have become institutions.

To seize an object is *occupare*, to abandon one *derelinquere*. The institutions *occupatio* and *derelictio* never occur in the Roman sources. To transfer something to the heir is *transmittere ad heredem*; *transmissio* is first met in a law by Justinian.[19] How slow this kind of abstraction was in making its way is shown by the absence from the classical texts of so basic a concept as *acquisitio*; they speak only of *acquirere*; the noun emerges at a snail's pace in post-classical ones.[20]

Much can be learned by taking note of the earlier or later birth of one action noun compared with another. In contradistinction to *acquisitio, alienatio* is classical. General rules about making over property - one may think of groups with restricted powers, women, prodigals - were formulated by the jurists long before general rules about receiving property. *Auctio* is frequent already in Plautus:[21] that special case of *augere*, a public bidding competition, very early became an established thing.

As for the agent noun[22] - baker, seer, from bake, see - it is often narrower than the verb, singling out him who performs the action in a striking fashion. A baker bakes for a living, a seer sees

what is invisible to others. An illustration from Roman obligations
is *sponsor*, describing not everyone who *spondet*, promises, but only
him who, peculiarly, promises in support of another person, the sure-
ty. The use of *auctor* in the law of property is not so dissimilar.
This term designates not everyone who *auget*, augments, but only him
who, remarkably, augments, warrants, somebody else's title.

VI

For the past fifty years or so, the contact of Roman law with
rhetoric has excited much interest;[23] and for the past twenty-five,
quite a few writers in this field have speculated on the role of the
rhetorical doctrine of the *topica*, arguments which, though rational,
yet lack absolute cogency.[24] We possess Aristotle's and Cicero's
versions of this doctrine. For Viehweg,[25] it forms the backbone of
the casuistic method of the leading classics who proceeded, not from
a system into which the problem in hand would be fitted, but from the
particular problem to be solved by bringing together and weighing up
any relevant considerations. His first illustration is a discussion
of usucapion by Julian.[26]

A significant contribution may be found in Dieter Nörr's mono-
graph on *praescriptio longi temporis*, the protection of one who has
been in possession of an object for a long time. This institution,
unlike many, did not grow up in the obscurity of the early Republic:
it dates from the late classical period, around A.D. 200. Yet it
presents an extraordinary number of doubtful features. According to
Nörr, this is due neither to the scarcity of texts about it nor to
deficient modern analysis but to its "topical" nature. Its creators,
that is, pragmatically gave prominence now to substantive law, now to
procedural; now to possession, now to presumption of title; now to
security, now to the analogy of usucapion; now to one figure for
"long time," now to another.[27]

One of the stimuli behind this involvement in rhetoric is the
desire to place Roman law in a living context. It - or much of it -
was meant, after all, to serve or obstruct a party to a dispute. Of
considerable importance, too, is the - by now pretty universal - recognition that the quasi-mathematical logic that used to be attributed to Roman law was an illusion. Even the logic of the sciences
has been taken down a peg or two: we have become very self-critical,

there are no more gods among us. The latter development indeed plays
a somewhat paradoxical part in the debate about the influence of the
topica on the jurists. At first blush, it would seem to support the
side believing in this influence. In reality, it has been held to
speak against it. The way the jurists set about their task is so
general, it has been maintained, that there is no need to bring in
the *topica*.[28] Clearly, one of those controversies which may never be
settled to the satisfaction of all or even a majority.

VII

In a sense, the question of Roman law and rhetoric is a segment
of the general one of foreign input. Here, fashions and idiosyncracies play an extraordinary part. It is not only that a discovery
like that of the *Code of Hammurabi* or a cache of papyri may produce a
wave of interest. Quite apart from this, scholarly attitudes vary to
an astonishing degree in different periods, countries, persons. Apparently deep emotions favouring a positive or negative approach are
involved.

Nor should we overlook mundane factors. For instance, the alien
material is often in a difficult language, which must make it tempting *a priori* to deny its relevance. (The treatment of modern writings in an unaccustomed tongue provides analogies. Some while ago,
I received a Bulgarian treatise on Roman law. I can plough my way
through Russian, but Bulgarian is beyond me. So I console myself
with the thought that the book probably contains little that is new.)
While it would be wrong to assume that no gifted linguist will defend
the autarky of the classics, as a rule no one but a gifted linguist
will be keen on discovering foreign influence. One of the conclusions Alan Watson reaches in his work *Legal Transplants* is: "most
changes in most systems are the result of borrowing."[29] Such a statement is not likely to come from one who is unilingual.

Pignus, pledge, was a mode of real security which left the debt-
or owner of the object pawned: the creditor obtained only possession.
In course of time, it became possible to pawn a thing without even
handing it over. The creditor, that is, would have a possessory remedy or an action *in rem* only when the debt was due. In most texts,
this relaxed variant goes under the old designation *pignus*. A fair
number of them, however, call it *hypotheca* - a Greek word. Some

authorities conclude that the idea originated in Greece; others that
the texts concerned are spurious; yet others that, while the institution is native, already middle and late classical lawyers made occasional use of a distinction met in Greek terminology. The third
view - advocated, for example, by Wolfgang Kunkel[30] - appears the
most attractive to me.

VIII

This brings us to interpolations, alterations of classical
statements by later editors and Justinian. In the first third of the
century, there was intense preoccupation with them. Especially in
Germany, the enactment of the *Bürgerliche Gesetzbuch*, by turning the
Corpus Juris into a purely historical monument, no longer to be
treated by anyone as a consistent, unitary legislation, opened the
way to uninhibited critical probing. As a result of such enthusiasm,
many a passage was held spurious on inadequate grounds. By now the
climate is different, perhaps owing not only to the normal swing of
the pendulum but also to a longing for security. In fact, there may
be a little too much zeal to pronounce in favour of genuineness.

A fragment from Ulpian runs:[31] "Ownership has nothing in common
with possession; and therefore one who has begun a real action for
the thing is not refused the interdict *uti possidetis*; for by bringing the real action he is not considered to have renounced possession."

Beseler, in an article published in 1925, maintains that the initial clause, "Ownership has nothing in common with possession," is
without substantive content and lends no support to the opinion. The
classical utterance starts "One who has begun a real action," and the
reason for the verdict comes at the end, "for by bringing the real
action" etc.[32]

Probably no colleague of mine nowadays accepts any of this. The
text is constantly quoted, never with any question-mark.[33] In Buckland and McNair's *Roman Law and Common Law*, it figures as epitomizing
the Roman distinction between ownership and possession.[34]

Yet I wonder whether a grain of truth may not be salvaged.
Beseler in this piece is out to prove that the classics do not employ
et ideo, "and therefore." No doubt he goes too far. But the phrase
is indeed a rather easy connective and frequently resorted to by the
compilers when they abbreviate or re-arrange the original.

That one who has sued - scil. unsuccessfully - by means of the
interdict may go on to sue by means of the real action is mentioned
by Paul.[35] The ban on suing twice for the same thing does not operate since, as he remarks, the interdict has regard to possession, the
real action to ownership. This solution can never have been questioned. A foremost function of the interdict is precisely to prepare
the real action, i.e. by determining possessor and non-possessor to
allot the superior role of defendant and the inferior one of plaintiff in the action about title. Paul here gives the theoretical justification for the practice: the statement comes from his chapter
on the bar to a second process about the same matter.[36]

Ulpian's problem is not simply the reverse: may one who has
lost the real action go on to institute the interdict? What he asks
is whether the latter may be instituted by one who has begun the
former, scil. while it is on. One can think of situations where this
might plausibly be wanted; for instance, it is only after commencing
the real action that plaintiff comes upon evidence showing defendant
to have been allowed onto the land by plaintiff's deceased father
precario, under a revocable licence - so his possession is no good
against plaintiff.[37] It should be noted that Ulpian must be dealing
with a dispute about land: the interdict he names is *uti possidetis*.
And the fragment, as we know from Lenel,[38] goes back to a part of his
work mainly devoted to defective possession, i.e. possession obtained
by force, clandestinely or by licence. (But Lenel did not see how
the fragment fitted into this part.[39] He would have been pleased
with my suggestion.)

How is he likely to have answered? Presumably he made a preliminary reference to the inapplicability of *non bis in idem*: to assert
possession is not the same as to assert ownership. But his observation would be far more subdued than the present opening. For the
chief difficulty of the case lies elsewhere. It stems from the principle that the real action is brought by the non-possessor against the
possessor. Plaintiff in a real action, therefore, may be said to be
acknowledging defendant's possession. Has he not, then, debarred himself from turning around midway through the litigation and demanding
that the roles be reversed?

To go by the report before us, Ulpian declared that he is not
estopped. Perhaps he did take this straightforward, liberal stand.
Quite possibly, however, it is substituted by the compilers for

something a little less absolute; say, the interdict is feasible till
litiscontestatio moves the real action from the magistrate to the
judge. In Justinian's procedure, this division no longer exists; so
the limitation would be crossed out.

Three conclusions emerge as pretty certain. First, the jurist's
exposé contained more detail than is preserved. At least, there must
have been a brief indication of the circumstances (such as *precarium*
granted by the *de cuius*) in which the problem could arise. Secondly,
the opening sentence reveals a type of rewriting Justinian is given
to: a sober classical explanation of a decision is changed into a
maxim.[40] Indeed, as often, the latter is too sweeping. That "ownership has nothing in common with possession" is an exaggeration. Actually, *nihil commune* stands in front, which makes the denial of any
tie even more emphatic - "Nothing in common has ownership with possession." (Already Buckland apparently found it a bit much: he
calls it "a strong statement.")[41] Thirdly, "and therefore" papers
over one of the cracks resulting as the codifiers revised the discussion.

IX

This may be the place for a reminiscence.

In the late 1920s and early 30s I often visited Lenel, then in
retirement at Freiburg. My parents' house was Goethestrasse 35, a-
bout seven minutes on foot from his Holbeinstrasse 5. In his whole
long career he had in fact only two personal pupils (at least that is
how he saw it): Josef Partsch, who died at age 43 in 1925 and whose
obituary in the *Savigny Zeitschrift* - a moving tribute - was written
by Lenel,[42] and me. Which lends Kantorowicz's reconstruction of
Lenel's academic genealogy[43] - showing an unbroken chain of transmission right from Irnerius around 1100 - particular meaning for me and
my personal pupils.

One morning when I called on him, he showed me a postcard just
received from Beseler:

+

considerare

R. I. P.

Which meant that yet another word was to be consigned to the post-
classical rubbish heap. To appreciate the communication, one must

remember that in 1925 Lenel had sounded the alarm against hypercriti-
cism, singling out A. Albertario and G. V. Beseler.[44] The title of
the paper, *Interpolationenjagd*, "Interpolation hunt," became a slo-
gan. From then, he repeatedly opposed Beseler's radical methods.[45]
The latter, besides replying in print,[46] took a naughty boy's pleasure in needling authority - hence this frivolous announcement designed to shock the old master. He definitely succeeded. Lenel sad-
ly shook his head and looked at me as if imploring help.

Beseler, besides absolute command of the material and a natural
affinity with classical legal thinking, had a genius's flair for the
subtleties of Latin usage. He also had many a genius's knack of putting people's backs up. At the time of this incident, though he far
surpassed most others in his field, he was still *Honorarprofessor* at
Kiel, where he had begun as *Privatdozent* some twenty-five years before. No university ever offered to make him *Ordentlicher Professor*.
Lenel was the greatest Roman lawyer, *stricto sensu*, since Julian
whose Edict he reconstructed.

X

What fashions may we expect in the next decades? I hope for
two, above all.

1. The position of women in regard to property needs re-exami-
nation. Not enough attention has so far been paid to subtler modes
of discrimination - for example, *privilegia odiosa*, fake privileges
which, while ostensibly helpful, in reality degrade.[47] Taxation may
be one of the areas in need of re-evaluation.

2. Anthropological and psychological - even psychoanalytical -
insights should be put to greater use. The earliest meaning of *con-
trectare* seems to have been "to touch obscenely." When the jurists
employed it as a criterion of theft, were they "personalizing," even
"sexualizing," property? We are not surprised to hear a sailboat referred to as "she;" and to many a youngster his motorcycle or car offers a relationship passing the love of women. The Romans may have
gone further.[48]

FOOTNOTES

1 Varro, *Res Rusticae* 1.37.4. Translation based on W. D. Hooper,
   Cato, *On Agriculture*, Varro, *On Agriculture* (Loeb Classical
   Library), 1936, pp. 261 ff.

2 *Digest* 5.3.27 pr., Ulpian XV *ad edictum*.

3 See e.g. P. F. Girard, *Manuel Élémentaire de Droit Romain*, 4th
   ed., 1906, p. 247.

4 *Digest* 22.1.28.1, Gaius II *rerum cottidianarum*, Justinian's *Institutes* 2.1.37.

5 *Op. cit.*, p. 247.

6 See W. W. Buckland, *The Roman Law of Slavery*, 1908, p. 21.

7 How M. Kaser can say that "it remains with the mother" and invoke
   humanitarian motives (*Zeitschrift der Savigny-Stiftung*, vol. 75,
   1958, p. 199), I do not understand.

8 *Tulane Law Review*, vol. 42, 1968, pp. 291 ff., *The Law of Property
   in the Roman Republic*, 1968, p. 216.

9 I have it from him: it has not appeared in print. - A slight
   contretemps. I sent him a xerox of my draft asking whether I re-
   ported him correctly, and I interpreted a prolonged silence as approval. But he was abroad, and now, at the proof stage, I hear
   from him as follows: "Your paraphrase of my suggestion is accurate, though what I really meant to emphasize was that the exception which the *partus ancillae* rule forms in usufruct would have
   been intolerable had there been a blood link between the usufructuary and the child; but as the *original* usufructuary was a woman,
   such a link was biologically impossible and so the curious rule
   avoided giving, so to speak, human offence. It is not necessarily part of this reflection that the *dominus nudae proprietatis* would
   typically be the child's father - if he lived on the premises, of
   course this would very regularly be the case - but it might equally be the offspring of a male slave living in *contubernium* with
   the mother." So his phantasy is more restrained than I represented it as being. But where does this leave me?

10 See A. Rodger, *Owners and Neighbours in Roman Law*, 1972.

11 Cp. A. M. Honoré, in *Oxford Essays in Jurisprudence*, ed. by A. G.
    Guest, 1961, p. 114.

12 See E. Rabel, *Zeitschrift der Savigny-Stiftung für Rechtsges-
    chichte*, vol. 36, 1915, Rom. Abt., pp. 341 f., M. Kaser, *Eigentum
    und Besitz im Älteren Römischen Recht*, 1943, pp. 3 ff.

13 John 8.22. See D. Daube, *Philosophy and Public Affairs*, vol. 1, 1972, pp. 395 f., repr. *Suicide and Life-Threatening Behaviour*, vol. 7, 1977, pp. 140 f.

14 Justinian's *Institutes* 2.2. See D. Daube, in *Studi Solazzi*, 1948, pp. 49 ff. of reprint.

15 See R. von Jhering, *Geist des Römischen Rechts*, part III.1, 6th and 7th ed., 1924, p. 323: *Recht der Arbeit*.

16 See F. de Zulueta, *The Institutes of Gaius*, Part II, 1953, p. 79.

17 See D. Daube, *Zeitschrift der Savigny-Stiftung für Rechtsgeschichte*, vol. 90, 1973, Rom. Abt., p. 5 (in German), *Juridical Review*, vol. 18 N.S., 1973, pp. 128 f. (in English).

18 See D. Daube, *Roman Law*, 1969, pp. 11 ff.

19 Justinian's *Code* 6.30.19.1, A.D. 529.

20 E.g. Ulpian's *Regulae* 19, rubric.

21 E.g. *Menaechmi* 5.9.93 ff., 1153 ff.

22 See D. Daube *op. cit.*, pp. 2 ff.

23 Sparked by J. Stroux, *Summum ius summa iniuria*, 1926.

24 This line was initiated by T. Viehweg, *Topik und Jurisprudenz*, 1954.

25 *Op. cit.*, 5th ed., 1974, pp. 46 ff.

26 *Digest* 41.3.33, Julian XLIV *digestorum*.

27 D. Nörr, *Die Entstehung der longi temporis praescriptio*, 1969, pp. 6 f., 42 ff., 62, 112 f. The main results of the book are already offered in *The Irish Jurist*, N.S. vol. 3, 1968, pp. 352 ff., but with no explicit reference to the *topica*. - In a letter written to me after I showed him a xerox of my draft, he informs me that in the meantime he has revised his views about the topical in law. An article by him on the question will appear in the forthcoming *Festschrift* for H. J. Wolff.

28 See F. Horak, *Rationes Decidendi*, vol. 1, 1969, pp. 45 ff.

29 See Alan Watson, *Legal Transplants*, 1974, p. 95.

30 See W. Kunkel, *Römisches Recht*, on the basis of P. Jörs, 3rd ed., 1949, p. 156.

31 *Digest* 41.2.12.1, Ulpian LXX *ad edictum*. Translation by F. de Zulueta, *Digest 41, 1 & 2, Translation and Commentary*, 1922, p. 57.

32 See G. V. Beseler, *Zeitschrift der Savigny-Stiftung für Rechtsgeschichte*, vol. 45, 1925, Rom. Abt., p. 479.

33   See e.g. M. Kaser, *Das Römische Privatrecht*, vol. 1, 1955, p. 325.

34   See W. W. Buckland and A. D. McNair, *Roman Law and Common Law*, 2nd ed. by F. H. Lawson, 1952, p. 62.

35   *Digest* 44.2.14.3, Paul LXX *ad edictum*.

36   See O. Lenel, *Palingenesia Iuris Civilis*, 1889, vol. 1, p. 1085.

37   *Digest* 43.26.8.1., Ulpian LXXI *ad edictum*, 43.26.12.1, Celsus XXV *digestorum*.

38   See O. Lenel *op. cit.*, vol. 2, p. 822.

39   See O. Lenel, *Das Edictum Perpetuum*, 3rd ed., 1927, p. 469 n. 13 where, despairingly, he labels it as an excursus or appendix to either defective possession or *interdicta utilia*.

40   See D. Daube, *Zeitschrift der Savigny-Stiftung für Rechtsgeschichte*, vol. 76, 1959, Rom. Abt., pp. 176 ff., P. Stein, *Regulae Iuris*, 1966, pp. 117 ff.

41   See W. W. Buckland and A. D. McNair *l.c.* *Cp.* also W. Kunkel, *Römisches Recht*, on the basis of P. Jörs, 3rd ed., 1949, p. 113 n. 11: *nicht immer werden indessen Eigentum und Besitz einander so scharf gegenübergetreten sein*.

42   See O. Lenel, *Zeitschrift der Savigny-Stiftung für Rechtsgeschichte*, vol. 45, 1925, Rom. Abt., pp. V ff. This issue of the *Zeitschrift* was curiously focal in my early days as a Romanist. Besides the obituary of Partsch and the article on *et ideo* quoted above, it contains Lenel's *Interpolationenjagd*, to be mentioned presently, as also W. Kunkel's debut, a brilliant if slightly overbold attack on the classicality of *diligentia* and *neglegentia* (pp. 266 ff.). Four years later, he left Freiburg for Göttingen and I followed him as his student. When Hitler came to power, I found refuge at Cambridge; Lenel had given me a letter to H. F. Jolowicz, who sent me to W. W. Buckland. Buckland thought Kunkel's thesis far too extreme: in *Studi P. Bonfante*, vol. 2, 1929, pp. 85 ff., *Law Quarterly Review*, vol. 48, 1932, pp. 217 ff. Kunkel's rejoinder may be found in W. Kunkel, *Römisches Recht*, on the basis of P. Jörs, 3rd ed., 1949, p. 177 n. 23 and p. 178 n. 31.

43   See H. Kantorowicz, *Zeitschrift der Savigny-Stiftung für Rechtsgeschichte*, vol. 50, 1930, pp. 475 ff.

44   See O. Lenel, *Zeitschrift der Savigny-Stiftung für Rechtsgeschichte*, vol. 45, 1925, Rom. Abt., pp. 17 ff.

45   See e.g. O. Lenel, *Zeitschrift der Savigny-Stiftung für Rechtsgeschichte*, vol. 49, 1929, Rom. Abt., pp. 7 ff.

46   See e.g. G. v. Beseler, in *Studi P. Bonfante*, vol. 2, 1929, p. 62.

47   See D. Daube, in the forthcoming Memorial Volume for Walter Fischel.

48   More comments on this in a forthcoming paper by me on Lucrece.

Susan Treggiari examines the attitude of the Roman aristocracy toward property, especially landed estates and slaves. Wide examination
of the sources suggests that the Romans did not view land and slaves
in a purely commercial way as commodities to be bought and sold, as
has sometimes been argued in the literature. There is evidence that
the Romans felt emotional ties to both land and slaves which must be
taken into account in a complete portrait of Roman property relationships.

SENTIMENT AND PROPERTY: SOME ROMAN ATTITUDES

The poet Horace, in one of his verse letters on philosophical
themes, describes his attempt to become wise and good and says he is
trying to subordinate things to himself, not himself to things,
"...mihi res non me rebus subiungere conor."[1] *Res* or things can mean
both external circumstances and property. The ancient moralists were
much exercised by the context in which a man's moral life took place:
could he be good and happy in unfavourable circumstances? They come
sometimes to surprising conclusions, such as the notorious Stoic doctrine that a good man can be happy even on the rack.

Wealth and property are among the most noticeable of externals
and philosophers held various views about them. One extreme view is
epitomised by Diogenes the Cynic, who held that a philosopher should
divest himself of all worldly goods except the bare essentials. Asceticism in this extreme form had a wide appeal in the late Roman Empire, when the monastic movement began, and we find, for instance,
two young people of the highest Roman aristocracy, Melania the Younger
and her insignificant husband Pinianus, frantically shedding all their
properties (which included a house in Rome, a palace just outside the
City and estates all over the West), freeing eight thousand slaves and
transferring others, and withdrawing from society to live, first in
Africa and then in the Holy Land, in revolting and much-respected
squalor.[2]

A more moderate philosophical opinion held that wealth was morally neutral, that a wise man would choose to have it if he could do so
without compromising his virtue, but that he must be able to do without it if necessary. The technical word for the morally neutral, desirable object is *prokekrimenon*. This moderate line is taken by Romans such as Seneca, an extremely rich man who occasionally practised
doing without his usual comforts, and Horace, who claims that he
would be prepared to give up his position and possessions if they
threatened his independence of mind.[3] There is also very strongly
present in Horace the idea that a modest competence, which commands
the necessities of a leisured life but not dangerous luxuries and
display, is to be desired: "If a man has the luck to have enough, he
must not want anything more."[4]

The central concern is with what wealth does to its possessor,
that it may make him anxious not to lose it, soft and self-indulgent
and greedy for more. Although avarice may deprive others of their
possessions, there is little emphasis on the social injustice of
large concentrations of wealth in the hands of individuals. Nor do
ancient writers insist on the moral duty of the rich man to administer
his wealth for the good of others. The moralist stereotypes the vices
of the rich man as *avaritia* and *luxuria*. The danger to which Horace
realises that he himself is prone is much more interesting. As a man
who is *pauper*, which means comfortably off but neither rich in Roman
terms nor poor in our terms, he may become too attached to his way of
life and to his worldly goods and forget to put moral goodness first.
In particular he knows that he may love his Sabine farm too much and
forget that he is only a temporary owner. To quote his famous re-
minder to Postumus, in a prose translation.

> The land must be left and house and pleasing wife
> and of the trees here you cultivate none will go
> with you, their short-lived owner, except the
> dreaded cypresses. An heir more worthy of it will
> drink the Caecuban now guarded by a hundred locks
> and he will stain the tiled floor with that proud
> wine, finer than that at pontifical dinners.[5]

Horace is not, of course, saying that it is wrong to love possessions
of this sort - indeed this eclectic bachelor rates a compatible wife
among the *prokekrimena* - but he is saying that we must be prepared to
give them up. Horace must own things and they must not own him.

It is not acquisitiveness which will be discussed, but attachment to beloved possessions and, in particular, the pull which certain
types of property may exert on their owner. We shall consider two
kinds of property which it is easy to anthropomorphise, so that we can
say they have an effect on us: land and slaves.

I

The Romans saw land as the safest investment and as socially and
morally respectable, in contrast with commerce. As Cicero says, explicitly expounding a Stoic theory,

> But commerce, if it is on a small scale, must be
> thought sordid, but if it is large-scale and
> wholesale, bringing in many products from all
> over the world and distributing them without
> false advertising to many people, it is not
> really to be decried, but rather, if sated or,

> better, satisfied with its gains, as in the old
> days it went from the sea to the harbour, it
> takes itself now from the harbour to the country,
> it seems that it can perfectly justifiably be
> praised. For of all profitable pursuits agri-
> culture is the best, sweetest, pleasantest and
> most proper for a free man...[6]

Improving landlords could make remarkable profits in a few years;
others, like the younger Pliny in the early second century, found administration of land full of problems.[7] Many capitalists, thanks to
the inefficient Roman methods of accounting,[8] were probably satisfied
with low returns from their investment in land. Nevertheless, let us
posit at least some hard-nosed businessmen who were in land for financial profit. The Cicero passage has already shown one form of
sentiment about land - that it provides the proper occupation for a
free citizen. For the Romans, the Greek philosophical idea that farming is better than urban work complements nostalgia for a mythical
past, when consuls and dictators had ploughed their own fields. Tough
physical work produced the disciplined, loyal, brave and simple-minded
infantryman who had won an empire. His farm gave him independence and
enough time to exercise his citizen rights. Selling only a surplus
of primary products, he did not have to stoop to dishonest practices,
such as advertising, as an urban craftsman did.

This sentiment about country life is very common in city-based
and leisured Latin writers.[9] We shall not explore it, nor love of a
whole "country" as a physical and emotional object, which Vergil expressed so splendidly in his praises of an Italy which in his day had
only recently become a political unity,[10] nor love of a particular
type of landscape.[11] What will be isolated is sentiment for a particular piece of land, which is often linked with ownership of it, but
which in any case includes a sense of attachment and duty to it and
perhaps a sense of history and continuity. It is this attitude towards landed property which stands at the opposite extreme to the
treatment of land purely as investment.

Often in modern literature we find a writer who describes a special relationship between a person, often himself, and a piece of
land. For example, Rudyard Kipling (who had a typical Anglo-Indian
childhood, spent formative years of his early working life in India,
attempted to settle permanently in Vermont with his American wife
and only in his late thirties started putting down roots in Sussex)
often explores this feeling in his later work. It is one of the

major themes of *Puck of Pook's Hill* and *Rewards and Fairies*, and is
the subject of the short story, "An Habitation Enforced", published
in 1909.[12] In this story, an American businessman, recovering from
a nervous breakdown, and his neglected wife, run across a decayed
and abandoned house in Sussex, buy it and restore it for fun, only
to find that they have acquired a position and duties to tenants,
employees and villagers. Eventually the wife discovers that her
family had emigrated to the States from the same district a century
before. The "simple peasants" had found this out for themselves
weeks earlier. The birth of a son completes the take-over. In the
final scene, the husband, who wants to have a footbridge rebuilt in
larch, is compelled to use oak. Otherwise, says his tenant,

> "...by the time the young master's married it'll
> have to be done again. Now, I've brought down a
> couple of as sweet six-by-eight oak timbers as
> we've ever drawed. You put 'em in an' it's off
> your mind for good an' all. T'other way - I
> don't say it ain't right, I'm only just sayin'
> what I think - but t'other way, he'll no sooner
> be married than we'll 'ave it *all* to do again.
> You've no call to regard my words, but you can't
> get out of *that*."

"No," said George after a pause; "I've been realising that for some
time. Make it oak, then; we can't get out of it."[13]

In "My Son's Wife," written in 1913, the unsympathetic Londoner,
Midmore, is metamorphosed by a small estate inherited from an aunt.
"Ther Land, as they call it down here... Ther Land is brown and
green in alternate slabs like chocolate and pistachio cakes, speckled
with occcasional peasants who do not utter."[14] The aesthete's final
capitulation to the land and his engagement to a healthy fox-hunter
are produced by a charging piglet who bowls them over. The romanti-
cism is firmly realistic.

I doubt if we can find detailed expressions of this feeling before Gray's Elegy. It belongs to a literary vein of recent date, un-
touched by the Romans. It is discussed here in order to represent an
extreme sentimental view of land.[15]

For the Romans, let us first examine a paper by Elizabeth Rawson,
called "The Ciceronian Aristocracy and its Properties," which she produced at a Cambridge seminar. The paper focuses on the first century
B.C. and the evidence of Cicero, chiefly his letters, which are our
best documents on upper-class life in the whole of the Roman period.[16]

Her arguments will be analyzed in a broader context, in part to suggest modifications of her views. Because she sets out and uses the
sources so judiciously and has often foreseen and parried counter-
arguments, part of her work will be quoted directly.

Rawson begins her discussion of upper-class attitudes to land by
saying: "From the corpus of Cicero's letters we get an impression of
the Roman upper class as not only deeply concerned with real property,
its main form of investment, but indeed feverishly engaged in property
deals." The evidence of these personal letters might be skewed because Cicero and his brother were upwardly mobile and perhaps bought
and sold more than most people. Some landowners were losing land because of civil war and proscription in the 80s and 40s, or, in the
intervening period because they bankrupted themselves by extravagance
or political ambition or were condemned in the lawcourts and exiled.

> Yet more basic, doubtless, is the absence of
> any strict system of primogeniture and entail,
> and the tendency for a man to leave fractions
> of his wealth to a number of different persons,
> in token of esteem and obligation. The proper-
> ties concerned were perhaps often sold up, the
> proceeds redistributed in cash, and the various
> legatees would then very likely re-invest in
> real estate, as the best and safest investment
> there was. Even if one bought out the rest,
> these would still have money to re-invest in
> the same way. The contrast is great with what
> one may call the classical English system,
> where property was usually strictly entailed
> on the eldest son, but was encumbered with
> charges for dowagers, dowries, younger sons
> and other dependants; and where, in the
> eighteenth century at least, it was very dif-
> ficult to buy land, so firmly did landowning
> families hang on to their estates, in a poli-
> tically stable period when agriculture was in-
> creasingly profitable and mortgages easy to ob-
> tain. Finally, the Romans often preferred to
> own a number of smaller estates, rather than
> one great one, and this would tend to multiply
> the number of deals that took place.[17]

She goes on to illustrate the rapid turnover of property by citing the five owners, including Cicero, of his grand house on the
Palatine, which he bought after his consulship in order to maintain
the dignity of a senior senator. She also cites the four owners in
25 years of a villa at Misenum; four owners in 25 years of Cicero's
villa at Tusculum and five in approximately 50 years of another villa
at the same popular weekend resort near Rome. She makes a telling

comparison with the relative stability of country houses in the same
area from the 16th century on, when papal nobles kept places at Fras-
cati in the same family for centuries. She then cites Cicero's sale
of a seaside house at Anzio and some sales of farms by him and others,
and points out that renting was inconsistent with upper-class dignity.[18]

> By contrast, in late eighteenth- or in nine-
> teenth-century England, it was so distasteful
> and inglorious to sell one's country estate
> that owners in difficulties would let - mostly,
> inevitably, to *nouveaux riches* without estates
> of their own, but still to persons of consider-
> able standing. Conversely, while the really
> great magnates or those closely attached to a
> London life would also own a house in the capi-
> tal, it was perfectly proper for a country gen-
> tleman to hire a house for the Season, and this
> was even more true of resorts such as Bath or
> Brighton. I make no apology for using the evi-
> dence of Jane Austen. It will be remembered
> that Sir Walter Elliot, Bart., of Kellynch Hall
> in Somerset, fell into financial troubles. "He
> had condescended to mortgage as far as he had
> the power; but he would never condescend to sell.
> No; he would never disgrace his name so far."
> He is consequently forced to let Kellynch - to
> Admiral Croft, an excellent man but not quite,
> Sir Walter thinks, his equal socially, and re-
> tires to a rented house in Bath....
> Sir Walter's emotional identification with
> Kellynch, and his convoluted relationship
> with his nephew and heir, that is in part a
> result of it, is not to be paralleled even by
> Cicero's attitude to his ancestral property at
> Arpinum; not even though his family cults were
> established on the place.... Doubtless he would
> not have sold it unless very hard-pressed; but
> there is never a word, as there might be in
> England, about regarding the estate as a trust
> for his descendants. In fact young Marcus is
> never mentioned at all in connection with any of
> Cicero's properties....[19]

Several comments seem to be in order. First, the implied comparison between Cicero and Sir Walter Elliot, suggestive though it is, is
incompletely valid because Sir Walter, as a baronet, comes at the top
of the gentry but below the peerage. Moreover, he is a *country* gentleman: we may contrast him with the younger sons of gentry or peers
who worked in the City or overseas as merchants, lawyers or in the
army or navy. But Cicero, though by origin a member of the ruling-
class of a country town which had had the Roman citizenship only for

a century, had risen to be a member of the top class in the Roman state, that of the senators, and, as an ex-consul, despite his middling financial status and lack of an ancient name, was among the more eminent senators. Secondly, for a senator who did not have military abilities or ambitions, Rome was the centre of the universe. Cicero would spend most of the year at work, attending meetings of the Senate or appearing in the lawcourts. He needed his great town house in order to cut a proper figure, to receive his clients in the morning before going down to the Forum with an impressive train, to entertain more valued acquaintances at dinner. When he acquired this residence, he passed on the old family house, in an equally smart but less convenient neighbourhood, to his younger brother.[20]

Cicero had learnt early in his career how important it was to be on the spot, and he impressed this lesson on his younger friends: "The City, the City, my dear Rufus, stay in it and *live* in its sunlight... All foreign travel... is skulking and paltry to men whose work could shine at Rome."[21] On short public holidays it was only possible to slip away for a weekend or so to a country-house near at hand, so this is why he bought a villa at the fashionable hill resort of Tusculum. (Tivoli and Albano were favoured by some).[22] If one had a week or more, then the Latin coast or the Bay of Naples became attractive, especially in spring. We must remember that Cicero and probably most of his contemporaries liked to travel, when on holiday, at a rate of about 25 miles a day. This means that his town house at Anzio was a day away, Formia three, Cumae five, Puteoli five and a half, and Pompeii six. He had houses at all these places, though not all at once. The Formian villa might possibly be a family property; all the rest were purchased or inherited from friends.[23] They were reached by the Appian Way. The old home in the hills at Arpino was reached by a two-day journey along the Latin Way as far as the valley of the Liri and then a side-road of whose condition we know nothing. It was not an area much frequented by senators and its climate would be most attractive during the summer, particularly August and September, the time of the Senate's long vacation when the heat made Rome dangerous. The frosty Apennines in winter beckoned most Romans in vain.[24]

The parallel to this high social position, largely urban life, and wide dispersion of country properties, is surely not that of a

country baronet, but that of the Whig nobility. A member of the House
of Lords, or even a commoner from a well-established family and with a
seat in the Commons, might have a principal estate, usually ancestral,
a town house (possibly rented), and other farms or estates scattered
around England (and perhaps Ireland and Scotland). But he would not
need to own holiday residences at watering-places like Bath or the
seaside resorts which began to be fashionable, such as Brighton.[25]
So perhaps we should think of the Duke of Omnium rather than Sir Walter Eliot. Gatherum Castle, his chief seat, had to be opened from
time to time, to entertain political colleagues and toadies and to
maintain the Duke's connections with the parliamentary borough at its
gates. But the Duke and Duchess much preferred to live at Matching
Priory, their smaller country house.[26]

Thus, in response to Rawson's comparison, it should be noted that
the Ciceronian senatorial upper class was peculiarly urban, partly because Rome was still in theory a city state. Cicero spent much more
of his year in the capital than did the gloriously part-time and ama-
teurish prime ministers of Victoria's day, Wellington or Plantagenet
Palliser, not to mention those of the eighteenth century. Senators,
along with a few of the next class down, the *equites*, were immeasur-
ably wealthy compared with most of the population.[27] For eighteenth-
century England Mingay calculated that there were roughly 27,000 country gentry, and 160 to 170 English peers before the Younger Pitt's new
creations brought the numbers up to nearly 300. A duke might have had
an income of from ten to thirty thousand pounds, a poor peer three to
four thousand, while many of the gentry had more, and a poor gentleman a few hundred.[28] In the late Republic 600 senators and a few
thousand *equites* had the lion's share: we find Cicero, with a bit of
an effort, paying 3½ million sesterces for his house. To Pompey, after he conquered the East, or Caesar, when he came home from Gaul,
such a sum would not seem so much, but to a common soldier, after
Caesar had gratefully put up his pay, it represented the income of
3,888 years, not allowing for booty or stoppages.[29] Sir Walter Eliot,
a baronet who needs to cut his expenses, would be approximately on the
level of the *eques* and *domi nobilis*, the members of the ruling class
of an Italian town such as the father of Catullus, with his town house
in Verona and his country estate at Sirmione, or the grandfather of
Cicero who was a big fish in the small pond of Arpino. But there was

no solid middle class below the *equites*. Apart from a few successful
new citizens and freedmen, nobody could rise to the richer classes;
only *equites* could ascend to the Senate.

A second point which *Omnium Gatherum* may suggest is that "the
family seat" has a particular sentimental value even if you personally
dislike it. There is an eighteenth-century letter which puts this in
a nutshell. It was written by Bryan Fairfax to his kinsman young Lord
Fairfax, who wanted to sell the ancestral estate:

> I don't find, that by any way you can make £100
> p.ann. more by parting with Denton than by keeping
> it, which with humble submission I don't think
> equivalent to more valuable considerations. It is
> a great disgrace (if possible to be avoided) to
> have sold one's whole estate, and in the eye of
> the world I think a lord with his paternall seat
> and by the name of which he has been always dis-
> tinguish'd may make a better figure in England
> than one with much more money in his pockett,
> like a merchant, that has not a foot of land and
> consequently no more interest. And if you think
> the help of great men may be of use to you, by
> keeping this estate you may sometime or other
> expect to find it from your countrymen such as
> the Dukes of Somersett, Devonshire, Newcastle,
> the Earl of Burlington, and besides the general-
> ity of the gentry who have all sometime or other
> courted the family and perhaps may have occasion
> again, which should you part with they respect no
> more than a Scotch or Irish lord being able to do
> them no service here. I shall not mention those
> imaginary arguments of family, of the place where
> your ancestors were born and bury'd and which name
> your descendants must go by.[30]

As Rawson rightly says, landowning was not as important for elec-
toral interest in Roman times as it was in unreformed England, so we
must ignore the political part of Fairfax's letter. But the rest, and
particularly the last sentence, finds Roman parallels. The Romans did
not believe in denying family pride, and long-standing connections
with a particular place, if possible going back into the mists of leg-
end, were often part of family tradition.[31] Although Romans belonged
to voting units based on areas where an ancestor had resided, even if
they themselves had ceased to own land there, there was enough stability in the system for it to be worth Cicero's while, as a candidate
anxious to know and conciliate key men in all the tribes, to familiar-
ize himself with patterns of landholding, so that, we are told, on all
the main roads he could reel off the names of owners as he passed

their land.[32] This does not suggest a rapid turnover of property, except that we might credit Cicero with a good enough memory to keep up
with transfers to or by people of his own class.

Let us look first at Cicero's attitude towards his own ancestral
estate a few miles outside the town of Arpino in southern Latium. If
we can trust a letter to his most intimate friend, Atticus, Cicero did
not often invite city friends to this comparatively backward and un-
fashionable district, for in the spring of 59 he is not sure if Atticus will enjoy a vist there and it sounds as if Atticus has never
been.

> ...No use inviting you to Arpinum.
> "Rough land, but breeds good men; and as for me,
> I can see no sight sweeter than my home."[33]

The comparison with Ithaca, the rough island home to which Odysseus
struggled to return through ten years and half the *Odyssey*, is significant. It may suggest that Cicero had the same feeling for his roots
as Odysseus, but only rarely and indirectly reveals it. Atticus, who
perhaps never got there in the spring of 59, is officially introduced
to the Arpinate land seven years later in the philosophical dialogue
on the Laws, where Atticus, Cicero and his brother Quintus, in the
course of a stroll, take a rest on an island in the Fibrenus. Cicero
makes Atticus say, "I used to think there was nothing around here except rocks and mountains... and I was surprised that you liked this
part of the country so much. But now instead I wonder why you go any-
where else when you leave Rome." Cicero answers,

> I do come to this beautiful and healthy place
> when I can get away for several days, especially
> at this time of year, but I hardly ever get the
> chance. But I have another reason for liking
> it, which doesn't apply to you, Titus. What is
> that? Because it's our own country (*germana
> patria*) to my brother here and me. We come from
> a very old family of these parts, our cults,
> people and many relics of our ancestors are here.
> More than that - you see this villa, now rebuilt
> in more luxurious style by our father, who lived
> most of his life here in literary pursuits be-
> cause of his weak health. While my grandfather
> was still alive and this was a small old-fashioned
> villa, ... I was born in this very place. So
> there is something deeply hidden in my mind and
> feeling which perhaps makes me like this place
> more, just as that wise man, as the poem says,
> gave up the chance of becoming immortal just so
> he might see Ithaca again.

Atticus then gracefully says that Cicero has a very good reason for
loving Arpinum, and that he likes it more because Cicero was born and
grew up there. He had had the same increased delight in Athens because of the famous men who had lived, debated and been buried
there.[34]

Rawson, though she cites this passage, seems to underrate it,
perhaps because she thinks it is more rhetorical than real. But it
seems that Cicero deliberately advertises a feeling which the im-
itation of Platonic form did not impose on him, and that the comparison with Odysseus was a natural expression of his attitude.

Apart from sentiment about one's own, the point that it was particularly disgraceful for a man to lose properties which had belonged
to his father was familiar to Cicero, who quotes appreciatively the
sarcasms of an older orator against a man who had had to sell various
inheritances.[35] Cicero had to defend a client of his own against the
smear that he had squandered three patrimonies (inherited probably
from father, maternal grandfather and perhaps mother).[36] The accusa-
tion was standard in Roman rhetoric and testifies eloquently to common opinion.[37]

The poet Horace is an eloquent witness to the preciousness of
things passed down from father to son, and with good reason. His
father had been a slave, and after being freed, owned a farm which he
must have acquired through his own efforts. Horace had at least one
idyllic memory of his early childhood in the mountains on the borders
of Apulia. The young Horace, thanks to his father, had the best education obtainable and when studying in Athens, at the same time as
young men of senatorial family such as the son of Cicero, he was
caught up in the clever recruiting campaign of Brutus, who came back
to the lecture-rooms after murdering Caesar.[38] Horace served as an
officer in the campaign of Philippi, with the result that his paternal
farm was confiscated. Later, he won the patronage of Maecenas and obtained a farm in the Sabine Hills above Tivoli large enough to support
five tenants and a home-farm run by a steward. (It is always assumed
either that this was a gift to him, or that it was obtained with the
help of his patron.) Horace himself lightheartedly says he used to
get a bit of exercise by helping with the hoeing, to the amusement of
onlookers.[39] In the light of this biography, it is hard to believe
that Horace is not serious when he writes of the farmer's happiness as
he ploughs his paternal land with his own oxen and owes money to

nobody,[40] or of the displaced poor man, driven out by the land-hungry
rich, who goes away with his wife and scruffy children, carrying his
little paternal gods.[41] Or there is the man who is contented with a
simple life, a modest table with just a salt-cellar inherited from his
father. Alfred Noyes made the attractive suggestion that a saltcel-
lar was all that Horace had been able to keep as a memento of his own
father.[42]

The confiscations suffered by small as well as great landowners
in the disturbed years after the death of Caesar also influenced
Vergil, whether or not he was touched himself. It is the theme of
two of his pastoral poems. When in the ninth eclogue, Daphnis is encouraged to graft pear trees and told that his grandsons will enjoy
the fruit, he is not just to believe that the graft will take and the
trees go on bearing for a long time. Pear trees often do live to a
great age. The point is that Daphnis and his family will enjoy undisturbed possession of their land, a blessing not granted to other
peasants in the *Eclogues* or to some in real life.[43]

Confiscation or the threat of confiscation of ancestral or paternal property did not seem a light thing to Vergil or Horace, and it
is doubtful that it seemed so even to wealthier people who owned many
properties apart from old family homes and who risked losing them to
Sulla, Pompey, Caesar, Antony, Octavian and their various hangers-on.
The distinction between properties which come to you from a parent
and those acquired by other means is clear from the Younger Pliny, a
senatorial administrator and orator with an Italian equestrian background like Cicero's; he maintained strong ties with his home town of
Como despite its remoteness from Rome. A friend of his wanted to obtain a farm on the lake; so, with the generosity which he so often
documents, he offered her any of his farms she liked except those he
had inherited from his father or mother, which he would not give up
even for her.[44] Elsewhere, asking a friend if he enjoys his newly-
bought farms and suggesting that we always like things better before
we get possession of them, he implicitly contrasts such purchases
with lands which have a sentimental value: "The farms I had from my
mother don't treat me very well, but I delight in them because they
were my mother's and anyway I've grown inured to the trouble they
cause me..."[45] Three hundred years later Sidonius Apollinaris, the
Bishop at Clermont-Ferrand, implies that a prejudice in favour of an

old family property would seem natural when he praises an estate in
Auvergne which came to him as part of his wife's dowry, saying that
it was even sweeter to him, because it was his wife's, than the property at Lyons which he had inherited from his father.[46]

At this point it is useful to consider briefly the vocabulary
used by the Romans to express the concepts under discussion. *Paternus*
and *maternus*, meaning "of a father" and "of a mother" cause no problem. *Avitus*, the cognate adjective for a grandparent, which is often
linked with *paternus*, is trickier, since it is also the usual Latin
word for "ancestral" in general. This means that when a Roman says
his land is *avitus* we cannot be sure whether he is counting back to
his grandfather or further. This may perhaps reveal what the Romans
felt was a sufficient claim to ancient right, or it may just indicate
a limitation in the language. In any case, what is clear is that if
something came to you from a grandfather you were a well-established
and respectable owner. Horace was so well turned-out when he went to
school that anyone would have thought that the expense was taken care
of by ancestral wealth (*avita ex re*) though as an ex-slave's son he
could not even have a grandfather.[47] Seneca, saying that we really
only hold land in trust for humanity, imagines an owner claiming that
his comes from his father and grandfather and that it is unjust to
drive him out. Celsus, talking of people who have mistakenly built
on land which belongs to someone else, says it is particularly unfortunate if it is a poor man who will have to lose his father's home
and the tombs of his grandfathers. Ammianus also has owners driven
out of the homes of their fathers and grandfathers and mentions loving one's country as if it were a house which had belonged to one's
father and grandfather.[48] Finally, although the English word "home"
is notoriously unique, in Latin *lar* or *lares*, the household gods, tend
to occur in this context, even in dispassionate legal writing, and
these words have high emotional content.[49] Poor people would only
have their own private family gods if they lived in the country, since
apartment-dwellers had to be content with cross-road shrines. The
shrine of the *lares* means a settled home, continuing devotion to the
spirits of departed ancestors, family unity.

In the light of these instances of Roman attachment to land, Rawson's suggestion that "the Roman landowner's relation to his land was
much less emotional than that of the English landed gentleman" may be
modified. The emotion Cicero felt for his ancestral estate outside

Arpino may have been deeper than she allows. It should also be noted
that most of the property sales which Rawson uses to indicate lack of
emotional attachment were deals involving investment or recreational
property, notably the Tusculan villas. Conversely, it is difficult to
point to recreational villas which are known not to have changed hands.
John D'Arms has only two examples from Campania of villas known to
have been in the same family for two generations, and one of those is
less than certain.[50] But absence of evidence may be partly due to the
patchiness of our sources. Land tenure is only occasionally discussed
in any detail in the speeches of Cicero; his letters, our best source,
cover only a quarter of a century, and are primarily concerned with
the passing moment and with the people and places he knew. Yet this
is the best-documented period for the sort of enquiry we are making.

Cicero could not often get to Arpinum, he tells us, but he
seems to have gone as often as he could, even for a short holiday of
five days, and he may have gone more often than we know.[51] It is also
true, as Rawson says,[52] that we never hear of Pompey staying on his
ancestral estates in Picenum - but why should we? Cicero was unlikely
to meet him there and no one else is likely to tell us where the Great
Man went for his summer holidays. *Argumentum ex silentio* is weak, if
the silence can be explained. There are two other important points in
her discussion. First, Cicero in July 45, in the middle of a passage
on his finances, emphatically tells Atticus, "My little holdings give
me more annoyance than delight. For it gives me more pain not to have
anyone to pass them on to than pleasure to have enough for myself."[53]
His beloved daughter Tullia had died early that year and Rawson is
quite right in saying that he is "thinking of course of his daughter,
... and not at all of his son." But there were reasons for this. His
mind was on Tullia for dreary months after her death; he was probably
closer to her than he ever was to her younger brother, and Marcus' behaviour as a student in Athens was giving Cicero reason to worry whether he would turn out well. Moreover, by "little holdings," Cicero
might mean the villas he had bought and not the property at Arpinum.

After Tullia's death at the Tusculan villa, he refused to go
near it, though it was a favourite, and instead withdrew to a house he
had just bought on the edge of the Pomptine Marshes, which held no mem-
ories of Tullia and where he would see no one. So in this passage
Cicero is expressing a revulsion to the villas which he had bought and

beautified with such delight, a revulsion which eventually faded.
Lastly, it might be suggested that Marcus is ignored here partly because it was obvious that he would inherit the ancestral home, but
Cicero had hoped to leave his own purchases to his daughter, who, one
might conjecture, had enjoyed them as much as he did.

The second important passage cited by Rawson belongs to the same
year. After Tullia's death Cicero spent months on an abortive plan
to build her a shrine and so make her immortal. Surprisingly late in
the planning (as far as we know) he refers to the possibility of placing the shrine at his Arpinate villa, on the island. But he at once
dismisses the idea because Arpinum was too far out of the way for a
shrine there to become an objective of pilgrimage.[54] Cicero's object,
incredible though it may seem to moderns, was to secure Tullia's im-
mortality by making her shrine a permanent tourist attraction, which
is why Cicero had been trying for months to find a suitable piece of
land near Rome. So he rejects Arpinum without discussing any advantage of possible continuity in the family of the Tullii Cicerones.
This passage tells us nothing about what Cicero thought of the chance
of the Arpinate property staying in the family.

The above evidence on the feeling of sons for their family homes
may go some way to counteract the shortage of evidence, apart from the
Vergil quotation, about what fathers hoped for their sons and grandsons. It is worth remarking that the Roman writers who survive produced remarkably few children. Horace and Vergil were bachelors; most
of the rest - Suetonius, Pliny (despite his three wives), Seneca (after
losing a son), and Tacitus (as far as we know) - were childless. The
Roman upper class, it appears, failed to replace itself. On the whole
authors had no children for their heirs. Childlessness would be a
more important cause of breaks in continuity than civil war or political change. Upper-class men who were anxious for their family to continue might adopt a sister's son or some other relative and make him
heir,[55] which might lead to consolidation of family property. Conversely, an estate might be split among a number of heirs, either relatives or outsiders. Consolidation and fragmentation took place simultaneously. A rich man might hold large blocks of land, nuclei of family property to which he added by buying neighbouring farms; he might

also own scattered farms bought or inherited individually, and in some
of these he might hold only part-shares with other heirs. So we get
what A. H. M. Jones calls "the complexity and dispersion of the average
senatorial fortune."[56]

Unfortunately, although we can sometimes reconstruct most of the
genealogy and some of the political activity of a given family over
more than a century, we never have details of property over a considerable time, except for that of the Caesars, which soon ceased to be
private property and which will not be considered here. As John Crook
says, "Ancient families surviving for many generations in genetic and
property continuity are not characteristic of Rome."[57]

Elizabeth Rawson's hypothesis is that a basic reason for this rapid turnover of property "is the absence of any strict system of primogeniture and entail, and the tendency for a man to leave fractions of
his wealth to a number of different persons, in token of esteem or
obligation."[58] These three factors are closely related. Roman law
gave no preference to the eldest son over his brothers and sisters, or
to male over female children. If a father died intestate, all children
(including grandchildren) who were under his control at the time of
his death (*in patria potestate*) and who now became independent auto-
matically inherited equal shares. This was later modified to allow
appeal by descendants who had been freed from *patria potestas* before
the *paterfamilias* died. If a man made a will, he could exclude his
children as long as he disinherited them explicitly, but even so it
was open to them to bring a case that the will was "undutiful" and have
it altered.[59] Society frowned on fathers who cut their children out of
their wills except for very serious misbehaviour. For instance, a man
who married an elderly second wife and cut out all the children of his
first marriage had his will overturned by Augustus.[60]

A lack of primogeniture in the legal system can lead and indeed
has led (in countries whose law is based on Roman law) to the splitting
of land into smaller and smaller portions.[61] But social pressures may
modify these effects. It would seem that a number of modifying factors were present in Roman society. The first is that a particular importance was attached to the eldest son. In the republican upper
class, he almost invariably took his father's first name. (Roman nom-
enclature becomes more complicated later on and cannot be explored
here). Marcus Cicero's father, grandfather and only son were all
Marci. The only son of his younger brother Quintus was another

Quintus. If Marcus had had a second son, he would have been Quintus;
conversely, if Quintus had had another, he would have been Marcus, and
this pattern would have been perpetuated. A glance at any of the bet-
ter-attested family trees will confirm this. Age usually also counts
in the succession to the Principate: thus the adopted son of Claudius,
Nero, supersedes the younger Britannicus and Titus precedes his younger
brother, Domitian, in the imperial power. Priority for males is also
well established. A second modifying factor was a low birthrate. This
made an enormous difference, as becomes clear when we compare it to the
relatively high fertility of rural France in the eighteenth century.

Next, let us see how people actually disposed of their property.
We may suppose that most Romans who had property to dispose of would
make wills (unless they just wanted it to pass as it would on intestacy).[62] Now, do we find them making wills which simply gave equal
shares to all their children? The answer is "not usually," neither in
those wills which we know about from literary sources, nor in those
discussed in the jurists, who, it must be admitted, might have a preference for a more complicated sort of will and so might skew the evidence. In Roman law, the testator had to institute an heir, or several
heirs, who would act as executor or executors, and who, according to a
law of the late first century B.C., had to inherit at least 25% of the
property. The heirs could be given various fractions: thus Augustus,
for instance, left his adopted son heir to two-thirds and his wife (who
also by his will became his adopted daughter) heir to one-third.[63]
This meant that the heirs became joint owners of every item in that
proportion. As Crook puts it, if a man is heir to half, "he owns a
half share of every field of land, half of every chair and spoon, and
half the cat."[64]

A joint heir who found this wearisome could come to an arrangement
with his fellow heirs, but quite often joint ownership continued, so
that joint ownership, for instance of land or slaves, is commonly mentioned in the legal sources. Augustus' heirs continued to own a number of his slaves jointly, as is indicated in their tomb inscriptions.
This is not surprising, as the heirs were mother and son, and the son
also became his mother's heir. Sometimes a man would make all his
children joint heirs in this way, to equal or unequal shares. But he
might think it more convenient to make one his heir and give the others
legacies. This would work well unless he had more than four children

or too many creditors or others, whom he wished to remember in his
will.[65] He could make one child heir to a quarter and give legacies
totalling (roughly) a quarter of his property to each of the other
three.

One could also give legacies of specific items, say a house or a
farm, to the heir or heirs. A few examples will illustrate these various solutions. Titius, Maevius and their sister Seia (these are conventional names like John Doe and Richard Roe) are left as joint heirs
of their mother and they divide the property so that nothing is left
in common ownership. (Unfortunately Titius cheats by taking some gold
out of the pool before the division).[66] Or a father makes several
children his heirs, but entrusts his seal-ring to his eldest daughter.[67] Or a son and daughter are both heirs but the son gets more in
legacies,[68] or in another case the daughter is the one who is supposed
to get a legacy in compensation for freeing a certain slave, but the
father unfortunately forgot to put the legacy down on paper.[69] Quite
often the testator explains the reasons for his discrimination. For
instance, one father, instituting two children of "diverse sex", asks
the son to pay all legacies, and permits the daughter to keep everything he had given her during his lifetime, explaining that she is
given a smaller share as heir because his son is taking on the obligations to the legatees.[70] It is clear that often a daughter would have
had more of her fair share during her father's lifetime since she
would often have had her dowry.

It was, then, open to a father to keep a family property in the
hands of his eldest son by making a legacy of it to him, even though
other children might be joint heirs. Or he could do the opposite by
making the eldest son the sole heir, and bequeathing to the other children properties other than the ancestral farm which he wished to go to
the eldest.

Bequest of estates to the eldest son is less documented than one
would like in the jurists, but then it is the sort of thing which would
not create a legal problem and would therefore only be mentioned to
give an air of artistic verisimilitude. What did create problems was
the attempt to tie up property in order to keep it in the family. The
jurists discuss a number of cases where a testator tries to prevent
farms or houses from going out of the family. A son is forbidden to
sell or mortgage a farm during his lifetime, on pain of its confiscation to the state, the intention being that it should never go out of

the family (*de nomine vestro numquam exeat*), but the jurist decides the son is free to will it away to outsiders, because the father only explicitly ruled out alienation in the son's lifetime. Unfortunately we do not know if this was an eldest son or a special farm.[71] Another man institutes his son and his son's sons (who have been freed from *patria potestas*) as heirs and states very firmly in Greek that he wishes his houses not to be sold or mortgaged but to stay in the family "for all time." A joint heir who wished to sell could only sell to a co-owner.[72] In another will, if the brother to whom a certain house is bequeathed sells it or institutes an outsider as heir, members of the family can sue him.[73]

If you had no relations of your name, you could fall back on your freed slaves, whose name was the same.

> A man instituted as heirs his freedmen Stichus and Eros with the proviso, "I forbid my Cornelian farm to go outside my name." One of the heirs, Stichus, manumitted the slavewoman Arescusa in his will and bequeathed his part of the farm to her. I ask whether Eros and the rest of Stichus' fellow-freedmen can sue the heir of Stichus for that part of the farm in accordance with the *fideicommissum*.

The jurists's answer, if the text is right, was "no," presumably because a slavewoman freed by Stichus would carry the name, although perhaps her heirs would not.[74] In another instance, a farm goes to a daughter for her lifetime and then reverts to the testator's surviving freedmen.[75] The reason is that the daughter's children would probably not bear her father's name, or perhaps her father knew when he made his will that she would not have any children. It is worth noting here that a man may object to his property going to people either not of his name or not of his blood. Although in the Republic a woman would only pass on her family name to her children if they were not born in civil law marriage, about the time of Augustus a custom begins to arise in the upper classes of naming some children after their mother even when they are fully legitimate. This is particularly likely to happen when the mother's family was important. When Augustus' daughter married Marcus Vipsanius Agrippa, her two daughters were not named Vipsania Major and Minor, as they would have been earlier, but one Agrippina, from her father's surname, and one Julia, after her mother.[76] So if it were a matter of retaining a grandfather's property, it might be worth arranging to give his name to his daughter's child.

We have already seen various attempts to keep the property in the
possession of the same family name. A last example, drawn from the
same *Digest* section as several of the others, gives a nicely documented story of inheritance by female relatives, not necessarily of the
same name. Julius Agrippa, a senior centurion and otherwise unknown
to us, provided that his heir should not alienate or mortgage his
tomb, suburban estate or "greater house". His daughter and then *her*
daughter inherited and then the latter left the property to external
heirs. Should it go to them or to the centurion's great-niece, Julia
Domna (who, we notice, shared his name)? The lawyers decided it could
properly go to the outsiders.[77]

So we have found considerable evidence of testators trying to tie
up property for succeeding generations. Despite the reluctance of
Roman law to allow this, the decisions of the lawyers were by no means
always against the testator's wishes.[78] The vocabulary for keeping
things in the family became standardised over time, which is another
indication of the frequency of such attempts in wills. Another way of
trying to keep things in the family was to persuade daughters to marry
relations. There are various references in the *Digest* to legacies to
daughters if or when they marry in the family, which probably refer to
this practice.[79]

But sometimes there was no son, no daughter, no brother, no relation who could be adopted. If a man chose to honour a social equal by
making him heir, rather than naming a freedman or freedmen who at
least bore the family name, then the inheritance went to an outsider.
Some Romans felt as strongly about this as Mrs. Bennet in *Pride and
Prejudice* felt about her husband's property being entailed. Precau-
tions were often taken to exclude the heir from the family tomb.[80]
In Horace, the theme of inheritance by an uncaring heir recurs often,
in the context of the precariousness of life and good fortune. He re-
minds Dellius that he must die:

> You will leave your bought pasturelands and your
> house and your villa which the yellow Tiber washes,
> you will leave them and an heir will take possession
> of your heaped-up riches.[81]

Or, as we have already seen, Postumus must remember that he will leave
land, house and wife and that an heir who knows how to enjoy himself
will drink the previous vintages which Postumus has carefully kept,
and, with less discrimination, will spill them on the floor.[82] Finally, the heir with his "greedy hands" appears again in one of the

loveliest odes of the last book, of which there is a tolerable translation by A. E. Housman (although he omits the adjective):

> Torquatus, if the gods in heaven shall add
> The morrow to the day, what tongue has told?
> Feast then thy heart, for what thy heart has had
> The fingers of no heir will ever hold.[83]

We shall not be exaggerating if we say that the heir in Horace inten-
sifies his sense of the transitoriness of earthly happiness and that
surely, for him, this callous individual is the *externus heres*, the
outsider, even the "unknown heir"[84] not the son. There is no survival,
even through children.

So we have seen that, although the law did not encourage entail
or primogeniture or even preference for the male line, there is considerable evidence for social pressures working the other way. This
is not to contradict Rawson's proposition, but only to show the variety of factors and attitudes which operated in the Roman context.[85]
Romans, at all times in their history, were capable of an emotional
attachment to their homes and land. In the Late Republic and in other
times of disturbance, they may have had to cultivate a stoical acceptance of the possibility of losing it, and very often a man lacked
children to whom he could leave his possessions. Some property, particularly that bought as an investment or for fun or that left by mere
acquaintances, would sometimes have little sentimental value, but ancestral land and houses were in a different category and might even be
regarded as a trust to be passed on to one's descendants. So, although
there seems no evidence of any Romans reaching the fine sensibility of
the extreme modern attitude described at the beginning, many of them
are far removed from the opposite extreme of mere common sense.

II

Slaves are also property, live tools, extensions of the master
which can be operated even at a distance. But it was difficult to dis-
pel totally the idea that they were human beings. For instance, Cicero
wrote to Atticus about the death of a boy whom he had employed as a
reader and apologised for being so upset at the death of a slave.
Sometimes slaves seemed not just human beings, but good human beings.[86]
In law, however, they were mainly considered as articles of property,
to be bought, sold, pledged, bequeathed, hired-out, bred from. Humane
treatment is attested, but chiefly as a feature of sensible property-
management or of an imperial policy intended to safeguard the majority

of slave-owners by discouraging the brutality of a dangerous minority.
But human relationships refuse to be neatly categorized. Among the
special relationships which occurred there are two which are neglected
by literary sources (except the satirists): that of lovers and that
of parent and child.

It made a difference whether the slave-owner had been a slave.
Although slaves could not legally marry, they did take mates, and for
a man (particularly) it might be preferable to buy his mate (either
before or after the start of the sexual relationship) so that she was
a slave belonging to a slave, part of the property which he held on
sufferance and which his master might claim when he was freed. Supposing the man was freed and allowed to keep the woman, he was then a
free citizen, but she was still a slave and would remain so unless he
freed her. The same would apply to any children they had had, unless
his owner had claimed them. Normally, one supposes, the ex-slave man
would free his family as rapidly as possible.[87] The family relationships reflected in upper-class jurists will therefore *mostly* be between a freeborn Roman and his slave mistress and children. Lest it
be thought that there is undue emphasis on the male slave-owner, it
should be pointed out that sexual relationships between a free woman
and her male slave were feared and condemned, and if a woman wanted to
free a man in order to marry him, the only justifiable reason was that
they had been slaves together and she had been freed and he given to
her precisely in order that she might free him and marry him.[88]

Several juristic texts mention natural children. If the lawyers
want to suggest a convincing reason why a man would be particularly attached to a slave, it is the blood-tie that occurs to them. For example, Paul in discussing damages for the accidental killing of a slave,
says

> If you have killed my slave, I do not think a valu-
> ation has to be based on feelings, for instance if
> someone has killed your natural son whom you would
> have been willing to buy at a high price, but the
> valuation will reflect his value to anyone and
> everyone. Sextus Pedius too says that the prices
> of goods are fixed by the general market, not by
> the feelings of an individual or their usefulness
> to an individual, so a man who had possession of
> a natural son is not richer because if anyone else
> possessed him he would pay a large sum to get him
> back, nor does someone who has possession of some-
> one else's son, have that amount of money, for
> which he would be able to sell him to his father.[89]

Or, when discussing agreement between two owners to manumit, he says

> My natural son is your slave and your natural son
> is my slave: we agree between ourselves that you
> shall free my son and I yours: I have manumitted
> your son but you have not manumitted mine; the
> question is what sort of legal action I should
> take against you.[90]

If a bankrupt is sold up, Ulpian says

> ...we do not include things which it is reason-
> able to suppose a debtor would not have mort-
> gaged individually, for instance his furniture
> and clothes must be left to the debtor and those
> servants which he uses in such a way that it is
> certain he would not have pledged them. Similar
> considerations apply to services which are abso-
> lutely essential to him or those which touch his
> feelings.[91]

We are told more specifically in other texts that this means natural children and concubines or foundlings whom a man is bringing up.[92] Here we have, cheek by jowl, consideration of slaves who can be cate- gorized as an essential convenience like furniture or clothes, and mention of slaves who "belong" to his feelings. The Latin word trans- lated here is *affectio*, the primary meaning of which is a mental con- dition, state of feeling, frame of mind, mood or emotion. But it is also used to mean a feeling evoked by a particular object, an inner sentiment, and so, more broadly, feelings of attachment, affection or love. (In order to play fair, these translations have been taken from the most up-to-date authority, the *Oxford Latin Dictionary*). A re- lated word, *affectus*, has very similar meanings and in the context un- der discussion may be regarded as synonymous.

  Affectio occurs in two of the passages about natural children, the one from Ulpian about the bankrupt and the one, quoted first, from Paul about damages. In the latter *affectio* is explicitly contrasted with *utilitas*, usefulness.[93] There are four other passages linking *affectio* with slaves. In the first, Ulpian brackets slaves with wife, children or daughter-in-law and describes them all as persons who are subordinated to our power or affection.[94] Slaves always, children usually, wives and daughters-in-law sometimes, but hardly ever in Ulpian's time, were under the power of the *paterfamilias*. *Affectus* here will therefore refer at least to wives and daughters-in-law but probably also to children and slaves. Papinian, in discussing a clause sometimes inserted in contracts of sale which barred the pur- chaser from prostituting a slave, says that if he breaks his word the

seller can sue because the buyer has "both put the slavegirl to shame
and injured the feeling and perhaps the moral principles of the seller."[95] This *affectio* could be a serious and avowable feeling. The
Augustan law, which prohibited manumission of slaves under the age of
30 or manumission by owners under 20, allowed owners to apply for ex-
emption from the rule in special circumstances. Intended marriage was
a permissible reason, for male slave-owners. "The judges in approving
reasons for manumission," says Ulpian, "should remember to approve
reasons which derive not from extravagance but from affection, for we
must believe that the Aelian and Sentian law gave full freedom to proper feelings (*iustis affectionibus*) and not to frivolous infatua-
tions..."[96]

And finally there is a passage which neatly joins a sentimental
reason for wanting to gain possession of land with a sentimental reason for getting hold of a slave. A patron may want to claim half of
the property of a dead freedman (which in certain circumstances he was
legally entitled to do) even if the freedman was insolvent (which
would mean that the patron would have to take on his debts). Javolenus suggests the following motives:

> for example if there are some estates in the freed-
> man's property which contain the tombs of the ances-
> tors of the patron and the patron attaches great im-
> portance to having the right to the freedman's pro-
> perty as far as concerns that portion, or there is
> some slave, whom the patron wants not for his in-
> trinsic worth but because of his sentimental value
> (*quod non pretio sed affectu sit aestimandum*).[97]

So we have found a word which in some contexts it seems fair to trans-
late as "sentimental value" and which is used very commonly in connection with slaves with whom an owner has a close personal relationship.
This use of *affectio* to mean "sentimental value" is peculiar, I think,
to the jurists, who need an objective technical term to describe subjective feelings as neutrally as possible.

This short discussion of sentimental attitudes to slaves has been
confined to a small area and body of evidence, chiefly because of its
intrinsic interest and because slavery, like land, provides a testcase.
In the following passage, the semi-technical word *affectio* is used, not
of slaves, but of land. Ulpian is talking about a piece of property
which a man did not want to be sold, "because he has a particular feeling for it either because it is convenient or in a good neighbourhood
or has a good climate or because he was brought up there or his parents
are buried there..."[98]

We have now come full circle and to the conclusion that the Romans even in pragmatic legal documents recognised values other than those of the market-place and took into account emotional ties which might exist between an owner and a piece of property, whether that was a piece of land or a human chattel.

FOOTNOTES

1 *Epistles* 1.1.19.
    Much of the research on which the latter part of this paper is
based was done during my sabbatical leave in 1976/1977 and during
my tenure of a Canada Council Leave Fellowship. I should like to
express my gratitude both to my own university and to the Canada
Council, *sive quo alio nomine fas est nominare*. My thanks are also
due to the Principal and Fellows of Brasenose College, who made the
hospitable environment of Oxford more hospitable even than usual.
I am indebted for helpful discussion to Drs. R. Elaine Fantham of
the University of Toronto and Julian Gwyn and Martin Kilmer of the
University of Ottawa. Discussion with participants at the workshop and a perceptive letter from Elizabeth Rawson have removed
several errors and sharpened my awareness that only a fine line separates her position and mine. I am especially grateful to her for
allowing me to take some account below of the points which she made
in her letter.

2 See *Vita Sanctae Melaniae Junioris*, of which the Greek version is
most accessible in *Sources Chrétiennes* (Paris: Editions du Cerf,
1962), 90, the Latin (which has some extra details on property) together with the Greek in Cardinal M. Rampolla, *Santa Melania giu-
niore, senatrice romana* (Rome: Tipografia Vaticana, 1905). In the
Greek version, estates in Spain, Campania, Sicily, Africa, Maure-
tania and Britain are mentioned (11).

3 On Seneca, see Miriam T. Griffin, *Seneca, a Philosopher in Politics*
(Oxford: Clarendon Press, 1976), especially chaps. 8 and 9.
Horace: *Epistles* 1.7 etc.

4 *Epistles* 1.2.46 and what follows. Cf. *Epodes* 1. 23-24, *Odes* 2.16.
13, 2.18.1 ff., 3.16.25 ff. etc.

5 *Odes* 2.14.21-28. The translation is from Gordon Williams, *Tradition
and Originality in Roman Poetry* (Oxford: Clarendon Press, 1968),
585.

6 *On Duties* 1.151.

7 The standard book is K. D. White, *Roman Farming* (London: Thames and
Hudson, 1970) to which may be added the substantial review by P. A.
Brunt, *Journal of Roman Studies* 63 (1973) 153-158. Pliny: R.
Duncan-Jones, *The Economy of the Roman Empire. Quantitative Studies*
(Cambridge: Cambridge University Press, 1974), Chap. 2; V. A.
Sirago, *L'Italia agraria sotto Traiano* (Louvain: Université de Lou-
vain, 1958), Chap. 1 (particularly useful for the present topic).

8 G.E.M. de Ste Croix, "Greek and Roman Accounting," A. C. Littleton
and B. S. Yamey eds., *Studies in the History of Accounting* (London:
Sweet and Maxwell, 1956), 14-74.

9   W. E. Heitland, *Agricola. A Study of Agriculture and Rustic Life
    in the Greco-Roman World from the point of view of Labour* (Cam-
    bridge: Cambridge University Press, 1921), especially Chaps. 20
    and 29, is still useful.

10 *Georgics* 2.136-176. On local patriotic feeling for particular
    towns or regions ("la petite patrie"), see Madeleine Bonjour, *Terre
    Natale. Etudes sur une composante affective du patriotisme romain*
    (Paris: Les Belles Lettres, 1975). This book, which I read after
    the workshop, discusses many of the literary passages used.

11 L. Friedländer, *Roman Life and Manners under the Early Empire*, tr.
    A. B. Gough (London: Routledge, 1908), I, 380-394.

12 *Actions and Reactions* (London: Macmillan, 1909), 1-50. Charles
    Carrington, *Rudyard Kipling. His Life and Work* (London: Macmil-
    lan, 1955), 410-411, rightly refuses to see the story as autobio-
    graphical. But on Kipling's own love of Sussex see, e.g., "Sussex"
    in *Rudyard Kipling's Verse. Definitive Edition* (London: Hodder
    and Stoughton, 1940), 213-216.

13 The more humble labourer or small farmer may have a far longer con-
    nection with the land than do successive owners. This is explicit
    in "The Land", *Verse* (n.12), 601-603, where one Hobden after anoth-
    er, from Diocletian's time onwards, politely tells the incoming
    owner how to manage.

14 *A Diversity of Creatures* (London: Macmillan, 1917), 333-376. The
    quotation: 335.

15 Further examples, unmethodically selected: Hilaire Belloc (e.g.
    "Duncton Hill," *Collected Verse* (London: Penguin, 1958), 100);
    John (Cecil) Moore (e.g. *Brensham Village* (London: Collins, 1946),
    The Blue Field (London: Collins, 1948)).

16 M. I. Finley ed., *Studies in Roman Property* (Cambridge: Cambridge
    University Press, 1976), 85-102.

17 *Ibid.*, 85-86.

18 *Ibid.*, 86-87.

19 *Ibid.*, 87-88.

20 Plutarch *Cicero* 8.3; Cicero *To Quintus* 2.3.7.

21 Cicero *To his Friends* 2.12.2.

22 Tusculum was full of consular families (Cicero *Defence of Plancius*
    19-20); villa-owners in Cicero's time include Balbus, Brutus, Hir-
    tius, Lucceius, Lentulus Spinther. Tivoli (Tibur): Cicero *On the
    Orator* 2.224, Horace *Odes* 1.7 etc., Albano: Curio (Cicero *To Atti-
    cus* 9.15.1), Pompey (*ibid.* 4.11.1, 7.5.3, 7.7.3). Further details
    may be found through the indices of I. Shatzman, *Senatorial Wealth
    and Roman Politics* (Brussels: Latomus, 1975).

23 25 miles: D. R. Shackleton Bailey, *Cicero's Letters to Atticus*
    (Cambridge: Cambridge University Press, 1965-1970), 2.230, citing
    earlier work. For a survey of Cicero's villas see W. Warde-Fowler,
    Social Life at Rome in the age of Cicero (London: Macmillan,
    1908), 251-260. For Campanian villas, John H. D'Arms, *Romans on
    the Bay of Naples: A Social and Cultural Study of the Villas and
    their Owners from 150 B.C. to A.D. 400* (Cambridge, Mass.: Harvard
    University Press, 1970) is the standard work. Cicero's Formian
    villa is first mentioned in 66 (*To Atticus* 1.4.3). The earliest
    letter in the collection (sparse for the 60s) belongs to 68. The
    villa may have been a recent acquisition in 66, but we cannot tell.
    Its easy communications with Arpino up the valley may have attract-
    ed Cicero or an ancestor. (More will be known soon about the roads
    and settlements of the Cassino Gap area thanks to the work of a
    McMaster team which began a survey in 1977). In this paper, for
    the sake of clarity and at the expense of elegance, Latin and Ital-
    ian place-names have been mixed, the more familiar being chosen
    (Tivoli, not Tibur). "Arpino" is used for the town, "Arpinum"
    (which Cicero would call "Arpinas") for Cicero's villa, which was
    a few miles outside the town, on the Liris.

24 Arpinum: Cicero praises the cool of its hill-streams in summer
    (*Laws* 2.1-6, *Tusculans* 5.74, *To Quintus* 3.1.1). He also went there
    in March-April (*To Atticus* 8.9.3) and even November (*ibid.* 15.13a).
    Apennines: e.g. Cicero *Against Catiline* 2.23; Horace *Odes* 1.9,
    Epistles 1.7.9-11.

25 Rawson (n. 16) 88.

26 The reference is to the six Palliser novels of Trollope (especially
    The Prime Minister) and to several of the Chronicles of Barset.

27 For the basic modern bibliography see Treggiari, "Roman Social
    History: Recent Interpretations " (*Social History/Histoire Sociale*
    8 (1975), 150-153, to which Shatzman (n. 22) must now be added.

28 G. E. Mingay, *English Landed Society in the Eighteenth Century*
    (London: Routledge, 1963), Chaps. 1 and 2, especially pp. 6-10.

29 3½ million: Cicero *To his Friends* 5.6.2 Soldiers' pay: 900 ses-
    terces *per annum*.

30 *B. Mus. Additional MSS* 30306, f. 110, quoted by L. Namier, *The
    Structure of Politics at the Accession of George III* (London:
    Macmillan, 2nd ed. 1957), 411-412.

31 Cf. T. P. Wiseman, "Legendary Genealogies in Late-Republican Rome,"
    Greece and Rome 21 (1974), 153-164.

32 Plutarch *Cicero* 7.1-2. Rawson rightly points out to me, however,
    that Cicero "may merely be thought of as knowing who all the influ-
    ential people in different areas are, not that their connection
    with their estates is important."

33 *To Atticus* 2.11.2, Bailey's translation; cf. 2.8.2, 2.14.2, 2.15.3,
    2.16.4 (especially), 2.17.1.

34 *Laws* 2.1-6, probably set in 52. Cf. Bailey (n.23) 1.378, suggesting that this really was Atticus' first visit.

35 *On the Orator* 2.222-226. I owe this reference to Dr. R. E. Fantham.

36 *Defence of Milo* 95, with Asconius *ad loc*.

37 Cf. Paulus *Sententiae* 3.4a.7.

38 The standard account of Horace's life is E. Fraenkel, *Horace* (Oxford: Clarendon Press, 1957), Chap. 1. Childhood: *Odes* 3.4.9-20. Education: *Satires* 1.6.45-92.

39 Horace *Epistles* 1.14 especially 1-3, 39.

40 *Epode* 2, especially 1-4. Until the final stanza the poem appears to be straightforward, but then we find that the speaker is a city usurer. This typical Horatian irony need not invalidate my point.

41 *Odes* 2.18.23-28.

42 *Odes* 2.16.13-14; Alfred Noyes, *Portrait of Horace* (London: Sheed and Ward, 1947), 2.

43 *Eclogues* 1; 9 especially 50. Servius and Conington saw the point, which some other editors miss.

44 Pliny *Letters* 7.11, on which see J. A. Crook, "Classical Roman law and the sale of land," Finley, *Studies* (n.16), 71-83, at 82. On Pliny's property in general see R. Duncan-Jones (n.7) Chap. 1.

45 *Letters* 2.15.2.

46 Sidonius *Letters* 2.2.3.

47 *Satires* 1.6.79-80. Legally slaves had no parents: cf. the taunt of Martial 11.12.1-2.

48 Seneca *Moral Letters* 88.12; Celsus *Digest* 6.1.38; Ammianus Marcellinus 19.11.1, 27.6.9. Cicero's "expulsion" from his Palatine house and his villas (confiscated when he was exiled but later recovered) rankled bitterly. See for example *On his House*, especially 106-109, 143-147, with the commentary of R. G. Nisbet. My thanks to G. W. Pinard for reminding me of these passages.

49 Celsus l.c. (n.48); Horace *Odes* 1.12.43-44; Cicero *Verrines* 3.27; Valerius Maximus 7.7.1, Martial 12.57.1-2. Cicero *On his House* 1, 106,108,143-144, gives a good sample of vocabulary: apart from *lares*, there are *penates*, altars, hearths. In *Defence of Sestius* 145 he is again driven away from altars, hearths and *penates*.

50 *Op. cit.* (n.23) 172-173 (Mark Antony) and 224-225 (perhaps Vatia, praetor in 25 B.C.). In Latium, the Lamiae may have had a villa at Formia for generations, but this was probably the family seat (Treggiari, "Cicero, Horace and Mutual Friends: Lamiae and Varrones Murenae," *Phoenix* 27 (1973) 245-261 at 246-247).

51   We hear of him there in ?61 (*To his Friends* 7.23.1); 59 (*To Atticus*
     2.17.1 etc.); 56 (*To Quintus* 2.5.4: five days; 3.1.1: later in the
     year); 51 (*To Atticus* 5.1.3); 49 (ib. 8.9.3); 46 (ib. 12.1); 45
     (ib. 13.9.2); 44 (ib. 15.3.1, 15.26, 15.13a: three separate vis-
     its).

52   *Op. cit.* (n.16), 89.

53   *To Atticus* 13.23.3. *Ibid.* 12.18a.2, of March 13, 45, mentions the
     complaints of his divorced wife Terentia about his recently-made
     will, which presumably replaced one made before Tullia's death or
     the birth of her child a few weeks earlier. Cicero claims to have
     made generous provision for this grandson, who probably died soon
     after. Cicero had similarly complained about Terentia's will in
     47 (*ibid.* 11.16.5, 11.24.2 etc.), apparently because he thought it
     insufficiently generous to their children. In rhetorical flights
     he was capable of saying that it was enough if he left his children
     (*On his House* 147) or his son (*To his Friends* 2.16.5) nothing but
     his glorious name.

54   *To Atticus* 12.12.1. On the whole subject see Shackleton Bailey
     (n.23) 5 Appendix III, "Tullia's Fane."

55   Familiar examples of such adopted sons are Atticus, the Younger
     Pliny or C. Julius Caesar Octavianus, grandson of a sister of
     Caesar.

56   *The Later Roman Empire 284-602. A Social, Economic and Administra-
     tive Survey* (Oxford: Blackwell, 1964), 2.782. The best example of
     a complicated estate which Jones cites is that of the sixth-century
     bishop, Remigius (785). Joint ownership of small urban properties
     is well documented at a much later period by Robert Brentano, *Rome
     before Avignon: A Social History of Thirteenth-Century Rome* (New
     York: Basic Books, 1974), 27-29.

57   J. A. Crook, *Law and Life of Rome* (London: Thames and Hudson,
     1967), 132, quoted with approval by Rawson, *op. cit.* (n.16), 89. I
     would add "as far as we know," with the caveat that we know little
     about any but senatorial families. Possibly the leading families
     in some country districts and even small peasants or shop-keepers
     could show continuity. I have noticed two interesting passages on
     recovery of property: the fictitious freedman Trimalchio, after
     recouping his fortunes in trade, bought back all his patron's farms
     (Petronius *Satyricon* 76.8: it is unclear whether they were part of
     the property he had inherited from his patron); Sidonius supports
     a *vir spectabilis*, Donidius, who wants to recover part of a farm at
     Ebreuil which had long been in the family and where he had crawled
     as a baby: his motive was not greed but proper family feeling
     (*Letters* 3.5).

58   *Op. cit.* (n.16), 85.

59   See, e.g., Crook, *op. cit.* (n.57), 118-128; Barry Nicholas, *An
     Introduction to Roman Law* (Oxford: Clarendon Press, 1962), Part
     4, Chap. 5.

60   Valerius Maximus 7.7.4. There is a whole title in the *Digest*
     (5.2).

61 See, e.g., Nicholas, *op. cit.* (n.59), 264. Arthur Young was par-
    ticularly opposed to the evils of parcelling-up farms, but his
    Travels in France During the Years 1787, 1788, 1789 (Cambridge:
    Cambridge University Press, 1929) shows that uneconomically small
    holdings were characteristic of certain districts only, not of the
    whole country.

62 See J. A. Crook, "Intestacy in Roman Society," *Proceedings of the
    Cambridge Philological Society* 19 (1973), 38-44, with references
    to earlier scholarship.

63 Suetonius *Augustus* 101.

64 *Op. cit.* (n.16), 182 n.35.

65 Nicholas, *op. cit.* (n.59), 252.

66 *Digest* 2.14.35, Modestinus.

67 *Digest* 31.77.21, Papinian.

68 *Digest* 35.2.94, Scaevola.

69 *Digest* 31.34 pr., Modestinus.

70 *Digest* 31.34.6, Modestinus.

71 *Digest* 32.38.3, Scaevola.

72 *Digest* 31.88.15, Scaevola.

73 *Digest* 31.69.3, Papinian.

74 *Digest* 32.38.1, Scaevola. Cf. 31.77.15, Papinian, where the heir
    is an outsider and farms are left to freedmen to keep them in the
    family name. 31.77.27 is similar.

75 *Digest* 32.38.2. Similarly the right of burial in a family tomb may
    be left to freedmen and their descendants as long as they bear the
    name (*Corpus Inscriptionum Latinarum* 5.381).

76 Roman upper-class men of the first century B.C. normally had three
    names, *praenomen, nomen gentile* and *cognomen,* women only the *nomen
    gentile.* As men find the *gens* name insufficiently distinctive,
    they emphasise the *cognomen* and often add an extra surname.
    Agrippa himself stopped using the undistinguished name Vipsanius
    and called himself M. Agrippa. Some women had already added *cogno-
    mina* (e.g. Caeciliae Metellae) and in the late first century B.C.
    they become individualist like the men, as may be seen from the
    Julio-Claudian stemma. If this fashion spread to lower-class wom-
    en, it will affect our estimates of family-structure, since in-
    scriptions attesting children who bear the name of the mother and
    not of her husband are generally held to show illegitimacy or pre-
    vious marriage.

77 *Digest* 32.38.4, Scaevola. There seems to be no reason why this
    should not be *the* Julia Domna, wife of the emperor. See A. R.
    Birley, *Septimius Severus, the African Emperor* (London: Eyre and
    Spottiswoode, 1971), 297.

78 Crook, *op. cit.* (n.57), 122.

79 27.2.4.pr., Iulianus; 32.27.pr., Paul; 32.41.7, Scaevola; 33.5.21,
    id.; 35.1.15, Ulpian; 36.2.21.pr., Paul; 40.5.41.16, Scaevola. The
    phrase is *in familia nubere*. None of the passages explains what it
    means. 32.41.7 describes a daughter who makes three such mar-
    riages, which may, if my interpretation is right, suggest that an
    extended family is intended.

80 See Crook, *op. cit.* (n.57), 135-137.

81 *Odes* 2.3.17-20.

82 *Odes* 2.14.21-28.

83 *Odes* 4.7.17-20. Housman's version, "Diffugere nives," is in *More
    Poems*. Rawson replies (personal letter) that this "cuts both
    ways. Horace's friends may lament the *externus heres*, but the fact
    remains that this is not a *topos* in English verse, in spite of
    strong Horatian influences in the eighteenth century, because there
    hardly ever was an *externus heres*: at worst there was a nephew or
    cousin. Conversely, you note how in Rome there often was no son:
    yes, and the desperate desire to produce an heir to the family
    estate *is* a *topos* in English literature, especially novels, but not
    in Roman literature, where people seem relatively content with *or-
    bitas* or adoption."

84 Cf. *Odes* 2.18.5-6.

85 A small piece of evidence against my thesis about the Roman prefer-
    ence for eldest sons is that the estate in Auvergne which Sidonius
    Apollinaris obtained from his wife's dowry may have been her family
    seat, even though she had two brothers. Cf. C. E. Stevens, *Sidon-
    ius Apollinaris and his Age* (Oxford: Clarendon Press, 1933), 20,
    n.2.

86 Cicero *To Atticus* 1.12.4, 7.4.1; *Digest* 30.71.4, Ulpian.

87 Slave blood-ties are probably the main reason for the ruling that
    a master, even if under 20, may free a slave, even if under 30, if
    the latter is a natural son, daughter, brother or sister (*Digest*
    41.2.11, Ulpian; Gaius *Institutes*). There is a striking instance
    of a slave son, not freed and aged 16, who ran a shop for his fa-
    ther and is known from an inscription at Philippi (*Inscriptiones
    Latinae Selectae* 74-79). *Digest* 30.71. 3, Ulpian, mentions inheri-
    tance from a father, mother or natural brothers, probably by a
    freedman.

88 *Digest* 40.2.14.1, Marcianus. Even this was disputable.

89 *Digest* 9.2.33. There is some confusion between "you" and "me" at
    the beginning.

90 *Digest* 19.5.5.pr.

91 *Digest* 20.1.6.

92 *Digest* 20.1.8, Ulpian; 42.5.38.pr., Paul. I shall not discuss here
    36.1.80.2, Scaevola, which involves another slave's natural son.

93 *Utilitas* would be the particular value of an individual slave to an
    individual owner. For instance, if you kill my research-assistant,
    his special suitability for my research interests will not be taken
    into account, only his market value as a scholar.

94 *Digest* 47.10.1.3.

95 *Digest* 18.7.6.pr.

96 *Digest* 40.2.16.pr.

97 *Digest* 38.2.36.

98 *Digest* 38.5.1.15.

Anthony Parel gives a systematic exposition of Aquinas' doctrine
of property. The Thomistic theory of property is rooted in metaphysics
and ethics, in Greek, Roman and patristic thought, according to which
temporal goods exist as means to higher goods, and do not exist solely
to be enjoyed for their own sake but also to be used for the attainment
of felicity on earth and beatitude in eternity. Private property ex-
cluding the right to common use does not exist according to natural law,
but is an institution evolved by men, and therefore depending on the
sanction of human law. It is beneficial as long as acquisitiveness does
not replace felicity/beatitude as the end of life, and as long as the
right to private property does not interfere with the right to common
use.

AQUINAS' THEORY OF PROPERTY

A subvention from the University Research Policy
and Grants Committee of the University of Calgary
enabled me to do part of the research involved in
this essay. I hereby express my gratitude to the
University for its support.

Aquinas' doctrine of property forms part of his wider teaching on
the nature and destiny of man, of his humanism. It is the humanistic
values embodied in his teaching on property that are of permanent value
and therefore of interest to us today. The notions that the use of
earth's goods belongs to mankind in general, and not to any "owners";
that the ontological essence of property is its common use, not private
ownership; that the good social order requires the subordination of
ownership to use; that the only justification for surplus is social
use; that felicity of mind is the true end of man rather than accumulation and consumption of material things; that the balance between the
inner force of virtue and the outer force of coercion of just laws is
the basis for a humane organization of property - these are all ideas
germane to Aquinas' teaching on property. They are also constitutive
of his doctrine of man.

Although in the existing literature the emphasis has generally
been on the juridical question of private property, it is important to
realize that for Aquinas the question of property raises ethical and
philosophical, political and social questions of the first magnitude.
As Thomistic ethics is founded on metaphysics, so his juridical views
are founded on ethics. Accordingly, in this paper I shall synoptically
explore Aquinas' thought on: (1) the philosophical basis of man's relationship to material things in general; (2) property as the object
of sensory appetites to be regulated by right reason; (3) the basis of
private property; (4) the social evils that result from the emancipation of sensory appetites for property from the rule of right reason,
especially avarice and usury; (5) the ethical remedies specifically
applicable to evils related to property, namely liberality and justice;
and (6) the institutional remedies supplied by law and politics.

Aquinas was a metaphysician and it is natural that certain metaphysical assumptions should underlie his ethical thinking. This approach should not be dismissed as some form of pre-Kantian or

pre-Comtean aberration. For every serious approach to the problem of
property involves explicit or implicit metaphysical assumptions. Even
non-metaphysicians make use of metaphysics despite their protestations,
which makes their non-metaphysical metaphysics sometimes astonishingly
attractive. Just as Marx's doctrine of property cannot be understood
except in the light of his philosophy of doctrinaire materialism, and
the liberal doctrine of property except in the light of its implicit
practical materialism, so Aquinas' doctrine cannot be understood except
in the light of his philosophy of hylomorphism, matter and form, act
and potency. And just as for Marx human existence, taken in its totality, is the process which, originating in primitive communism, leads
to the self-achieved perfection of communism, so for Aquinas, human existence is the dynamic process according to which man, created in the
"image of God" (which consists of human reason), moves towards the fellowship of God and of redeemed humanity by the conjoint activity of
reason and grace. The role that is assigned to grace need not detain
us, for Aquinas recognizes (and this recognition is his peculiarity as
a philosopher) the indispensable and valid role that reason plays in
the drama of human existence. As he states in the very first Question
of the *Summa theologiae*, grace does not abrogate nature but perfects
it: *gratia non tollat naturam sed perficiat*....[1]

Man is a composite of body and mind. The consubstantiality of the
two, denied later by Descartes, as well as the Idealists and the Ma-
terialists, has important consequences for the matter at hand. In man,
the diverse exigencies of mind, sensation, vegetative and physico-
chemical forces, each without losing its proper good, meet. Reason
brings about the necessary harmony, and acts as the principle of an
ordered diversity. The major Thomistic assumption is that all imper-
fect things tend towards perfection,[2] and therefore the less perfect
should be governed by the more perfect. Man, says Aquinas, is a
microcosm:

> Man in a certain sense contains all things: and
> so *according as he is master of what is within himself,*
> *in the same way he can have mastery over other things.*
> Now we may consider four things in man, his reason,
> which makes him like the angels; his sensitive powers,
> whereby he is like the animals; his natural forces,
> which liken him to the plants; and his body itself,
> wherein he is like the inanimate things. Now in man rea-
> son has the position of a master and not of a subject....
> Over the sensitive powers, as the irascible and con-
> cupiscible, which obey reason in some degree, the soul

> has mastery by commanding.... But of natural powers
> and the body itself man is master not by commanding,
> but by using them....[3]

Although part of the material, vegetative and sensory world, man transcends them by virtue of his rational powers. Human reason has at certain levels an independent subsistent activity. For his moral, aesthetic and intellectual activities no exemplar can be found in brute creation. The capacity of reason for subsistent activity makes man a person, which, says Aquinas, is the most perfect thing in all nature.[4] Because of the ontological capacity for subsistent activity, the species or any smaller group may not totally absorb the human person. Since by personality man transcends nature, a purely secular conception of felicity bound by time, *saeculum*, even that resulting from the activity of creative labour, cannot fully satisfy him. Only beatitude, an activity of the mind, can be the true ultimate end of human existence.

Autonomy is the essential attribute of the human person, and it differentiates him from the rest of nature:

> Man differs from irrational animals in this,
> that he is master of his actions. Wherefore those
> actions alone are properly called human of which
> man is master. Now man is master of his actions
> through his reason and will, whence free will is
> defined as the faculty and will of reason. There-
> fore those actions are properly called human which
> proceed from a deliberate will.[5]

This means that man is more properly human in the activity of the mind than in the activity whose *terminus ad quem* is the good of the senses or of the body, e.g. accumulation and consumption of property.

Since reason is capable of knowing universal truth, and the will of desiring universal good,[6] only participation in universal truth and good can satisfy the human potential. It is in man's rational nature to seek to become all things through knowledge. The activity by which man can attain his perfection is an activity immanent to the subsisting reason. When attained in this life, it is called *felicity*; when attained in its perfection, which is possible only in the extra-temporal, transhistorical existence, it is called *beatitude*.

The doctrine of felicity/beatitude is crucial for our investigation for three main reasons. First, being man's ultimate end, felicity/beatitude penetrates every subordinate end and every subordinate activity. Second, the good of material things can have no goodness

autonomous of the good of felicity/beatitude. Thirdly, history or time
or *saeculum* taken even in its totality cannot provide the perfection of
human happiness.

Since happiness is a perfect and sufficient good, it excludes
every evil and fulfills every desire. But in this life every evil cannot be excluded; life is subject to many unavoidable evils: to ignor-
ance on the part of the intellect, to inordinate affection on the part
of the appetite, and to many penalties on the part of the body. Likewise neither can the desire for good be satisfied in this life. For
man naturally desires the good which he has to be abiding. Now the
goods of the present life are transitory, like life itself which we
naturally desire to have and would wish to hold abidingly, for man
naturally shrinks from death. Wherefore it is impossible to have true
happiness in this life.[7]

In a series of arguments, which we need not explore here, Aquinas
eliminates riches, honours, glory, power, bodily well-being, sensory
pleasures, even self-preservation as the ultimate end of human life.[8]
What should interest us is Aquinas' general views on the role that material things play with respect to felicity/beatitude. They have only
an instrumental or use value, and they are necessary only as means, as
bonum utile. The desire for material things, only insofar as they are
conducive to an end which transcends the use of property, is natural to
man.[9] But they do not contribute to the essence of felicity:

> For the imperfect happiness such as can be had
> in this life, external goods are necessary, not as
> belonging to the essence of happiness, but serving
> as instruments to happiness, which consists in the
> operation of virtue. For man needs in this life,
> the necessaries of the body, both for the opera-
> tion of contemplative virtue, and for the opera-
> tion of active virtue, for which latter he needs
> many other things by means of which to perform
> his operations.[10]

For Aquinas productive work, which is referred to by the mediaeval
term *ars* (art), has only an instrumental reality. In the *Contra
Gentiles* he writes:

> For the knowledge that pertains to art is prac-
> tical knowledge. Accordingly it is ordered to an
> end, and is itself not the ultimate end. The ends
> of art operations are artifacts. These cannot be
> the ultimate end of human life, for we ourselves are,
> rather, the ends for all artificial things. Indeed
> they are all made for *man's use*. Therefore ultimate

felicity cannot lie in the operation of art (*cum
magis nos sumus fines omnium artificialium, omnia
enim propter hominis usum fiunt*).[11]

Man is master of material things by using them; the product of his
skilled labour is for his use. But for Aquinas, what is the precise
meaning of use? The use of a thing, says Aquinas, is its application
to some activity. Thus the use of a horse is riding. In using things,
the internal principle of action and choice, namely the will, is acti-
vated; there is also some rational deliberation. Thus only rational
creatures can, properly speaking, use things; a response to a stimulus
is not use.[12]

Use also implies that something is ordered to something else as
its end (*uti semper est ejus quod est ad finem*).[13] Thus "use" and
"end" are distinct notions: *frui* (to enjoy) is not the same as *uti*
(to use). (*Frui importat absolutum motum appetitus in appetibile; uti
importat motum appetitus ad aliquid in ordine ad alterum*).[14] Enjoyment
is the result of attaining the end; one does not so much use an end as
enjoy it. If Aquinas' conception of use is correct, it follows that
material things, insofar as they are used, are not, strictly speaking,
enjoyed. At least one must not seek enjoyment in them, an enjoyment
unrelated to or underived from the enjoyment of the transcendent end,
unless one wants to look upon them somehow as ends which, of course,
one may not. Thus an avaricious man enjoys rather than uses his
wealth. But a virtuous man uses his wealth and enjoys felicity. Accordingly, to look upon consumption as the end of property, and to
speak of human society as a consumer society would not be in strict
agreement with the Thomistic doctrine of property.[15]

The problem arises because of the relationship the *bonum utile* of
material things has with the *bonum delectabile* of sensory pleasures.
Unless this relationship is maintained strictly under the harmonizing
influence of right reason, *bonum utile* can be falsely estimated and
evaluated as *bonum delectabile*. How this change could occur is explained by Aquinas in his treatment of concupiscence. And it is to the
consideration of concupiscence that we must now turn.

II

Property, though ontologically a *bonum utile*, is simultaneously
an object of sensory desire or concupiscence. Now concupiscence in man
belongs both to body and soul; but thanks to the consubstantiality of
body and soul, of the senses and mind, sense appetites participate to

a certain extent in reason. It is because of this participation of
concupiscence in reason that man is said to have a capacity for virtue.
But sense appetites have a motion of their own (*aliquid proprium*), and
claim a certain "equality" with mind. Accordingly, the mind does not
have a despotic power over them, as it has over the limbs, but only
political power, which is a power that equals exercise on equals; that
is why sensory appetites can turn in the direction of either vices or
virtues, depending on how they accept the directives of right reason.[16]

Further, the good of the concupiscence is the good of the total
human being, of the person, not just of the senses. Sensory pleasure
in man cannot be a purely sensory pleasure the way it is in animals.
The consubstantiality of body and mind requires no less. Thus man,
like other animals, enjoys eating and drinking, but, unlike other animals, he can consciously know and desire the good in eating and drinking. Knowledge of a certain type accompanies such pleasure: desire
follows knowledge. Sense pleasures, in other words, acquire a certain
affinity to reason or, as Aquinas states, participate in reason.[17] He
calls this aspect of concupiscence *concupiscentia cum ratione*.[18]

It is because of the affinity of sense appetite to reason that
human concupiscence could desire its absent objects *in infinitum*.[19]
For it is in the nature of reason to proceed *in infinitum*. Thus, as a
means to health, one may need only one drink a day, but one could
"desire" drinks *in infinitum*, even though right reason may forbid it,
and delight in it as good and desirable. In this way a rational creature, who does not live by right reason and who looks to material
things as ends, tries to overcome the finitude of material possessions
and the insecurity of possession which necessarily accompanies the enjoyment of the good of any finite material thing. It is in the nature
of the good of material things not to be able to satisfy human desires
completely: (*corporalia bona, cum adveniunt, non perpetuo manent, sed
deficiunt*).[20] But thanks to sense appetites' affinity to reason, man
can compensate for this deficiency (but of course deludedly) by thinking or imagining and delighting about the good of sense objects *in
infinitum*.

It is in this way that Aquinas explains how man comes to desire
property, in the form of money, *in infinitum*: "when a man desires
riches he may desire, not riches up to a certain limit, but simply to
be as rich as he possibly can."[21] When this happens, property has already ceased to be a means for use, but has become (falsely no doubt)

an end to be enjoyed. The proper end of every sensory desire is, of
course, to serve as a means to the final end of felicity, under the
direction of right reason. But because of a false perception brought
about by a sense appetite and sensory knowledge against the direction
of right reason and rational knowledge, property is desired as an end.
The desire for the means to a given end, says Aquinas, cannot properly
be infinite - the means is desired to the extent that it leads to attaining the end:

> Thus a man who has made wealth his end has a
> desire for wealth without limit; whereas one who
> desires wealth as a necessary means to supporting
> life desires only limited wealth - as much, that
> is, as is needed to support life.[22]

III

Now it is the role of virtue to bring about the rule of right reason in the world of concupiscence, and to free man from his false conceptions about the nature of property and to dispose him to right action. Intellectual virtues remove all conceptual delusions about property, and moral virtues introduce the proper order in the operations
of concupiscence, in this case in the use and ownership of property.
Before we proceed to consider the vices and virtues specifically associated with property, we must first investigate the specific question
of right and modes of ownership or private property.

The first and fundamental issue that interests Aquinas is the
wider question of man's, i.e. of every man's, not just the owner's,
relationship not just to property but to material things in general.
Aquinas' terminology is not without interest here. The terms he almost
always uses are *res* or *bona*, modified by adjectives such as *exterior*,
temporalis, *materialis*, and *sensibilis*. This is significant in two
ways. First, private property is only a part of the larger issue.
Secondly, use of the adjectives *exterior*, *temporalis*, *materialis*, *sensibilis*, indicates that throughout the discussion one may not forget
the interior, extra-temporal, spiritual, and intellectual things, and
that an adequate discussion of the problem of property must involve
both empirical and metaphysical considerations.

Thus the question is raised whether it is natural for man to possess external things? The answer is based on an important distinction
between the nature of material things and their use. As to the nature
of material things, man has no *dominium* over them, only God has it.
As for use, man has a natural *dominium* over them:

> ...for he has a mind and will with which to use
> them for his benefit. They seem to be made for him
> insofar as imperfect things are for the sake of the
> more perfect.... Further, this dominion over the
> rest of creation, which is natural to man as a crea-
> ture possessed of reason, in which exists the image
> of God, is manifested in the very creation of
> man....[23]

The *dominium* that is the foundation of any possession is the philosophical notion of *dominium* which reason has over its own acts, over
the acts of mind and will. "According as man is master of what is
within himself, in the same way he can have mastery over other things."
This is a characteristic of man *qua* man. It is not to be confused with
the legal notion of *dominium* such as *dominium jurisdictionis* (over
men), and *dominium proprietatis* (over one's own things). The *dominium*
which man has over acts of mind and will extends to material things as
well. This is so because of the principle that the less perfect must
be for the sake of the more perfect, i.e. the use of material things
has its proper finality only in the higher activities of the mind. An
added reason why man has a natural *dominium*-relation with material
things is because he needs the use of them for his full development as
a rational being. *Dominium*, then, is a broad, indeterminate power that
every man has with respect to both internal acts of mind and will as
well as to the use of the things of this world. It is an analogical
notion. Possession, as distinct from *dominium*, is a specification and
an extension of the latter to material things.

Turning to the next question,[24] the basis of private property,
Aquinas' very phraseology of the question suggests its derivatory or
secondary character. Whereas *dominium* is extended to man as such and
covers material goods in general, private possession is confined to
only certain things (*res aliquas*) and the right itself is *quasi pro-
priam* and the mode is permissive (*liceat*). *Dominium naturale* did not
specify the mode of possession; its requirement was that possessions
be for use and that, too, of all mankind. The primary requirement of
use applied, whether the mode of possession was private or not. Private mode of possession or private property had only conventional
justification of a historical and empirical nature. Whatever its human sanction, private possession had the obligation to realize the
primary purpose of property, namely, use. In a twofold answer Aquinas
makes his point clear:

Man has a two fold competence in relation to
material things. The first is the power to care
for and exchange (*potestas procurandi et dispensandi*).
As for this power, it is permitted that many may
possess things as his own. It is even necessary
for three reasons: First, because each person
takes more trouble to care for something that is
his sole responsibility than what is held in common or by many - for in such a case each individual
shirks the work and leaves the responsibility to
somebody else, which is what happens when too many
officials are involved. Second, because human affairs are more efficiently organized if each person
has his own responsibility to discharge: there
would be chaos if everybody cared for everything.
Third, because men live together in greater peace
where everyone is content with his task. We do,
in fact, notice that quarrels often break out
among men who hold things in common without distinction.

The second point concerns man's competence
with regard to the use of external things. In
this respect man ought to possess external things,
not as his own, but as common, so that he may more
readily share them with those in need.[25]

The justification of private property, then, is not in the *domin-*
ium naturale referred to above. It is to be sought rather in historical conditions which vary from time and place and culture. Assuming
that men are better motivated to care for material things if owned
privately, assuming further that there will be less social conflict
on the basis of private ownership, and assuming still further that each
owner will be content with the satisfaction of his own legitimate need
and will not invade others', private ownership may be necessary and
beneficial. But this is something for the times, for the cultures and
the good legislators to determine. Natural law itself is silent on
how private property should be arrived at. That is left to human law,
to *jus gentium*. Private property, in other words, is a historical institution.

...community of goods is said to be part of the natural law not because it requires everything to be
held in common and nothing to be appropriated privately (*quasi proprium*) but because according to
natural law there is no distinction of possession,
but rather according to human agreement (*secundum*
humanum condictum), which pertains to human law.
Hence private possessions are not contrary to natural law, but are added to natural law by the invention (*adinventionem*) of human reason.[26]

The right of use, which we may call the primary right, which comes from
dominium naturale has precedence over the power to acquire and exchange

(*potestas procurandi et dispensandi*), which is ownership and private
property, and which we may call the secondary right. If there is conflict between use and ownership, there was no doubt in Aquinas' mind
which should prevail. This is brought out very clearly in his attitude
towards surplus and urgent need.

With respect to surplus, Aquinas points out that it can happen only if someone else suffers want. The superabundance of one can only be
at the expense of another. This is so because of the very nature of
material things: "with material possessions it is impossible for one
man to enjoy overabundance without someone else suffering want, since
the resources of this World cannot be possessed by many at one time."[27]
Positive law may well justify surplus, but, says Aquinas, it has no
justification in natural law except for its social use: "...wherefore
division and appropriation of things which are based on human law do
not preclude the fact that man's needs have to be remedied by means of
these very things. Hence whatever certain people have in superabundance is due, by natural law, to the purpose of helping the poor."[28]
And, of course, for Aquinas, no good positive law may violate the precept of natural law.

The second instance which illustrates the primacy of use over ownership is *urgens necessitas*. Where such necessity exists one is permitted, either secretly or openly, (*sive occulte sive manifeste*) to expropriate the surplus without being guilty of theft or rapine. Indeed,
he cites with approval St. Ambrose's dictum, "Let no man call his own
that which is common," and "He who spends too much is a robber" (*plus
quam sufficeret sumptui, violenter obtentum est.*)[30] Thus Aquinas neatly balances the permissive right of acquiring and exchanging, which is
what the right of private property is, with the equally permissive
right of legitimately expropriating any surplus in case of urgent necessity.

In ST I-II, q.105, a.2, Aquinas complements the above moral obligation to use surplus in socially beneficial ways with the legal obligation which the legitimate authority and the community as a whole must
impose. Citing Cicero's famous definition of people (*populus coetus
multitudinis juris consensu et utilitatis communione sociatus* - a people
is a society held together by consensus on what is the law and the
sharing in material things), Aquinas argues that common sharing of material things (*utilitatis communio*) pertains to the very notion of
civil society. No matter what freedom private owners may have in

matters of acquisition and exchange of goods, when the question of common use is involved, civil law has the obligation to regulate that
freedom in the interest of society as a whole. Irregularities in private possessions, says Aquinas, following Aristotle, are the very
source of societal destruction.[31]

What is said of the right of private possession is applicable to
the right of private acquisition as well. It should be clear from the
primary principle of use that the mode of acquisition confers no exclusive right over the use of the produce. Thus, one who cultivates a
piece of land which hitherto belonged in common may appropriate its
produce, but the fact that he cultivated it does not give him an exclusive right of use of that land, and may not prevent another from using
it.[32]

One mode of acquisition and accumulation that Aquinas was familiar
with was usury. It is interesting to see how he himself applied his
principles of use and ownership to this concrete historical economic
institution. He was not supportive of it. His critique of usury is
well known and stated many times over.[33] And if there are common elements between usurious accumulation and modern modes of accumulation,
Aquinas' views should be of practical interest even today.

The key issue for Aquinas is the nature and purpose of money, and
whether in using it the intrinsic requirements of social justice are
realized or frustrated. Following Aristotle, Aquinas holds the strict
view that the first and proper use of money is to facilitate exchange
of property.[34] Money is a constant, neutral element in all exchange of
goods. Accordingly, to take an interest on a loan is to demand something that does not exist and thereby to set up an inequality between
the lender and the borrower. To make his point clear, Aquinas employs
the distinction between two classes of exchangeable goods.

First, there are some things the use of which consists in their
being consumed. The use of these things cannot be exchanged apart from
the things themselves. For example, we use wine for drinking, and when
we sell wine we transfer the use as well as the ownership of the wine
itself. Anyone who sells the wine and the use of the wine separately
would be selling the same thing twice, or selling something that does
not exist. Similarly, in lending wine, one lends both the use and the
ownership of wine. To ask for anything more than return of the same
amount would be to ask for an interest for the use of the wine, which
is unjust.

Secondly, there are other things, the use of which does not consist in being consumed, where use and ownership can be separated. Thus
a house or land could be loaned for the use of others without transferring ownership. And charging for the use in this type of goods (rent)
would not be usurious or unjust.

Money, however, is like the first category of goods: in loaning
it one transfers both the use and the ownership. And usury is to
charge for something which you do not own but which comes in the use of
others. Money, in other words, is not an exchangeable commodity; it is
not saleable.

What is forbidden in usury is the violation of justice in selling
something that is strictly not saleable. So long as the rule of justice is not violated, taking compensation is permitted. Thus, a lender
may accept compensation so long as it is not measurable in terms of
money, e.g. good will.[35] Again, a lender is within his rights to settle terms of compensation for the loss of any advantage which he is entitled to enjoy, for here no selling is involved but only avoiding
loss. The lender, however, is not entitled to make a contract to secure compensation for the loss that consists in not being able to use
the money lent, because one should not sell something which one has not
yet got and which one may be prevented in many ways from getting. Similarly, one may seek a share of the profit in an investment in a trading or manufacturing company, for here there was no lending strictly
so called.[37] Finally, rent on land and dwelling is legitimate for the
reason mentioned above.[38]

The question of profit as a mode of acquisition and accumulation
arises. The profitable economic institution Aquinas was most familiar
with was trade and commerce. His attitude towards it was governed by
the principle of the primacy of social use over private ownership.[39]
In Aquinas' eyes, business in the strict sense seemed to lack a social
purpose. Insofar as profit for profit's sake was the essence of business, it was a form of asocial pure self-assertion through accumulation
of property. Following the Aristotelian distinction between natural
and unnatural "business" (exchange), natural business, i.e. business
that has a social purpose, is not and could not be the responsibility
of businessmen at all, but of heads of families or of governments
(oeconomicos et politicos). And only business that is socially justified can be morally acceptable. And by social justification Aquinas
means social use or the satisfaction of "natural" i.e. ethically

justifiable needs:

> What men are in business for is the making of
> exchanges. But as Aristotle points out, there are
> two sorts of exchanges. The first is natural and
> necessary, and consists in the exchange of commodity
> for commodity or of commodity for money, for the
> *maintenance of life*. And such exchanges are the re-
> sponsibility not, strictly speaking, of businessmen,
> but of heads of families and governments, who have
> the responsibility to provide for the necessities of
> life for the household and the city. The other sort
> of exchange is money for money, or even of any com-
> modity for money, though now *for the sake of making
> a profit*, and this sort of exchange belongs to busi-
> nessmen in the strict sense. According to Aristotle,
> the former sort of exchange is praiseworthy because
> it responds to natural needs, whereas the second
> sort is rightly open to criticism, since *in itself,
> it responds to the acquisitive urge which knows no
> bound but tends to increase in infinity*. It follows
> that "business" as such, considered *per se*, has some-
> thing shameful about it insofar as it is not intrin-
> sically calculated to fulfill right or necessary
> ends.[40]

It must be pointed out that Aquinas is not against profit as such.
Profit that is socially beneficial and profit that accrues as the just
reward for labour are recognized as legitimate. On this point, Aquinas
goes beyond Aristotle. Thus, although business in the strict sense
does not carry the notion of anything right or necessary, neither does
it carry the notion of anything evil and contrary to virtue. "There
is, therefore, nothing to stop profit from being subordinated to an activity that is necessary and right. And this is the way business can
become justifiable." Thus business conducted for the purpose of making
moderate profit for support of the family, or the poor, or the public
good, is justifiable. Likewise one is permitted to make profit from
his work, not as the end of the work, but as a reward for it - *non quasi
finem, sed quasi stipendium laboris*.[41] Similarly, speculative buying
excepted, one may sell a commodity for a higher price than one paid for
it if between buying and selling the price has increased, or if the
buyer has improved the quality of the commodity "in some fashion,"
presumably by labour, or if the price has gone up because of local
changes, or of transportation risks. In these and similar instances,
neither the purchase nor the sale is unjust.[42]

Summing up the right to possess and to acquire private property,
it is clear that such right: 1) does not come from *dominium naturale*
but from human convention and human law that must always be in

conformity with natural law; 2) is justified only in terms of given
assumptions about human motivations and social and political organizations; 3) is subject to the primary right of use by all mankind;
4) limits the actual quantity both by reason of the transcending spiritual end of man and by reason of equality required by justice; 5) requires that surplus, whether acquired by labour, investment, or commerce, be socially justified; 6) requires that money not be misused as
a commodity.

IV

The discussion of the right to acquire and to accumulate property
took us to the essential and normative aspect of the question. We must
now turn to the question of how acquisition and accumulation operate in
the actual, historical world, given certain human motivations and social conditions of the existential order. And this takes us to
Aquinas' discussion of avarice.

The importance of avarice to Aquinas' theory of property can hardly be exaggerated. Being primarily an ethical theory, his theory of
property is directly challenged by avarice.

Avarice is opposed to the true end of human existence because it
replaces felicity with money, and through money the limitless acquisition of property. What avarice does is nothing short of proposing an
alternative end of human existence and an alternative ethic of conduct.
Freed from the status of a means, property has become an end. Where
good depends on a given measure, argues Aquinas, evil results from exceeding or falling short of that measure. As to things existing for
the sake of an end, such as property, the good consists in a determinate measure demanded by the end. Consequently, the human good in property consists in that a person seeks to possess it only to the degree
that is necessary for his growth and development. To go beyond this
measure is evil, namely the will to acquire and accumulate property
excessively. Avarice involves this, and so is clearly an evil.[43]

Money enters into the notion of avarice, because it is money that
facilitates acquisition of the false sense of infinite possession.
Thus, to define avarice strictly, avarice is the immoderate appetite
for temporal things which are meant for the use of human beings, and
which can be measured by money.[44] The immoderate affection is extended
not only to what one actually possesses but also to what one does not

possess. Thus avarice is broadened to include every sort of unchecked appetite to have any sort of thing that has a measurable monetary value.[45]

Avarice could not be the great evil it is had it not been for the misuse of money. Although money is the means of obtaining material things, because of the disorder in appetites it comes to be seen as the end of all material values and the very rival of felicity itself. Aquinas writes:

> ...the end sought above all is beatitude or felicity, the last end of human life. Thus the more anything shares in the qualities of beatitude the more desirable it is. One of these qualities is all-sufficiency, as Boethius remarks; and Aristotle explains this by saying, "Money serves us as a guarantee of possessing all things," and Ecclesiastes, "All things obey money."
>
> It is true that money is subordinated to something else as its end; still to the extent that it is useful in the quest for all material things, by its power it somehow contains them all...this is how it has some likeness to beatitude.[46]

Avarice is an interior disorder of concupiscence, and succeeds in making reason the servant of passions, thus reversing the right order of things and thereby disposing the person to "enjoy" instead of "using" property. Accordingly, it dehumanizes man and makes him desire as end the least lovable in the hierarchy of goods:

> Among all human goods, the good in material things is the least; it is less than that of the body (like health) and this in turn is inferior to the good of the soul (like knowledge); and good of the soul is exceeded by the divine good.[47]

What is worse, avarice once contracted becomes incurable. The incurableness of avarice has its basis, writes Aquinas, in the constant deterioration which it brings about in our nature. Thus the more needy a person becomes, the more he needs the relief allegedly supplied by temporal things and so the more easily slips into avarice. To gain inner rectitude of affection it is necessary to combat avarice *in affectu*. Such inner freedom for Aquinas is a precondition for, and more important than, external legal regulation of property.[48]

The external consequence of avarice, *avaritia in effectu*, is social disorder. Clearly it involves taking things that rightfully belong to others. Aquinas calls it the source of all sins against justice: inhumanity, callousness, restlessness, violence, deceit, falsehood, perjury, fraud, treachery, lying, false-witnessing, and rapacity.[50] Among all virtues, writes Aquinas, it is justice which chiefly

demands the right use of reason, for justice is the habit or disposition of the rational appetite. Hence the undue use of reason appears
chiefly in vices opposed to justice, the chief of which is covetousness
or avarice.[51]

The false likeness of avarice to felicity has already been noted.
It follows that, just as felicity is the final cause of both personal
and social harmony, so avarice is the source of all evil. Aquinas al-
ternately calls it the genus or the root of every human evil, for ultimately it involves the maximum alienation of man from his proper finality, and an inordinate turning towards a "commutable" good: covetousness is the root of all sins in that it gives sustenance to them
like the roots do to the whole tree. "For we see that by riches man
acquires the means of committing any evil whatever, and of satisfying
his desire for any evil whatever, since money helps man to obtain all
manner of temporal goods.... In this sense desire for riches is the
root of evil."[52]

By making accumulation of property the end of human existence,
avarice subverts the entire moral and social order. As practical secular materialism, it represents the total, incurable dehumanization of
man, based on a false knowledge of ends. The question now arises as
to what Aquinas sees as the way of humanizing man and of restoring to
him his *dominium naturale*, his freedom and mastery over material
things. And this takes us to his doctrine of virtues, especially the
moral virtues directly concerned with property, namely liberality and
justice.

V

Moral virtues are operative habits of right reason according to
which concupiscible appetites attain their objects (*bonum sensibile*) in
a manner agreeable with right reason. The desire for property, as
noted already, belongs to the concupiscible appetite. Such desire is
good and necessary for man so long as it is under the direction of
right reason. It becomes evil and harmful, to the person as well as
to society, if sought outside that limit. Whether it will become beneficial or harmful to man and society will depend in the first instance
on the power of virtues.

It is against this background of Aquinas' theory of virtues that
we should approach liberality and justice. The proper exercise of the
primary and secondary rights of property requires the rectification of

the interior disorders of sensory appetites affecting use and possession. Thus the immediate objects of liberality are the interior passions according to which man is affected towards money, and all that
can be measured by money.[53] Now the good of money and all that can be
measured by money consists in its being a means for man's use. Therefore the proper act of the virtue of liberality is the right use of
money and wealth.

The money and wealth liberality refers to is one's own, acquired
justly.[54] And the right use may consist of either spending on oneself
(consumption) or giving to others. In the latter case, what is essential is not the amount given but the attitude of the giver (*liberalitas
non attenditur in quantitate dati, sed in affectu dantis*).[55] In short,
liberality creates an attitude of indifference towards one's own possessions and creates an inner freedom which alone can enable us to use
property without having to enjoy it. For Aquinas, possession and acquisition of wealth cannot be separated from the liberal use of it:
one acquires property and owns it not as an end to be enjoyed but as a
means to be used.

No wonder then that Aquinas views liberality, lowly though it is
with respect to its object (the material good of things), as a founda-
tion-virtue of a good society. For without the inner freedom from
property it is not possible to love the common good or the higher good
of the body or of the mind or the divine good. From the fact that one
is not a lover of wealth (*amativus pecuniae*) one is enabled to use
one's property properly both with respect to oneself and others. In
this respect liberality has a certain preeminent excellence, for without it neither moral nor intellectual nor theological virtues can be
practised.[56]

Justice is the other moral virtue concerned with the proper use of
property. Whereas liberality is concerned with the interior affections, justice is concerned with external (or social) actions respecting equality of possessions among men.[57] Whereas liberality is concerned with the use of one's own property, justice is concerned with
property that belongs to others. And whereas liberality is concerned
with moral obligation in the use of one's own property, justice is concerned with legal, that is, public obligation, in the exchange of property. Unlike liberality, which is concerned with the rectification of
concupiscence, justice is concerned with the rectification of human actions, the rectification particularly of the rational will.

Justice effectively consists in the will to give each one his due. Giving each one his due requires the knowledge of the right proportion between things, and between persons and things. Now to render each one his due is wholly beyond the capabilities of sensory appetites, for the simple reason that sensory knowledge does not extend to the apprehension of the proportion of one thing to another. Such knowledge properly belongs to the mind. Hence justice cannot be in the sense appetite but can only be in the rational appetite, i.e. the will guided by right reason.[58] And this is how justice brings about rational rectitude in our social relations.

Insofar as justice involves actions affecting others, the focus of justice is the common good or the public good. Giving each one his due is a necessary requirement of social living. Although the juridical concept of justice emphasises the effective rendering of their due to others, the ontological basis for it must be sought elsewhere, viz. in equality. If something is designed for the use of all, then the sharing or the distribution of that thing has necessarily to be on the basis of equality. Thus, for Aquinas, the substantive basis of justice is equality: *Nomen justitiae aequalitatem importat* - justice signifies equality;[59] *justitia est circa actiones debitas inter aequales* - justice is concerned with obligatory actions between equals; again, *Hoc autem dicitur esse suum uniuscujusque personae quod ei secundum proportionis aequalitatem debetur* - only such things are one's own which are owed according to the proportion of equality.[61] And in the relation of the individual to the group, distributive justice maintains such equality, which is geometrical in character. And in the exchange relation between things, an arithmetical equality is maintained. We cannot here go into the detailed analysis of Aquinas' thought in the application of distributive and commutative justice. For our purpose here, it is sufficient to note that the rule of equality is a rational rule of justice and that it prevails over every consideration of ownership.

To sum up, the ontological nature of property (common use) requires that man maintain both an inner freedom and external equality in the private possession and use of things. There is a complex relationship between man's composite nature, the ordered satisfaction of various needs, the attainment of felicity, and the use of property.

VI

Turning now to the last point, namely the institutional remedies against the disorders arising from the abuse of property, we need only indicate here the main lines of Aquinas' thought. On the ontological and normative planes the ideal of property relations is clear: man ought to strive for felicity, not property. On the actual historical plane, on the other hand, the realization of the ideal is subject to the imperfections of human nature. Accordingly, the realization of human perfection is necessarily developmental, which is to say incomplete at any given moment in time. Thus the metaphysician could say: *Natura humana est mutabilis. Et ideo id quod naturale est homini potest aliquando deficere* - human nature being changeable, man sometimes falls short of the perfection of which he is capable.[62] This means that the realization of the full human potential is subject to correction of actual deficiencies, which is a matter of human freedom, and therefore contingent. History therefore could not be said to have one necessary end that should be realized in one particular set of social institutions.

Aquinas' discussion of the *best* regime is not therefore a discussion of the *necessary* regime. While it is necessary to have a regime, to have a particular regime is not a matter of necessity. Where many free wills operate, it is necessary to have a directing authority charged with the common good. Such an authority is a requirement of social organizations as such, and not a function of any particular economic relations. And it is the task of such authority to strive to bring about a just property relation.

As to the question of how particular regimes strive to bring about such a result, Aquinas does not look to metaphysics for the answers, but to culture as influenced by metaphysics. The nature of particular regimes depends on the character of culture so understood. Thus, if a culture is based predominantly on virtue, the political regime would be aristocratic; if on property, an oligarchy; and if on liberty, a democracy. His understanding of how metaphysics operates on history, or ought to operate on history, makes him a pluralist with respect to political regimes.

This is not to say that law and regime ought not to have transcending rational aims, other than their cultural capacities. The philosophical justification of regimes always rests on the common

good, the realization of which, as we have already noted, is possible
only with the aid of virtues. Beyond this, Aquinas does not commit
himself, for the simple reason that the imposition of a temporal end
without the combination of virtue and culture would be foolishly tyrannical. The contact of culture to metaphysics is necessary in order
to enable the former to strive for the ideal.

Finally, the fact that Aquinas was a theologian, which one must
never forget, gave him a certain confidence in humanity's ability to
attain its final destiny. This, in turn, gave him a decent tolerance
of the imperfections of history. Faith had assured him of the avail-
ability of grace with which to overcome the imperfections of nature
and to attain beatific vision. Reason corroborated this position inas-
much as it was reason's own conclusion that no temporal good could satisfy to the full the human potential. Hence Aquinas could not have
made the realization of a perfect regime of property a necessary or
even a desirable end of human existence.

FOOTNOTES

1   *Summa theologiae* (hereafter ST) I, q.1, a.8, ad 2. I have consulted available English translations in making my own translations of particular passages.

2   ST. I-II, q.16m a.4: *Omne imperfectum tendit in perfectionem.* Again, II-II, q.66, a.1: *Imperfectiora propter perfectiora.*

3   ST. I, q.96, a.2. Emphasis added.

4   ST. I, q.29, a.3: *Persona significat id quod est perfectissimum in tota natura, scilicet subsistens in rationali natura.*

5   ST. I-II, q.1, a.1: Compare Engels and Marx: "Men can be distinguished from animals by consciousness, by religion or anything else you like. They themselves begin to distinguish themselves from animals as soon as they begin to produce their means of subsistence, a step which is conditioned by their physical organization." *German Ideology*, ed. C. J. Arthur (London, 1974), p. 42.

6   ST. I-II, q.5, a.1.

7   ST. I-II, q.5, a.3.

8   The entire ST. I-II, q.2 in 8 Articles is devoted to this discussion. See also *Contra Gentiles*, Bk. III, chs. 27-36.

9   ST. II-II, q.118, a.1, ad 1. For the distinction between *bonum utile, bonum delectabile*, and *bonum honestum*, see I-II, q.5, a.6; II-II, q.145, a.3.

10   ST. I-II, q.4, a.7.

11   *Contra Gentiles*, Bk. III, ch. 36. Emphasis added.

12   ST. I-II. q.16, a.1-4.

13   *Ibid.*, a.3.

14   *Ibid.*, a.2, ad 1.

15   See Marcus Lefebvre, "'Private Property' According to St. Thomas and Recent Papal Encyclicals," in the Blackfriars Translation of *Summa theologiae*, Vol. 38 (London: Eyre and Spottiswoode, 1975), pp. 275-283.

16   ST. I, q.81, a.3, ad 2; also ST. I-II, q.56, a.4.

17   ST. I-II, q.56, a.4.

18   *Ibid.*, q.30, a.3, ad 2.

19   *Ibid.*, q.30, a.4.

20 *Ibid.*

21 *Ibid.*

22 *Ibid.*

23 ST. II-II, q.66, a.1.

24 *Ibid.*, a.2.

25 *Ibid.*

26 *Ibid.*, ad 1.

27 *Ibid.*, q.118, a.1, ad 2.

28 *Ibid.*, q.66, a.7.

29 *Ibid.*

30 *Ibid.*, a.2, ad 3.

31 ST. I-II, q.105, a.2.

32 ST. II-II, q.66, a.2, ad 2.

33 See John T. Noonan, *The Scholastic Analysis of Usury* (Cambridge, Mass., 1957).

34 ST. II-II, q.78, a.1.

35 *Ibid.*, a.2.

36 *Ibid.*, ad 1.

37 *Ibid.*, ad 5.

38 *Ibid.*, a.4.

39 *Ibid.*, q.77, a.4.

40 *Ibid.* Emphasis added.

41 *Ibid.*

42 *Ibid.*, ad 2.

43 *Ibid.*, q.118, a.1.

44 ST. I, q.63, a.2, ad 2.

45 ST. II-II, q.118, a.2; also q.78, a.2.

46 *Ibid.*, a.7. See also ST. I-II, q.2, ad 1 and 3: "Many foolish men think that all corporeal things obey money, but these are men who are conscious only of goods which can be acquired with money. But our judgement about human goods should be taken, not from the foolish but from the wise...."

"The desire for natural wealth is not infinite because at a certain point the needs of nature are satisfied. But the desire for artificial wealth is infinite because it is subject to disordered concupiscence which observes no measure, as Aristotle shows. There is a difference between the infinite desire for wealth and the infinite desire for the ultimate good, since the more perfectly the infinite good is possessed the more it is loved and other things despised, for the more it is possessed, the more it is known...but with respect to desire for wealth and any temporal good it is the converse, for as soon as any such thing is possessed despised and other things are desired.... The reason for this is that we recognize their insufficiency more when we possess them; this very fact shows their imperfection and that the ultimate good does not consist in them."

47 ST. I-II, q.118, a.5.

48 *Sententia Libri Politicorum*, Rome, 1971, II, 9.

49 ST. II-II, q.118, a.1, ad 2.

50 *Ibid.*, a.8.

51 *Ibid.*, q.55, a.8.

52 ST. I-II, q.84, a.1.

53 ST. II-II, q.117, a.3.

54 *Ibid.*, a.4, ad 3.

55 *Ibid.*, a.2, ad 1.

56 *Ibid.*, a.6.

57 *Ibid.*, a.2, ad 3; q.58, a.8, ad 3.

58 *Ibid.*, q.58, a.4.

59 *Ibid.*, a.2.

60 ST. I-II, q.61, a.3.

61 ST. II-II, q.58, a.11.

62 *Ibid.*, q.57, a.2, ad 1.

James Tully's paper situates Locke in terms of the discussion of
property which was current in his day. He shows that Locke did not
draw the same type of distinction between private and common property
which is made today. The problem for Locke was to explain the individuation of property in the world which had been given by God to mankind in common. Further, Tully demonstrates that Locke's usage of
terms like "property" and "rights" is closer to that of the Thomists
such as Suarez and Vitoria than to his immediate predecessors, such as
Filmer, Grotius, and Pufendorf. The latter had justified exclusive
private property as a natural right, whereas Locke returned to the
Thomistic idea that exclusive property rights had to be balanced by
inclusive claim rights to common use.

THE FRAMEWORK OF NATURAL RIGHTS IN LOCKE'S ANALYSIS OF PROPERTY:
A CONTEXTUAL RECONSTRUCTION

This paper has two aims.[1] The first is to throw light on one aspect of the theory of property which John Locke intended to convey in the *Two Treatises of Government*. The second is to recommend a way in which we might come to understand political writing in past time.[2] The two aims come together in that my interpretation of Locke is an application of the way of approaching texts which I present and defend in the paper. The relevance of the paper for contemporary discussions of property is indirect and chiefly by way of contrast. Locke conceptualizes property in a manner different from our mutually exclusive concepts of private property and common property. He does not use the modern concept of private property, which, like its modern antithesis of common property, emerged in the eighteenth century. Understanding Locke's thought will help us to see the limits of the way in which we normally think about property.

It is now well known that Locke's immediate audience received his work predominantly with silence, and, when noted, with abuse.[3] The first point at which it became an important element in a philosophical and practical political movement was in the early nineteenth century. Locke was read as the father of modern socialism in England by the "Lockean" socialists.[4] This was paralleled by a socialist reading of Locke in France by Etienne Cabet and in Germany by Karl Grün.[5] We can gauge the importance of this interpretation by Marx's attack on it when he began to move against the unscientific socialists in *The German Ideology*.[6] The last socialist reading of Locke that I have been able to locate is an article by Charles Driver in 1928.[7] The second major wave of interpretation is the liberal one, which can be said to have been securely established in the 1930s.[8] This also marks the first appearance of the view that Locke's analysis is confused and superficial, a view which remains a constituent of present day liberal readings.[9] The immensely influential works of Leo Strauss and Professor Macpherson give rise to the third interpretation - that of the illiberal Locke. Locke is said to have defended and recommended "possessive individualism" and unlimited accumulation and to have freed ownership

of social obligations.[10] A fourth interpretation, which now appears
to be common, is that Locke leaves it up to governments to define property as they see fit.[11]

These four major interpretations rest on a common methodological
premise. This is the central tenet of the Whig view of history: that
twentieth-century political theories and institutions "grew out of,"
or "evolved from," or have their "roots" in seventeenth-century theories and institutions.[12] The normative use of metaphors of development, growth and evolution, which informs most if not all of these
studies, came under sustained attack in the late 1960s.

One line of attack was launched by the post-structuralists in
France, especially Louis Althusser and Michel Foucault.[13] Evolutionary assumptions were shown to predispose us to look for our own set of
problems, in primitive form, in past writers, thus imposing an alien
interpretive framework on the text and so yielding an unavoidably circular argument.[14] This critique was carried forward in England by
Maurice Dobb's pupil, Dr. Keith Tribe, and, *inter alia*, applied to
Locke scholarship.[15] He argued that to impose a primitive capitalist
market as an explaining factor causes us to misunderstand the uniqueness of seventeenth-century economic structures and so to misinterpret
Locke.

Another criticism came from the revival of interest in hermeneutics, especially by Hans Georg Gadamer and Charles Taylor.[16] It was
argued that to recover the meaning of a text it is necessary to situate it in its intersubjective matrix of conventions and assumptions,
in light of which the text can be said to have meaning for the author
and his audience. John Dunn and Quentin Skinner went on to link the
sense of meaning involved in hermeneutics to the author's intention in
writing, or what the author was doing in writing it.[17] Thus, the meaning exists for a subject but is equally dependent upon the intersubjective and conventional vocabulary available for its articulation.
In *The Political Thought of John Locke* John Dunn showed that it is
necessary to interpret Locke's writings in light of the normative theological vocabulary available to him and in terms of which his theory
is written if his meaning is to be recovered.[18] Professors Hundert,
Neale and Pocock have all presented studies along these lines which
throw into question the four major interpretations outlined above.[19]

The primary criticism of the methodology exemplified by the Whig
historical approach rests on a distinction between explanation and

understanding.[20] An agent can be said to have performed an action only
if the description under which the action is defined and performed is
available to him.[21] To redescribe and so explain a complex linguistic
action, such as a text, in terms of an explaining factor unfamiliar to
the author seems to provide an interpretation which he would not recognize. It would not be the meaning the author intended. What stands in
need of interpretation - the meaning the text had for the author and
his audience - is elided by redescribing it in terms of an explaining
factor more familiar to us. Understanding, as opposed to explanation,
turns on recovering the meaning the author intended to convey by reading the text in light of the conventions and assumptions available to
him, and so of coming to understand it in those terms. This is what I
attempt to do for one neglected but important aspect of Locke's writings on property.

II

The range of normative vocabulary available to Locke and in terms
of which he articulates his theory is the language of seventeenth-century natural law and natural rights discourse. Thus interpretation
should take place in light of other natural law writers whom he recom-
mends or who can be seen, for historical and textual reasons, to be
important in understanding Locke. This is essential in order to make
explicit the conventions usually adopted in natural law discussions of
property. It enables us to see which aspects of Locke's writings are
conventional, in which he wishes to endorse or reassert prevailing
norms and assumptions. It also provides a backdrop against which it
is possible to gauge where Locke diverges from the norm and presents
his audience with something new and different. Other natural law writers, therefore, function as objects of comparison which throw light on
Locke's work in virtue of their similarities and dissimilarities.

In addition, this method permits the demarcation of intersubjective beliefs which the audience had no reason to doubt and thus could
function as public criteria for justifying arguments.[22] I am of course
aware that natural law was not the only discursive mode available and
that an historical form of political argument was more popular in
England in the 1680s.[23] One of the merits of the approach I adopt is
that it explains why Locke chose to write in natural law language rather than in the normal historical mode.[24]

It is also necessary to situate the *Two Treatises* in the context
of the range of social and political action Locke addresses in writing
on property. We can scarcely understand Locke unless we recover the
forms of political and social action which he intends to recommend or
to repudiate at various points in his arguments. Therefore it is essential to outline this ideological context.

The leading issue to which Locke responds in the *Two Treatises* is
arbitrary and absolutist government. He mounts a blistering attack on
its most popular defence: the political tracts of Sir Robert Filmer
(1588-1652). In its place Locke reasserts a radical constitutionalist
theory, or theory of popular sovereignty, and an individualist theory
of resistance to arbitrary government.[25] Filmer's treatises, a Royal-
ist defence of absolute monarchy, were written between 1638 and 1652,
and originally published in 1648, 1652 and 1653. They were republished
in 1679 and again in 1680. *Patriarcha*, the locus of Locke's attack,
was published for the first time in the 1680 collection.[26] The occasion of their republication was the Exclusion Crisis (1679-1681), en-
gendered by the Whigs' attempt to exclude James, Duke of York, the son
of King Charles II, from accession to the throne of England. The Tories pressed Filmer's writings into service as an ideological justification of James' promotion. The perceived threat on the basis of which
the Whigs resisted the King was a combination of popery and arbitrary
government. The Tory defence was based on Divine Right and passive
obedience to hereditary succession, even if this entailed a Roman Catholic monarch.[27]

As a result of Mr. Laslett's painstaking efforts to date the composition of the *Two Treatises*, it is apparent that Locke began to move
against Filmer in this context as early as his reading of the 1679 edition of Filmer's work in that year.[28] Thus, insofar as the Tories described and so legitimated court action in terms of Filmer's writings,
Locke was necessarily attacking their position in attacking Filmer.
This ideological point shows that Locke's refutation of Filmer is a
positive Whig contribution to the Exclusion Crisis without being what
Mr. Laslett calls an "Exclusion tract."[29] The continuing appeal of
Filmer during and after the Glorious Revolution of 1688 explains
Locke's publication of the *Two Treatises* in 1689.[30]

To refute Filmer and to provide an alternative theory in terms of
natural law and natural rights, Locke had to answer the objections
brought against natural law by Filmer in his tract entitled

Observations on Hugo Grotius' The Laws of War and Peace. Locke's complete project would have seemed ridiculous to his audience unless he
replied to Filmer's claim that there were inconsistencies in Grotius,
inconsistencies which threw the whole natural law mode of political
discourse into question. The contradictions which Filmer alleged to
have found are in Grotius' treatment of property (*dominium*). Therefore, it was necessary for Locke to develop a theory of property which
would answer Filmer's critique and so save natural law as a viable
form of argument.

The constraints of the context thus make a theory of property
the necessary precondition for Locke's main and explicit aim of over-
throwing Filmer's modern theory of absolutism and of reasserting the
older and more traditional constitutionalist or consent theory of government.[31] However, the situation is even more complex than this.
Hugo Grotius (1583-1645), the Dutch scholar statesman and jurist, in
The Laws of War and Peace (1624), and Samuel Pufendorf (1632-92), the
German jurist, historian and political theorist, in *The Law of Nature
and Nations* (1672), both use the normative vocabulary of natural law
to present rationalist theories of absolutism.[32] In addition to saving
natural law from Filmer's attack, Locke is faced with the task of using
natural law vocabulary to construct a theory of property different from
the compact theory which both Grotius and Pufendorf set up as a means
of establishing their absolutist conclusions. Locke requires a theory
which will yield, or be consistent with, a non-absolutist or limited
theory of government, grounded in the consent of the people.[33]

III

In his criticism of Grotius, Filmer pounces on the apparent inconsistency that natural law is said to sanction common property in the
state of nature and private property in political society. "Grotius,"
writes Filmer, says

> that by the law of nature all things were at first
> common, and yet teacheth, that after propriety was
> brought in, it was against the law of nature to use
> community. He does thereby not only make the law
> of nature changeable, which he saith God cannot do,
> but he also makes the law of nature contrary to
> itself.[34]

This problem in Grotius, of natural law endorsing both common and private property, is a result of the radical innovation Grotius introduces
in the treatment of rights. In his early work, *De Jure Pradae* (1604),

written at the age of twenty-one, he makes a decisive break with the
Scholastic orthodoxy of the previous century. To see the full importance of Grotius' move, and of Locke's later repudiation of it, it is
necessary to view it in light of the theory he rejects.

In the autumn of 1535 the Dominican theologian Francisco de Vitoria began his lectures in the University of Salamanca on the second part
of Aquinas' *Summary of Theology*, lectures which were to provide the
theoretical support for the Catholic counter-reformation. One of Vitoria's pupils, Domingo de Soto (1494-1560), published his *Ten Books on
Law and Justice*, based on Vitoria's lectures, and it ran to twenty-
seven editions in the sixteenth century alone. This work was carried
forward by the Jesuit Luis de Molina (1535-1600) and by another Jesuit,
Francisco Suarez (1547-1617), in *The Laws and God the Lawgiver* (1612)
and *The Defence of the Catholic and Apostolic Faith* (1612). They
sought to reestablish Aquinas' concept of natural law as the foundation
of moral and political philosophy.[35] However, they were faced with the
emergence and widespread use of the concept of subjective rights after
Aquinas' death. A subjective right is a right which an individual is
said to have or to possess, such as a right to education or to a material object. This is distinguished from the objective concept of
right, when we say that such and such is right or is the right thing to
do. Aquinas seems not to employ the subjective concept of right and
its appearance is usually dated in the early fourteenth century.[36]
During his student years at the University of Paris in 1507-1522, Vitoria had been exposed to the last advocates of an unlimited subjective
rights theory associated with Jean Gerson (1363-1429). The task of Vitoria and his followers was to use the language of subjective rights,
but to give political theory a more objective basis, and subjective
rights a more limited purchase, by grounding both in natural law.
Suarez' work is the culmination of this school of Vitorian neo-Thomists
and it provides the best object of comparison for understanding Grotius.

Suarez develops his concept of a subjective right by considering
two accepted meanings of justice (*iustitia*).[37] First, he writes that
"right" (*ius*) has the same meaning as "that which is just" (*iustum*)
and "that which is equitable" (*aequum*). These are the two objects of
justice. Thus "right" will have two meanings corresponding to the two
objects of justice. Justice in turn stands for (1) every moral virtue,
since every moral virtue is, in some way, directed towards and brings

about equity, and (2) a special moral virtue which renders to another that which is his due.[38] Thus a just man in the first or generic sense is just in all his relationships, whereas a man would be just in the latter or specific sense by acting justly in a specific sort of relationship.

Suarez writes that "right" in the generic sense is what is fair and in harmony with reason, this being the general object of virtue in the abstract. "Right" in the specific sense, the object of justice in the specific sense, refers to the equity which is due to each individual as a matter of justice.[39] Having distinguished "right" from justice, and having identified it primarily with the object of justice in the specific sense, he redescribes "right" in this objective sense in terms of two subjective rights. First he writes,

> According to the latter and strict acceptation of right, this name is properly wont to be bestowed on a certain moral power which every man has, either over that which is rightfully his own or with respect to that which is due to him.

He defines "right" in the strict sense above as that which is due to a person as a matter of justice, as opposed to justice, which is the rendering of that which is due. Then he unpacks this formulation to show that it contains two traditional objects of justice: that which is rightfully one's own (*rem suam*) and that which is rightfully due a person (*ad rem sibi debitam*). The reason why the moral power which a man has with respect to these two objects (which are right) can itself be called "right" in the subjective sense is that the moral power cannot but be right in the objective sense. That is, the moral power is objectively right because it is a moral power with respect to what is right by definition: one's own and one's due. Thus subjective right is derived from and limited by natural law, the standard of what is objectively right. The basis is laid for a subjective rights theory limited by natural law, the sort of theory Locke reasserts sixty years later.

Suarez goes on to distinguish between the moral power that one has with respect to that which is rightfully one's own and one's due:

> For it is thus that the owner of a thing is said to have a right in that thing (*ius in re*) and the worker is said to have a right to his stipend (*ius ad stipendium*) by reason of which he is declared worthy of his hire. Indeed, this acceptation of the term is frequent, not only in law, but in Scripture; for the

law distinguishes in this way between a right already established in a thing (*ius in re*), and a
right to a thing (*ad rem*).

The right to a thing (*ius ad rem*) is a claim right to that which is
due to a person as a matter of justice (e.g. a stipend) but which he
does not yet possess. As Suarez redescribes it: "a right to claim a
thing which in some way pertains to him." The right in a thing (*ius
in re*) is a right in that which rightfully belongs to a person and
which he does possess. In each case, the object belongs to him, but
in different senses of "to belong."

To use Locke's terminology, in fulfilling his obligation the person who possesses a right to a thing "comes to have" a "right in" or a
"property in" the object.[40] Suarez' translation of right in the objective sense into two subjective rights allows a person to discuss the
two objects of justice in terms of subjective rights.

A right to a thing (*ius ad rem*) and a right in a thing (*ius in re*)
as defined by Suarez and Locke are conceptually linked in a way which
can be illustrated by a modern example. The claim right to ride on
public transportation is a right not to be excluded from riding and
correlates, we may say, with a positive duty on the part of the community to provide the necessary transportation. When an individual is exercising his claim right by using public transport he comes to have a
right in the use of the seat he occupies. This is now a right to exclude others from the use of the seat while it is occupied. The claim
right is a right not to be excluded (to be included) and so may be
called an inclusive right. The right in the use of the seat, which is
necessary to complete, or make good, the claim right, is a right to exclude others, temporarily, from using it and so may be called an exclusive right.[41] The example illustrates the crucial logical point
that a claim right of this sort requires some kind of exclusive right
in what is claimed, and some criterion of "coming to have," for it to
be exercised.

Suarez' analysis of property (*dominium*) begins, as does Aquinas'
and Locke's, with the premise that there is common ownership of all
things (*communitas rerum*).[42] He argues against an Adamite theory similar to Filmer's and states that there is no original donation of private dominion, either from God directly to Adam or from natural law.[43]
Genesis 1.28 is to be interpreted as giving mankind dominion in common.

The original dominion in common is power to use the world and the inferior creatures:[44]

> Nature has conferred upon all men in common dominion
> over all things, and consequently has given to every
> man a power to use those things; but nature has not
> so conferred private property with that domain.

This exposition is similar to Aquinas in its sharp distinction between
dominion in common and any form of private or exclusive property (*proprietas*). Suarez continues by redescribing Aquinas' concept of dominion in common in terms of a natural, subjective claim right: "for we
have said that 'right' is sometimes 'law' while at times it means *dominium* or *quasi-dominium* over a thing; that is, a claim to its use."[45]
He makes it clear that this is an inclusive claim right to use that
which belongs to all: "a positive precept of natural law to the effect that no one should be prevented from making the necessary use of
the common property."[46]

Suarez's further analysis of the individuation of property takes
place within this framework of the world belonging to all men in common. Once property has been distributed within a society in accordance
with various criteria, some natural and some conventional, the natural
claim right remains as the foundation for a positive theory of charity.
Not only is Locke's theory similar, but his theory of charity develops
from the same foundation. The striking feature of this sort of theory
is that private and common property are interdependent rather than mutually exclusive concepts; private or exclusive property is necessary
to individuate and so distribute common property.

Grotius' early work, *De Jure Pradae* (1604), gives a completely
different picture. He informs his reader that *dominium* used to mean
the common right to use common property. *Dominium* used to mean a kind
of common possession different from *proprietas*. However, this is no
longer the way in which the terms are to be used. *Dominium* means solely its Roman sense of exclusive possession. Use (*usus*) means only exclusive use:[47]

> Accordingly, it must be understood that, during the
> earliest epoch of man's history, *dominium* and common
> possession (*communio*) were concepts whose significance
> was different from that now ascribed to them. For in
> the present age the term *dominium* connotes possession
> of something peculiarly one's own, that is to say,
> something belonging to a given party in such a way
> that it cannot be similarly possessed by any other
> party; whereas the expression "common property" is
> applied to that which has been assigned to several

parties, to be possessed by them in partnership, so
to speak, and in mutual accord, to the exclusion of
other parties. Owing to the poverty of human
speech, however, it has become necessary to employ
identical terms for concepts which are not identical. Consequently, because of a certain degree of
similitude, and by analogy, the above mentioned expressions descriptive of our modern customs are applied to another right, which existed in earlier
times. Thus, with reference to that earlier age,
the term "common" is nothing more nor less than the
simple antonym of "private" (*proprium*); and the word
dominium denotes the power to make use rightfully of
common property. This attribute the Scholastics
chose to describe as a concept of fact but not of
law. For the legal right now connoted by the term
"use" (*usus*) is of a private nature.

In his great work, *The Laws of War and Peace* (1624), Grotius continues and clarifies his break with the Thomist tradition. He defines
"right" (*ius*) in three ways.[48] First, "right" in the objective sense
signifies that which is just (*iustum*). The second, subjective sense is
a "moral faculty annexed to a person, enabling him to have or to do
something justly." He then collapses the concept of a subjective right
into a right in that which one actually possesses, an exclusive right,
thus eliding the concept of an inclusive claim right to one's due:
"lawyers call a faculty that right which a man has to his own, but we
shall hereafter call it a right properly and strictly taken." It is
impossible to speak of Suarez' subjective right which redescribes ownership in common using Grotius' concept of a right. *Dominium* for Grotius is solely an exclusive right over one's possessions, the same kind
of right as that which one has over one's liberty, children and
slaves.[49] Grotius' *dominium* is the same as Filmer's "private dominion." Translated as "property" in the English editions abstracted from
its regulative absolutism, it passes into legal theory in the eighteenth century in the works of Sir William Blackstone:[50]

> the right of property, or that sole and despotic
> dominion which one man claims and exercises over
> the external things of the world, in total exclu-
> sion of the right of any other individual in the
> universe.

Thus when Grotius discusses the origin of property he uses *dominium* and *proprietas* interchangeably, since they both denote the same exclusive right.[51] The right which each man is said to have is not an
inclusive claim right but rather an exclusive right to use the things
which one happens to come to possess (*ius in res*). He uses Cicero's

simile of the theatre to show that originally the world belongs to no
one but is open for the first taking of anyone: "although the theatre
is common for anybody who comes, yet the place that everyone sits in
is properly his own."[52] On this model, if the theatre fills to capacity, the people excluded have no rights. Suarez' inclusive claim
right, on the other hand, suggests that the theatre (world) belongs to
everyone and those excluded have a claim right on the basis of which
they may impose the duty on others of moving over and making room.

Pufendorf, in *The Laws of Nature and Nations* (1672), differs from
Grotius in many respects, but he continues Grotius' fundamental revision in the concept of a subjective right: "*proprietas* or *dominium* is
a right whereby the substance, as it were, of something belongs to a
person in such a way that it does not belong in its entirety to another
person in the same manner."[53] Pufendorf draws the important conclusion
that it is no longer conceptually possible to speak of community, of
everyone owning the same object in the same manner, as a form of property. With Grotius' concept of dominium it is possible to speak of
individual *dominium* and *dominium* in several, but not of *dominium* in
common:[54]

> I say "in the same manner" for nothing prevents, and,
> indeed, it very often happens, that the same thing be-
> longs to different persons according to their different
> ways of holding it. Thus, over the same land a state
> has eminent, the owner direct, and the user useful *do-
> minium*. It was also said "in its entirety" for also
> several persons can possess the same thing in the same
> way of holding, but each one for his own share and not
> in its entirety.

For Pufendorf, as for Grotius, "common" means that it belongs to no one
and is open for the appropriation of anyone. For Suarez "common" means
that the object belongs to everyone and so must be individuated such
that each realizes his claim.

III

Our passage to Locke is facilitated by the commentary on Grotius
and Pufendorf by Jean Barbeyrac (1674-1744), a French legal theorist
and historian. He annotated a Latin edition of Grotius' *The Laws of
War and Peace* (1735) and annotated and translated into French Pufendorf's *The Law of Nature and Nations* (1725). He corresponded with
Locke, learned English in order to read the *Essay Concerning Human Understanding*, and wrote a history of natural law political theory which
situates Locke in the context described above.[55] As Mr. Laslett writes

of Barbeyrac, "no man was in a generally better position than he to
know about the relationship of his [Locke's] writings with the natural
law jurists and with the whole tradition of social and political theory."[56] Many of his notes on Pufendorf consist of references to the
Two Treatises, with unreserved enthusiasm for Locke's superiority. His
note on Pufendorf's definition of *dominium* is precisely what one would
expect from a person familiar with Grotius' and Pufendorf's collapse of
the vocabulary of property into exclusive rights: "our author [Pufen-
dorf] gives us a notion of a particular kind of *dominium*, rather than
of *dominium* in general."[57] He refers his reader to Locke's refutation
of Filmer for clarification.

     Locke hammers out the foundation of his rights theory in the *First
Treatise*, in the course of his refutation of Filmer. When Filmer
speaks of property or private dominion he means the same kind of exclusive right as we have seen in Grotius and Pufendorf. Locke paraphrases
this concept of property and draws special attention to its unlimited
and unlimitable nature:[58]

>   This *Fatherly Authority* then, or *Right of Fatherhood*,
>   in our A___'s sence is a Divine unalterable Right of
>   Sovereignty, whereby a Father or a Prince hath an
>   Absolute, Arbitrary, Unlimited, and Unlimitable Power,
>   over the Lives, Liberties, and Estates of his Children
>   and Subjects; so that he may take or alienate their
>   Estates, sell, castrate, or use their Persons as he
>   pleases, they being all his slaves, and he Lord or
>   Proprietor of every Thing, and his unbounded Will
>   their Law (1.9).

Locke's aim in the *First Treatise* is to overthrow this unlimited rights
theory and to establish the framework for a limited rights theory
bounded by natural law. He does this by arguing for a rival interpretation of Scripture and by showing that his limited rights can be derived from natural law.

     The scriptural text to which both Filmer and Locke appeal is *Gene-
sis* 1.28:

>   The words of the Text are these; "And God Blessed
>   them, and God said unto them, be Fruitful and Mul-
>   tiply and Replenish the Earth and subdue it, and
>   have Dominion over the Fish of the Sea, and over
>   the Fowl of the Air, and over every living thing
>   that moveth upon the Earth." (1.23)

Filmer interprets this as granting to Adam *"Private Dominion* over the
Earth, and all inferior or irrational Creatures" (1.23). Filmer calls
this private dominion "property" (1.23). Locke agrees that there is

"nothing to be granted to *Adam* here but Property" (1.24). However, property is not the same as private dominion according to Locke. He writes (1.24):

> I shall shew...That by this grant God gave him not *Private Dominion* over the Inferior Creatures, but right in common with all mankind; so neither was he Monarch, upon the account of the Property here given him.

As Barbeyrac comments, property is "right in common with all mankind... a right common to all."[59]

Locke then gives a more extensive redescription of *Genesis* 1.28: "Whatever God gave by the words of this Grant...it was not to Adam in particular, exclusive of all other men: whatever *Dominion* he had thereby, it was not a *Private Dominion*, but a *Dominion* in common with the rest of Mankind" (1.29). This is the first characterisation of Filmer's private dominion as exclusive and particular, and he contrasts this with dominion in common. He argues for this conclusion and states that "God in this Donation, gave the World to Mankind in common, and not to *Adam* in particular" (1.30).

He then repeats that this right in common is property (1.36, 39, 45-47). Dominion in common is then defined in terms of subjective rights: "God gave his sons a Right to make use of a part of the Earth for the support of themselves and Families" (1.37). Locke's concept of property at this point is different from Filmer's in two respects. First, it is predicated of all men, not just of Adam. Second, it is a claim right to use the world for support, a right not to be excluded from such use. It says nothing yet about actual possession. Property is the same kind of inclusive claim right as we have seen in Suarez. As Locke reiterates, "God...himself gave them all a Right, to make use of the Food and Rayment, and other Conveniences of Life, the Materials whereof he had so plentifully provided for them" (1.41). Locke's concept of property here is, as he points out, community translated into the language of rights: "this Text is so far from proving *Adam* Sole Proprietor, that on the contrary, it is a confirmation of the original Community of all things amongst the Sons of Men" (1.40).

Having established that common property is consistent with Scripture and that it can be discussed in terms of a natural claim right to one's due, Locke goes on to show that this right can be derived from natural law. The fundamental law of nature for Locke is that mankind ought to be preserved.[60] He derives three natural rights from this, the third of which is the claim right to use the world for the sake of preservation. He does this by enunciating the law of nature in two ways: first, carrying the substantive "preservation"; and second, carrying the verb "to preserve."[61] In the first case he writes that *"the fundamental law of Nature* [is] *the preservation of Mankind"* (2. 135). This is nothing but the continued subsistence of the human race and he gives each man a right not to be denied it: "Men, being once born, have a right to their Preservation" (2.25).

In his second enunciation he writes that "all the members of the Society are to be *preserved"* (2.159). This is redescribed as a duty of all men to preserve themselves and others (2.6). There will always be a natural right in this case: "they will always have a right to preserve what they have not a power to part with," namely their lives (2.149). He calls this the "original right" (2.220), or *"the Right of Preserving all Mankind"* (2.11).

These two natural rights, as Father Copleston notes, are unique.[62] We normally think of the duties involved in a particular right as correlative with it, although there are exceptions.[63] That is, if a person has a right then others are said to have a correlative duty either to abstain from (a negative duty) or to provide (a positive duty) the object to which the right refers. A right to a piece of land correlates with a negative duty on the part of others to abstain from the use of that land unless the consent of the rightholder is given. A right to an education correlates with the positive duty of others to provide educational facilities. Locke's two natural rights have correlative duties but, in addition, they are tied to other duties in a unique manner.

We usually think of a right as a liberty, the exercise of which is at the possessor's discretion. Locke's two natural rights, of preservation and to preserve oneself and others, are not liberties. They are natural rights directly resulting from, or entailed by, the natural duty to preserve mankind. Their exercise is not at the rightholder's discretion; their exercise is the exercise of the natural law duty to preserve mankind. It may seem redundant to say that each man has a claim right to exercise his duty of ensuring preservation and of preserving mankind, but Locke's point is well taken. These perpetual duties could be blocked by, say, the unlimited rights of property in a society modelled on the theories of Grotius or Filmer. In these cases a person may require natural claim rights in order to override the

conventional rights of property, to preserve himself and his family
and, if need be, others.

Locke illustrates his point by applying his third natural right in
such a case. The third natural right is derived from the logically
prior right to preservation. He writes that, "Men, being once born,
have a right to their Preservation, and consequently to Meat and Drink,
and other such things, as Nature affords for their Subsistence" (2.25).
That is, every man has the natural right to the means to preserve himself: "He that is Master of himself, and his own life, has a right too
to the means of preserving it" (2.172). This claim right is entailed
by both the right to preservation and the right to preserve oneself and
others (2.26). This third right is property; it is identical to the
natural right which Locke derives from Scripture, as we have seen.

He explains how his natural rights would work in a society in
which property is distributed in such a way that some are legally excluded from the means of preservation. His natural right, or property,
gives the needy the moral justification to take what they need from the
conventional property of others (1.42):

> But we know that God hath not left one man so to the
> Mercy of another, that he may starve him if he please:
> God the Lord and Father of all, has given no one of
> his children such a Property, in his peculiar Portion
> of the things of this world, but that he has given his
> needy Brother a Right to the Surplusage of his Goods;
> so that it cannot be justly denied him, when his pres-
> sing Wants call for it.

The moral claim to the means of preservation overrules the purely legal
description of such an act as theft. The man's need creates a title *in*
the goods of another, thus individuating his natural right not to be
excluded from the means of preservation: "*Charity* gives every man a
Title to so much out of anothers Plenty, as will keep him from extream
want, where he has no means to subsist otherwise" (1.42). This is similar to Aquinas' formulation.[64] Also, the proprietor cannot use the
man's need to force him to work for his subsistence (1.42). This theory of charity is a repudiation of the negative theories of Grotius and
Pufendorf and a reassertion of Thomist theory. It should be read as an
illustration of how natural rights would work in a society not constituted in accordance with natural law. In the *Two Treatises* Locke is
primarily concerned with showing how property would be distributed in a
society organized in accordance with natural law, such that the above
circumstances would not occur (2.135).

V

Locke carries his framework of natural, inclusive claim rights forward to the *Second Treatise*, where it functions as a premise. His famous chapter entitled "Of Property" begins with a recapitulation of the argument we have traced in the *First Treatise*. Natural law teaches that each man has a claim right to the means of preservation, and this is logically equivalent to saying that the world belongs to all in common (2.25):

> Whether we consider natural *Reason*, which tells us, that Men, being once born, have a right to their Preservation, and consequently to Meat and Drink, and such other things, as Nature affords for their Subsistence: Or *Revelation*, which gives us an account of those Grants God made of the World to *Adam*, and to Noah, and his Sons, 'tis very clear, that God, as King *David* says...*has given the Earth to the Children of Men*, given it to Mankind in common.

As in Suarez, this inclusive concept of property necessarily leads to the problem of individuation or distribution. Locke writes, "But this being supposed, it seems to some a very great difficulty, how any one should ever come to have a *Property* in any thing...I shall endeavour to shew, how Men might come to have a *property* in several parts of that which God gave to Mankind in common" (2.25). The "great difficulty" is one which Filmer voiced in his criticism of Grotius: "where there is community there is neither *meum* nor *tuum*."[65] Filmer is correct only if "community" means belonging to no one, as with Grotius. If "community" means belonging to everyone in the same manner, as their due, then mine and thine are not only logically possible, but are logically necessary if each man's due is to be realized. Thus natural law can be seen to consistently sanction common property and private property in this special, interrelated sense.

A theory in which private property exists as the individuation or realization of common property constitutes a concept of property different from a theory in which private and common property are construed as mutually exclusive. One linguistic feature which Locke uses to tie his analysis together is to call the right involved in a claim right to something and a right in something "property." This wide use of the term "property" was first noted by Barbeyrac:[66]

> Mr. Locke means by the word "property" not only the right which one has to his goods and possessions, but even with respect to his actions, liberty, his life, his body; and, in a word, all sorts of right.

Locke goes on to show in Chapter V of the *Second Treatise* how common property can be individuated naturally and how the common property
of a political community can be individuated conventionally, both in
accordance with natural law.[67] In both cases the inclusive sense of
property provides a framework within which the distribution takes
place. It is not, as J. P. Day assumes, a "justification of private
property."[68] "Locke wants to explain," writes Professor Yolton, "how
particularisation of the common is possible."[69] It is an attempt to
work out the distribution of common property as defined and constituted
by his natural rights framework.[70] This however is a complex story and
falls outside the confines of the paper. I would like nonetheless to
briefly outline one point: the way in which Locke's framework limits
exclusive rights.

That each man has the claim right to use and to enjoy the good
things of the world naturally limits the amount of things which any
particular person can come to have a property in. It is noteworthy
that Locke uses the locution "a property in" to describe an individual,
exclusive right which a person comes to have as a result of exercising
his natural claim right in accordance with natural law. This locution,
it seems to me, is simply his translation of the Latin *ius in re*.[71]
If a man comes to have a property in things to the extent that it excludes others from the exercise of their claim right, then his possessions cease to be his property. This is the major difference between
Grotius and Locke. Grotius, like Professor Nozick, starts with the
primitive concept of an exclusive right and, if he is interested in
limiting it in some way, he must introduce limits based on a different
principle. By working with exclusive rights as rights in what the exercise of an inclusive right realizes, Locke has a theory in which exclusive rights are self-limiting.[72] The limits which Locke introduces
are internal limits which follow from the nature of the original position - of the world belonging to all in the same manner and of man under the direction of natural law (2.4).

For example, the first limit derived from the original position is
that a man is entitled to what he acquires by the labour of his person
only "where there is enough, and as good left in common for others"
(2.27). If this criterion is fulfilled then Locke can answer his own
question in the negative: "Was it a Robbery thus to assume to himself
what belonged to all in common?" (2.28). If the world belongs to no
one, as with Grotius and Pufendorf, then the question of robbery cannot

arise until after first occupancy. This would be the first appearance
of the concept of belonging to, which is the logical precondition of
robbery. As a consequence, robbery is defined with reference to the
primitive concept of exclusive rights.[73] Locke's reassertion of the
Thomist logical priority of the world belonging to all in common turns
the concept of robbery around. The question for Locke is this: is an
exclusive right an instance of robbery, given that the world belongs to
all? For him, the primitive concept of belonging to is the inclusive
one. An exclusive right is not robbery solely because, as a right in
the means to realize the end for the sake of which the world exists, it
is a common gift.[74]

The argument that I have attempted to recover would not seem unto-
ward to Locke's audience. Each man possessed Locke's claim right in a
legal form. The parish authorities had a duty, not merely to provide
the local poor with welfare, but to provide them with the means by
which they could make bread and so on, and so preserve themselves and
their families.[75] Each man had the legal right and the legal duty to
work.[76] Locke's argument "makes sense" within the intersubjective assumption of the economy (if we may call it that) as a large household,
as carefully reconstructed by Karl Polanyi and Dr. Keith Tribe.[77]

Appealing to a concept of natural law which enjoys widespread consensus, Locke alters it slightly in order to arrive at a concept of
property, or exclusive right, within a framework of common property
consistent with natural law, thus replying to Filmer's criticism. In
so doing he establishes a rights theory which functions as a precondition for his major task of enunciating a theory of popular sovereignty.[78] The concern here, as I have attempted to show, is not with capitalist accumulation. That sort of debate, as Professor Pocock shows in
his contribution to this volume, emerges in the eighteenth century in
quite different circumstances.[79]

FOOTNOTES

1   This paper is a presentation of one theme in my forthcoming book,
    A Discourse on Property: Locke in the Natural Law Tradition, Cam-
    bridge University Press, 1979. I am indebted to the following
    scholars for discussions on some of the points covered in the
    paper: John Dunn, Anndale Goggin, Edward Hundert, Greg Ostrander,
    Alan Ryan, John Shingler, Quentin Skinner, Charles Taylor, Keith
    Tribe, Richard Tuck and John Yolton. It goes without saying that
    all the shortcomings are wholly my own property.

2   The methodology which I present is unoriginal with me and owes
    everything to John Dunn and Quentin Skinner. Refer to note 17 for
    further readings.

3   See M. P. Thompson, "The Reception of Locke's *Two Treatises of
    Government* 1690-1705," *Political Studies* 24, 2 (1976), 184-191;
    Mark Goldie, "Edmund Bohun and *Jus Gentium* in the Revolution De-
    bate," *The Historical Journal* 20, 3 (1977), 569-586; J. P. Kenyon,
    Revolution Principles: The Politics of Party 1689-1720 (Cambridge:
    Cambridge University Press, 1977); and John Dunn, "The Politics of
    Locke in England and America," in J. W. Yolton ed., *John Locke:
    Problems and Perspectives* (Cambridge: Cambridge University Press,
    1969).

4   Max Beer, *The History of British Socialism* (London, 1921), 101-279;
    and A. Menger, *The Right to the Whole Produce of Labour*, tr. M. E.
    Tanner, (London, 1899).

5   Etienne Cabet, *Voyage en Icarie, roman philosophique et social*
    (Paris, 1842), 485; K. Grün, *Die soziale Bewegung in Frankreich
    und Belgien. Briefe und Studien* (Darmstadt, 1845), 261.

6   Karl Marx and Frederick Engels, *Collected Works* (London: Lawrence
    and Wishart, 1976-) 50 volumes, vol. 5, 520-24.

7   C. H. Driver, "John Locke," in *The Social and Political Ideas of
    Some English Thinkers of the Augustan Age 1650-1750*, ed. F. J. C.
    Hearnshaw (London: G. G. Harrap, 1928), 69-97.

8   P. Larkin, *Property in the 18th Century with Special Reference to
    England and Locke*, (Cork, 1930); J. L. Stocks, *John Locke*, (Ox-
    ford: Oxford University Press, 1933); G. Sabine, *A History of
    Political Theory* (New York: Holt, 1937); and J. D. Mabbott, *The
    State and the Citizen* (London, 1947).

9   P. Laslett, ed., *Two Treatises of Government* (Cambridge: Cambridge
    University Press, 1970), 92-120.

10 Leo Strauss, *Natural Right and History* (Chicago: Chicago Universi-
    ty Press, 1950) 202-252; C. B. Macpherson, *The Political Theory of
    Possessive Individualism* (Oxford: Oxford University Press, 1962).

11 Hillel Steiner, "The ·Natural Right to the Means of Production,"
    Philosophical Quarterly 27 (1975), 45; Gordon Schochet, *Patriar-
    chalism in Political Thought*, (Oxford: Basil Blackwell, 1975),
    253; and Thomas Scanlon, "Nozick on Rights, Liberty and Property,"
    Philosophy and Public Affairs 6, 1 (Autumn 1976), 23. Professor
    Nozick's work, *Anarchy, State, and Utopia* (Oxford: Basil Black-
    well, 1974) represents a transition between these last two inter-
    pretations: beginning with an endorsement of the illiberal view,
    he goes on to acquiesce in the most recent orthodoxy (see p. 350,
    n. 9).

12 For example, Macpherson, *Possessive Individualism*, and his *Demo-
    cratic Theory* (Oxford: Oxford University Press, 1975).

13 Louis Althusser, *Pour Marx* (Paris, 1966); Michel Foucault, *L'Arché-
    ologie du savoir* (Paris: Editions Gallimard, 1969).

14 Foucault, *L'Archéologie*, chapter 1.

15 Keith Tribe, *Ground Rent and the Formation of Classical Political
    Economy: A Theoretical History*, Ph.D. dissertation, Cambridge
    University, 1977 (to be published by Macmillan in 1978).

16 Hans Georg Gadamer, *Truth and Method* (London, 1975); Charles Tay-
    lor, "Interpretation and the Sciences of Man," *Review of Meta-
    physics* 25 (September 1971), 3-51; and see Alaisdair MacIntyre,
    "Ideology, Social Science and Revolution," *Comparative Politics* 5,
    3 (April 1973) 321-342.

17 John Dunn, "The Identity of the History of Ideas," *Philosophy*
    (April 1968); "Practising History and Social Science on Realist
    Assumptions," in *Action and Interpretation: Studies in the Philo-
    sophy of the Social Sciences*, ed., C. Hookway and P. Pettit (Cam-
    bridge: Cambridge University Press, 1978); Quentin Skinner,
    "Meaning and Understanding in the History of Ideas," *History and
    Theory* 8, 1 (1969), 3-53; "Conventions and the Understanding of
    Speech Acts," *Philosophical Quarterly* 21, 79 (April 1970), 113-38;
    "'Social Meaning' and the Explanation of Social Action," in *Philo-
    sophy, Politics and Society*, 4th series, ed., P. Laslett, G. Run-
    ciman and Quentin Skinner (Oxford: Basil Blackwell, 1972) 136-157;
    "On Performing and Explaining Linguistic Actions," *Philosophical
    Quarterly* 21, 82 (January 1971) 1-21; "Some Problems in the Analy-
    sis of Political Thought and Action," *Political Theory* 2, 3 (Au-
    gust 1974) 277-303; "Hermeneutics and the Role of History," *New
    Literary History* 7 (1975-76), 209-32.

18 John Dunn, *The Political Thought of John Locke*, (Cambridge: Cam-
    bridge University Press, 1969).

19 E. J. Hundert, "The Making of Homo Faber: John Locke between Ide-
    ology and History," *Journal of the History of Ideas* 33, 1 (1972),
    3-22; "Market Society and Meaning in Locke's Political Philosophy,"
    Journal of the History of Philosophy, 15, 1 (January 1977), 33-44;
    R. S. Neale, "The Bourgeoisie historically, has played a most revo-
    lutionary part," in *Feudalism, Capitalism and Beyond*, ed., E. Ka-
    menka and R. S. Neale (London: Edward Arnold, 1975) 84-101; J. G.
    A. Pocock, "Early Modern Capitalism: The Augustan Perception,"

ibid, 62-84; and see Alan Ryan, "Locke and the Dictatorship of the Bourgeoisie," *Political Studies* 13, 2 (1965) 219-30.

20 See George Henrick von Wright, *Explanation and Understanding*, (London: Routledge and Kegan Paul, 1971).

21 See Alaisdair MacIntyre, "A Mistake about Causality in Social Science," in *Philosophy, Politics and Society*, 2nd Series, ed., P. Laslett and W. G. Runciman (Oxford: Basil Blackwell, 1962).

22 That problematic norms are standardly justified by an appeal to criteria which are public (enjoy a consensus) is, of course, one of the central lines of Wittgenstein's later work. See Ludwig Wittgenstein, *On Certainty*, tr. G. E. M. Anscombe and G. H. von Wright, (Oxford: Basil Blackwell, 1974); and John Richardson, *The Grammar of Justification*, (Sussex: Sussex University Press, 1976).

23 Quentin Skinner, "History and Ideology in the English Revolution," *The Historical Journal*, 8, 2 (1965) 151-78; Kenyon, *Revolution Principles*; J. G. A. Pocock, *The Ancient Constitution and the Feudal Law* (Cambridge: Cambridge University Press, 1957).

24 See Chapter I of my forthcoming book on Locke.

25 See John Dunn, *Political Thought of John Locke*. For a meticulous placing of Locke within the constitutionalist tradition see Quentin Skinner, *The Foundations of Modern Political Thought* (forthcoming, Cambridge: Cambridge University Press, 1978).

26 P. Laslett, ed., *Patriarcha and other Political Works of Sir Robert Filmer* (Oxford: Basil Blackwell, 1949) 1-48.

27 John Dunn, *The Political Thought of John Locke*, 43-58; P. Laslett, *Two Treatises*, 45-67.

28 P. Laslett, *Two Treatises*, 60-67; John Dunn, *The Political Thought of John Locke*, 48.

29 P. Laslett, *Two Treatises*, 61.

30 See M. P. Thompson, "The Reception of Locke's Two Treatises;" and Mark Goldie, "Edmund Bohun."

31 See the title page of the *Two Treatises* and the first treatise, section 6 (1.6) where Locke states his intention to return to the older mode of political discourse.

32 For an account of Grotius see Richard Tuck, *Natural Rights to Locke*, Ph.D. dissertation, Cambridge University, 1977 (to be published by Cambridge University Press, 1978), an excellent study to which I am greatly indebted. For Pufendorf see Leonard Kreiger, *The Politics of Discretion: Pufendorf and the Acceptance of Natural Law* (Chicago, 1965).

33 For recent attempts to situate various aspects of Locke's political writings in this context see Karl Olivecrona, "Appropriation in the State of Nature: Locke on the Origin of Property," *Journal of the*

History of Ideas, 35, 2 (April-June 1974), 211-31; "Locke's Theory of Appropriation," *The Philosophical Quarterly* 24, 96 (July 1974), 220-34; and Patrick Kelly, "Locke and Filmer: Was Laslett so wrong after all?", *The Locke Newsletter* 8 (summer 1977), 77-91.

34 Robert Filmer, *Patriarcha and other Political Works*, ed., P. Laslett, (Oxford; Basil Blackwell, 1949), 274.

35 For detailed studies of this school see Richard Tuck, *Natural Rights to Locke* and Quentin Skinner, *Foundations of Modern Political Thought*.

36 Michel Villey, "La genèse du droit subjectif chez Guillaume d'Occam," *Archives de Philosophie du Droit*, 9 (1964) 97-127.

37 Francisco Suarez, *De legibus ac Deo legislatore* (1612), in *Opera Omnia* (Paris: 1856-78), 28 volumes, vols. 4 & 5, sections 1.2.4-5 (hereafter referred to as *The Law*). I have used the following translation whenever possible: F. Suarez, *Selections from the Three Works*, ed., G. L. Williams (Oxford: Clarendon Press, 1944).

38 Suarez is applying Aristotle's two senses of "justice": Aristotle, *Nicomachean Ethics*, 1129a3-1134a16.

39 Suarez notes his agreement with Aquinas, *Summa theologiae*, II, II, 57.1.

40 Locke, *Two Treatises*, second treatise, section 25 (2.25).

41 For a recent discussion of the concepts of inclusive and exclusive rights to which I am indebted see C. B. Macpherson, *Democratic Theory*, 120-42.

42 Suarez, *The Law*, 2.14.14; and Aquinas, *Summa theologiae* II, II, 66.

43 Suarez, *The Law*, 3.2.3.

44 Suarez, *The Law*, 2.14.16.

45 Suarez, *The Law*, 2.14.16.

46 Suarez, *The Law*, 2.14.17.

47 Hugo Grotius, *De Jure Pradae*, Latin-English edition, ed., G. L. Williams (Oxford: Clarendon Press, 1950), 12.3.

48 Hugo Grotius, *De Jure Belli ac Pacis*, Latin-English edition, ed. F. W. Kelsey (Oxford: Clarendon Press, 1925), 1.1.3. (Hereafter referred to as the *The Laws*).

49 Grotius, *The Laws*, 1.1.5.

50 Sir William Blackstone, *Commentaries on the Laws of England*, (London: 1778, 8th ed.), 11.1.1.

51 Grotius, *The Laws*, 2.2.1.

52 Grotius, *The Laws*, 2.2.2.

53   Samuel Pufendorf, *De Jure Naturae et Gentium*, Latin-English edi-
     tion, ed. C. H. Oldfather and W. A. Oldfather (Oxford: Clarendon
     Press, 1934), 4.4.2. (Hereafter referred to as *The Law*).

54   Pufendorf, *The Law*, 4.4.2.

55   Jean Barbeyrac, "A Historical and Critical Account of the Science
     of Morality," in his annotated edition of Pufendorf's *De Jure
     Naturae et Gentium* (1725).

56   P. Laslett, *Two Treatises*, 306 n.

57   Jean Barbeyrac, ed., Samuel Pufendorf, *The Law of Nature and Na-
     tions*, tr. Basil Kennett (London: 1729), 4.4.2 n.

58   All quotations from the *Two Treatises of Government* are from P.
     Laslett's edition (Cambridge: Cambridge University Press, 1970).
     The first number in the bracket refers to the treatise, the second
     to the section.

59   Barbeyrac, ed., Pufendorf, *The Law of Nature and Nations*, 4.4.3
     n.1.

60   Locke, *Two Treatises*, 1.86, 2.6, 2.7, 2.11, 2.16, 2.23, 2.60, 2.79,
     2.129, 2.135, 2.138, 2.149, 2.155, 2.159, 2.168, 2.171 and 2.200.
     By making the preservation of mankind, rather than self-preserva-
     tion, the foundation of his natural rights Locke is consciously
     writing in opposition to Hobbes. As he writes in his journal: "An
     Hobbist, with his principle of self-preservation, whereof he him
     self is to be the judge, will not easily admit a great many plain
     duties of morality" (reprinted in Lord Peter King, *The Life of John
     Locke*, London: 1830, vol. I 191).

61   Preservation: 1.86, 2.129, 2.135, 2.149, 2.159, 2.170, 2.182,
     2.209. To preserve: 1.88, 2.6, 2.8, 2.11-16, 2.159, 2.220.

62   F. Copleston, *A History of Philosophy* (New York: Image Books,
     1964), vol. 5, part 1, 139.

63   See H. L. A. Hart, "Bentham on Legal Rights," in *Oxford Essays in
     Jurisprudence*, 2nd. series, ed., A. W. B. Simpson (Oxford: Claren-
     don Press, 1973), for the analysis of a legal right constituted by
     duties in a manner similar to Locke's natural rights.

64   Aquinas, *Summa theologiae*, II, II, 66.7.

65   Filmer, *Patriarcha*, 264.

66   Barbeyrac, "A Historical and Critical Account of the Science of
     Morality," in Pufendorf, *The Law of Nature and Nations*, ed., Bar-
     beyrac, tr. Kennet (London, 1725), 4.

67   See Locke, *Two Treatises*, 2.117-120, 2.138.

68   J. P. Day, "Locke on Property," *Philosophical Quarterly*, 16 (1966)
     207.

69 J. W. Yolton, *Locke and the Compass of Human Understanding* (Cambridge: Cambridge University Press, 1970), 187.

70 See Dunn, *The Political Thought of John Locke*, 67, n. 4.

71 See especially *Two Treatises*, 1.86, 1.87, 1.90, 1.92, 2.25, 2.173.

72 As he claims at *Two Treatises*, 2.31.

73 Professor Nozick argues in a manner similar to Grotius, and, as a consequence, finds taxation and redistribution to be forms of robbery, defined with reference to a primitive concept of exclusive rights. Nozick, *Anarchy, State, and Utopia*, 169-72, 265-68.

74 See *Two Treatises*, 2.28, 2.33, 2.37, 2.38, 2.46.

75 See "Act for the Relief of the Poor," 43 *Elizabeth*, c.2 1601, 1.

76 See Sir William Holdsworth, *A History of English Law*, 3rd edition (London: 1922-26), 9 volumes, vol. 4, 375-85.

77 Karl Polanyi, *The Great Transformation* (Boston: Beacon Press, 1944); Tribe, *Ground Rent*.

78 See how Locke's property as the natural right to the means to preserve oneself functions as the foundation for the right to resist arbitrary government at *Two Treatises*, 2.149.

79 See Professor Pocock's article in this volume.

This essay by John Pocock offers a distinctive interpretation of the history of property theory in the century "from Locke to Bentham." There was not a simple, linear growth of the "bourgeois" conception of private property. Rather, the author traces the complex interplay of "civic" and "juristic" views of property. The civic view emphasized property as the material support of the gentleman-citizen in public life, while the juristic view stressed the rights of acquisition, ownership, and transference. Both dimensions must be understood if history is not to be distorted.

James Moore's commentary supports Pocock's general thesis and also adds supplementary information dealing with certain special aspects of the history of this period: the critical reaction of Hume and others to schemes of public credit, the connections between commercial and "polite" society, and the four-stages theory of history.

THE MOBILITY OF PROPERTY AND THE RISE OF EIGHTEENTH-CENTURY SOCIOLOGY

We have been discussing property under a number of heads, which might be summarized as follows: First and foremost, there is the tradition begun by Aristotle and continued by Aquinas, in which property appears a moral and political phenomenon, a prerequisite to the leading of a "good life" which is essentially civic. In the form of the Greek *oikos*, a household productive unit inhabited by women, minors and slaves, it provided the individual with power, leisure and independence, and the opportunity to lead a life in which he (not until John Stuart Mill do we study a thinker seriously interested in adding "she") could become what he ought to be. Property was both an extension and a prerequisite of personality (and we should by now be aware of the possibility that different modes of property may be seen as generating or encouraging different modes of personality.) The citizen possessed property in order to be autonomous and autonomy was necessary for him to develop virtue or goodness as an actor within the political, social and natural realm or order. He did not possess it in order to engage in trade, exchange or profit; indeed, these activities were hardly at all compatible with the activity of citizenship. Greek politics were not based on bourgeois concepts, which seems odd when you consider that "politics" and "bourgeois" have the same root meaning of "living in a city." The *polis* and the *bourg*, *Burg* or borough were profoundly different places, and it is hard to estimate the amount of confusion caused by the circumstance that the German word for "citizen" is *Bürger*.

Professor Hunt's article demonstrated not merely that Karl Marx can be considered a thinker among the classical Western moralists, but that the Western moral tradition displays an astonishing unity and solidarity in the uneasiness and mistrust it evinces towards money as the medium of exchange. Where Marx quoted Martin Luther with approval, Luther was elaborating in his own manner upon the dictum of Aquinas, to which Professor Parel drew attention, that money had a constant tendency to substitute itself for beatitude. Because so many of the components of the good life can be had for money, we are under a constant temptation to mistake money for the *summum bonum*, and an individual drawn wholly into the life of monetarized exchange relationships would be living in a commodified parody of the natural and divine order,

tempted to regard himself and his wealth idolatrously. In every phase
of Western tradition we have considered, there is a conception of virtue - Aristotelian, Thomist, neo-Machiavellian or Marxian - to which
the spread of exchange relations is seen as presenting a threat. In
this perspective those thinkers of the seventeenth through nineteenth
centuries who argued on individualist, capitalist or liberal premises
that the market economy might benefit and transform human existence appear to be the great creative heretics and dissenters.

      In the form of *oikos* within *polis*, property appears as an item
within a scheme of relationships which are essentially political and
obtain between citizens set free by their property to engage in them.
But there is another face of the Western tradition of no less importance to the understanding of property: the language of jurisprudence,
inaugurated by the Roman civilians, strongly present in Aquinas, and
carried on by a succession of jurists and natural-law theorists into
the age of Locke. In this tradition property, without losing any of
its significance to personality, was defined less as that which makes
you what you are than as that to which you have a right. With this interpretation we entered upon that fascinating and elusive relationship
between the notions of right and ownership, and upon that world of language in which "property" - that which you owned - and "propriety" -
that which pertained or was proper to a person or situation - were interchangeable terms. The distinction between persons and things gained
in prominence; and instead of being the mere prerequisite to political
relations between persons, property became a system of legally defined
relations between persons and things, or between persons through
things. Since the law defined justice in terms of *suum cuique*, it was
possible to define the good life in terms of property relations, or of
human relations as the notion of property served to define them, though
the thought which stemmed from the *polis* constantly asked whether this
definition of justice was adequate. The social relations which law and
property defined included many which obtained between men engaged in
transferring, exchanging and conveying possessions and even rights; and
the vision of the law was therefore less hostile than that of the *polis*
towards trade, profit and accumulation. Because jurisprudence and the
jurist's conception of justice were concerned with men and things, they
were less concerned with the immediate relations between men as political actors or with the individual's consciousness of himself as living the good life. Consequently under jurisprudence, the notion of the

political itself changed and became less the system of relations between citizens and more the system of relations between authorities and
subjects which was necessary to a life lived under law.

Both views, however, as we see in the unity to which Aquinas reduced them, incorporate the notion of property in, and subject it to,
a complex moral universe; and in both contexts we have learned to talk
about an "ancient" view of property as opposed to a "modern." We associate "modern" ideas of property with both capitalism and socialism
which entail those very complex schemes of production and exchange
which we call "economics," a word derived from the ancient *oikos* and
oikonomike which it supplants; and we see reason to believe that the
transition from ancient to modern was bound up with the advent of capitalism. We also incline to think that as this transition took place,
two other things happened: the notion of unlimited acquisition es-
caped from many if not all traditional moral restraints - an escape
which was itself legitimised - and the increasingly complex and dynamic
relationships and processes which we call "economics" began to surpass
in importance the political relations among people, swallowing up the
ancient *polis* as they swallowed up the *oikos*. It is reasonable to in-
quire after the actual or perceived effects of this upon personality.

I dwell on all this because I want to establish a setting in which
to pursue the next phase of the transition from ancient to modern notions of property: the problem posed by Professor Macpherson and re-
opened by Professor Tully. I aim to present an interpretation of that
period in the history of thought about property which Macpherson label-
led by use of the phrase "from Locke to Bentham," but my interpretation
will differ from his in a number of ways. He laid down the paradigm
of an unrestricted right of acquisition emerging from legal and moral
constraints, which were those of the scholastic jurisprudence elaborated by Aquinas and Suarez. I am uneasy with this, and I am going to
put forward an alternative, in which I shall lay emphasis on the revival in the period defined of ideas about classical politics and the
view of property that went with it. I shall suggest that it was a-
gainst these civic, rather than juristic, conceptions of property that
new economic forces were recognised and defined as asserting themselves, in such a way that capitalist property was recognised as historically new because it was post-classical and modern, and man as
proprietor and political animal was seen as existing in the historical
dynamic which economic and moral forces created. But if one employs

the paradigm of classical politics, rather than that of natural jurisprudence in interpreting this great revolution in the concept of property - this transformation of the relations between *polis* and *oikos*,
and between polity and economy, in the words of Joseph Cropsey[1] - one
is not discounting the importance of ideas about property derived from
natural jurisprudence. In his article Mr. Tully shows us that these
ideas were operative in the case of Locke; Duncan Forbes has insisted
on their importance in the case of Hume.[2] We shall have to return to
them, but for the present it will be contended that the story can be
better understood by operating with the ideas of classical politics.

In England after 1649, a shattering collapse of civil authority
faced theorists with the necessity of re-conceptualising it from its
foundations. In this enterprise both ways of thinking about property
played a role. Thomas Hobbes operated within the paradigm of natural
jurisprudence; he showed individuals acting in and from a state of
nature, extending their power over things and in so doing coming to
interact with one another, acquiring possession and right over things
against one another, and even acquiring possession over rights in such
a way that they could transfer them to a sovereign whom they instituted by the act of transfer.[3] His individuals move from the pre-
possessive to the possessive, the pre-political to the political, the
pre-human to the human.

James Harrington operated within the paradigm of classical politics so completely that the concepts of right and obligation make no
appearance in his works at all.[4] His individuals never occupy a state
of nature; they are naturally political, having been created by God in
His image as capable of intelligent self-rule. But because they live
between heaven and earth, they occupy a dimension of secular history,
which is partly governed by fortune. This agency redistributes property, which is to redistribute the capacity to act as fully political
beings. Property brings power: the power of masters over servants,
the power of masters over themselves; but whenever fortune has brought
about the existence of a sufficient number of masters, these may leave
the domain of power and enter that of authority. Authority is not distributed by property, but by the free masters' recognition of one another's political capacity; in instituting it among themselves, they
enter upon the world of political relations and begin to act as the
images of God which they are.

Property and power are the prerequisites of authority and virtue. They discharge no other function than that of the *oikos* in Aristotle and need not possess any other social or economic characteristics than those which distinguish masters from servants. Because they are liable to redistribution by fortune, they bring to Harrington's politics an historical dimension, and he was able to organise history around the distributions of property; but at bottom his theory of history is simple, binary and cyclical. The *oikos* exists in sufficient numbers, or it does not. In the ancient republics it existed in the form of the yeoman smallholding of the citizen warriors; then it was overcome by the *feudum*; now it is restored in the shape of the yeoman or gentleman freehold, and military and political capacity are restored with it. One should note, however, that Harrington's first readers early assumed what he had never said, that the breakup of feudal tenures had had something to do with trade. There was a perception of such a thing, though it had small enough place in the vocabulary of classical politics.

Since Harrington thought it the function of property to provide a large but limited number of people with the basis of independence from which they could practise the equal relations existing among republican citizens, he found that this could be best performed by the relative stability of landed realty. But there were others (of whom, *pace* Macpherson, Hobbes is not necessarily the best example) who aimed to present men as acquisitive and competitive beings whose activities required regulating by a powerful and independent sovereign. Some of these theorists found that a commercial society best illustrated both the subject's competitiveness and the sovereign's independence. In their hands mobility, exchange and acquisition furnished so many arguments for absolute monarchy; and some latter-day criticisms of a liberal order were in this sense anticipated and acknowledged.

A generation later, Sir William Temple produced a carefully constructed anti-Harringtonian statement when he declared that "power," which he called "strength" and "riches," was always on the side of the governed, and nothing but what he called opinion (a crucial term in this story) could prevail on them to submit to the "authority" of government.[5] The next century was to be passed in elaborating the theme that it was in the multiple activities of commercial, cultivated and specialised societies that opinion in Temple's sense could best develop. The commercial, which Marxists call the bourgeois, order was

from its first appearance in theory geared to the stabilisation of
authority.

But the 1670s saw the revival of Harringtonian theory. Neo-
Harringtonianism supplied an idealisation of propertied independence
with which it was hoped to mobilise the country gentry in parliament
against the crown's revived power of parliamentary patronage, known as
corruption. Here classical politics became for the first time a
staple of English political rhetoric; and its persistence for more
than a hundred years in the face of every discouragement and defeat
suggests that it answered some fairly profound ideological needs.
From then on there were to exist two parallel and competing doctrines
of propertied individualism: one which praised the gentleman's or
yeoman's independence in land and arms as performing the functions of
the *oikos* in an English or Virginian *polis*, and one which praised the
mobility of the individual in an increasingly commercial society as
teaching him the need for free deference to authority.

In pursuit of the dialectic between these two modes of individualism, these two definitions of the political function of property, we
shall not linger upon that remarkable episode in the history of property theory associated with the names of Filmer and Locke. If we
fully analysed the debate of the 1680s, we should doubtless learn a
great deal; but in a history of property theory organised around the
duality of classical and commercial politics, it is difficult to retain the image of Locke as the hinge on which history turned. As
Professor Tully showed, he stands in the lineage of those thinkers who
approached the politics of property through the language of natural
jurisprudence. He was, as far as can be told, utterly indifferent
(though at the same time very close) to that revival of classical politics taking place in the neo-Harringtonian ideology of the country opposition. He cared nothing for the virtue of independence threatened
by corruption, and it is tempting to try and place him among the philosophers of the commercial order. But neither the refutation of Filmer
in 1680 nor the justification of revolution nine or ten years later
necessitated the assertion of the commercial order; it was not yet a
crucial issue in English ideological debate. Within a very few years
it was to become so, and Locke was to be personally involved; but its
presence is not to be detected in his *Treatises on Government*, and
when the great debate began it is hard to detect Locke's presence in
it.

I am alluding here to what we now call the Financial Revolution of
the middle 1690s, which saw the foundation of the Bank of England and
the successful and lasting creation of a system of public credit whereby individuals and companies could invest money in the stability of
government and expect a return varying in proportion to the success of
the government's operations.[6] Over the quarter-century that followed,
contemporaries came to hold that this had led to the creation of what
they called a "monied interest," and that this new class of creditors
and speculators was tending to dominate politics. This conviction led
critics like Swift[7] and Bolingbroke to say what had certainly not been
said before, that a new form of property had arisen, one unknown in
previous history. Consequently the relation of property to power,
studied by Harrington, and the relation of property to the need for
government, studied by Locke, seemed to have been transformed and to
need reconsideration. This was a momentous intellectual event: there
had been a sudden and traumatic discovery of capital in the form of
government stock and a sudden and traumatic discovery of historical
transformation as something brought about by the advent of public credit.

The century that followed the Financial Revolution witnessed the
rise in Western thought (something not dissimilar may have been occurring in contemporary Japan)[8] of an ideology and a perception of history
which depicted political society and social personality as founded upon
commerce: upon the exchange of forms of mobile property and upon modes
of consciousness suited to a world of moving objects. This eighteenth-
century perception of "commercial society" was not based in the first
instance upon a perception of trade, or upon an increased hold which
market values were gaining upon the thought of social theorists. If we
pay attention to the actual records of debate, to the concerns which
were expressed and the doctrines which were developed, we find that the
origins of commercial ideology lay in the controversy between "virtue"
and "corruption" and in the associated debate between "landed interests" and "monied interests" which was revitalised by the Financial
Revolution.[9] There existed an ideal of the social and political personality epitomised by the term "virtue," entailing a conception of
property which had more to do with Harrington than with Locke and more
to do with classical than with feudal values. It extolled the image
of the "patriot," the individual rendered independent by his property
and permitted an autonomous engagement in public affairs. This image

was regularly opposed to that of the man of commerce and the latter had
to fight its way to political recognition in the teeth of the "patriot"
ideal. Though the image of the patriot was of comparatively recent
vintage, its roots were deep in classical antiquity, and on these
grounds it asserted a rejection of feudal values as vigorous as anything in "commercial" ideology.

 Thus we can no longer hold that the beginnings of a modern political theory of property are to be found in Locke's refutation of Filmer,
or in any simple transition from feudal to bourgeois values. We must
think instead of an enduring conflict between two explicitly post-feu-
dal ideals, one agrarian and the other commercial, one ancient and the
other modern. The roots of the conflict in the world of theory and
ideology lie not in the perception of two conflicting ways of gaining
wealth, so much as in that of two conflicting ways in which property
might determine the relations of personality to government. The ideal
of the patriot or citizen entailed the image of a personality free and
virtuous because unspecialised. The function of his property was to
give him independence and autonomy as well as the leisure and liberty
to engage in public affairs; but his capacity to bear arms in the public cause was an end of his property and the test of his virtue. As
far back as Harrington, we find it stated that while in principle the
function of assuring arms and leisure can be discharged by property in
goods as well as in land, in practice merchants and craftsmen will find
it harder than will landowners and tenants to leave their productive
activities to engage in self-defence. Therefore a commercial and manufacturing society like Holland is likely to be defended by mercenaries
and governed by oligarchs. By the end of the century, this had been
expanded into a general history of society. Medieval Europe was presented in a highly non-feudal light as a society of warrior freeholders. But with the revival of commerce and culture in the fifteenth
century, these freeholders succumbed to the temptation to pay mercenaries to defend them while they pursued the profits and pleasures of
civilisation, and so they passed under the rule of absolute kings, the
specialists in government by whom the specialists in warfare were
paid.[10] The freeholders' loss of liberty was identical with a loss of
virtue.

 Here for the first time we hear that there is a process of specialisation in history and that specialisation may be incompatible
with the unity of the moral personality which can only be found in the

practice of civic virtue. It is also clearly implied that moral personality in this sense is possible only upon a foundation of real property, since the possession of land brings with it unspecialised leisure and the opportunity of virtue, while the production and exchange
of goods entails activities too specialised to be compatible with citizenship. The merchant and the consumer are mistrusted as liable to pay
the mercenary and the bureaucrat; yet it is seldom dogmatically stated
that they constitute an inferior and banausic class. It was not the
merchant trading upon his own stock who transformed and corrupted the
relation of property to government; he might - though he would find it
difficult - retain his civic virtue, his autonomy and his right to keep
and bear arms. The danger lay with the owner of capital, great or
small, who invested it in systems of public credit and so transformed
the relations between government and citizens, and by implication between all citizens and all subjects, into relations between debtors
and creditors. It was not the market, but the stock market, which pre-
cipitated an English awareness, about 1700, that political relations
were on the verge of becoming capitalist relations; and this awareness
could never have developed as it did without the unspecialised agrarian
ideal of the patriot to serve as antithesis. The merchant became involved in the indictment of capitalism, and the credit society became
known as the "commercial" society, because it was observed that there
was a fairly obvious relation between trade and credit. However, an
obstinate conviction survived that the individual entrepreneur ought to
be free from the machinations of those who determined the rate at which
capital might be got. There was always urban as well as agrarian opposition to the alliance of government and bank.

If this alliance - developed with varying degrees of success by
Dutch, English, Scottish and French projectors - was to be successfully
defended against its critics, an ideological defence of specialisation,
speculation and exchange would have to be provided. Though Locke took
a hand in the Recoinage of 1696, one of the major proceedings of the
Financial Revolution, he did not engage in the ideological manoeuvres
which characterise the defence of credit politics. To understand this
profound shift in sociological and historical perspective, we have to
turn to other publicists, such as Daniel Defoe and Joseph Addison.
Defoe argued vigorously that society could defend itself better against
its own professional soldiers by controlling the money that paid them
than by sending its citizens to serve in their place. Out of this

thesis he developed a contrast between a commercial society which could
pay to have services performed and one without money which could secure
them only in return for grants in land.[11] The stereotype of a pre-
commercial "feudal" society - or one more primitive still, like that of
the Scottish Highlands - was in large measure the invention of defenders of the Whig system of government. It was harder to meet the neo-
Harringtonian argument that a people who paid others to rule them would
be exploited in both purse and liberty by their rulers. Here Defoe was
on the brink of depicting a people engrossed in their commercial and
personal concerns, who maintained a constitutional system of government
with a view to keeping their rulers in leading-strings by retaining the
power of the purse.

The conventional wisdom of today refers to this image as "liberalism" - though the word was unknown in this sense during the eighteenth
century - and encourages us to think that it obtained paradigmatic dom-
inance during the century which divided John Locke from Adam Smith.
The challenge of virtue to commerce and specialisation remained constant and only half met; otherwise there would never have been a Rousseau. The reason of most importance to our purposes emerges quite
clearly from the record of debate. The criticism based upon the concept of virtue presented a clear and coherent image of the unity of human personality, in its relation to both society and property. Arguments like Defoe's, which clearly implied that the ideal of patriot
virtue was being abandoned and treated as historically unreal, could
not be complete until an alternative image of personality had been provided. It is possible to show how this was done, and the story is in
some respects familiar. Yet we cannot tell it properly if we ignore
the complex struggle between the two images, or treat one as antique
and the other as taking its place; both were formulations of the late
seventeenth century. There is, however, extremely strong pressure from
the existing paradigms to take the triumph of "liberalism" for granted.
Both the classical and the socialist critics of modern society appear
to need the "liberal" antithesis so badly, as a prelude to stating
their own positions, that they exaggerate its paradigmatic control
while simplifying and antedating the history of its emergence.

We have now to consider what problems necessitated the construction of a new image of social personality and why these problems were
hard to overcome. It was common ground that the political individual
needed a material anchor in the form of property no less than he needed

a rational soul. If he found that anchor in the shape of land, it
guaranteed him leisure, rationality and virtue. If he acquired land
by appropriation or by inheritance, these things were guaranteed him
as part of a natural order. Locke had argued that this was not enough
to necessitate government and that a pattern of exchange relationships
must figure among its preconditions. But Locke was ever indifferent
to the ideal of patriot virtue, and it was this which the Financial
Revolution seemed to challenge. Government stock is a promise to repay at a future date; from the inception and development of the National Debt, it is known that this date will in reality never be reached, but the tokens of repayment are exchangeable at a market price in
the present. The price they command is determined by the present state
of public confidence in the stability of government, and in its capacity to make repayment in the theoretical future. Government is therefore maintained by the investor's imaginations concerning a moment
which will never exist in reality. The ability of merchant and landowner to raise the loans and mortgages they need are similarly dependent upon the investor's imaginations. Property - the material foundation of both personality and government - has ceased to be real and has
become not merely mobile but imaginary. Specialised, acquisitive and
post-civic man has ceased to be virtuous, not only in the formal sense
that he has become the creature of his own hopes and fears; he does
not even live in the present, except as constituted by his fantasies
concerning a future. The National Debt has rendered society more Hob-
besian than Hobbes himself could ever have envisaged, since it has
placed the performance of covenants forever beyond the new Tantalus's
reach and left him to live by dreaming of it.[12]

When the stability of government in the present became linked to
the self-perpetuation of speculation concerning a future, something
happened which forms an important part of the history of ideas concerning unlimited acquisition and accumulation. Government and politics seemed to have been placed at the mercy of passion, fantasy and
appetite, and these forces were known to feed on themselves and to be
without moral limit. This is not to suggest that this was the origin
of the idea of unlimited acquisition or of the need to legitimate it;
Joyce Appleby's studies of early market theory may well have shown
that observation of mercantile behaviour itself generated a good deal
of thought upon this question.[13] But what I do want to suggest is
that it was observance of the revolution of public credit that

generated the idea that political relations were becoming relations between debtors and creditors - a thought which the publicists of Queen
Anne's reign discussed unendingly - and that this was seen as leading
not merely to corruption, but to the despotism of speculative fantasy.
Booms and busts, bulls and bears, became the determinants of politics.
The value of public stock - the Dow Jones ratings of the eighteenth
century - became the index to the stability or instability of governments, and all this was seen as placing politics at the mercy of a
self-generated hysteria.

The intellect of the early eighteenth century can be seen applying itself to the stabilisation of this pathological condition. Defoe
and others wrote about the conversion of "credit" into "opinion,"[14]
Montesquieu about the conversion of *crédit* into *confiance*.[15]
Defoe, a moralist, meant that men should behave in such ways as to
give one another good grounds for believing that promises would be performed and expectations fulfilled; Montesquieu, a Machiavellian, meant
that by making themselves promises, men would discover that they had
increased their credit, wealth and power. Both had in mind the conversion of the pure fantasies of speculation upon the future into the
well-grounded opinions of continued experience in an on-going and dynamic political economy. It was the problem of how the bags of wind,
which we meet in the imagery of Addison as well as Montesquieu, might
be filled, and seen to be filled, with real gold.[16] (The problem of
paper currency is acutely relevant here.) Such thinkers had recognised that, in the credit economy and polity, property had become not
only mobile but speculative: what one owned was promises, and not
merely the functioning but the intelligibility of society depended
upon the success of a program of reification. If we were not to live
solely in terms of what we imagined might happen - and so remain vulnerable to psychic crises like those of the Darien Scheme, the South
Sea Bubble and the Mississippi Company - experience must teach us when
our hopes were likely to be fulfilled, and *confiance* teach us that we
might create conditions in which their fulfilment would be more likely.

The conversion of passion into opinion was only one of the programs which theorists devised for the remedy of the situation. Albert
Hirschman's *The Passions and the Interests* suggests another, and there
is a clear relation between the problem of speculative politics and
economics, and the existence in the eighteenth century of so many moral and philosophical writings on the conversion of passion into reason

and of rational egoism into socially desirable behaviour.[17] But there
was far more at work here than a mere recognition that English society
had been taken over by hard-faced *homines economici* obedient only to
the laws of market behaviour. These laws were present and there was
thought about them. There was an anxious desire to discover what these
laws were; but it is equally true, and perhaps more prominent, that it
was the hysteria, not the cold rationality, of economic man that dis-
mayed the moralists. Systems of rational egoism were devised less to
explain and legitimise what he was doing than to offer him means of
controlling his own impulses. It might be possible to distinguish between "hard" and "soft" rationalisations of this order, of which the
former accepted the uncontrollable acquisitiveness of entrepreneurs who
knew what they were doing, and the latter hoped to teach self-disci-
pline and self-understanding to entrepreneurs who did not. Mandeville
might be a "hard," Addison a "soft." But there is reason to believe
that the latter might preponderate; and certainly a main theme of
Hirschman's study is the emergence of a strategy whereby passion and
commerce could be presented as self-limiting forces in a new and remarkable way.

Economic man as masculine conquering hero is a fantasy of nineteenth-century industrialisation (the *Communist Manifesto* is of course
one classical example). His eighteenth-century predecessor was seen
as on the whole a feminised, even an effeminate being, still wrestling
with his own passions and hysterias and with interior and exterior forces let loose by his fantasies and appetites, and symbolised by such
archetypically female goddesses of disorder as Fortune, Luxury, and
most recently Credit herself. Pandora came before Prometheus: first,
because to pursue passions and be victimised by them was traditionally
seen as a female role, or as one which subjected masculine *virtù* to
feminine *fortuna*; and second, because the new speculative image of economic man was opposed to the essentially paternal and Roman figure of
the citizen patriot. Therefore, in the eighteenth-century debate over
the new relations of polity to economy, production and exchange are
regularly equated with the ascendancy of the passions and the female
principle. They are given a new role in history, which is to refine
the passions; but there is a danger that they may render societies effeminate - a term whose recurrence ought not to be neglected.

A contrast in these terms between "patriot" and "man of commerce,"
between "virtue" and "politeness" or "refinement," emerges during the

first half of the eighteenth century, with Montesquieu as not the first
but an authoritative exponent. The patriot's virtue - his autonomy and
engagement - cannot well be questioned, so long as there exists a *polis*
or republic in which it may be exercised; but it can be shown to have
rested on an archaic and restrictive foundation. The ancient city existed in a world where neither commerce nor agriculture were properly
developed, and for this reason, argues Montesquieu[18] (Josiah Tucker
half a century later greatly enjoyed turning this argument against the
Virginians),[19] the virtuous citizen was usually a slaveowner. His devotion to the laws of his city was characteristic of a world in which
neither commerce nor culture - frequently bracketed as "the arts" -
furnished social ties capable of holding men together and only the
"stern *paideia*" (the phrase is Marvin Becker's) of civil discipline
could perform the task. It was a world in which there was no god by
Lycurgus and Plato was his prophet. With the rise of commerce and culture, new forms of social relationship emerged and virtue in the antique sense became archaic. Yet Montesquieu, though he describes at
length how "*le doux commerce*"[20] refines and moderates behaviour - how
polis is replaced by politeness, even as *oikos* is absorbed by economics - does not give the name of "virtue" to that which takes the place
of the old. Consequently, though we can glean from his text that something comes after the republic whose principle is virtue, he does not
explicitly categorise what it is and does not escape from the possibility that modern refinement corrupts antique virtue without replacing it.

     Notions of refinement and politeness, then, were crucial elements
in the ideology of eighteenth-century commerce. We have examined some
epistemological reasons why this should have been so. If speculative
man was not to be the slave of his passions, he had to moderate these
by converting them into opinion, experience and interest, and into a
system of social ties which these things reinforced; and the reification followed by exchange of the objects on which his passions focussed was an excellent means of socialising them. When the polite man
of commercial and cultivated society looked back into his past, what
he necessarily saw there was the passions not yet socialised, to which
he gave such names as "barbarism" and "savagery;" and his debate a-
gainst the patriot ideal could be far more satisfactorily carried on if
he could demonstrate that what had preceded the rise of commerce and
culture was not a world of virtuous citizens, but one of barbarism. To
demonstrate that the citizens of antiquity were barbarians themselves

was plausible, but for most people too destructive. The apologists of commerce therefore preferred, to any scheme of history based on civic humanism, those schemes of natural law and *jus gentium* propounded by Grotius, Pufendorf, Locke and the German jurists, which stressed the emergence of civil jurisprudence out of a state of nature, since the latter could be readily equated with barbarism.[21] The tradition of natural jurisprudence thus makes its reappearance in the story - though there are scholars who would say that I ought to have been telling it in these terms all along - joining hands with many moral philosophies which focussed on the notion of passion, and using the state of nature to show how the passions were moderated in history by the progress of commerce and politeness.

We are contrasting a conception of property which stresses autonomy and civic virtue with one which stresses exchange and the civilisation of the passions, and thereby disclosing that the debate between the two is a major key to eighteenth-century social thought. What is perhaps of greatest concern in the present context is the spectacle of property moving from a situation in a structure of norms and rights to a situation in a process of history, of which changes in its character and function are seen as being largely the occasion; but we have not yet reached the point where the concept of property becomes absorbed into the larger scheme of productive relations. That point lies only a little way ahead, however, and we shall not have to distort the history of social theory in order to get there.

It may have been the injection into the debate of a concept of barbarism, that social or pre-social condition in which there was neither ownership nor exchange - or so it was thought - which helped occasion the still imperfectly-understood appearance in Western theory of the famous four-stages theory of human history: that men were first hunters, then shepherds, farmers, and finally merchants.[22] To us, and soon to contemporaries, this meant a series of stages of production; but it is in the logic of the historical debate that it should have been primarily a scheme of the rise, diversification and control of the human passions, which the preoccupation with property served to anchor in history. It was by this time common ground that the passions were aroused and satisfied (if satisfied at all) by material goods and by perceptions and expectations of human behaviour importantly, if not exclusively, associated with the distribution of these goods, their reality or non-reality being an important part of the problem. The

relation between commercial society and its possible predecessors had
done much to make this a historical problem and to make it hinge upon
the refinement of the passions. The four-stages theory marked an important step in the direction of a historicisation of the human personality, in which the character and control of the passions, together
with the psychologies and epistemologies associated with the notion,
were organised into a historical sequence of the modes of production.

The ninth chapter of Gibbon's *Decline and Fall*, in which he ela-
borates upon Tacitus's account of the primitive Germans, is an excellent specimen from which to illustrate what operations could be performed with the aid of this schema.[23]   Gibbon tells us that the German
tribes were pre-agricultural and illiterate; consequently they lacked
both money and letters, the two principal means of communication by
which goods and information are exchanged within more civilised societies. By placing exchange ahead of ownership, Gibbon indicated a historical perspective in which agriculture, which he calls "the useful
parent of the arts," is seen rather as a necessary pre-condition of
commerce than as a stage of society existing in its own right. He
places himself in that tradition which we have traced from Defoe rather
than from Locke and in which to exchange is seen as more important than
to possess. But he does not neglect to emphasise that because the Germans lacked an effective agriculture, they lacked a sense of property
which could reinforce and moderate the sense of self. The tribesman's
passions were violent but unfocussed; he alternated between periods of
lethargy and melancholy and moments of uncontrolled warrior action
which roused him, says Gibbon, to "a more lively sense of his existence." For this *Angst* the only remedy was property. Had the German
possessed land of his own to till, productive labour would have cured
his physical and psychic lethargy. The sense of honour - of an exposed
and vulnerable personal identity - which Gibbon tells us was all that
the tribesman understood of liberty, would have been transformed into
a sense of law and a capacity for military discipline by an awareness
of responsibility for his material possessions and for the relations
with others which possession involved.

There are obvious enough echoes of Locke here, though Gibbon does
not make them explicit by citation. It may be added, on the one hand,
that he is repeating Machiavellian doctrine about property as the sole
source of social responsibility in the warrior as well as Machiavelli's
views about mercenary and citizen militias. But on the other hand, a
level of sophistication, not to be derived simply from Locke, is to

be found in Gibbon's association between property and the passions.
Property as such does what *"le doux commerce"* was seen to do by writers
such as Montesquieu: it refines and moderates the passions by making
us aware of what we share with others; without it there can only be a
barbaric sense of honour based upon a profound psychic insecurity. Unless the passions are focussed upon objects outside the self, the self
cannot be socialised or reconciled to its own existence. This is not
the moment to embark upon a history of the concept of alienation, but
certainly the above is an early statement of its association with the
notion of property. If we are to be social beings, then we must become
what we own in relation to others, what we share and exchange with
others; and since the concept of labour has put in an appearance
(though I do not ascribe to Gibbon a labour theory of value) the step
from exchange to production is not far away.

In the same chapter, when writing of the history of sexuality,
Gibbon makes further use of the concept of honour - the only value
which can arise from the pre-social and pre-commercial self's awareness
of its identity.[24] Echoing Tacitus on the role of women in primitive
German society, he tells us that they were as warlike as the men and
were respected as their equals. This occurred because warrior honour
was literally the only value available at this stage of human development and was consequently adopted as one by either sex without differentiation. Since honour and equality are valuable, the tribal women
were and are to be respected; and they added another value possessing a
sexual basis: that of a ferocious chastity, since "the first honour of
the sex has ever been that of chastity." But what was the role of
women as property relations developed in society? We know that it
was the perceived function of property and commerce to refine and polish human passions and behaviour. At this point Gibbon joins himself
to a widespread and momentous tendency in eighteenth-century thought -
that of ascribing precisely the same role to women and associating
their performance of it with the rise of commercial society. It would
be easy, and entirely justified, to point out how far this association
was based on the still surviving view of women as a species of property, or as a medium of exchange between proprietors. However, a case
might be made for the view that women could expect more mobility, and
even active agency, from a commercially conceived society than from
the alternative model of the masculine and self-contained classical
patriots.

The Enlightenment certainly saw women in the role of cultural
entrepreneurs, encouraging the exchange of politeness and refinement
in a variety of forms. The notions of commerce and culture were, as
we have seen, intimately allied. But it is noteworthy that Gibbon,
having remarked that the women of the German tribes might be admirable
but not very feminine, goes on to express the fear that as property
and commerce civilise society and as women play their role in the promotion of refinement, the latter may grow less chaste. Chastity's
"most dangerous enemy," he says, "is the softness of the mind. The re-
finements of life corrupt while they polish the intercourse of the
sexes." Gibbon is saying about sexuality precisely what Montesquieu
had said about commerce itself, and there is more at work here than the
standard imbalances of intersexual perception. We are being told that
something is lost with the disappearance of barbaric honour and that
the process of civilisation is at the same time a process of corruption. The unity of the undifferentiated personality - whether property
or sexuality be seen as the source of differentiation - may have been
relegated to a savage and irrecoverable antiquity, but it has not lost
its uniqueness as a value.

The associations in Gibbon's ninth chapter between property and
personality and between commerce and sexuality are not the only threads
which may guide us in tracing the history of the ideology of commerce,
and they are far from being confined to his writings alone. His contemporary William Robertson, for example, in his *History of America*,
goes so far as to indicate (following Buffon) that the savage - in this
case the Amerindian - is sexually cold, or at least devoid of affection
in his sexual relationships, because he is not producing and distributing a sufficient diversity of goods to permit his passions to begin
growing towards sociability and civilisation.[25] The point in the four-
stage series (or was it really a cycle?) at which the sexual and economic Arcadia might be found, Robertson left Rousseau to determine;
but in his companion work on India he depicted an Asian society so far
civilised by commerce that Europeans might trade with it and be neither
impoverished nor corrupted.[26] Given the presumptions of the time, he
would have to admit that Indians understood law but not liberty, private but not public virtue, thereby raising the question of whether
European public values could have existed without the antithesis of
the commercial principle - without barbaric and feudal honour, without
classical citizenship and virtue.

In his *View of the Progress of Society in Europe*, Robertson attempted what may in the proper sense be called a "bourgeois" interpretation of history by isolating the growth of trading towns as the agency which had introduced into feudal society the principles of modern
liberty.[27] But the contrast with Asia was alone enough to show that
the pre-commercial component must be allowed some positive role in the
process. Gibbon touched on the same problem when he wrote, in language
once again significantly sexual, that "the fierce giants of the north"
- the savage Germans - "broke in" to a Roman world privatised to the
point where personality had been stripped of its civic relationships.
"They restored a manly spirit of freedom; and after the revolution of
ten centuries, freedom became the happy parent of taste and science."[30]
What happened during those ten centuries, whether savage freedom became
civic virtue, and whether freedom fertilised politeness or politeness
freedom, Gibbon does not tell us, since the later *Decline and Fall* does
not focus on the history of the medieval West; but the essays of David
Hume on the relations between liberty and the arts are enough to tell
us that the problem was a difficult one.

We have seen how property moved from being the object of ownership
and right to being the subject of production and exchange, and how the
effect of this on the proposition that property was the basis of social
personality was to make personality itself explicable in terms of a
material and historical process of diversification, refinement and perhaps ultimate decay and renewal. We have now to consider more closely
the politics of the commercial ideology, and in this regard it is crucially important to recall that the ideological necessity throughout
had been to provide an alternative to a view of politics as founded upon the autonomy and unity of the patriot personality. The relegation
of that unity to a barbaric or economically primitive past, in which it
must itself disintegrate and seem never to have existed, was a powerful
critical weapon in the hands of the modernists. Yet the ideal of unity
obstinately refused to disappear. We find this interestingly illustrated in the writings of Josiah Tucker, a vigorous and original con-
servative - he calls himself a constitutional Whig - of the era of the
American Revolution.[29] In *A Treatise Concerning Civil Government* which
he completed in 1781, Tucker set out to deny that political capacity
could be immediately anchored in human personality; but he did not locate the doctrine he attacked - as his language shows he knew he might
have done - in concepts of classical citizenship or of man as by nature

a political animal. He located it instead - as his choice of a title
reveals - in the political theory of Locke, whose doctrine of property
he did not explore because he believed himself confronted by English
and American democrats who were using Locke to divorce property from
personality and make the latter alone the sufficient and necessary condition of political right. If moral personality entailed a right of
consent, and if without that consent government could have no authority
over the individual, then government would be forever philosophically
as well as practically impossible, for moral rights and obligations
could not be deputed by one individual to another, whereas all government was founded upon the transfer of rights to representatives and
rulers. Talk of "inalienable rights" was therefore political nonsense,
and if - as Tucker believed - it was as a moral being that Locke supposed the individual to possess the right of consent, that premise made
the latter incapable of choosing a representative to exercise his
rights for him: a truth which only the "honest, undissembling" - but
unfortunately mad - Rousseau had been able to perceive and declare.
The capacity to transfer rights and become the subject and beneficiary
of government must be sought for in man not as a moral, but as a social
being; and the two, declared Tucker, who was an Anglican clergyman with
an acute sense of sin, were not simply identical.[30]

Tucker was not a stupid man, and we should have to work hard to
demonstrate that Locke was on his side and not, as he thought, against
him. But when he puts forward his account of the social origins of
government, he says things which the conventional wisdom of modern
scholarship has encouraged us to deduce largely from the supposed principles of Locke. Government, he says, originates not in the inherent
moral nature of men, but from the diversity of social activities in
which they engage. These set up a variety of relationships among men,
in which some individuals necessarily exert greater authority than
others; in their origin these may be violent and unjust, but by experience men learn to recognise their necessity and conduct them properly.
The various patterns of authority cohere into what may be called a
"government" or "state," which experience similarly vests with codes of
rules and systems of elaborate conventions. Though certainly constitutional in character, nothing prevents this government from exercising
an ultimately uncontrolled sovereignty. At least it is not controlled

by any rights or other moral characteristics inherent in men, which
need be understood as preceding and going into the making of government.[31]

Tucker was a correspondent of Hume's, and we may recognise the
latter's voice in some of the things he says. But it is of greater importance to see that he was situating himself in a by no means discon-
tinuous tradition descending from Sir William Temple, who had written a
hundred years before that nothing but opinion could prevail upon property to submit itself to authority; and what had happened during the
interval was that it had become increasingly possible to see how property might itself be the source of opinion. Tucker uses the term
"natural authority" when describing its civil and social genesis, but
he repeatedly makes it clear that the "natural society" which this term
entails can only exist by becoming a commercial society. Not only is
the paradigm of commerce necessary in order to describe the diversity
of activities which generate "natural authority"; Tucker also emphasises that in the pre-commercial society - and here he mentions the
classical *polis* to which republicans appeal - the exchange of goods and
services is so underdeveloped that the normal human relationship is
that between master and slave, lord and serf.[32] Only as commerce develops do social relations become capable of generating civil authority. Tucker uses no English equivalent for *bourgeoisie*, because there
isn't one, but he does argue at length that it was the growth of the
borough, under the patronage of the kings and barons of medieval England, which permitted the conversion of the latter from barbaric into
civil rulers, exercising "natural authority."[33] Commerce, and the complexity of exchange which it generates, teaches both rulers and subjects the conventions according to which government must be conducted.
Being rooted in experience, these lessons take the form of opinion, and
we have heard enough by now of the process through which it had been
decided, since Temple, that the conversion of passion into opinion was
the function of commerce.

In this projection, the personality was related to government only
through a series of social relationships of which commerce was the paradigm if not the efficient cause. Government was restrained and determined by convention but not by natural right; and far from there being
any such things as "inalienable rights," the very foundation of government lay in the alienation of rights and, in a certain sense, of personality itself. For if government is merely the aggregate of the

diverse forms of "natural authority," there is no one social or political relation to which the personality as a whole, or in its unity,
is naturally committed.

Today we call this political theory "liberalism," and though the
word itself was not so used in the eighteenth century, the criticisms
which we use it to express were in many cases already in circulation.
The indictment to be levelled against such a system would be not only
that it denied the individual his natural right and his liberty of consent, but that it denied him his virtue. Commercial man might be asocial but he could never be a wholly political being. There was no moment at which he addressed himself undividedly to the public good;
consequently he risked the privatisation which Gibbon had seen over-
coming the Romans of the middle empire and which Adam Smith thought a
criticism to be most validly levelled at the conditions of life in commercial society.[34] He might under modern conditions have the social
solidarity necessary to resist the barbarian invaders who had brought
down ancient society, but it was a good deal less certain that he could
resist the corruption of society from within. For if all his political
relationships were mediated, he must in the last analysis be governed
by intermediaries, whether these took the form of mercenaries, cour-
tiers, clergy or representatives; and every theory of corruption, without exception, is a theory of how intermediaries substitute their own
good and profit for that of their supposed principals. The theory of
surplus value itself may be considered an extension of corruption theory from the political to the economic realm. Virtue - a synonym for
autonomy in action - was not merely a moral abstraction, but was declared to be a human necessity.

To all this the apologists of commerce replied that the unity of
personality in political action was imaginable only under conditions
so archaic and remote that it could not currently exist and, if we looked closely, would appear not to have existed even then. They added
that the growth and diversification of human potentialities through the
development in history of the capacity to produce and distribute was
the true story of the human personality in society and that any loss of
virtue which specialisation entailed was a price well paid for the increase in economic, cultural and psychic capacity. But the fact that
the apologists so regularly admitted the possibility of a loss of virtue is a proof that the ideal of the undifferentiated personality,
even when driven from history, refused to disappear as a norm.

Montesquieu had called it "le plainte de Platon" that "le commerce corrompt les moeurs pures,"[35] and we may call it "le plainte de Rousseau" that "les moeurs pures" had never been fully realised in a history conceived as a process of commerce and specialisation. There were innumerable treatments of the tension between virtue and commerce, and innumerable attempts to resolve it, some of which satisfied their authors and may satisfy the modern critic; but I would like to suggest that there is no greater and no commoner mistake in the history of social thought than to suppose that the tension ever disappeared, that the ideals of virtue and unity of personality were driven from the field, or that a commercial, "liberal" or "bourgeois" ideology reigned undisturbed until challenged by the harbingers of Marx.

We have been tracing, from the era of Hobbes and Harrington to that of Hume and Rousseau, a complex dialectic based first on the perception that there were now two ways - an ancient and a modern, a classical and a commercial - in which property might be seen as the foundation and determinant of social and political personality, and second on an increasing awareness that the latter way furnished the human creature with a history, the former with a means of protesting against it. Real and mobile property formed the substratum of a quarrel which ended as that between the unity of personality and its increasing diversification in history, and it is hard not to link the problems perceived by Rousseau and Smith with Marx's indictment of specialisation and diversification, though I shall not attempt to consider how this link might be established. The problem of personality persisted as the core of the matter. But by the time of Marx there existed the powerful paradigm of the classical economics, of which Adam Smith was said to be the father and Locke the somewhat shadowy ancestor.

There is an enterprise, to which Joyce Appleby is the most recent contributor, of providing Smith with a pedigree of earlier analysts of market behaviour; but she does not seem to have shown how the analysis of the market could become a problem in political theory, and her dismissal in a footnote of all anti-commercial ideology as "reactionary" (and so presumably not worth thinking about) appears to disable her from doing so.[36] I suggest that we cannot understand the vindication of commercial society unless we understand the grounds on which it was assailed and accept the attack's continuous vitality. This obliges us to take a route which leads through Mandeville and Hume to Ferguson and Smith, and to encounter classical economics at the end of it, after long debate between virtue and commerce, virtue and corruption, virtue and passion. In a recent work by Donald Winch,[37] Smith is interpreted in this light, and we are reminded that he was a professor of moral philosophy and his first major work was a study of the theory of moral sentiments.

But if classical economics emerged in this way, if the last of the civic humanists was the first of the Scottish economists, if the quarrel of the ancients and moderns furnished the context in which the developing understanding of market relations took on problematic meaning, then the classical economics seem rapidly to have hardened into a paradigm which operated to deny the ambivalent historicism of late Whig culture. Bentham and the elder Mill, as well as McCulloch and Ricardo, would seem to have much to do with this, and we are left trying to see how their thought emerged in history. The space "from Hobbes to Bentham" is replete with problems and possibilities.

FOOTNOTES

1 Joseph Cropsey, *Polity and Economy* (The Hague: Nijhoff, 1957).

2 Duncan Forbes, *Hume's Philosophical Politics* (Cambridge University Press, 1976).

3 See Quentin Skinner, "The Context of Hobbes's Theory of Political Obligation," in Maurice Cranston and R. S. Peters. eds., *Hobbes and Rousseau* (New York: Doubleday, 1972), and "Conquest and Consent: Thomas Hobbes and the Engagement Controversy," in G. E. Aylmer, ed., *The Interregnum, The Quest for Settlement, 1646-1660* (New York: Anchor, 1972).

4 See J. G. A. Pocock, ed., *The Political Works of James Harrington* (Cambridge University Press, 1977).

5 *The Works of Sir William Temple* (London, 1770), I, pp. 29-57; "An Essay on the Origin and Nature of Government," written in or after 1672.

6 P. G. M. Dickson, *The Financial Revolution in England: A Study in the Development of Public Credit, 1688-1756* (London, Macmillan, 1970).

7 Jonathan Swift, *The History of the Four Last Years of the Queen* (ed. Herbert Davis, Oxford, Basil Blackwell, 1964), pp. 68-78.

8 See Masao Maruyama, *Studies in the Intellectual History of Tokugawa Japan* (Tokyo and Princeton University Press, 1974).

9 J. G. A. Pocock, *The Machiavellian Moment* (Princeton University Press, 1975), pp. 436-61.

10 *The Machiavellian Moment*, pp. 427-32.

11 *The Machiavellian Moment*, pp. 432-35.

12 This theme is developed in J. G. A. Pocock, "Modes of Political and Historical Time in Eighteenth-Century England," in Ronald C. Rosbottom, ed., *Studies in Eighteenth-Century Culture*, vol. 5 (Madison: University of Wisconsin Press, 1976).

13 Joyce Oldham Appleby, *Economic Thought and Ideology in Seventeenth-Century England* (Princeton University Press, 1978).

14 *The Machiavellian Moment*, pp. 440-1, 454-6.

15 *Esprit des Lois*, book XIX, Chapter 27.

16 *The Spectator*, no. 3; *Lettres Persanes*, CXLII.

17 Princeton University Press, 1976.

18   *Esprit des Lois*, IV, 8.

19   *A Treatise Concerning Civil Government* (1781), pp. 167-8.

20   This phrase is not Montesquieu's (for its history, see Hirschman, *op. cit.*), but "partout où il y a des moeurs douces, il y a du commerce; et partout où il y a du commerce, il y a des moeurs douces" (*Esprit des Lois*, XX, 1).

21   See Duncan Forbes, *op. cit.*

22   Ronald L. Meek, *Social Science and the Ignoble Savage* (Cambridge University Press, 1975).

23   For the following references, see J. B. Bury's edition of the *History of the Decline and Fall of the Roman Empire* (London, 1902), vol. 1, pp. 218-26.

24   Bury ed., I, pp. 227-8.

25   *The Works of William Robertson* (London, 1824), IV, pp. 297-8.

26   "An Historical Disquisition concerning Ancient India," Section II; *ed. cit.*, IX, pp. 44-86; cf. Gibbon, Bury ed., I, pp. 54-56.

27   *Works*, III, pp. 36-46 IV, pp. 52-54.

28   *Ed. cit.*, pp. 56-58.

29   He was one of those insignificant Englishmen of whom the history of political thought so largely consists. This remark is dedicated with irritated affection to Judith N. Shklar.

30   *Treatise*, pp. 27, 32-3, 167-8, 236-8.

31   *Treatise*, section II, generally. Tucker relies heavily on Robertson's *America*.

32   *Treatise*, pp. 130-2, 167-8, 170-201.

33   *Treatise*, section III.

34   "Of the Influence of Commerce on Manners," *Lectures on Justice, Police, Revenue and Arms*, Part II, Division 2, section 3.

35   *Esprit des Lois*, XX, 1: "On peut dire que des lois du commerce perfectionnent les moeurs, par la même raison que ces mêmes lois perdent les moeurs. Le commerce corrompt les moeurs pures: c'était le sujet des plaintes de Platon: il polit et adoucit les moeurs barbares, comme nous le voyons tous les jours."

36   Appleby, *op. cit.*, p. 268, n. 61.

37   Donald Winch, *Adam Smith's Politics: An Essay in Historiographic Revision* (Cambridge University Press, 1978).

A COMMENT ON POCOCK

Professor Pocock's argument in this paper is an elaboration and a further refinement of a theme which will be familiar, at least in part, to anyone who has read the later chapters of *The Machiavellian Moment*, the introduction to his edition of *The Political Works of James Harrington*, and articles published over the last fifteen years, some of them collected in *Politics, Language and Time*. His theme (if one may epitomize it in a few sentences) is that the distinctive character of theories of property in early modern political thought, particularly in British political thought in the seventeenth and eighteenth centuries, can be adequately appreciated only if one recognizes the continuity through this period of a tradition of thought which may be called the civic humanist or the classical republican tradition. It was a tradition which upheld the ideal of a society composed of citizens in arms, of men who regarded property not as the basis for productive life, but as a safeguard or guarantee of material autonomy or independence, who attached therefore special significance to real property, or property in land, which alone provided the conditions which permitted a man to realize his potential for citizenship. For the landed citizen possessed the means to bear arms in defence of the republic; he had sufficient leisure to cultivate the virtues requisite for a life of public debate and action; he enjoyed liberty, and could be relied upon to insist that governments must be so constituted that the spirit of liberty might animate the conduct of its public men; and most significantly in the present context, the participation of the patriotic citizen was stabilized by his attachment to the land, with its indissoluble connection with the country and its traditions of public and private life.

It is against this classical background, Professor Pocock has told us, that we can recognize most clearly the distinctive features of the theories of commercial society which figured so prominently in eighteenth-century thought. In this perspective the ideal of commercial society was not so much a construction of thinkers in the natural jurisprudence tradition such as Hobbes and Locke; the critical moment in the conception of the model of commercial society was the debate which accompanied the financial revolution in England in the

last decade of the seventeenth century. It was the establishment of a
system of government borrowing, intended initially to finance Britain's
involvement in a succession of wars with France, which seemed, particularly to its critics, to inaugurate a new form of property, government bonds and stocks in government companies, and a new social class,
the "moneyed interest," upon whom governments depended for credit, and
who, in turn, depended on the continued legitimacy of the government
and its ability to make repayments on its debts. The new financial
order seemed to its republican critics as dramatic a transformation of
the classical priorities as any they could imagine. The funds obtained by public borrowing permitted governments to maintain standing armies which threatened to make obsolete the citizen militias of the
classical ideal; the multiplication of offices, places, and pensions
in the military and civil service made interest in securing public office and rewards more relevant for the fulfilment of political aspira-
tion than the cultivation of public virtues; and the dependence of
governments upon their creditors, and the support which creditors,
pensioners, placemen, and office holders unquestioningly gave to governments could not help but undermine the spirit of liberty.

The implications of the new financial order for constitutional
government, devastating as they were for the prospects of classical
politics, were compounded by problems of another type; and while constitutional questions are not absent from the present discussion, they
are explored more fully elsewhere, by Professor Pocock and by others.[1]
In the paper before us the emphasis falls upon the psychological and
sociological dimensions of commercial society and the response it provoked in its republican critics. For the identification of public
credit as the novel and problematic feature of commercial society may
also be attributed to the observed effects of the passions generated
by dealings on the stock exchange. The periodic crises in commercial
society in the eighteenth century could be linked to the fantastic
expectations and the equally unbalanced moods of despair of investors
and dealers in public stock. And such emotional crises would not fail
to appear peculiarly excessive when contrasted with the stability,
perhaps stolidity, of the patriotic citizen's affection for his land.
In this light the preoccupation of successive theorists of commercial
society with the problem of controlling the passions and the imagination may become more comprehensible, as may the emergence of theories
of society as theoretical histories of the manner in which the

passions have been polished and refined. In the course of these social inquiries the rise of commercial societies became identified with
the rise of polite societies, and the psychology of commercial society
was contrasted with the ruder passions of the classical period and the
appetites of a still more primitive phase of savage or barbarous societies. It is in this context that we should locate the emergence of
the four-stages theory of social history, which may have been inspired,
at least in part, by an attempt to explain how the stage of society
typified by commerce and politeness superseded earlier ruder stages of
society, among them the agricultural society of the patriotic citizen.

It is impossible, no doubt, to restate the argument of Professor
Pocock's paper in this highly condensed manner without losing much of
the complexity and nuance of the presentation, but the main outlines
of the argument may stand out more obviously in an abridgement of this
kind. The points which seem to me outstanding and to call for comment
are three: the recognition that public credit was the most controversial feature of commercial society in the eighteenth century; the
identification of commerce and politeness; and, finally, the advent of
the four-stages theory of social history and the theoretical factors
which must be taken into account in explaining its emergence. Professor Pocock's insistence that little sense can be made of any of
these matters if one neglects the continued vitality and relevance of
the classical republican or neo-Harringtonian tradition seems to me
undeniable; and more generally I find myself so much in sympathy with
the perspective that he brings to bear upon these problems that to
belabour the many points of agreement and points which call for commendation might well be wearisome to the reader. At all events, it
may be more fruitful for this discussion to attempt to bring to light
the relevance of other contexts and traditions for the themes he has
identified, and in all three cases, these traditions intersect with
the dialectical world Professor Pocock has brought before us.

1) It is true no doubt to say that the institutional arrangements of public credit would not have been perceived as the most controversial feature of commercial society without the critical response
to those arrangements of thinkers in the neo-Harringtonian tradition.
And the constitutional, psychological and sociological reasons for
their antipathy were, as we have seen, very far reaching indeed. But
there were other political theorists, among them David Hume, who, in
his frequently reworked essay on this subject, opposed public credit

primarily on the grounds that it was damaging to commerce, and because
it made possible a foreign and colonial policy wholly inconsistent with
the interests, properly understood, of commercial society. The point
of departure for Hume's thinking (and also for Montesquieu's) on the
subject of public credit was a debate among French theorists of commercial society in the first half of the eighteenth century.

It had been contended by John Law, early in the century, and by
Melon, Dutot, and Dupin in the 1730's and 1740's, that commerce could
not fail to benefit from the issuance of government stock, for trade
in stock increased the circulation of goods and services, and made new
forms of credit available to manufacturers, merchants, and other employers of labour.[2] Their arguments concealed, in the judgment of
Montesquieu and Hume, an ambiguity in the term circulation: the volume
of dealings in the stock exchange was not coextensive with the exchange
of commodities or goods and services; the latter was beneficial to commerce,

> But what production we owe to Change-alley, or even
> what consumption, except that of coffee, and pen,
> ink, and paper, I have not yet learned; nor can one
> foresee the loss or decay of any one beneficial com-
> merce or commodity, though that place and all its in-
> habitants were forever buried in the ocean.[3]

Some marginal advantage for commerce might follow if the owners of
public stock were also merchants, for revenue from investment might
permit merchants to sell their commodities at lower prices. But this
advantage was trifling when weighed against the various impediments to
commerce imposed by public credit: taxes on commodities must be raised
to pay interest on the public debt, and higher taxes must result in
higher prices and higher wages; the use of public stock as a medium of
exchange must depreciate the value of the currency; the number of un-
industrious persons and also of foreign creditors was bound to increase
and cities become enlarged beyond their capacity to provide healthy and
orderly conditions of civic life. There is much in this part of Hume's
indictment of public credit which would be agreeable no doubt to a
classical republican critic; but it is worth remarking that the critique of public credit is couched entirely in terms of its effects on
commercial society. The landed citizen has yet to make an appearance
in the debate.

But there was another aspect of the attack on public credit in
the writings of Hume, Adam Smith, and others, which was more serious
in their view than the effect of government borrowing on domestic

commerce: this was the use of public credit to finance ever more cost-
ly wars of trade and colonial aggrandizement. This policy, pursued with
indifferent virtuosity by Great Britain in the 1740's, but with unprecedented success in its own terms by the elder Pitt in the Seven Years
War, inspired Hume to rhetorical levels of impassioned denunciation
usually reserved in his writings for discussions of the effects upon
society of religious belief. In this context, it has been observed,
the language of civic humanism reappears in the argument;[4] the funds
required to service the new debt (more than doubled in the course of
the war) would exhaust the revenue available from taxes on commodities,
and require the government to raise taxes on land to the ruin of the
landed gentry. The rhetoric of Hume's discussion is entirely reminis-
cent of the attacks on public credit and commercial society of the Augustan humanists; but there is, I should want to affirm, a crucial difference. The classical republican critics of public credit did not
doubt that commerce depended upon wars of trade and imperial expansion:
Davenant's misgivings about standing armies did not extend to navies,
and Bolingbroke was not averse to advocacy of wars of this kind.[5] In
this respect both may be recognized as subscribers to an older republican conviction that commonwealths or mixed governments have a particular capacity for territorial expansion.

It was this conviction which Hume, and later Smith, were to challenge most forcefully: the great danger of public credit was not merely that it would be ruinous to landowners; it would be, but landowners
were not devoid of resources or of a degree of influence upon their
neighbours which stockholders rarely enjoyed.[6] The problem of public
credit was that it promoted a foreign policy at odds with the interests
of commerce properly understood. For commerce was best served, not by
the conquest or impoverishment of neighbouring states, but by their
continued commercial strength and their readiness to trade. In sum,
there were commercial grounds for opposing public credit, which sometimes, but not always, complemented the arguments directed against it
by its classical republican critics.

(2) If public credit was the most controversial feature of commercial society in eighteenth-century Britain, and William Lecky once
observed and Sir Lewis Namier agreed, that no subject was more often
debated in parliament in that century,[7] the characteristic of commercial life which might well have been remarked upon most often in week-
ly journals and by moral philosophers was the politeness of the man of

commerce. The emphasis on politeness by theorists of commercial society in the eighteenth century might easily be mistaken for mere man-
nerism or literary affectation of not much significance for the historian of philosophy or political thought; but such a presumption, should
it exist, would be unfounded. Shaftesbury, Mandeville, Hume, Smith,
Ferguson, the outstanding political thinkers of eighteenth-century
Britain, were all, in their different ways, impressed by the affinities
of commerce and politeness. There were thinkers (Shaftesbury was perhaps prototypical in this respect) who related commerce to natural politeness or sympathy, to an instinctive tendency to identify with the
feelings or passions of others. And this disposition to sympathize
with the pleasures of other proprietors was recognized by Hume and
Smith to have fundamental significance for the psychology of commercial
life. But there was another dimension of politeness, no less fundamental for Hume and Smith, which may be called artificial politeness,
a propensity to check or restrain instinctive feelings or passions in
deference to the sensibilities of others. The main inspiration for
theories of politeness of the second kind[8] was no doubt Mandeville,
and more remotely, the worldly Augustinian moralists of seventeenth-
century France, who had shown how passions which had been regarded traditionally as voices were turned into socially useful channels productive of commerce and refinement.[9]

The connections between commercial society and polite society
might also be approached critically and for purposes of contrast with
the ruder virtues of the ancient world. This was the design of the
patriotic moralists who found an instructive contrast between French
refinement and the more rugged virtues of ancient Britain, and a similar dialectic pervades the work of Adam Ferguson. John Pocock has explored, here and elsewhere, the many facets of the comparative sociology which was extrapolated from the contrast of virtuous societies and
polite societies. And in this context Montesquieu must be regarded as
indeed "not the first but an authoritative exponent." But I am puzzled
by his suggestion that "though we can glean from his text that something comes after the republic whose principle is virtue, he does not
explicitly categorize what it is, and does not escape from the possibility that modern refinement corrupts antique virtue without replacing
it." Was it not part of Montesquieu's argument that the principle of
honour which inspires the conduct of subjects under a properly constituted (hierarchical) monarchy is entirely compatible with commerce and

with the social stratification found in commercial societies? In Book
VII of *L'Esprit des Lois* he seems to countenance Mandeville's view that
honour in commercial societies is in fact vanity; that members of commercial societies constantly strive to appear to belong to a rank higher than the one they in fact occupy; but that such vanity is useful.
In Book XX he warns to be sure against the involvement of the nobility
in commerce, such involvement having contributed to the decline of the
nobility and thus to the weakening of the monarchy in England. But he
finds it consistent with the spirit of monarchical government that merchants should aspire to a degree of wealth which would enable them to
purchase titles and thus enter the ranks of the nobility. The honour
so acquired, he seems to say, may well be a false honour, "mais il y a
des gouvernements où un tel honneur serait utile".[10] In sum, there is
an important distinction between the honour that traditionally inspired men to occupy a certain rank or station in society and the vanity which inspires the quest for status or rank in commercial society.
But while the two species of honour are distinguishable they also overlap in ways that may be useful, and in their coincidence provide a
principle that may replace the virtue of the classical republics.

> (3) "In a history of property theory organised around the
>   duality of classical and commercial politics, it is
>   difficult to retain the image of Locke as the hinge
>   on which history turned."

An incipient orthodoxy may be emerging on this matter, if we consider John Pocock's presentation together with the previous paper by
James Tully, and look beyond them to John Dunn's well known exercise
in debunking the image of Locke as a political thinker of significance
in the first half of the eighteenth century.[11] Happily the proposition that Locke's theory was unimportant in this period can be phrased
in Popperian terms as a negative generalization, open to challenge if
one can discover contexts in which Locke's political thinking was significant. There were, I believe, at least three distinguishable contexts in British political thought in the early eighteenth century in
which Locke figured in important ways, and more pertinently, in ways
which relate to the rise of the four-stages theory of social history.

The first was the eighteenth-century historiographical debate
concerning the origin of the English constitution, the phase of English
historiography which supersedes the common-law historiography of the
ancient constitution. The terms of this debate were set in large part
by the extended response to Brady's Tory history by Locke's friend

James Tyrrell, who represented the origin of the English constitution
as an original contract successively confirmed, violated, and vindicated. His *General History of England* marked the beginning of what
might be called, without anachronism, the Whig interpretation of English history.[12] It must be acknowledged that Locke himself made little or no contribution to this historical endeavour. Tyrrell wrote frequently to Locke requesting his assistance,[13] but Locke's replies would
seem to have been unfailingly abrupt and unhelpful. It cannot be
doubted, however, that Tyrrell thought that his historiography
"perfectly agreed with Locke's theories of property and power";[14] and
through the agency of Tyrrell, a version of Locke's views may be said
to have exercised considerable influence on English historiography in
the first half of the eighteenth century.

The second context is the response of Locke's sometime pupil and
friend, the third earl of Shaftesbury, to what Shaftesbury took to be
the selfish theory of ethics propounded in Locke's philosophical and
political writings. Shaftesbury is a pivotal figure in the moral and
political philosophy of eighteenth-century Britain: we know from his
correspondence that the refutation of Locke was the major critical objective of his work; but out of courtesy to his former tutor, he re-
frained from mentioning Locke's name in his published writings.[15]
Shaftesbury's work takes us directly into the dialectical world described by John Pocock: he was a classical republican, and he was also
one of the major philosophers of polite society. And his emphasis on
the social affections or social passions was a major influence on the
reorientation of moral and political philosophy in the direction of
the moral and common sense approach of Hutcheson, Smith, Kames, Reid,
and the Scottish enlightenment.

But there is a third context which can also be traced in part to
Locke, which intersects with the second, and which leads, I should like
to propose, directly to the four-stages theory. It was the attempt by
Scottish natural jurists of the eighteenth century to modify the Roman
law of property in a manner which would accommodate the different concerns of Locke and Shaftesbury. Hutcheson's predecessor in the chair
of moral philosophy at the University of Glasgow, Gerschom Carmichael,
would seem to have been the first of the Scottish jurists to call
attention to Locke's theory of property and its significance for the
rule of occupation in Roman law. In notes appended to an edition of
Pufendorf's shorter work, *De Officio Hominis et Civis* (Edinburgh,

1724), Carmichael may be found referring the reader repeatedly to
Locke's treatment of themes developed by Pufendorf. Like Jean de
Barbeyrac, to whom reference was made earlier by James Tully, Locke's
labour theory of property seemed preferable to Pufendorf's account
mainly on the grounds that it was unnecessary according to the labour
theory to wait upon the agreement or consent of others before occupying
or appropriating things for one's own use.[16] Carmichael's annotated
text of Pufendorf was particularly recommended by Francis Hutcheson
when he drafted his own treatise of natural jurisprudence, and in the
preface to the same work he recommended to his students that they read,
along with Grotius and Pufendorf, Cumberland, Shaftesbury, Harrington,
Bynkershoek and Locke.[17] Hutcheson made extensive use of the labour
theory of property in his exposition: it obviated the need to "have
recourse to any old conventions with Grotius and Pufendorf, in explaining the original of property: nor to any decree or grant of our first
parents with Filmer."[18] The labour theory best explained how the passions and affections could be enlisted in preserving mankind, for
"without a property ensuing upon labour in occupying and cultivating
things fitted for the support of life, neither our self-love nor any
of the tender affections would incite men to industry."[19] But notwithstanding the centrality of the labour theory in Hutcheson's account of
property, he acknowledged that Locke's theory rested on doubtful epistemological grounds. He suspected that "the difficulties on this subject emerge from some confused imagination that property is some physical quality or relation produced by some action of men."[20] This problem in Locke's theory of property had been noted by Hume in *A Treatise
of Human Nature*.[21] But a solution to Hume's difficulty seemed at hand
in Shaftesbury's theory of the natural affections. If it were recognized that property depended, not upon the imagination, but upon the
sentiments and affections which dispose men to labour, and, still more,
upon those sentiments (of benevolence, humanity, etc.) which prompt
others to approve of men's appropriation of the things on which they
have laboured, then property could not fail to rest upon a more solid
or more natural foundation.[22] Some years earlier, and independently,
it would seem, Henry Home had arrived at a similar conclusion: the
best justification for property was to be found in the natural affections. This was the context in which Adam Smith addressed the Roman
law of property in his *Lectures on Jurisprudence*, and, in so doing,
launched the four-stages theory of social history.

FOOTNOTES

1   See J. G. A. Pocock, "Early Modern Capitalism: The Augustan Per-
    ception," in *Feudalism, Capitalism and Beyond*, ed. Eugene Kamenka
    and R. S. Neale (London: Edward Arnold, 1975). Isaac Kramnick,
    "Bolingbroke and his Circle," *op. cit.*, Ch. V and Ch. VI.

2   The relevant texts of Law (1705), Melon (1734) and Dutot (1738) are
    conveniently collected in Eugene Daire, *Economistes financiers du
    XVIIIe siècle*. Paris, 1843.

3   David Hume, "Of Public Credit," *Writings on Economics*, ed. Eugene
    Rotwein (Edinburgh: Thomas Nelson and Sons, 1955). Montesquieu,
    De L'Esprit des Lois, (Paris: Société Les Belles Lettres, 1958),
    Vol. 3, Book XXII, Ch. 17, pp. 170-171.

4   *The Machiavellian Moment*, pp. 496-7. See also Professor Pocock's
    discussion of Hume's treatment of public credit in his latest cor-
    respondence in "Hume and the American Revolution: The Dying
    Thoughts of a North Briton," in *McGill Hume Studies: Papers from
    the McGill Bicentennial Hume Congress*, ed. David Norton, Nicholas
    Capaldi, and Wade Robison (San Diego: Austin Hill Press, 1978).

5   See *The Machiavellian Moment*, p. 442, and H. T. Dickinson, *Boling-
    broke* (London: Constable and Co., 1970), p. 190.

6   David Hume to William Strahan, August 1771, in *The Letters of David
    Hume*, ed. J. Y. T. Grieg (Oxford: Clarendon Press, 1932), Vol. 2,
    p. 248.

7   W. E. H. Lecks, *A History of England in the Eighteenth Century*
    (London: Longmans, Green and Co., 1883; 3rd edition), pp. 433-4.
    Sir Lewis Namier, *England in the Age of the American Revolution*
    (London: MacMillan and Co., 1961; 2nd edition), pp. 33-34.

8   The implications of the two theories of politeness for Hume's phil-
    osophy are explored in my article "The Social Background of Hume's
    Science of Human Nature," in *McGill Hume Studies*, *op. cit.*

9   Nan Keohane's forthcoming book on French political thought will no
    doubt be indispensable for an appreciation of the Augustinian moral-
    ists. See also Albert O. Hirschman, *The Passions and the Interests*,
    op. cit.

10 Montesquieu, *De L'Esprit des Lois*, Vol. 1, Book VII, Ch. 1, pp.
    178-179; Vol. III, Book XX, Ch. 22, pp. 65-66.

11 John Dunn, "The Politics of Locke in England and America in the
    Eighteenth Century," in J. W. Yolton, ed., *John Locke: Problems
    and Perspectives* (Cambridge: University Press, 1969).

12 James Tyrrell, *The General History of England* (London, 1696-1704, 3 volumes). See also his *Bibliotheca Politica; or an enquiry into the ancient constitution of the English Government in thirteen dialogues* (London: 1694, mod. ed. 1702), esp. dialogue X: "Of the original contract as the fundamental law of England."

13 His letters to Locke (some sixty-three in all) are collected in the Bodleian Library, Locke Mss. C. 22. See the recent discussion by J. W. Gough, "James Tyrrell, Whig Historian and Friend of John Locke," *The Historical Journal*, Vol. XIX, 3 (1976), pp. 581-610.

14 Tyrrell was convinced that Locke was the author of *Two Treatises of Government* and told Locke in August 1690 that:

> whoever writ it whether yourself or any other; I thought him very much in the right in most things: that he agreed perfectly with my conceptions...which I spoke on purpose that you might then take occasion to deny it if I were mistaken, which since I found you did not, but rather declined discourse, and turned it off to another subject. I must confess I did then (as I do still) entertain some suspicions of your being the author of it....

See Gough, pp. 597-598.

15 *The Life, Unpublished Letters and Philosophical Regimen of Anthony, Earl of Shaftesbury*, ed. Benjamin Rand (London, 1900), pp. 403, 415-416.

16 Samuel Pufendorf, *De Officio Hominis et Civis*, ed. Gerschom Carmichael (Edinburgh, 1724), p. 216, and *Of the Law of Nature and Nations*, ed. J. Barbeyrac (London, 1729), IV, IV, IV, 4.

17 Francis Hutcheson, *Philosophia Moralis Institutia Compendiara*, (Edinburgh, 1742), translated as *A Short Introduction to Moral Philosophy*. (Glasgow, 1747).

18 Francis Hutcheson. *A System of Moral Philosophy* (Glasgow, 1755), Vol. 1, p. 331.

19 Hutcheson, *A Short Introduction to Moral Philosophy*, p. 150.

20 *Ibid.*, p. 158.

21 See James Moore, "Hume's Theory of Justice and Property," *Political Studies*, XXIV, 2 (1976), pp. 114-115.

22 *A Short Introduction to Moral Philosophy*, p. 153, and *A System of Moral Philosophy*, pp. 319-320.

This essay by James MacAdam is a systematic exposition and analysis of the remarks on property which are scattered throughout Rousseau's works. The author treats three logically interrelated topics: man's existence in the state of nature without property; his enslavement to other men through the institution of property; and his liberation from this condition of alienation. Rousseau provides no easy way to achieving this liberation, for men have voluntarily subjected themselves to property and cannot be expected to renounce it readily.

In her commentary on MacAdam's paper, N. O. Keohane deals with the same three topics. However, she arrives at a somewhat different conclusion. She argues that man's liberation from the evils of property is, for Rousseau, adequately accomplished in the formation of a state based on popular sovereignty and the general will, as described in the *Social Contract*.

ROUSSEAU: THE MORAL DIMENSIONS OF PROPERTY

A Reference to Previous Discussion

The most useful historical introduction to Rousseau is by way of his agreement and disagreement with Hobbes. Rousseau agrees with Hobbes that the defect of all modern systems of natural law is their incapacity to deal with the fact that modern peoples are motivated by self-interest. As Rousseau argues in the *First Version of the Social Contract*, it is useless and pernicious to say that one should act upon universal, rational, moral principles of natural law if one lacks good reason to believe that others will conform to natural law. If justice and self-interest are to be united, then the moral values of natural law must somehow be embodied in positive law.

Where Rousseau disagrees with Hobbes is in regard to Hobbes' belief that humans are by nature self-interested. The peculiar self-interested behaviour of modern man is itself caused by insane social relations. If social relations were governed by the general will, then, and then only, man could live up to his nature. Within the insane social relations, on the other hand, self-interest becomes *amour propre*, and under its influence man seeks property to enhance and realize his personality or human nature. That is, man covets material goods in order to realize spiritual goodness. This foolish substitution, becoming part of humanity's profound mistake, aids in making slaves of all of us.

Preface

The original intention in writing this essay was to answer two questions: What does Rousseau mean by "property," and are his arguments concerning it sound? But the more one studied the material, the more impossible the original intention became. Rousseau's remarks upon property (plus those upon wealth, luxury, commerce and economics) are scattered throughout his writings. Nothing could be found amounting to a succinct, coherent theory of property appropriately supported by argument. Moreover, none of Rousseau's critics fill this gap. Accounts of "Rousseau on Property" which attempt to deal with the complexity of what he is saying are few, and the basic questions raised above have yet to be answered.[1] One also finds, in reading Rousseau,

that his pronouncements are frequently contradictory and that either
this is overlooked by his critics or, when noted at all, the contradictions are not taken seriously.

Hence, it was decided that the main aim should be to provide an
account of what Rousseau means to say. This account is based mainly
on *The Discourse on Inequality* and *The Social Contract* because they
provide the best theoretical foundation. However, it also became obvious that a decision as to which writings are most helpful is far
from enough. It is necessary to construct a plausible argument out of
the materials Rousseau offers, and this can be done only if one at
least indicates a general interpretation of his political philosophy.
Without one, it is impossible to see how his statements on property
fit together and how they fit into his philosophy as a whole. It is
also difficult to know what is important and what is not.

First, an interpretation will be presented to provide the necessary background for the rest of the paper. We shall begin with a hypothesis that is meant to capute a fundamental principle of his
thought and then go on to suggest the framework of argument accompany-
ing it.

The hypothesis is as follows: Contrary to Hobbes, human nature
has as its final end the realization of moral nature. Human beings
ought to exist cooperatively as moral agents. This final end is not
now actual and may never come about, but if it is to exist then it
must come about through historical development. Mankind must pass
through developmental stages which are necessary conditions to the
realization of human nature as moral nature. Man as he exists is an
alienated, estranged, contradictory being who has not realized his nature. We shall call this hypothesis Rousseau's idea of developmental
natural law.

Developmental natural law is a hypothesis in the sense that it
provides a fruitful way of understanding the argument of the *Discourse*
and its relation with that of the *Contract*. Developmental natural law
is never presented explicitly and coherently as a principle in any of
Rousseau's writings. But we do find intimations of it, for instance,
in several introductory proclamations in the *Discourse*. It may be
present in the quotation from Aristotle which appears on the title-
page and which says that we do not look for what is natural in depraved beings, but in those which are well-ordered   (*O.C.*, III, 109);[2] in
Rousseau's avowal that the Socratic "know thyself" is basic to the

study of man (III, 122); in his passionate support of Buffon's claim
that we deny our nature by "living outside ourselves" and are preoccupied with "augmenting the exterior of our being," (III, 195-6); and
in his description of the *Discourse* as a history of man through successive stages which is, at the same time, "a criticism of contemporaries." (III, 133). It seems most strongly present in what he says
of *perfectibilité*:

> [T]here is a very specific quality which distin-
> guishes [man from animals]...it is the faculty of
> man to perfect himself: a faculty which with the
> aid of circumstances, develops successively all
> the others...It would be sad for us to be forced
> to acknowledge, that this distinctive and nearly
> unlimited faculty is the source of all the unhap-
> piness of man...and renders him at length, tyrant
> of himself and of Nature. (III, 142).

The framework of argument which supports developmental natural
law itself involves three stages, the first two of which are presented
in the *Discourse* and the third in *The Social Contract*. They can be
summarized as follows:

1. All humans would be equal in an original state of nature because:
   (a) in a situation where few exist in a state of plenty, needs
        and desires would be the same; humans would desire only
        what they need.
   (b) Men would not be afflicted with *amour propre*.
   (c) Men are independent: "the relations of servitude [are]
        formed only from the mutual dependence of men and the recipro-
        cal needs which unite them." (III, 162).
This is not a state of moral equality or inequality. It is an amoral
state.
2. All civilized peoples are equal in being slaves. Civilization is
a condition of universal moral inequality: inequalities of rank, deference and distinction obtain, but humans do not treat one another as
moral equals.
   (a) Men live to satisfy sensual desires.
   (b) All are subjects of *amour propre*.
   (c) All are mutually depraved and dependent.
3. All humans would be morally equal.
   (a) There would be neither a situation of plenty, nor of scarcity.
        Each would have enough, but not enough to own another.

(b) Humans would not suffer from *amour propre*. Each would respect
     his own moral nature and that of his fellow humans.

(c) Although politically, economically and morally dependent in
     one sense, they would in another sense, be politically, eco-
     nomically and morally independent.

Along with these three stages, three questions should be recognized and answered:

1. How do free men become slaves?

2. If men were free, how could they live in free association?

3. How do slaves become free?

It will be suggested later that Rousseau attempts to answer questions
one and two and that question three is the source of most of his difficulties.

In what has preceded, the outline of an interpretation has been
indicated within which Rousseau's views on property can be understood.
With reference to this interpretation, the essay will attempt to answer
the following questions:

1. Is it possible to reconcile Rousseau's contradictory pronouncements
on property?

2. What are the moral grounds of Rousseau's criticism of property? If
there is a sense in which all humans are slaves, is there one in which
all are property?

3. What is Rousseau's concept of private property? Is private property a natural right? a thing owned by an agent (a possession)? the
alienation of human nature? a conditional legal power? a right of
the general will and thus a democratic right?

4. What is the difference if private property is understood as a
product of law, that is, of the sovereignty of the general will? Does
property as legal power promise a good moral effect? Especially, does
the connection of property with law and the sovereignty of the general
will overcome that dependency which is slavery and thus enable self-
mastery?

These sets of questions suggest four headings under which they
can be discussed. "Contradictory Pronouncements," "The Moral Dimensions," "The Concept of Property," and "Property, Law and Freedom."
Since we have already suggested the complexity of Rousseau's treatment,
the reader may appreciate a forewarning of the path of argument prior
to discussion of the questions. We shall begin with a mere list of
Rousseau's contradictory positions, then explain the moral

considerations which govern Rousseau's treatment. Once these are clar-
ified there should emerge a certain logical relationship amongst the
contradictions and the variety of possible concepts. The logical relation stems from the fact that Rousseau considers the development of
the nature of property itself. Hence, the contradictions can be considered as different responses to something - property - which is itself changing. Similarly, the variety of concepts of property are
comprehensible as different philosophical categories or attempts at
understanding property undergoing a change in its nature. Once we have
dealt with these contradictions and their relationships, then it will
be possible to consider, with reference to the fourth question, just
how successful Rousseau is in responding to his own moral criticisms as
raised in relation to the second question.

Contradictory Pronouncements

A short way of illustrating the contradictions is by summarizing
assertions made in his principal political writings. For example, in
the *Discourse on Inequality* we find Rousseau's most famous words on
the subject of property:

> The first one who, having enclosed a piece of land,
> took it upon himself to say, "this is mine," and
> found men foolish enough to believe it, was the
> true founder of civil society. What crimes, wars,
> murders, miseries and horrors would Mankind have
> been spared by one who, uprooting the stakes or
> filling in the ditch, had cried out to his fellows:
> Beware of listening to this imposter: you are lost,
> if you forget that the fruits belong to all and the
> land to no one. (III, 164).

Property is the conspicuous cause of law and the system of justice,
and of "devouring ambition," slavery and alienation. Actual states
began when the rich tricked the poor into adopting a mode of government
which made the rich richer and protected their wealth by enlisting the
common force, while worsening the lot of the poor.

According to received opinion, Rousseau's essay on *Political Economy* was written at about the same time as the *Discourse*. Yet there
Rousseau seems to forget the bitter denunciations which characterize
the *Discourse*. For in *Political Economy* we are told:

> It is certain that the right of property is the
> most sacred of all the rights of citizens and
> more important in certain respects than liberty
> itself...[P]roperty is the true foundation of
> civil society. (III, 262-3).

Yet vestiges of the *Discourse* are also in *Political Economy*. Are not, he asks, all the advantages of society for the rich and powerful? If a rich man in his coach finds his way blocked by a wagon, then are not his servants ready to beat out the brains of the wagon driver? Is it not better that fifty honest pedestrians should be crushed to death rather than delay one rich man? Such is a rich man's right. But the lot of the poor man? Rousseau answers: "I take him for lost if he has the unhappiness to have an honest heart, a lovable daughter and a powerful neighbour." (III, 272).

In *The Social Contract*, Rousseau seems to contradict himself again. In the only legitimate act of social contract, by which one becomes a citizen of the state, apparently the sacred right of property is profaned, for the consenting individual is required to give up all his rights, unquestionably including those of property (III, 360).

Comparable disparities are to be found elsewhere in these and other writings. Some of the most scathing criticism ever delivered against wealth, luxury, trade and commerce are found in Rousseau. This is true not only of the three main political works, but also of *The Discourse on the Arts and Sciences*, certain fragments on politics, the *Constitution for Corsica* and *The Government of Poland*. But again, by contrast, when in *Emile* and *La Nouvelle Héloïse*, Rousseau creates his fictional characters (and presumably he makes them as he wishes), they are pointedly persons of property.

In these condemnations and approvals, of con and pro attitudes, we have contradictions enough to warm the enthusiasm of any Hegelian. Later, we shall return to see what sense can be made of them.

The Moral Dimensions

One strain of Rousseauist criticism emphasizes the biographical, arguing from Rousseau the man to his thought. To understand Rousseau's critique of property, such a critic might urge, it is pertinent to note that Rousseau was neither a lawyer, nor an economist, nor even a philosopher, if the last is defined as a drawer of fine and firm conceptual distinctions. Instead, he will insist, Rousseau was a moralist, a servant, a man of the people and an intellectual. In consequence, he judged property morally, emphasized the hypocrisy and cruelty of the rich, wanted control of property to belong to the people, and was personally disdainful of possessions. But although this observation has much in it, it is not what is needed.

The first priority must be to fathom the connection between property and voluntary and universal slavery. However, we have to approach this problem gradually. A plausible beginning is to suggest
that Rousseau passes from a literal meaning of slavery to one that is
increasingly metaphorical and philosophical.[3]

With reference to the literal meaning, Rousseau supposes that
property is altered radically and decisively influences human life,
when division of labour and economies of scale are applied to agriculture, mining and manufacture. Wealth becomes concentrated, the many
are employed by the few. Some may sell themselves into actual slavery
(i.e., literal alienation of self) but most do "as good as" because
they sell their birthright. Every man has a right to preserve his life
and, derivatively, a right to that property which is necessary to maintain existence. The working poor have no property but their bodies,
which they exchange for their subsistence. They "as good as" sell
themselves into slavery, "as good as" make themselves the property of
the rich. In sum, the working poor alienate their bodies, their only
property, voluntary and universally to become the slaves and property
of the rich. Some may question the aptness of "voluntary" in this context, but the rich do offer a choice: "my money for your life."

However the voluntary enslavement of all, including the rich and
not so rich, must also be explained. This brings us closer to the
promised complexity and the extension of the metaphor. The full story,
as related in the *Discourse*, involves very complicated relationships
amongst *perfectibilité*, *amour de soi-même*, *amour propre* and successive,
necessary material (in Marx's sense) conditions. Since it cannot be
told here, we must try to abbreviate it as best we can. Both *amour de
soi-même* and *amour propre* could be translated by such words as "self-
love," "egoism," "self-valuing," "self-regard" and "self-esteem." But
Rousseau warns that they are passions different in kind and effect.
The first characterizes the state of nature: the second, civilization
and the state of slavery. The first is connected with the natural
right of property, since it is that passion which motivates self-preservation. But natural self-love, as we may call it, is causally defective in relation to *perfectibilité*. Natural self-love by itself
cannot explain human development to the level at which we know it--and
that is Rousseau's aim. If there ever existed a being whose desires
and needs coincided, if it desired only what it needed and the satisfaction were always guaranteed, then no development would occur. To

understand a moral being capable of moral relations with his kind, who yet denies his nature and treats others as animate instruments for his own ends, we must comprehend a being who must give his self away in order to regain his self.

What is causally effective in this connection is the relation between *perfectibilité* and *amour propre*. Buffon, from whom Rousseau apparently obtains the contrast between "living outside oneself" and "living inside oneself," uses the distinction to urge a simple moral prescription, meaning that one should follow one's conscience and resist a life of sensual pleasure. Rousseau uses the distinction both descriptively and prescriptively. "Living outside oneself" is an unavoidable necessity since human development is impossible without it. Rousseau tells the causal story by connecting "living outside oneself" with dependence and eventual slavery. It is one of growing and changing dependence upon the natural environment and fellow humans.

Curiously, the most significant cause is romantic attraction. Rousseau writes:

> Each began to look at others and to will to be looked at himself, and public esteem had a price...this was the first step toward inequality and, at the same time, vice... As soon as humans began to evaluate one another, and the idea of consideration was formed in their minds, then each claimed the right to it. (III, 169-170).

However, it is not quite so curious once one realizes that Rousseau is contrasting romantic with physical desire, that physical desire is identified with procreation and anyone who can satisfy the function, whereas romantic desire is the attraction to a person considered as more than a mere instrument of procreation and sexual satisfaction. Hence, the importance of the cause lies in the idea that at some stage of human development, humans desire to be valued individually by others and each claims the right to it. Hence, what is important about that self-esteem which is *amour propre*, considered as a causal agent, is that it is a form of self-evaluation and self-distinction which renders the person who desires acceptance totally dependent upon the evaluations of others. One is as one is valued. In the *Contract*, Rousseau says that the literal meaning of "to alienate" is "to give or to sell." In the structure of valuing which he is describing, one gives or transfers one's self, in the sense of the evaluation of one's self, to others. This process of self-alienation is important to the development of property.

In the quotation Rousseau holds that each claims the right to be
valued by others. But if someone lacks whatever natural attributes
are necessary to be valued, appearance is substituted for reality.
Property is important to self-valuing, because, although it is artificial in itself, it is causally interchangeable with natural attributes. Indeed, given the urge for acceptance, recognition and self-
distinction, property becomes causally more powerful than any natural
attributes as a criterion of human value. First, it is the most apparent of appearances, the most visible. Second, in relation to self-
distinction, it allows nearly infinite varieties of novel means for
setting oneself apart. Third, it allows social mobility. Fourth, it
creates "new needs." In consequence, it is perhaps not too much to
say that the very meaning of "personal property" alters. In the causal
story, it is now *not* the case that the person owns the property; rather
the person is his property and, at the same time, becomes the property
of it, owned by it, dependent upon it, alienates his self to it, becomes enslaved by it.

This transformation requires at least two steps to explain it.
First, the person thinks of himself as identical with his property,
since he and others believe that his value consists in what he owns.
Since he is--in his judgment and in that of others--what he owns, he
becomes his property. (In a part of Canada which I frequent a person
is identified by two questions: "What's his name? What's he drive?")
He is his property, not in Locke's sense that his person is his property, but rather in the logically opposite sense. It is not that he
owns himself, as Locke presumably intended. It is rather that others
own his person. He allows others, through the evaluative process, to
identify him with his possessions. This is perhaps the most important
sense in which he "lives outside himself." He is his property. He
voluntarily alienates his "self" as property. Second, since property
distinguishes him, he becomes dependent upon it for recognition. And
if he stands highest and shines brightest on that basis alone, then he
must give himself over to maintaining what he has and to acquiring
more. In this way, he becomes enslaved by property.

In this connection, it is important to realize that the cause of
alienation and of universal and voluntary slavery is not assignable to
individuals but to a certain social phenomenon, a certain structure of
valuation to which humans consent and which they support. Both Rousseau and superficial critics mislead when they suggest that property

is *the* cause of inequality, of law, the system of justice, human de-
gradation and enslavement. Rather, according to Rousseau's own account, property is on the one hand, a name of several social and economic mutations, and, on the other, one part of a causal nexus. Beyond
doubt, property is a necessary condition of the modern problem which
Rousseau seeks to describe. But it is not a sufficient condition and
there are other necessary conditions. Or, to put it another way, property by itself could not produce the effects which Rousseau and the
critics attribute to it unless property is defined to include the connections among the factors such as *perfectibilité* and *amour propre*.

Rousseau's account of property moves through the following stages.
Originally man appropriates things for his self-preservation, his physical well-being. As material conditions alter, a few may literally
alienate themselves into slavery. The working poor "as good as" alienate themselves to the rich, again for their physical well-being. *Amour
propre*, as the desire to be valued, causes the alienation of one's self
as a whole being, and not merely of one's body, to others. This is a
form of psychological dependence and is not merely physical. When it
is united with or, rather, expressed in property, then the self is
alienated from human nature as property.

In trying to encompass the complexity of Rousseau's account, one
is conscious of the inadequacy of what is offered, although in broad
outline it seems correct. One is conscious also that its significance
is misunderstood unless Rousseau's contribution is viewed in contrast
with that of Hobbes, Locke, Diderot, Voltaire, Mandeville and Hume. To
attempt that contrast here would be impossible.[4] However, I cannot resist the temptation to donate a sweeping statement which I believe
could be justified in detail.

In chapter 11 of *Leviathan*, Hobbes proposes a modern morality. It
consists of renouncing the idea that there is an ultimate end for man
and of accepting the principle that the good life is solely a matter of
satisfying successive desires and of having the power to satisfy them.
Goodness, then, is a matter of subjective desire. From this beginning,
the substitution of economic value for moral value is not difficult.
Goodness equals satisfaction of subjective desire, equals utility,
equals what persons think something is worth, equals what price they
will pay for it.[5] Goodness equals price. It might be suggested that
Rousseau's moral criticisms of his opponents and of "civilized"
peoples is that they allowed moral relations to become economic

relations and enabled economic and property relations to supersede moral and political ones. *The Social Contract* seeks to repair that fundamental error.

The Contradictions Reconsidered

On the basis of the foregoing moral criticism it looks as if many,
if not all, of the contradictions could be explained. We shall only
comment upon a few. With reference to the first fencer, it would have
been better if men had rationally devised a system of property more
congruent with man's whole nature. But that did not happen. What is
certain, Rousseau believes, is that the mere enclosing of the land does
not justify a right to the land. It was in this sense that the fencer
was an impostor: he pretended to a right to which he was not entitled.
It was an undisputed claim, but not an indisputable right.

Rousseau's statement that property is the foundation of civil society, law and the system of justice is, or is meant to be, a statement
of fact. It is not a favourable value judgment. Rousseau also believes, for instance, that all government is founded upon consent.
This claim may involve both a factual claim and a favourable value
judgment. To confuse property and consent in this way would be to interpret Rousseau as meaning that in fact and in right, property is the
foundation of government, law and justice. And this would be an error.
Moreover, the statement concerning property is causal. Once the habit
of *meum* and *tuum* become established, rules and social organizations
would come into being to protect property. Finally, it is no doubt
true that one can be taught to comprehend the accepted sense of justice in terms of property relations, but if these relations are unjust
in their effects (III, 608-9), they cannot be the basis of an understanding of genuine justice. Eventually justice must get its meaning
from the rights and duties of moral agents.

Even the most discordant statement of all:

> It is certain that the right of property is the most
> sacred of all...and more important in certain respects
> than liberty itself...

is less so in context. Indeed, when he explains these claims, the result is almost the opposite of the apparent meaning. He offers two
reasons. Property is necessary to human life, and however important
liberty may be, it is clearly meaningless if life is denied. Again,
property provides a method whereby the state can ensure that individuals fulfill their responsibilities to the common good and share

its duties as well as its benefits. Property, in other words, is the
means whereby the state can finance its activities.

Finally, although Rousseau is more critical of property in the
Discourse than in any of his other writings, he goes out of his way in
that work to deny that he advocates the abolition of private property
and revolution by force.

> Therefore, what? Must we destroy societies, annihi-
> late "thine" and "mine," and return to live in the
> forests with bears? A conclusion in the manner of my
> adversaries, that I prefer to anticipate, rather than
> to allow them the disgrace of drawing it. (III, 207).

Rousseau's considered view seems to be somewhat as follows. Ownership of goods is not intrinsically evil but can be evil in its effects. The latter is most obviously true when we allow property relations to swallow up and stand in the place of human relations. "It is
not without difficulty," he remarks in the same place, "that we have
succeeded in making ourselves so unhappy." But if ownership can be
regulated by correct moral principles, many of the apparent contradictions, which refer to misuse and abuse, can be understood and perhaps
reconciled.

The Concept of Property

Nowadays, property is one of the most difficult to comprehend of
all jurisprudential ideas. A decisive reason for this state of affairs
is not puzzling in itself. The common sense understanding of private
property is of objects which we buy or receive or make. But that idea
is much too crude for the law which must encompass notions of property
rental, inheritance, joint ownership by shareholders, dummy corporations, public ownership, joint private and public ownership plus myriad
other ways in which, to paraphrase Rousseau, we work hard to make ourselves unhappy! Trusting common sense might believe that private ownership is present whenever the words "my" and "your" are applicable.
(Although consider "my allergies," "my wife," "my professor" and "my
country!") But the law has been forced to conceptualize property as a
more or less arbitrary collection of positive and hypothetical rules
which assert that when certain legally described facts are in place
then certain legal prescriptions should be followed. However, the common sense idea of property as objects rather than legal abstractions
dies hard and creates conceptual cramps even among lawyers. A further
problem is that what Rousseau views as a matter of moral complaint,

namely, that all legal relations are thought of as property relations, is now viewed as a mere truism, although some might add that all relations of property are also nothing but legal relations.[6]

Contemporary jurisprudential concepts of property may seem worlds away from Rousseau; but it is surprising how much of the space between them and the common sense view he does cover. In trying to clarify his concept of property, a number of possible categories have been suggested: whether or not property is a natural right, a possession, alienated human nature, a legal power, a right of the general will and thus a democratic right.

Rousseau's general answer is that in specified conditions property can be said to be all of these except possession. And perhaps he might even admit that if possession spanned a sufficient period (whatever that might be) it would become *de facto* ownership. However, the main thrust of his thinking seems to turn on what might be called moral entitlement, which is related to what is necessary to development of human nature as moral nature.

Thus he may be said to support a natural right to property, but only in a very limited sense. The obvious support is that the individual is morally justified in preserving his own life. Hence, a person has a moral right to property if, and only if, it is necessary to existence. But otherwise, a natural right to property does not imply a right of ownership to property in the form of land.[7]

To justify ownership of land Rousseau provides a strict list of *sine qua non* conditions: 1) that the land be uninhabited, 2) that one take only so much land as is necessary for subsistence, 3) that one take possession not by ceremony but by labour, "the only sign of ownership which, in default of legal title, deserves the respect of others." (III, 366). The qualification in the third condition is unclear, but I take Rousseau to mean that the three conditions are jointly necessary: for example, it would not be enough to satisfy the first two, and the third by itself is insufficient. One reason for thinking that labour alone is not enough comes from the familiar story of Emile and the gardener. The pupil Emile is encouraged to plant and tend some beans. But although Emile "mixes his labour" with nature, the gardener is justified in ripping out the beans, since they were planted in the gardener's plot! (IV, 330-3).

Rousseau continues, in the chapter of the *Contract* entitled "Real
Property," to refuse the standard justifications: none of fencing, occupation, claims by sovereign powers, etc. are accepted. I think it
also follows from his moral criticisms that he would refuse Mandeville's formula that private vices make for public benefits and Locke's
argument to the effect that a right to unlimited property makes the
poor marginally better off. The rich must never be rich enough to buy
the poor.

Given that there is no natural right to property beyond need and
that none of the standard claims for possession provide sufficient entitlement to property, Rousseau is surely mistaken in asserting that
possession does not change its nature in coming under the control of
law and the sovereignty of the general will. (III, 365). The claim
is perhaps explainable in terms of his effort "to unite what right permits with what interest prescribes." Nevertheless, the denial is not
only mistaken, it obscures his argument.

Indeed, what Rousseau proposes in the *Contract* is the surrender by
the individual to the sovereignty of the general will of all his property in Locke's general sense: that is, the surrender of his life,
liberty and estate. Property, in this sense, then becomes a legal
right, given the identification of law, sovereignty and the general
will. Under these conditions, two changes become apparent. First,
private belongings are protected by the common force of the state.
Second, the sovereign regulates all ownership through universal rules
by reference to the standard of the common good. Reciprocity is involved: in return for security of possession, ownership is limited by
the common good as judged by the sovereign. Remember Plato's demented
knife-owner. In one sense, it is his knife: but it is not his to use
for whatever private ends he, in his demented condition, has. "Possession" of goods, as Rousseau himself notes, refers merely to an individual's own power to obtain and retain objects. "Property" in goods
refers to a legal power and right, supported but also regulated by the
state. It is false and misleading to say that "possession" does not
change its nature in becoming "property."

What is also surprising is that Rousseau seems unaware that he
offers no justifications for private ownership other than the somewhat
vague idea of a natural right to what is necessary for existence. In
a recent work, Becker lists several arguments in support of property,

arguments based upon "first occupancy," labour, social utility, liberty
and moral character.[8] So far as one can judge, Rousseau would not accept any of these as justifications. First occupancy and labour have
already been rejected. Property is not socially useful since it en-
slaves and, finally, it depraves moral character. Moreover, even on
the matter of the one natural justification he does recognize, he does
not argue that it necessitates private ownership. In fact, in the
chapter on property, he conceives the opposite possibility without
noticing that it undermines the one natural justification he advances.

> It could happen also that men begin to unite before
> possessing anything and that, taking possession of
> land sufficient for all, they enjoy it in common, or
> they divide it among them, equally or according to
> proportions established by the Sovereign. (III, 367).

Perhaps Rousseau's rejection of the standard justifications should
be qualified. Some or all may work, given that man is corrupt and enslaved. In that condition, pragmatic justifications are acceptable.
The best practices and justifications are those that do the least harm.
But taken in themselves, and palliatives apart, none are morally justified. From all this, it appears that the only criterion of justified
ownership given by Rousseau is that according to which property is a
product of that law which is authorized by the general will.

But law as it is, and not "laws as they could be," is clearly insufficient. Legal equality as it exists is, as Rousseau succinctly
notes, equality which is "only apparent and illusory: it serves only
to maintain the poor in misery and the rich in usurpation." (III,
367).

Property, Law and Freedom

What Rousseau's account of property comes down to, "the bottom
line" as men of property put it, is a distinction between property as
"it is" and as "it ought to be," and I do not doubt that there is a
positivist criticism which applies here in the same way that Bentham
believes it applies with regard to law. However, I want to consider
whether or not Rousseau's recommendations enable self-mastery.

Law authorized by the general will is law which comes from all
equally and applies to all equally. Crudely put, the legal rules
should apply generally, all should subscribe to them and all should
willingly subject themselves to them. These conditions can be satisfied, Rousseau thinks, if the standard of the rules is the common good.

With regard to property, my ownership would be a conditional legal
power or right in the sense that I could use, consume, sell or transfer it, subject to the condition that these activities be consistent
with the common good as judged by the general will.

Some would recognize moral (and prudential) benefits in this re-
commendation. Rousseau would first have to qualify what he means in
saying that laws apply equally and universally. Given his preference
for progressive taxation, gradations of wealth have to be somehow
singled out. But categories could be established and the rules applied universally within them. In that event, all within the category
could be treated fairly one with another, with no individual being
victimized. Along these lines property distribution, looking always
to the common good, could be regulated in such a way that none would
be too badly off and none too well off. Moreover, property would become a democratic right in that the citizen-sovereigns themselves
would judge which rules applied or should be replaced by others as circumstances altered. Disciples of Hobbes, Locke, Mandeville, *et al*
would be distinctly unhappy with property as a democratic right. Conspicuous consumption and natural rights to property sanctified con-
stitutionally would have no place in Rousseau's system.[9] Property
would, however, assume its rightful role as a means regulated by moral
values of liberty, equality and fraternity. Citizens would, conceiv-
ably, gain a sense of self-respect stemming from their nature as moral
beings and would respect that nature in others.

Thus one can see in broad outline, at least, how Rousseau views
property in relation to the questions:

(1) How do men become slaves?

(2) If men were free, how could they live in free association?

What remains unclear is an acceptable answer to the third question: How do slaves become free? One problem is easy to discern.
The slaves of property are voluntary: apparently they like it that
way: Hobbes and Co. have many supporters and they control the voting
shares. That is a practical problem which cannot be solved by moral
philosophy nor even, it seems, by political action if that means a
change in the mechanics of government.

However, philosophy can express Rousseau's problem more adequately and there may be value in that. Althusser has written a brilliant
essay, but its main thrust seems wrong.[10] He argues convincingly that

Rousseau sees man as an alienated being, but then he produces an elaboration of contradictions which Rousseau is supposed to have devised
to remove the problem of alienation. However, if that alienation is
social, as Rousseau, Althusser and I all agree, then Althusser's claim
that Rousseau sought a theoretical solution fails to convince. Social
alienation is not dissipated by fancy argument.

The source of Althusser's mistake probably arises from a failure
to distinguish between questions two and three i.e. how can free humans
live together? and how can slaves be made free? Althusser treats Rousseau's answer to question two as an answer to question three and, not
surprisingly, finds Rousseau's answer inadequate. Rousseau does not
confuse the two and plainly sees the difficulty embedded in the third
question. He expresses it by saying that in order for men to rule
themselves by the general will, it is necessary for them to be before-
hand that which they will become as a result of rule by the general
will. The effect, as he puts it, must somehow become the cause. (III,
383). That is, he seems to mean that the condition of the proper action of the rule of the general will is that humans be free and re-
spectful of human nature in themselves and others. Sovereignty of the
general will can create freedom and respect, but it also presupposes
them. Hence, the conundrum that the effect be the cause.

This leads into the fundamental difficulty revealed by the third
question: how can you free those who do not want to be freed, without
violating their freedom? The liberation of voluntary slaves is inconsistent with moral liberty, that liberty which alone ensures self-
mastery. (III, 365). Moral liberty is "obedience to a law which one
prescribes to oneself." Rousseau's "premise" is that humans consent
to slavery; his "conclusion" is that they must consent to be ruled by
the general will if they are to be free. But how is it possible to
get from the "premise" to the "conclusion" without contradicting the
"conclusion?" By liberating them without their consent? But if you
"force them to be free," you deny that very moral liberty which is
their only guarantee of self-mastery. Rousseau does not call upon the
slaves of the world to throw off their chains. If the inconsistency
is to be avoided, men must wait "to feel the beat of the angels'
wings." Some argue that humans are "living outside themselves" to a
degree that suggests that Rousseau's day of reckoning is not far off.

Let us conclude this essay with a qualification. There is one way in which our assertions could be wrong. At the beginning of the *Contract*, Rousseau says that he proposes "to take men as they are," and he says also that he does not know how the change from freedom to slavery came about. From this basis one might argue, stretching things a bit here and a bit there, that he wants to withdraw the assertion that humans are enslaved and treat them as being free. This interpretation involves repudiation of the argument of the *Discourse* and ignores many allusions in later writings to the enslaved condition of humans, including several in the *Contract* itself. The interpretation has been tried several times, consciously and unconsciously; but it gelds him and leaves him a tidy liberal *comme les autres*, which seems neither desirable nor correct.

FOOTNOTES

*This paper is based on work done with the assistance of a Canada Council research grant, a research grant in France sponsored jointly by Canada and France, and a Trent University research grant. I wish to express my gratitude for this support.

1   A preliminary search of the secondary literature revealed no work directly and exclusively devoted to the subject. However, the following are interesting and worth consulting:

    (a)   Baczko, B., *Rousseau: Solitude et communauté* (Paris: Mouton, 1974).

    (b)   Starobinski, J., *J.-J. Rousseau: La transparence et l'obstacle* (Paris: Gallimard, 1971).

    (c)   Lemos, R., *Rousseau's Political Philosophy* (Athens: The University of Georgia Press, 1977).

    (d)   Coletti, L., *From Rousseau to Lenin* (New York: Monthly Review Press, 1972).

    (e)   Althusser, L., *Politics and History* (London, 1972).

    (f)   Cobban, A., *Rousseau and the Modern State* (London: Allen & Unwin, 1964).

    (g)   Secrétan, P., "La Thème de la Propriété à Travers Rousseau, Hegel et Marx," *Revue de Théologie et de Philosophie*, 1970.

2   Jean-Jacques Rousseau, *Oeuvres Complètes*, tome III, *Bibliothèque de la Pléiade*, eds., B. Gagnebin et M. Raymond. Since all textual references are to volumes three (1964) and four (1969) of this edition, I shall hereafter cite only the volume and page *e.g.* III, 107.

3   On metaphor in political philosophy, see Margaret Macdonald, "The language of Political Theory," in A. Flew (ed.), *Logic and Language* (Oxford: Blackwell, 1955), pp. 167-186.

4   But see Coletti, 1 (d) above, pp. 143-193.

5   Compare L. Becker, *Property Rights* (Boston: Routledge & Kegan Paul, 1977), pp. 67-68.

6   For an excellent summary, see: S. Benn, "Property," *The Encyclopedia of Philosophy*, editor, P. Edwards, Volume Five.

    Other important sources are:

    (1)   Honoré, A. M., "Ownership," in *Oxford Essays in Jurisprudence* (First Series), edited by A. G. Guest (Oxford: Oxford University Press, 1968).

(2) *Salmond on Jurisprudence*, Twelfth Edition by P. J.
Fitzgerald (London: Sweet & Maxwell, 1966).

7 See R. Lemos, *Rousseau's Political Philosophy*, Chapter VII.

8 *Op. cit.*

9 The claim that Rousseau sanctions natural rights is a perennial.
In one sense, I think there is something in it. However, let me
give a final consideration to a claim for a natural right to property in relation to the general will, because it is here that the
real difficulty lies. In a state which has as its sovereign the
general will, Rousseau might offer four reasons for a natural right
to private property. One, it follows from a natural right to self-
preservation. Two, it follows from a natural right to liberty.
Three, it gives one a sense of place and of attachment to one's
community. (IV, 858). Four, it is necessary to the development
of moral nature. If we suppose these are Rousseau's reasons, we
have to admit they are unconvincing. The natural right to self-
preservation is, I hold, an unsupported claim. Even if it were
true that every human always has the strongest desire for self-
preservation, this would be a matter of fact and not one of right.
The objectives mentioned in the other three reasons are fulfilled
by the general will. If we suppose, consistently with developmental natural law, that the highest stage of moral development
for an individual or a people is rule by the general will, then
liberty is expressed by the general will and not in property. The
third reason collapses into the fourth. A sense of community is
necessary to development of moral nature. (IV, 858) And the development of moral nature, like the exercise of liberty, is best
realized by the sovereignty of the general will.

The consequence of this criticism of Rousseau's supposed defence
of private property places it, in Rousseau's thought, in much the
same position as government. In the *Contract* (Book III, Chapters 3
and 8), Rousseau argues that if the sovereign is the general will
then one can be pragmatic about the form of government. Presumably
the general will decides upon the suitable type of government given
the circumstances of the people. Except for obvious exceptions
specified in the essay, the same should hold for property. That
is, logically Rousseau should be indifferent to means of ownership,
private or public or a mix of both and depend upon the general will
to make the judgment in terms of the circumstances.

In the discussion Professor Macpherson objected to my conclusion
somewhat as follows: Rousseau could not be as indifferent as my
conclusion suggests. Rather, Rousseau is best understood as the
first and greatest apologist of the *petit bourgeois*. He cited the
quotation from *Political Economy* (III, 262-3) and the principle
that each should own enough but none, too much. (III, 367, footnote). What Rousseau supports, therefore, is an economy of small,
independent producers.

The question is difficult. Texts can be cited which suggest
an opposite conclusion, especially the important ones of the *Contract* and *Emile* (III, 381) and (IV, 249). There Rousseau claims
that the best state, ruled by the general will, is one whereby

"the self is transported into the common unity." The difference
in principle seems to be as follows. On the one hand, and in
certain places, Rousseau favours economic self-sufficiency such
that one man's economic dependence on another is minimal. On the
other hand, and in the places which I cite, he favours the greatest possible mutual dependency. In the second case, the independence of each is replaced by the dependence of each upon all others
such that none can do anything without the help of others. The
difficulty arises precisely from imagining exactly what the second
case means concretely: oddly, the same sort of problem arises in
trying to imagine property-relations in the future Marxist society. In a state governed by the general will, where all are united
by mutual respect, the importance of property-relations would,
presumably, wither.

10 See 1 (e) above.

ROUSSEAU ON LIFE, LIBERTY AND PROPERTY:
A Comment on MacAdam

Professor MacAdam set out to expound Rousseau's theory of property and could find nothing amounting to a theory to be expounded. This
is a frustrating experience but not an unfamiliar one. With only a
dash of Rousseauesque rhetorical exaggeration it could be said that
little "amounting to a succinct, coherent theory" on any subject "appropriately supported by argument" can be discovered in Rousseau.
Rousseau launches discussions of clusters of topics as they become
relevant for his concerns. To see how much overlap there is in these
discussions and how they shed light on one another is one way to tease
something like a "theory" out of Rousseau's social thought. Apparent
contradictions can sometimes be resolved when the several accounts of
a topic are carefully interwoven, as Rousseau promised us and MacAdam
has demonstrated persuasively. When tensions remain after this exercise has been attempted, they may indicate not sloppiness in Rousseau's
social thought, but his complex appreciation of the paradoxes that compose *la condition humaine*.

Rousseau's "theory" of property is notoriously one of the more
paradox-ridden or contradictory aspects of his social thought. In this
essay we will attack the problem by taking up MacAdam's three questions
and giving answers that are sufficiently different from his own to hint
at the various ways Rousseau's dicta on property can be read. The
three queries posed by MacAdam - how do free men become slaves? if men
were free, how could they live in free association? and how do slaves
become free? - have the great virtue of moving immediately to the central preoccupations in Rousseau's social thought: liberty and association. I will adopt MacAdam's framework without the hypothesis from
which it is derived, the idea of a "developmental natural law" in
Rousseau's work. I have reservations about this hypothesis as stated
but do not find it crucial to the three questions themselves, nor to
Rousseau's ideas on property.

Liberty and association are the heart of Rousseau's concerns.
Property is important to each of these, rather than a third topic of
equal importance in itself. This helps explain why it becomes relevant to Rousseau's arguments precisely at those points when it is

introduced, rather than requiring to be addressed directly and independently. Surely one of MacAdam's most important insights is that
there is for Rousseau no natural right to property in the Lockean
sense. Property is a product of human convention and devising. Like
all other products of human artifice, laws and institutions of all
sorts, it has a double-edged potential for good or evil in human life.
To explain why property, perhaps more than any other human institution,
has been the ground for evil in human experience and how it could under
carefully specified conditions be bent to good purposes instead, are
the main points Rousseau wants to make about it. This is what I take
MacAdam to mean by the "moral dimensions" of property, and on this I
am in full agreement with his reading.

Rousseau's concept of property is perhaps best approached by way
of a comparison with Locke. Although Rousseau dissents from the Lockean idea of a "natural right" to property, his discussions have certain
important features in common with those of the man he calls "le sage
Locke." Some of his passages appear to have been written with Locke
in mind, with the intention of showing where he went wrong and of
avoiding the abuses of the concept of property that Locke had himself
embraced. Like Locke, Rousseau names as the "constitutive elements of
human existence," which men form societies in order to protect, "their
goods, their liberties, and their lives;" but he does not subsume these
things under the general heading of "property."[1] He assumes, with
Locke, that the earth and its fruits are common to all members of our
species, made available to us by nature so that we may preserve ourselves. The right of self-preservation indicates that we may take what
we need as individuals from this common store and that we should not
take more than we can use to preserve ourselves, especially if this
means that other human beings will be deprived of the means to preserve
themselves. It is at this point that Locke and Rousseau diverge. For
Locke, the right of self-preservation is itself a right to property,
to the ownership of whatever we appropriate in the process of preserving ourselves. The mixing of our labor with this thing, even so simple a labor as stooping to pick up an acorn, makes it our property.
Governments are instituted to confirm and secure this right, but do
not create it. The limitations on the exercise of this right in the
simple theory of property - that I must leave enough and as good for
others and must not take more than I can use before it spoils - are

easily circumvented, for Locke, by the invention of money and the
structures of capitalist accumulation.

For Rousseau, the right of self-preservation cannot be extended
to cover any actions that involve taking more from the common stock
than we need for our immediate subsistence. It is not itself the basis
of a right to property. For a claim of ownership to make sense, something further is required. Rousseau also distinguishes between possession and property. The former is a claim that can be advanced in several ways: that I was the first occupier of this land, that I have
mixed my labor with it, that I have successfully taken it by force.[2]
Some of these claims may have more plausibility or carry more weight
than others, but none confers a right to property. Such a right comes
into existence only when human groups have established rules for distributing lands and legitimating ownership. Only by appealing to such
conventions can I make a statement about property.

Another way in which Locke's attitudes towards property and Rousseau's are similar and yet divergent is in an area this workshop has
wrestled with repeatedly: whether property relations are relations between men and men, or between men and things. For Locke and Rousseau
both dimensions are present; property relations are relations between
men and things that have crucial consequences for the relations between
those men and other men. For Locke, the most important of the two relationships is that between men and things; the consequences for other
men are derivative from this. If I own this land, in Lockean theory,
the most fundamental aspect of that ownership is what I do to this
land, working it, making it bring forth fruit. If others work on it
for wages at my behest, or as my slaves, this relationship between me
and my workers is dominated by my ownership of the thing itself that
makes such a relationship possible, and their potential relationship
to this thing, this land, is neutralized or blocked by my prior claim
of ownership. For Rousseau, the claim to own this land is on the face
of it a statement about a relationship between me and this thing, but
its most important aspect is a relationship between me and other human
beings. It is a notice to others to keep out, and it changes my relationship with them in certain crucial ways. The ownership of this
thing deprives them of the use of it and it becomes an obstacle to my
having a direct and unmediated relationship with them as other human
individuals. By owning a thing, I become dependent on it; but this
dependence is less important, less debilitating, than the dependence

on other human beings that also follows from the invention of property
and the complicated economic structures that accompany it. For Locke,
Robinson Crusoe on his island could have "made a property" by planting
a garden. For Rousseau, the existence of the garden would not constitute "property" since this notion has meaning only when there are other
potential claimants to be excluded from it.

With this general background in mind, we can turn to MacAdam's
three questions. A great deal of Rousseau's social thought could be
subsumed under the discussion of any one of them. In this essay I will
focus each of the questions on a particular episode in Rousseau's writings. Rousseau was fond of vignettes as a way of making more vivid the
ideas he wanted to express, and he also liked casting himself as one of
the participants in these episodes, more or less disguised. The three
vignettes I have chosen are among the most familiar in Rousseau's
works. MacAdam refers in passing to them all: the episode of the
first fencer in the *Discourse on Inequality*; the scene with the gardener in the second book of *Emile*; and the "moment of formation" of the
community in the *Social Contract*.

1. How do free men become slaves?

The first man to enclose a piece of ground and claim "this is
mine," asserts Rousseau, founded civil society and brought down upon
mankind a whole chain of evils that we might otherwise have been
spared. This first fencer, the symbolic representative of the notion
of possession and exclusive appropriation, is matched by an anti-
fencer, who has several traits Rousseau associated with himself. He
is a prophet who would have saved mankind by pulling up the stakes and
crying to his brethren that they were lost if they forgot the simple
truth that the earth belongs to no one and its fruits to all. The
prophet, alas, did not appear when he was needed, and free men set out
along the road that led to slavery. Savage man, carrying himself whole
and entire about him, acting from the desire for self-preservation - a
neutral *amour de soi* - began to extend himself into his possessions and
form the complicated relationships with other human beings that accompany an economy of ownership. From what sorts of ills, specifically,
would he have been spared if the anti-fencer had prevailed?[3]

The first fencer, in claiming that "this land is mine," is blamed
for introducing "the idea of property," which requires a number of
other complicated ideas for human beings to make sense of it.

Rousseau's argument is that once this idea has been grasped, it leads
men by terrible and easy stages to the institution of government which
alone can protect this claim against interference and establish it effectively as a "right" rather than a statement about ephemeral control
over something and an expression of intent. The idea of property is
shown to be directly associated with, even in a sense responsible for,
those conditions that enslave free human beings - debilitating dependence upon other men, submission to domination and finally government
itself. Unlike MacAdam, I do not think that Rousseau construes this
slavery as a form of property. Men in becoming enslaved submit to
chains and mastery; they lose their independence, their wholeness,
their control of their own lives. But they do not become "things" at
the disposal of other human beings who themselves remain free of enslavement. The rich and poor, the powerful and the underdog are all
enslaved; they all lack the independence, the autonomy that Rousseau
associated with freedom; none of them enjoys self-mastery and integrity. The institution of property is crucial in this process, but it
distorts Rousseau's argument, I think, to speak as if becoming enslaved for him means that some human beings become the property of
others.

The initial factor in the enslavement of free men is the deforma-
tion of neutral *amour de soi* into *amour propre*. The term *amour propre*
itself carries within it semantically and psychologically the taint of
la propriété. It is a form of self-love that regards the self as a
thing to be owned, advanced, invested in, and compared with other
selves to determine value in competitive situations. I am no longer
simply one individual among others, with pressing needs for subsistence. I regard my self as "mine," as peculiar and particular to me,
as an object to be cultivated and protected...as my property. But I
cannot validate my self by myself; this requires the admiration and
esteem of other human beings like but separate from myself. And thus
each of us begins to attempt to advance our properties in ourselves
competitively, to force or seduce recognition for our values as a self.
This makes each of us dependent on others in a debilitating struggle
and it also leads to the notion of property in other things, as extensions of myself, as exercises of my own self-activity, such as my hut,
my tools, my land.

The next step in this enslavement of free men is that as I become
more and more dependent on these things that I possess as extensions

of myself, I also become more and more dependent on other human beings, less and less sufficient to myself. The ownership of things engenders covetousness for more; the effort to advance and cultivate the self requires new goods, new things, which cannot be provided without the cooperation of other human beings. Rudimentary ownership leads to the division of labor as human beings develop new needs that can only be satisfied by a complex economy. Thus I am made dependent on others not only for my self-esteem, but for the cooperative labor that provides those artificial things that I have come to need.

The final steps are the establishment of domination as such and the legitimation of domination as government. Once complicated property relationships have been instituted, some men become richer than others, and this wealth itself becomes a source of domination. I can use my wealth to buy the services of others, which involves the ability to command them to do what I require. The more property I have, the more I fear losing it and the more vulnerable I am to robbery of the goods I have appropriated. It is at this point in Rousseau's developmental tale that the true status of the notion of property is analyzed most carefully. Referring to the rich, he says that "whatever color they might try to give to their usurpations," they know that fundamentally their possessions are founded only on "a precarious and abusive title," ordinarily nothing more than the successful use of force. Even those who have gained their wealth by their own industry have no better leg to stand on, since effort and industry alone cannot create right. The voice of the anti-fencer is heard once more, rejecting all these purported claims of entitlement:

> Who gave you this standing? and in virtue of what
> do you claim to reward yourself at our expense for
> a labor that we did not ask of you? Do you not
> know that a multitude of your brothers die or suf-
> fer dire need of that which you have in excess,
> and that the express and unanimous consent of the
> entire human species would have been needed to al-
> low you to appropriate from the common subsistence
> anything that went beyond what you needed for your
> own?[4]

Against Locke's assertion that labor confers right and that consent is not needed to found the right of property, Rousseau argues that nothing short of unanimous consent would serve to legitimate excess appropriation and that industry and effort in and of themselves confer no rights. Having no arguments to make in response to the eloquence of

the anti-fencer, the rich man pressed by necessity then hits upon the
clever notion of instituting government to protect and legitimate his
possessions, enlisting his adversaries as his defenders and giving mankind "other institutions as favorable to himself as the law of nature
was against him."

The ultimate enslavement of men originally free is thus predicated
on the need to protect property and secure to each man the possession
of what he owns, and the laws which favor the haves against the have-
nots thus become the most important chains binding enslaved humanity.
The "right" of property is shown not only to lack foundation in the
laws of nature, but in fact to be instituted in direct contravention of
what those laws enjoin.   Rousseau as head Leveller, as anti-fencer, as
the prescient prophet against property who did not appear in time, provides in the *Discourse on Inequality* one of the most scathing indict-
ments of the institution of property in all of social thought.   How
did free men become slaves?   By hitting upon this diabolical idea of
property.

2.   <u>If men were free, how could they live in free association?</u>
     In the education of Emile, the primary value is liberty, which is
identified with autonomy, the avoidance of dependence upon the wills of
other human beings and (less important, but still relevant) upon those
things one owns.   Emile is not solitary; he will live with other human
beings and yet avoid becoming subordinate to their wills.   Nor is he
an ascetic; he will own property and live comfortably, but avoid becoming so attached to his possessions that he becomes enslaved by his
need of them.   From birth, his training is directed towards making him
capable of independence in both these respects.   His needs and his powers are to be brought in balance, and he is to be taught to respect the
limitations provided by necessity, rather than the rules concocted for
his behavior by another man.[5]   The only rules he respects are the laws
made by the society of which he is a part, and his happiness and liberty are unavoidably threatened to the extent that the society is deficient in its lawmaking.   Emile is to be made as free as possible, but
only in an association with other free men could he be wholly free.
Emile itself cannot guarantee such an association; but it can show us
how one individual would achieve freedom for himself and suggest how
an association of such individuals would live together, as well as how
a single free individual must adapt himself to an unfree society.

In the second book of *Emile*, Rousseau attacks the problem of property from a direction quite different from the one employed by the
anti-fencer of the second *Discourse*. He gives us a further insight into the psychology of ownership by stating that "it is a disposition
natural to man to regard as his whatever is in his power."[6] The child
who has only to demand something in order to obtain it "thus thinks
himself the proprietor of the universe," and regards all other human
beings as his slaves, put there expressly to help him carry out his
will. This is the first impulse that an education for freedom must
combat. And since a child before the age of reason is incapable of
understanding moral arguments, of construing his relationship with
other human beings on moral grounds, his first experiences must be
those of impersonal strength and weakness, of the necessary consequences of his own acts, not those of authority and submission or duty and
obligation. His attempts to order others to carry out his will must
be ignored, and no one must give him commands. The first lessons he
learns must not be lessons in how to deal with other human beings as
moral beings, but lessons in necessity and in how to deal with things.
He must be taught to respect those things that cannot defend themselves
against his will; and this means, says Rousseau, that the first idea to
which he should be introduced is the idea of property. Property is
thus given an educative function at the very beginning of Emile's education, the first positive notion that he must understand.

The episode of the gardener and the ill-fated beans is Rousseau's
depiction of the learning-experience constructed by Emile's tutor (who
is of course a manifestation of Rousseau himself) to implant the idea
of property. We are told specifically that it involves "going back to
the origin of property," and this is identified with agricultural labor, the planting and tending of vegetables as a sign of human creative
power and activity.[7] On this point the accounts of property in *Emile*
and the second *Discourse* are in complete harmony; it is agriculture,
and the distribution of land that accompanies it, which is identified
with the primordial notion of property in the discussion of inequality.
Emile has seen gardens and wants to become a gardener. Together with
his tutor he takes possession of a piece of land by the labor of planting a bean. This act, together with the process of caring for the
beans from day to day - giving his time, his labor, even "his person"
to this project - is explained to Emile by his tutor as what it means
that something should "belong" to him.

One day, however - "ô spectacle! ô douleur!" - Emile hurries up
with his watering can to discover that the beans are all pulled up.
The spot chosen by the two would-be gardeners was part of the land
controlled by the real gardener of the household, who had planted pre-
cious Maltese melons in the very spot later appropriated by Emile for
his beans. This conflict is resolved in several stages. It seems at
first that the gardener's prior labor gave him title to the land; but
no, it was because the land was tilled by his father before him. All
the land is now occupied by such inheritors, so that the activity of
laboring itself has become irrelevant as a basis for establishing
claims of ownership. Property is thus shown to rest on the foundation
of human convention, to be distributed effectively by laws of inheritance, which confirm and protect the rights of the "original first oc-
cupiers" in ages long past and make the claims of the expenditure of
labor irrelevant to present economies.

The lesson is deftly taught. Emile learns first of all the primitive Lockean joys of labor as a basis for taking possession and then
has such a sensation rendered rudely irrelevant by the complicated
structures of modern Lockean society. He learns that things are in
fact owned by other people and that the phenomenon of ownership involves exclusion of other human beings from whatever it is that forms
a property, unless they secure the express consent of the owner. But
underneath this apparently simple and charming little episode there are
other problems suggested and left unresolved. To anyone familiar with
the fifth chapter of Locke's *Second Treatise*, the fact that it is the
gardener who claims the right to exclude Emile from the land requires
mulling over. It is the servant of Emile himself, who "cut the turfs"
and planted melons to enhance his table, who denies him property. To
anyone familiar with Rousseau's own second *Discourse*, it is significant
that good sturdy beans, a staple of human subsistence, are ousted in
civilized society by the superior claims of luxurious Maltese melons.

After this first complicated lesson, little attention is given to
property in this treatise until the very end. Emile's final lesson,
like his first, is about property. He comes to understand the extra-
ordinarily complicated relationship between ownership of things and
mastery of oneself. Both extremes in the sphere of property lead to a
loss of liberty. If Emile clings to his wealth, he becomes dependent
on the things he owns and is not able to control his own desires and

needs; if he renounces all possessions he becomes anxious and needy for
subsistence and this comes to dominate his life.

> What then shall I do with this fortune my parents
> have bequeathed to me? I will begin by not depend-
> ing on it in the least; I will loosen all the ties
> that attach me to it; if I am left with it, it re-
> mains with me; if someone takes it from me, they do
> not take away my own self with it. I will never
> torment myself to hold on to it, but I will rest
> steady in my place. Rich or poor, I will be free.[8]

So Emile takes up his inheritance, marries Sophie, and in becoming a
property-owner and head of a family, becomes a citizen and confirms his
mastery of himself. Since the government of his *pays* is only a "simul-
acrum" of a free association, he cannot be truly a free citizen among
others; but he can welcome the protection provided even by ill-made
laws and continue to display in his own actions the love of virtue and
consistent morality that are the consequence of his own freedom.

If men were free, how could they live in free associations? Emile
is free; but he does not live in a free association. He exemplifies
what it would mean to be educated as a free man from birth, prepared to
encounter other individuals on the healthy ground of their own autonomy, practicing simple virtues, and above all avoiding the extremes of
wealth and poverty that make a mockery of independence. But Rousseau
leaves unresolved a question he raises at the very outset of the book:
whether Emile, who is raised to be a man, could also be the citizen of
a free *patrie*. He indicates that the education of a citizen is diametrically opposed to that of a free man; yet by the end of the novel
this opposition is softened. It appears that Emile's education has
prepared him to be a citizen, to take his part in the affairs of a
well-constituted polity, to cooperate with other men in making the laws
that govern their lives. It is his misfortune that no such polity actually exists, so that he must "sacrifice his own interest to the common interest," even though all those around him continue to behave
selfishly and remain enslaved.[9]

3. How do slaves become free?

In educating Emile, the fortunate tutor begins with an unspoiled
infant and can raise him for freedom as an individual without first
having to free him from slavery. This process is difficult enough. To
free a group of slaves would seem many times more demanding; yet it has
the advantage, as a project in the cultivation of autonomy, that it

promises to produce an entire community of free men rather than an isolated virtuous individual. The *Social Contract* provides Rousseau's
answer to MacAdam's last question: men formerly enslaved by their own
appetites become free in achieving autonomy, in obeying a law they prescribe to themselves. They do so only with the aid of a legislator, a
superhuman dispassionate intelligence, which may be what MacAdam has in
mind when he refers to the "beat of angels' wings." But Rousseau does
not require that men themselves become angels, nor does he pose the
paradox of freeing enslaved men in such a harsh fashion that it becomes
impossible to resolve, which is what MacAdam asserts. The legislator
makes patriots of selfish men, teaching them to extend their self-love
into the love of the entire community, to identify their individuality
as part of a larger whole, to alienate themselves without fear of self-
loss, in order to discover their own autonomy in community.[10] In the
course of this process former slaves become full human beings, moral
entities, rather than animals subordinated to their own desires and to
one another.

By adopting the metaphor of the "social contract" Rousseau emphasizes the "moment of formation" of the community, a solemn and sacred
assembling of wills, a giving up of selves and goods that transmutes
individuals into citizens. This "moment" is clearly symbolic, since
the process of creating free citizens out of slaves is subsequently
shown to be a lengthy one of shaping and education. Rousseau may well
have projected aspects of himself as a creative social theorist into
the quasi-angelic legislator figure who makes the moment possible. It
is certain that his imaginative abilities allowed him to depict the
high drama of the "moment of formation" with unusual vividness, making
us feel that we, along with Rousseau himself, are present at the creation.[11] The important thing for our purposes is what happens to possessions in this moment and how it becomes the basis for the right of
property.

Rousseau asserts that "each member of the community gives himself
to it at the moment it is formed, just as he finds himself at that moment, himself and all his resources, of which the goods that he possesses form a part."[12] The giving of these goods to the community con-
veys to the sovereign (that is, the community of individual wills associated in the *volonté générale*) a specific type of mastery over those
things that is one of the attributes of sovereignty. It is a type of
possession, not of property. Rousseau is quite careful to draw his

distinctions here and to avoid making it seem that the sovereign "owns" these goods; and he does not fall into the confusions that MacAdam attributes to him. From the point of view of other sovereigns, the sovereign possesses the goods of all members of the community by the right of first occupier. From another point of view, the goods in land are brought together as the territory of the *patrie* itself. In giving up their possessions to the community, the citizens create a "public good" of lands and resources over which the sovereign has the right of control and disposition for public purposes. This ensures that the citizens are appropriately dependent on the community; by sharing control of their goods, by having legitimate access to them through taxation, the sovereign ensures their fidelity.[13] But the right of the sovereign over goods is not a proprietary right. This right, in Rousseau's social theory, can only be enjoyed by individuals and only after the community has been established that can provide the basis for such a right by means of law. Rousseau remains true to the semantic and traditional notions of "property" as something that individuals and families enjoy, as opposed to the type of mastery over goods and lands enjoyed by public authority. This makes it possible for the sovereign and the proprietor each to have valid rights over the same land.

This is what Rousseau means by the passage that troubles MacAdam, that "possession does not change its nature in changing hands and become property in the hands of the sovereign." Individuals before society is established cannot have property, but only possess their goods; this possession is transferred to the community at the moment of formation when the sovereign acquires possession, which is not yet property. Property is something new, something made possible only by association and only for individuals and families, a type of control that they enjoy over their goods in the security of civil association.[14] The notion of a "public property" would therefore not make sense to Rousseau; he does not use this phrase in describing a possible community that could come into existence among individuals who do not possess anything at all, but instead settle a new terrain at the time their community is founded, and can agree either to enjoy it in common or else to divide it up among themselves as property.

At the end of his discussion of the creation of property, Rousseau makes an important statement that connects the concerns we discovered in the *Discourse on Inequality* and in *Emile*. After asserting that the

primary consequence of the institution of society is the creation of a
"moral and legitimate" equality among men unequal in other ways, he
says:

> Under bad governments this equality is only apparent
> and illusory. It works only to maintain the poor man
> in his misery and the rich one in his usurpation. In
> fact, laws are always useful to those who possess some-
> thing and harmful tho those who have nothing; from this
> it follows that the social state is only advantageous
> to human beings when they all have something, and none
> of them has too much.[15]

In practice, the application of this rule requires that "no citizen
should be sufficiently wealthy to buy another, and none poor enough to
have to sell himself."[16] The moderate amount of wealth enjoyed by
Emile and his less than ferocious attachment to his property are appropriate to citizens of a free association. Possession of goods in
enough sufficiency to keep a man from having to sell himself ensures
his personal independence and makes it possible for him to join with
others in the collective autonomy of lawmaking on an equal basis. Thus
property is shown to be essential to the enjoyment of true liberty in
society - both the civil liberty of independence from the wills of other individuals and the moral liberty of participation in making laws.

How do slaves become free? By the paradoxical act of alien-
ating themselves and all their possessions to the community, whole-
heartedly and with a full patriotic understanding of the meaning of
this symbolic act. In so doing they gain not only freedom but also
property, neither of which can be enjoyed by disassociated slaves.

FOOTNOTES

1 *Discours sur l'origine de l'inégalité*, in Jean-Jacques Rousseau, *Oeuvres complètes*, ed. Bernard Gagnebin and Marcel Raymond, in four volumes (Paris 1959-1969), vol. III, p. 180; *Discours sur l'économie politique*, III, 248. Locke's most sustained and familiar discussion of property is the fifth chapter of his *Second Treatise of Government*.

2 *Du contrat social*, *OC* III, 366 (book I, ch. 9).

3 *Discours sur...l'inégalité*, III, 164; the image of the savage carrying himself "toujours tout entier avec soi" is on p. 136.

4 III, 176-177.

5 *Emile*, in *OC* IV, book I.

6 IV, 314.

7 IV, 330-333; *cf.* the *Discours*, III, 173, on "Cères Législatrice."

8 IV, 856.

9 IV, 858; this topic is discussed in Keohane, "'The Masterpiece of Policy in our Century': Rousseau on the Morality of the Enlightenment," *Political Theory*, VI, 4 (November 1978), an essay which makes evident my agreement with MacAdam's idea that Rousseau was bent on attacking a deficient "modern morality."

10 *Contrat social*, book II, chs. 6-12; David Gauthier has a fine discussion of this process in his paper for the Rousseau Bicentennial Congress held at Trent University in June, 1978.

11 Keohane, "Political Theory and the Uses of the Self," *Journal of Politics*, XXXVII (1975).

12 *Contrat social*, III, 365 (book I, ch. 9).

13 III, 366; this same point is reiterated in the *Discours sur l'économie politique*, III, 263.

14 This is borne out by Rousseau's discussion of property in the *Economie politique*, where he carefully distinguishes household or private economy from that general or public economy which is his topic and discusses taxation as the point where they intersect. There is one passage (III, 242) where he refers to property as "anterior" to public administration, but this is quite consonant with the reading offered here, since he is relying upon his familiar distinction between administration (or *gouvernement*) and *la souveraineté* (III, 244). Property is made possible by the creation of sovereignty and then becomes one of the objects to which administration must address itself.

15 *Contrat social*, III, 367 (book I, 9).

16 III, 391-392 (book II, 11).

Douglas Long makes a systematic presentation of Bentham's views on property from two perspectives: conceptual adequacy and humanistic concern. Along the former dimension, Bentham's conceptual apparatus is presented as he developed it through his many critiques of Blackstone. Along the latter dimension, Bentham is criticized for having little concern for distributive justice. He was so preoccupied with protecting the security of expectations in the present that he did not appreciate the necessity of a more equal distribution of property in the future.

BENTHAM ON PROPERTY

> ...The rich have feelings, if I can put it this way,
> in every part of their possessions...
>
> Rousseau
>
> ("...les riches étant, poour ainsi dire, sensibles
> dans toutes les parties de leurs Biens...",
> *Discours sur l'inégalité*, in *Oeuvres Complètes*
> (Pléiade), III, 179.)

Introduction

Jeremiah Bentham always hoped that his precocious son Jeremy would some day achieve power, glory and riches as a great lawyer-statesman. In a sense Jeremy Bentham laboured all his life to fulfill that dream according to his own lights. One might even say that in his own way he succeeded. But success, such as it was, came not in the public arena through the practice of law and the attainment of high public office but covertly and tardily in public recognition, widespread in Bentham's later years, of his role as counsellor to both lawyers and politicians. It was not Bentham's fate to grace (if the word can be used) the House of Commons, but it was his fate to have a "Character of Jeremy Bentham" given there and to have his influence on legal and political reform over-estimated, at least in some quarters, for generations after his death.[1] Unlike the jurisprudential foe with whose failings he remained obsessed all his life, he received no knighthood and never became a judge. One suspects, given his opinion of "judge-made law" (common law, which he found everywhere and always inferior to codified statute law), that had the opportunity arisen he would have refused it.[2]

It should surprise no one that Bentham never did and never could sit on the Bench where Sir William Blackstone perched with eminent comfort. Yet despite almost universal awareness of the stark contrast exhibited by the respective legal writings of Blackstone and Bentham, we have available to us surprisingly little detailed analysis of the precise nature of their accounts of the legal - and indeed the political - problems of their day. Certain modes of disagreement such as common law vs. statute law, natural rights vs. legal positivism and the general tenor of "everything as it should be Blackstone"[3] vs. the

shrill radical reformism of the young legal encyclopedist Bentham are
familiar to us; but a great many germane legal and political issues
seized upon in the course of the long (and somewhat one-sided) history
of Bentham's attacks on Blackstone and on his idolatrous worship of
the "matchless constitution" have yet to be seriously explored. A
cursory review of Bentham's early writings gives ample evidence of the
diversity of such issues. Bentham's *Fragment on Government* (1776),
probably his most readable and widely read publication, arose from critical reflection on one paragraph of one section of Blackstone's Introduction to his *Commentaries on the Laws of England* (1765-9). Bentham's *Comment on the Commentaries* (written in 1774-5) deals only incompletely with the concerns raised by his scrutiny of those same introductory portions of Blackstone's work. *Of Laws in General* (written
in 1778-1782) bears in its title and substance a notable similarity to
one section of Blackstone's *Commentaries* themselves.[4]   And the Bentham
Manuscripts contain a great deal more Blackstone-inspired material.

No single term or concept is better suited as the focus for an
attempt to probe the Blackstone-Bentham relationship than the idea of
property. Both men acknowledged it to be a notion of unsurpassed importance as an object of study and discussion. Blackstone wrote as
follows:

> There is nothing which so generally strikes
> the imagination, and engages the affections of man-
> kind, as the right of property; or that sole and
> despotic dominion which one man claims and exercises
> over the external things of the world, in total ex-
> clusion of the right of any other individual in the
> universe.[5]

It is absolutely clear from the contents of Bentham's early (though
unfortunately unpublished) manuscripts that the young "philosopher of
Queen's Square Place" made his first serious and sustained attempt at
an analysis of property in reply to that of Blackstone.

The present paper begins from this analysis in its reconstruction
of the development of Bentham's thoughts on property. Two lines of
development are traced. First, it seems clear that Bentham's life-
long concern with the family of legal terms relating to property,
terms such as "title," "conveyance," "occupation," "possession," "interest" and of course "property" itself, originated in his attempts at
clear definitions of these terms intended to supersede Blackstone's
jurisprudential cosmetic arts.[6]   Secondly, it is equally clear that

Bentham's "definitional" concern for property was matched by an "operative" concern for the protection of property set in a social context
much broader than that of a strict academic approach to the study of
the law. Political, economic and social vocabularies revolved around
the term "property" as much as did the legal idiom. If "title" and
"tenure" must be defined in relation to property, so must "power,"
"right," "security," "interest" and "happiness" itself.

Bentham clearly evolved in his own estimation from censorial
jurisconsult to full-blown social scientist, from an author of intra-
mural critiques of the legal profession and "digestor" of laws to the
founder of a utilitarian utopia.[7] As his theoretical scope widened,
so the socio-political implications of his view of property unfolded
in their diversity. It was inevitable, however, that definitional
niceties would suffer as a result of Bentham's increasing awareness of
reforming necessities. A comprehensive account of the varied perspectives on property entailed or implied by Bentham's myriad social reform projects could fill a very substantial volume. The present discussion will involve only a selective study of some of the innovative
practical proposals into which Bentham incorporated explicit "operative" views on property.

Wherever one turns for a sample of Benthamic utilitarian projects
with implications of one kind or another for property, in the end one
returns to the examination of one set of values, relationships and institutions - those embodied in the definitional and operative aspects
(69.31) of the civil law - and to one ultimate goal as the object of
the operations of that law, namely distributive justice. This is not
to ignore happiness. Happiness is surely Bentham's blanket term for
the essential stuff with which distributive justice is concerned, the
family of feelings by reference to which the meaning and value of justice, indeed of all "goods" is determined. Our intention here is simply to resist the fascination with the chameleon (not to say chimera)
of happiness which tends to mesmerize (and occasionally appall) students of Bentham's utilitarianism. We shall turn instead to an intellectual construct whose pedigree extends back at least to that
classical master scientist of politics, Aristotle, i.e. distributive
justice, seeking to map out the features of a just distribution of
good things as Bentham would have portrayed it. In such a portrait it
is assumed that the role of "property" as entitlement, in some sense
or other of that word, is undeniably central.[8]

Finally a more contemporary, if more speculative, issue is addressed briefly: the much admired and much discussed theory of justice propounded by Professor Rawls[9] is in large part, by his own assertion, an attempt to supersede a view of justice (the most influential and substantial of those he examines) which he attributes to utilitarians.[10] Is Rawls talking about Bentham when he discusses the
utilitarian view of distributive justice? If so, has he effectively
refuted the kernel of that view? If not, does our examination of Bentham's thought give any cause for Rawlsian reconsideration?

Having attempted in successive sections to elucidate the genealogy, the terminology, the practicalities and the significance of Bentham's notion of property, we conclude our discussion with an attempt
to arrive, by reaction to Bentham's work, at an understanding of certain features of a comprehensive theory of property and, by the same
token, of the shortcomings of the one he produced.

Blackstone and Bentham on Property

The young Bentham seeking to make his mark as a censorial scientist of jurisprudence[11] communed, though not quite in Machiavellian
fashion, with an array of jurisconsults from the past. Some, especially natural law partisans such as Grotius, Pufendorf and Burlamaqui, he left in undisturbed repose. Others, like Hale, Coke, Littleton, Barrington and the French constitutional jurist Jean-Louis
Delolme, he regarded more seriously as shapers of his legal world.[12]
But the figure of Sir William Blackstone loomed above them all.
Blackstone literally shaped Bentham's life. Bentham could sum up his
evaluation of other legal theorists - even those of the stature of John
Locke - in a phrase (69.43). Blackstone required a life-long diatribe.
He did more than evoke comment from Bentham - he catapulted him into a
critical study of the very idea of law whose depth, intricacy and sig-
nificance Bentham himself could not have foreseen before he began it.

We learn by antithesis and example. Though he might have denied
it, Bentham, it seems clear, learned from Blackstone in both ways.
Though the style and structure of his corpus of legal writings were
emphatically antithetical to Blackstone's, the topography of the socio-economic worlds mapped out by the two thinkers was surprisingly
similar. In important respects Bentham accepted Blackstone's char-
acterization of the social and political context in which legal strug-
gles were played out and even shared his objectives, though almost

never endorsing his methods and means of attaining them. There is no
better illustration of these surprising similarities than an examination of the two writers' comments on property.

Bentham had no inclination to disagree with Blackstone's account
of how the "right of property...engages the affections of mankind."
Nor had he any real quarrel with Blackstone's subsequent assertion that
"property" means "private property," the "exclusive" dominion of a
given individual over certain "external things." It was Blackstone's
opinion that

> Necessity begat property: and, in order to in-
> sure that property, recourse was had to civil society,
> which brought along with it a long train of insepar-
> able concomitants; states, government, laws, punish-
> ments,...[13]

For Bentham property was the offspring of desire, as basic to man as
the exercise of his own will. The "logic of the will" which Bentham
expounded over many years, contrasting it emphatically with Locke's
logic of the understanding, was a logic of desire, of possession, and
implicitly of property.[14]

"Necessity [or nature] begat property" would do nicely for Bentham. And there can be no doubt that he saw it as one of civil society's primary objectives to protect this child of necessity by protecting the socio-economic status quo:

> ...where the distribution of property and power is
> concerned, to keep things in the proportion in which
> they actually are, ought to be, and in general is,
> the aim of the legislator. His great purpose is to
> preserve the total mass of expectations as far as is
> possible from all that may interfere with their
> course.[15]

Whatever radicalism Bentham expressed in his critique of Blackstone's
accounts of "civil society, states, government, laws" or "punishments,"
it was not the radicalism of a democrat, a leveller or a partisan of
equality of social condition. He consistently opposed "community of
goods" and what he called the "levelling system" (88a.53-4), and his
denunciations became even more strident after the French Revolution.[16]
Anticipating that his proposal to replace taxation with escheat as a
source of revenue (a proposal defended on grounds that distant relatives of a deceased have no expectation of pecuniary benefit and therefore suffer no disappointment if government garners the estate instead)
would be attacked as "making a revolution in property," he contrasted
the French Revolution whose "characteristic" was "to trample in every

possible way upon the feelings of individuals," with his own measure,
which would "shew more tenderness to those feelings, than can be shewn
by the taxes to which it is proposed to substitute it."[17] He virtually
identified property with human feelings - pleasure, security, expectation. He viewed the idea of a revolutionary change in the distribution of property with "horror:"

> A revolution in property! It is an idea big
> with horror, a horror which can not be felt in a
> stronger degree by any man than it is by me...it
> involves the idea of possessions disturbed, of
> expectations thwarted: of estates forcibly rav-
> ished from the living owners, of opulence reduced
> to beggary, of the fruits of industry made the
> prey of rapacity and dissipation - of the levelling
> of all distinctions, of the confusion of all order
> and the destruction of all security.[18]

To anyone familiar with John Locke's *Second Treatise*, or for that
matter with any of the eighteenth-century works, up to and including
Blackstone's, which aped his opinions, the emphasis on protection from
violence, the sacredness of the fruits of industry and the supreme
value of security of possession are nothing new. What is new, or at
least what is given novel prominence, is the idea of expectation:

> Expectation is the basis of every proprietary right:
> it is this which affords whatever occasion there can
> be for giving a thing to one man rather than another.
> (29.6)

The defense of expectations meant the protection of inequality. "Inequality," he asserted, "is the natural condition of mankind...Abso-
lute equality is absolutely impossible."

> Subjection...is the natural and unavoidable state
> of at least two-thirds of the species, and if it were
> possible that anything like independence could subsist
> among any part of it it could only be among the remain-
> ing third. (88A. 69.70).

At his most extreme, when anxious for tactical reasons to avoid being
seen as a "dangerous" radical reformer, he could even contrive to defend the utility of the "aristocratical part of the constitution" and
of its "opulence:"

> Monarchy stands on the shoulders of the peer-
> age. Peers must be high, that the monarch may be
> the higher. The use of a peer is to command re-
> spect and to command it by his opulence. All cur-
> rents that bring in wealth to the peerage ought to
> flow without disturbance that in unquiet times
> there may not, in any part of the Kingdom, be want-
> ing a man who, by endowments less precarious than

personal ones, may be enabled, as well as by interest disposed, to contribute with effect towards the preservation of the peace.[19]

Whenever we hear Bentham eulogized as a democrat and a radical reformer, let us pause to make sure that "radical" is being used in an applicable sense. Though his passion for criticism penetrating to the
roots of legal, social and political theory and practice is obvious,
Bentham the radical could still aver that "the want of the regard due
to the existing interests of individuals" was "in many instances" by
itself "sufficient warrant" for "opposition...to plans of reformation." (100.177) There is more than a hint of Toryism in this "radical." (104.436-475).

We have observed that Bentham connected property directly with
human feelings, human desire and the individual's will and that he argued that the wills of "two-thirds" of the human species should naturally be "subjected" to the wills of the remaining one-third. Blackstone had postulated a direct connection between the will and the power to own property in his discussion of the franchise:

> [T]he true reason of requiring of any qualifi-
> cation, with respect to property, in voters, is to
> exclude such persons as are in so mean a situation
> that they are esteemed to have no will of their
> own.[20]

Though he differed with Blackstone on the nature of the franchise,
Bentham never retreated from the position that the very adequacy of
an individual's being, expressed through the purposeful and powerful
nature of his desires, was measured by his capacity to acquire and enjoy property. In fact the difference between Bentham and Blackstone
on this point seems to be that, while for Blackstone the correlation
between independence of will and independence of means was simply and
casually observed *en passant*, in Bentham the relationship between
those whose dependent "condition in life" made them essentially objects of "human property" and those men of property for whom independence of means had secured an essential independence of will was subjected to sustained - and justificatory - analysis. Moreover, Bentham's
treatment of the poor, the idle and the indigent in his Poor Law and
Panopticon schemes amply demonstrates this point.[21] Blackstone had
taken it to be axiomatic that

> ...a part only of society was sufficient to pro-
> vide, by their manual labour, for the necessary
> subsistence of all; and leisure was given to others

> to cultivate the human mind, to invent useful arts,
> and to lay the foundations of science.[22]

Bentham allowed that, even given the optimization of "the condition of
mankind as far as depends upon the law," for the labouring part of
society "toil even as now must be the prelude to subsistence: that
the few may be wealthy, the many must be poor..."[23]

Bentham's manuscript fragments of the 1770s and 1780s reproduce
faithfully the priorities established in Blackstone's treatment of the
"rights of Englishmen." An Englishman's fundamental rights are three:
"personal security, personal liberty and private property."[24] Yet
Bentham and Blackstone do hold divergent views on property and their
divergence arises from a consideration clearly raised by Blackstone.
The basic function and importance of property in civil society having
been established, he asserts,

> The only question remaining is, how this property
> became actually vested...[25]

Bentham wished to clarify the language and procedure of the law in relation to property. The vesting of title, the forms of conveyance,
these and other aspects of the law of real (Bentham preferred "immov-
able") property were the initial focus of his attention. He attacked
them in a particular manner, giving a pronounced emphasis to the analysis of individual terms. He saw this as a necessary prelude to more
concrete reform activity.

> Reform in the legal style...[is] the most important
> of all reforms - because a preliminary SINE QUA NON
> to every other. (153b, 354).

The Language of the Law

Blackstone had offered an interpretation of "the question" concerning property, and at least for a time Bentham was content to address that question, though in his own distinctive way. His comments
were penned as part of an attempt to reply to Blackstone's *Commentaries*
with a work of his own. He gave his envisaged *opus* different titles
at different times, but they all give some idea of its character. It
was to elucidate "The Elements of Critical Jurisprudence." It was to
provide "Preparatory Principles" for those interested in censorial
jurisprudence. It was to define "Key Terms" in critical jurisprudence.[26] One such term, given more space in these manuscripts than
most others, was "property."

Blackstone's question was "how...property became actually vested."
His answer was that title to real property was based on an individual's
initial occupancy of the property, occupancy constituting "a declaration that he intends to appropriate the thing to his own use."[27] Bentham accordingly investigated the terms "occupation," "possession" and
"title." As usual he found complexities where to Blackstone all had
been simplicity itself.

> A man may be said to *occupy* a thing when he per-
> forms any acts having their termination in that
> thing...the words *use* and occupation are in most
> cases nearly synonymous...

He defined "possession" as the physical or legal capacity or right to
occupy:

> Possession in general...may be said to be the
> absence of obstacles opposed to occupation: or
> in other words it is the liberty of occupation.

Legally sanctioned possession, i.e. legal right to occupy, is legal entitlement *de jure*. Legal recognition of *de facto* possession or
occupation is legal entitlement *de facto*.[28] The essential function of
the law of real property is to establish legal entitlement *de jure*
wherever possible. Blackstone had made the characteristic claim that

> ...the legislature of England has universally
> promoted the grand ends of civil society, the
> peace and security of individuals, by steadily
> pursuing that wise and orderly maxim, of assign-
> ing to every thing capable of ownership a legal
> and determinate owner.[29]

Bentham agreed that this was indeed the purpose of the law of real property, but as was his wont he could not share Blackstone's confidence
that the means of accomplishing this end had been properly, systematically, "scientifically" laid out. In his proposed work of "Critical
Jurisprudence" he planned to analyze not just the variety of possible
"objects of property" but also the distinction between a title to and
an interest in an object of property and a family of related questions
regarding entitlement such as length of tenure, conditions of tenure,
forfeiture, collective entitlement and methods of gaining entitlement.
This led him naturally into a consideration of "conveyancing": the acquisition, transmission or alienation of real property. Each of these
notions he carefully subdivided (he called his method "exhaustive bi-
furcation"). Transmission, for example, was by "dereliction" or "losing." Dereliction could be "*in durante vita*" or "*per mortem*."

> The Law on his behalf would form the matter of a
> code which might be entitled the Loser and Finder's
> Law. (69.33).

His reflections on the complexities of legally defining and settling entitlement induced him to focus his attention on the distinction
between what he called the "definitional" and "operative" parts of the
Law of property:

> ...so much of the Law, in a word, as respects
> Title, Tenure, Quantity of Interest, Time of En-
> joyment, Number and Connections of the Proprie-
> tors, comes under the description of the Defini-
> tional part of the Law of Property. The descrip-
> tion of the different ways of meddling with differ-
> ent punishments annex'd to each constitutes what
> may be called the operative. (69.31).

This distinction is replicated in his better known later efforts to
settle the relationship between civil (expository) and criminal (puni-
tive) law.[30]

The attention which Bentham initially lavished on questions of
real property was not sustained. His early manuscripts contain much
more material on property in general than on real property in particular. After an initial enthusiasm his involvement with real-property
law lapsed for almost 50 years. In 1826 it was suddenly reawakened.
James Humphreys, a well established conveyancer, lecturer in law at
University College London, member of Lincoln's Inn and friend of Sir
Francis Burdett, John Horne Tooke and James MacIntosh, published his
*Observations on the Actual State of the English Laws of Real Property,
with the Outlines of a Code*. Bentham was inordinately enthusiastic
about it. It combined attention to the long-lapsed subject of real
property with an attempt at Bentham's then-current passion, codifica-
tion:

> Before this work came out, CODE and CODIFICATION
> were rank THEORY,...and, as such, objects of sincere
> horror...NOW, at length, they are become PRACTICE;...
> and horror has given way to praise.[31]

The *Dictionary of National Biography* describes the work as

> ...the fruit of its author's association with...the
> new school of analytical jurists of which Bentham
> and Austin were the leaders[32]

It was influential in effecting a number of reforms in the laws of conveyancing and led to the appointment of a board of Real Property Com-
missioners to reform England's land laws.

Bentham generated almost 1,000 sheets of manuscript commentary on Humphreys' work, and his fascination with detail seemed endless. The spirit of his pages is summed up in a comment entitled "Beginning":

> If we do not great miscalculate, this work of
> Mr. Humphreys will [be?] an epoch, not only in Law,
> but in history. We do not intend [to] go as far as
> to say a revolution, [even] in law the foundation
> for [that] change having been laid already by other
> hands. (77.35).

The "other hands" may well have been Bentham's own, for the University College of London manuscripts contain an unpublished comment which speaks volumes: "Humphreys a Benthamite" (78.1). These manuscript notes formed the basis for his "Commentary on Humphreys' Real Property Code," published in the *Westminster Review*,[33] and he went on to submit to the Real Property Commission in 1831 an "Outline of a Plan of a General Register of Real Property."[34] When Bentham died in 1832 the Commission was still sitting.

What accounts for Bentham's failure to develop his thoughts on real property after a promising beginning in his early writings? The circumstantial evidence suggests that he was simply unable to sustain an analysis of one specific and narrow aspect of property or of law without gravitating towards a more general study in more fundamental terms. His examination of real-property law directed him back to a reconsideration of the definitional and operative aspects of law in general.

The elucidation of entitlement had its own way of leading to more general investigations. Entitlement seemed to him to be a particular kind of "interest," "applying to the whole thing, and to all its uses":

> Interest applies indifferently to the whole of a
> thing or any part or parts of it, and to the sum
> of its uses or any one or more of its uses. (69.31)

Thus arriving at the position that "[a]n interest in a thing is the right of making an use of it," Bentham then demarcated degrees of "interest" by equating them with modes of property. A "partial property" was a right "only to certain particular uses." An "integral property" was a right to put a thing

> to any use he has a mind to put it to, those
> alone excepted which he is precluded from
> putting it to on account of their being
> detrimental either to himself or to the pub-
> lic." (69.25)

This concept of a very strong and general property right raised
problems. Objects of property could be distinguished into (1) human,
(2) "irrational" but "sensitive" and (3) "irrational" and "insensi-
tive." (69.25) Should human beings be said to be the objects of "integral property?" Bentham decided, at least on first consideration,
that they should not. "Integral property" would "subsist in things
only." Even a general right of one man to the services of another
would be a "partial property" for "general" (as distinguished from
"special") purposes (69.30). Men were not to own one another in quite
the same way in which they owned things. In what sense, then, could
an individual acquire a "property or interest" in another "person or
persons?" One means, the least problematic possible, was by contract:

> A contract for special services is a partial
> conveyance of the person who is to serve to the per-
> son who is to be served...[and is] made either with
> the person himself who is the object of the property
> or with some other person who has a general property
> in his services. (69.31)

The true challenge was to establish the limits of a "general" property
of one man in another, and this Bentham attempted by advancing a fundamental utilitarian criterion:

> The dispositions made by the Law with respect
> to property ought to be and in general are influ-
> enced by this circumstance: viz.: that regard is
> paid by it to the interest of that being which is
> the subject of property. This is not the case with
> respect to property in things: though it ought to
> be with respect to such things as like people are
> susceptible of an interest: viz. of pain and
> pleasure. (69.31)[35]

Homo sapiens is a rational, sentient animal and must be treated as
such - no better and no worse.

For our purposes what is most glaringly absent from this analysis
is some recognition that the "interest of that being which is the subject of property" - or of him who is its object - may differ qualita-
tively, categorically from, or even be incommensurable with, the proprietary interest of the property-holder. In sum: the relationship
between property rights and human rights is not promisingly encapsu-
lated in the language of "interest" as it is used here.

The Vocabulary of Social Science

Jeremy Bentham conceived an enthusiasm for science well before he
was able to summon up any comparable motivation toward the study of
law. Indeed when he finally discovered a rationale for the pursuit of

of the study (if not the practice) of the law, it stemmed largely from
the realization that Blackstone's failure was precisely a failure to
employ scientific method in his legal explications. Bentham attacked
Blackstone's legal vocabulary as non-sensical. He never denied Blackstone's knowledge of the law as it in fact was. He ceaselessly ridi-
culed instead his predecessor's inability to either justify or criti-
cize the *status quo* in a logical, meaningful or persuasive (i.e.
"scientific") way. Bentham himself clearly set out to avoid such a
mistake. Definition and classification were the heart of his notion
of scientific method, and we have already seen that he used these processes to explicate property. But the "science of law" could never be
more than an aspect, albeit an indispensible one, of the "science of
man," and Bentham's analysis of legal language relevant to real property could not but prepare the way for a comprehensive utilitarian analysis of property as a set of social relations central to civil life.

Bentham's science of man owed a great deal to David Hume's science
of man, and a comparison of their views on property is instructive.
Bentham had extravagant praise for Hume's *Treatise of Human Nature*.
When he had read its third volume, "Of Morals," he said, "I felt as if
scales had fallen from my eyes."[36]   Yet on reflection his praise of
Hume was mixed with criticism:

> On some occasions the principle of utility was
> recognized by him as a criterion of right and wrong...
> but on other occasions the IPSE DIXIT principle, under
> the name of the moral sense, was, with the most incon-
> sistent oscitancy, seated by his own hands on the same
> throne.

The influence of his "moral sense" theory can be seen in Hume's discussion, in the same volume so extravagantly praised by Bentham, of the
"three different species of goods, which we are possess'd of," to wit:

> ...the internal satisfaction of our minds, the
> external advantages of our body, and the enjoyment
> of such possessions as we have acquir'd by our in-
> dustry and good fortune.

Hume took it as evident that the first two types of "goods" were secure. Loss (through transfer or theft) and scarcity could afflict only
our external possessions. He thus named instability and scarcity of
possessions, i.e. civil and economic dislocation and distress, as "the
chief impediment" to a comfortable civil life.[39]

Regardless of their shared interest in utility, Bentham's reasoning on property could hardly follow Hume's course. What but the

shadow of the moral sense theory could explain Hume's claim that our
minds and bodies and the "goods" ("pleasures" for Bentham) they provide are in some sense insulated from the pains and vicissitudes of
social life? Bentham assumed the very opposite of this insularity of
mind and body. His most feared enemies were disappointment, uneasiness, uncertainty and disorientation. Vulnerability, not insularity,
was his notion of the condition of mind and body alike and of the
"goods" ("affections" where Hume would say "virtues": 14. 297-8) arising from their condition.

Indeed, Bentham was completely open to the idea that some men
might in mind and/or body become the "human property" of others. Yet
he had no intention of allowing such power of proprietorship to go
unchecked. He was, for example, a clear if maddeningly cold-blooded
opponent of slavery.[40] In his discussion of "power over human property" he speaks not of "integral" but of "general" property, but his por-
trayal of it makes no reference to "the interest of that being which
is the subject of property," nor does he consider the possible "public
detriment" arising from abuse:

> With respect to human property, a man may
> [seize?] the object of his property when the
> interest he has in it is a general one. This
> happens in three cases: when the person who is
> the object of property is 1st a Wife; 2dly a
> child or Ward; or 3rdly an Apprentice. He may
> use force to put himself in possession of this
> kind of property, and that as well against the
> person who is the object of the property, as
> against all others. The power he has over a
> person so related to him is *in the first in-
> stance* uncontrolled. (69.29; emphasis J.B.'s)

Bentham made extensive plans for the employment of apprentices in his
imagined system of Panopticon. There were to be poorhouses blanketing
the United Kingdom, housing at least hundreds of thousands of children
in the condition of "human property" in relation to their owner - the
National Charity Company, prop. J. Bentham.[41]

Bentham went on, in the passage just cited, to distinguish a separate class of social relationships involving only "a special, a partial property:"

> A hired domestic servant...a working servant
> in husbandry, a superintending servant in husbandry -
> a Bailiff: a superintending domestic servant - a
> House-Steward: A servant superintending [one's]

> property in general - a Land-Steward. A ser-
> vant managing his Law-concerns - an attorney,
> an Advocate - a person bound by contract to
> do him any particular good offices personal
> or real. (69.29(4))

Such contractual relations for particular purposes created no "general"
proprietorship of man by man. But in the earlier case the only indication of consideration for the "interests" (if not "rights") of wives,
children and apprentices was Bentham's emphasis that controls on proprietors would be absent only "in the first instance."

At one point Bentham tackled directly the problem of distinguishing between offences against "person" and those against "property."
But his answer trivialized the issue. The classification arrived at
depended simply on whether person (seen as "body" in this instance)
or property absorbed the initial impact, the "direct...not consequential mischief" of the offence. Beyond this Bentham simply observed,

> There is scarcely any sort of offence against
> a man's person by which he may not come to be
> affected in his property...[and vice versa] (69.30)

The distinction which emerges is a purely physical, spatial one. It
has no moral content whatever. Yet Bentham was determined to retain
it. Perhaps misreading the dictum that "every man has a property in
his own person,"[42] he thought he saw personal and property injuries
conflated in Locke. He made a note:

> Locke - Every corporal injury not an invasion
> of property. (69.43)

Given Bentham's other statements on the subject, it is hard to know
whether this constitutes an assertion that Locke was wrong to regard a
man's person as his mere property or a denial that corporal punishment,
say, of an apprentice by a master, constituted an invasion, given the
master's general power of property! The former would argue a moral
stance regarding individuality for which Bentham gives us no evidence.
One is left with only the latter.

The most important respect in which Bentham preferred Hume to
Locke seems to have been in employing Hume's argument that property
was an essentially external relationship. Hence no man should be described as having a property in his own person. Property relations were
subject-object relations. However in common parlance the word property
was used to refer either to the relationship or to the object. Property, that is, could be "a right" or "a thing." (69.81) A man might
be said to "have a property" *in* a thing (i.e. to be in a certain

relationship to it) without having (possessing) the thing itself.
Whether physically appropriated or not, a thing could be seen as an
"object" (or "subject") of property. When he chose to focus on subjects of property in the sense of physical objects susceptible to human
use or acquisition, the journey from philosophical materialism to materialism of a more crass variety could be swift:

> The several subjects or...articles of pro-
> perty are the several sorts of Substances, the
> physical bodies that surround us; Animals,
> those even of our own species not excluded.
>
> The value these are/any of them/to us is
> either 1st as instruments of pleasure - [or]
> 2ndly as instruments of security.
>
> Money is the common pledge substitute and
> measure of the several instruments whether of
> pleasure or of security. He who has money may,
> generally speaking, have any of them in exchange.
> How this comes to be the case is matter of con-
> sideration for a work of another sort: it is
> sufficient for the present that the fact is so.
> (69.98)

Bentham divided the objects of property into "real," or "corporeal," and "fictitious" or "incorporeal." Real property he divided into
moveable and immoveable. One is amazed by the determination with which
he held to these classifications. The pages in which he initially defined the class of corporeal immoveable property dated, at the latest,
from before 1780. An eighteenth-century life-time (over 45 years)
later, one finds him, in his "Commentary on Humphreys' Real Property
Code," muttering somewhat petulantly about

> ...that species alone of property to which
> English lawyers, and they alone, have so absurdly
> and uncharacteristically instead of *immoveable*,
> given the name of *real*.[43]

Had Bentham had his way, one can only assume that sales and purchases
of land and houses would today be executed by corporeal immoveable
estate agents.

The classification "incorporeal objects of property" is in fact
more interesting than its corporeal counterpart. Bentham examined it
with some interest in his *Introduction to the Principles of Morals and
Legislation*. Where no concrete thing or person could be "brought to
view" as the object of a man's property, an "ideal being" was postulated in its place. "Men of science" (such as J. Bentham), in their
studies of the "operations of the law," characterized these fictitious

entities as "incorporeal."[44]   Indeed, scientists of jurisprudence had
"fabricated" them in "prodigious variety...almost out of every thing."
"Conditions in life," from that of trustee to that of apprentice, had
been lumped together as species of property. A man's reputation and
even his liberty were subsumed under the heading of his property. Bentham reiterated that he saw property as a relationship involving an
actor and an external object. He considered it a mistake to regard
one's own livelihood or skills as one's property - though they could
be someone else's. He accepted readily the implication of his own
analysis that such conditions in life as "master, servant, husband,
wife, steward, agent, attorney, or the like" involved "possessing a
property, or being the object of a property possessed by another."
Master-servant relations, to take only one possible example, ought not
on this view of the matter to be seen as an exchange, however lopsided,
of one human being's property in his own services and capacities in return for another's property in the form of a wage. Rather they are to
be seen as relations between one man capable of proprietorship and
another (dependent) who enters into a "condition in life" rendering him
in essence an "object of property." A relatively inclusive notion of
subjection is thus preferred to a relatively egalitarian notion of exchange.

In examining these examples of person-to-person proprietary relationships, Bentham meant to demonstrate simply that property relations often involved no "real" or "corporeal" objects. This initial
investigation of the new class of "incorporeal objects of property,"
however, raised problems which Bentham did not at this point address.
Were *all* the abstractions involved in human relationships to be regarded as objects of property? Evidently not. Many important abstract
notions, such as "reputation," "condition," "power," "rights," "liberty," "duty" and "obligation" were nowhere explicitly subsumed under the
heading of property. In fact they were distinguished from the objects
of property by the use of a brutally simple criterion:

> Property, considered with respect to the pro-
> prietor, implies invariably a benefit and nothing
> else: whatever obligations or burthens may, by
> accident, stand annexed to it, yet in itself it can
> never be otherwise than beneficial...it is created
> not by any commands that are laid on [the proprietor],
> but by his being left free to do with such or such an
> article as he likes.

> ...it is the master alone that is considered
> as possessing a property, of which the servant ...
> is the object: but the servant, not less than the
> master, is spoken of as possessing or being invested
> with a condition.[45]

He was not yet satisfied. In manuscripts which now form Appendix
B to *Of Laws in General*, he plunged once more into a morass of definitions and distinctions.[46] His dissatisfaction with the analysis print-
ed in the *Introduction* was intense: in the "cursed chapter about the
Division of Off[ences]," he had "given an exhaustive view of the system of possible offences," but had not thereby exhausted every aspect
of the subject of property:

> ...[I] found myself obliged to lay the founda-
> tion of another work by drawing up (without insert-
> ing) an analysis of the possible modifications of
> *property*.[47] [Bentham's emphasis]

There are important differences between the intent of this analysis,
now "inserted" by Bentham's editors as an appendix to *Of Laws in General*, and his previous efforts. On preceding occasions he had dealt
with property only for the purpose of showing (1) how an offence
against it could be identified and (2) how it, as the object of crimes,
could be distinguished from other human "possessions": person, reputation and condition. In all of this he had taken property as a "given"
in social life. In Appendix B he proposed to integrate "property" into
a new family of terms with a new relationship to law:

> Power, right, prohibition, duty, obligation,
> burthen, immunity, exemption, privilege, property,
> security, liberty - all these with a multitude of
> others that might be so named are so many ficti-
> tious entities which the law upon one occasion or
> another is considered in common speech as creating
> or disposing of."[48]

Such abstractions as these cannot be treated as mere formal classes or objects of offences. They are, he says, "fictitious *moral*
"goods." Moral goods for Bentham, however, are not so called because
they are intrinsically "virtuous," but because they are and ought to be
desired (14.297). They are and ought to be desired precisely in so far
as possession of them is justified by its social consequences, these
being measured in terms of pleasure and pain to individuals with a
discernible "interest" in them. The implications of this judgment
about moral values are spun out in Appendix B at such length that even
Bentham, that consummate master of prolixity, knew it was "uninviting"
to the reader. The basic point, however, can be relatively simply

stated for our purposes. Blackstone was not quite correct in stating
that "necessity begat property." Mere necessity begat no such "fictitious" entities. Rather man's desiring yet vulnerable nature begat
the sense of necessity, and the sense of necessity was focused mainly
(or at least most discernibly) on desired external objects. Necessity
was felt as need. Need begat occupation and possession. It was here
that the law stepped in. Bentham's position in this instance is not
as dramatically transformed as might at first have appeared. Law
transforms need and possession into right and title, into entitlement
in its two senses. Both Bentham's contemporaries and "the first authors of language" were found guilty of a regrettably faulty "ellipsis." It was "the mere work of the fancy: a kind of allegory" to say
that the law created or disposed of property - or of liberty, rights,
powers and so on.[50]

Law transformed the field of property relationships from a battle-
ground of conflicting desires into a chess board of reciprocal rights
and duties, powers and obligations. Bentham's achievement in this his
most sustained analysis of property was to clarify the legal process by
which, as Blackstone had put it, property was "vested" in its owners.
His failure, in our view, lay in his continued treatment of moral entitlement as simply analogous to (indeed reducible to) legal entitlement to real property. He felt he had exhausted the operations of the
law in relation to all forms of property by showing that it could either command or prohibit the use of things or the derivation of services from persons.

Bentham's attempt to define incorporeal objects of property ended,
knowingly or unknowingly, in the transformation of an enumeration of
legal objects into an evaluation of social relationships. Bentham may
have been aware of this. He argued that the essence of property was
the deriving of benefit (pleasure) from the performance of acts having,
as he put it, their "termination" in a given external thing or their
"commencement" in some "person" other than the actor. Property was
essentially a relationship, not an object. The combination of an appropriate external focus and a pleasurable relationship would make property a source of happiness. Bentham denounced the "violent ellipsis"
by which this operative relationship to some or all of the parts of a
thing or to the services of a person, strictly defined and

circumscribed in contractual terms, was described as simply making the
person or thing the actor's property. It seemed unsubtle to the point
of misrepresentation.[51]

Property properly understood need not always mean complete, unconditional and permanent possession. This point gains in importance
where it is read in Bentham's unpublished manuscripts alongside his
comments on "human property." He felt that the language of his contemporaries created a very real, though escapable, socio-political problem. By treating the proprietorship of men over men indiscriminately
as though it were the "integral" mode of proprietorship genuinely applicable only to things, legal theorists and political activists would
have to divide on an apparently invidious question: were men or were
they not to be the unconditional property of other men? This is the
essence of the warfare of rich vs. poor, of the "two nations," of
bourgeoisie vs. proletariat. And to Bentham it could have been fore-
stalled had public men paid more heed to the niceties of the vocabulary
of the "science of man." Ironically, however, Bentham's attempts at
what he saw as a more discriminating analysis of the language of property rights simply reinforced rather than removed the ubiquitous sociological battle-lines pitting proprietors against the "objects" of
their proprietorship in his day.

Distributive Law and Distributive Justice

As a result of his somewhat groping attempts to distinguish property from other human "possessions" such as person, reputation and
condition in life, Bentham uncovered for the first time in his career
some of the complexities afflicting the concept of property when it was
viewed not from the perspective of legality alone but in the context of
civil society in general. Legality, however, retained its leading
place in his social theory - to the detriment of his understanding of
the moral dimension of the theory of property. The *Introduction*'s social principles were essentially, almost solely, the principles of legislation - of laws as rules of command. Morality was distinguished
from law by its broader sphere, but the meaning of such a distinction
is indeterminate when no distinctions as to substance, as to the special nature of moral rules (or moral beings) accompany it. In Appendix
B to *Of Laws in General*, David Hume seemed to be vindicated: it was
after all the chief function of the laws of civil society to ensure
the stability and security of the relationships between individuals

and the external objects of their desires. Despite this broad agreement Bentham dismissed Hume because he was a moral-sense theorist
and attacked Hume's "goods" ("virtues") as "factitious entities"
(14.297). This was an indication of the direction in which Bentham's
theory of distributive justice was subsequently to develop. In his
practical reform projects of the 1780s and 1790s and in his pivotal
works on Civil Law and Political Economy in the same period, he concentrated on the process of distributing material "goods" to the virtual
exclusion of moral theory.

   In the 1770s and 1780s Bentham attended primarily to the pursuit
of theoretical niceties. The four major works of this period, the
Fragment on Government, the *Comment on the Commentaries*, the *Introduction to the Principles of Morals and Legislation* and *Of Laws in General*, showed an increasing abstraction and intricacy in his theoretical
treatment of property as time passed. Around the year 1790 a change
occurred. The French Revolution filled Bentham (and many others) with
an unprecedented sense of urgency: practical proposals for the protection of order and well-being in English society had to be promul-
gated without delay. Before 1790 Bentham's continuing obsession had
been with the requirements of scientific social theory. After 1790 he
was immersed instead in the gathering of the hard facts of social life.
"Political economy, finance, [and] the administration of justice"
(100.181) now occupied him. In the 1770s he had seen the analysis of
criminal law as his primary goal. In the late 1780s and the 1790s he
devoted immense energy to problems of a civil nature. By civil he
meant simply "distributive." His writings in the 1780s show a steady
rise to prominence and final ascendancy in his mind of the concept of
distributive law, specifically "private distributive" (civil) law and
"public distributive" (constitutional) law.[52] His earlier interest in
the classification of punishable offences against property is superseded by a preoccupation with the principles of distribution of both
corporeal and incorporeal objects of property. Bentham the censorial
jurist becomes Bentham the political economist.

   He is an ardent disciple of Adam Smith and a worshipper of wealth:

>   The parentage of Plutus' Wealth is no secret.
> He is the child of Earth by Labour...He has Earth
> for his Mother,...Labour for his Father, and Adam
> Smith for his head Genealogist. (153a.107).

Yet he realizes that his utilitarianism is in principle an interven-
tionist and managerial theory of government:

> I have not, I never had, nor ever shall have
> any horror, sentimental or anarchical, of the Hand
> of government. I leave it to Adam Smith...to talk
> of invasions of natural liberty, and to give as a
> special argument against this or that law, an argu-
> ment the effect of which would be to put a negative
> upon all laws. The interference of government, as
> often as...any the smallest ballance on the side of
> advantage is the result, is an event I witness with
> altogether as much satisfaction as I should its for-
> bearance and with much more than I should its negli-
> gence.[53]

Moreover, the principle which must govern the managerial activities of
governments, especially in relation to property, is absolutely clear:
"Enter now...the Disappointment preventive, or say Non-disappointment,
principle:"

> Because, of every part of the rule of action
> which has property for its subject matter - civil
> branch and penal branch taken together - this, next
> to the GREATEST HAPPINESS principle, is the main
> foundation. Because, in the genealogy of human
> feelings, this is the immediate lineal descendant
> of that same parent principle.[54]

The "Non-disappointment principle" is simply the principle of security of expectations renamed. And security of expectations was the
core of that general security to which Bentham gave highest priority
among the ends of distributive law. The appropriate ends of utilitarian legislation were many, he said, but could be grouped under four
heads: security, subsistence, abundance and equality. (100.136)
"Opulence" was a frequent alternative for abundance. With regard to
subsistence and abundance the case is simple, if unattractive: subsistence will be the goal and expectation of that two-thirds (sometimes Bentham's estimate could soar to "nineteen-twentieths") of the
populace who were fated to be human objects of property. The remaining
citizens, men of property all, could rightly expect the continuation,
even augmentation, of their opulence. Bentham laboured enthusiastical-
ly to bring forth proposals to increase the value of their currency,
lower their taxes (principally the Poor Rates) and otherwise enhance
the security of their expectations and the lavishness of the material
basis for their happiness. "Human property" on one hand, "the wealth
of nations" on the other - could this possibly be a basis for distributive justice? Disraeli's "two nations" spring irresistibly to mind.

Undertaking an "inventory of the sources of wealth," Bentham identified productive labour as "that which gives birth to all the others."
In "certain countries with predominantly agricultural economies," for
example, "the human beings attached to the soil and sold with it constitute its principal value." He attacked that "undefined mass of obligations" known as slavery simply because he held that liberty made
labourers more productive.[55] Emancipation was not humane, but utilitarian. There was "no reason for emancipation without indemnifica-
tion." As "experience had never shown them any other" condition,
slaves would not perceive their subjection as abominable (29.5). Bentham called mildly for "gradual abolition and intermediate modification" of the "personal obligations" constituting slavery.[56]

The life of all "human property" was essentially like that of the
slave. Having few expectations, wives, children, convicts, apprentices
and paupers could hardly be disappointed. He who has never hoped can
never despair. The perfectly obedient but poor subject was hardly significantly better off than the convict or the slave in Bentham's scheme
of things (xxv, 14). Discussing, with some reluctance, proposed "out-
relief" for paupers over 65 (a very great age for that day), Bentham
contrasted "the demands of indulgent humanity" with "those of rigid
justice":

> Humanity...requires that every individual
> should be made happy: justice...requires that of
> two members of the community,...equally innocent
> and equally deserving...one shall not be compelled
> to part with the fruits of his own labour without
> necessity for the benefit of another. (152b.534, 536).

The non-disappointment principle would suggest that, given "innocence"
(i.e. obedience), the rich deserve their opulence just as the poor deserve their fate. They are separate nations and live in separate
states. One state is Smith's competitive market economy, where men of
property use money and contractual agreements to enhance their aggregate wealth. The other is the state of the poor, where individuals are
not men but productive "hands,"[57] objects of property, characteristic-
ally governed by agreements conferring a "general," not a "partial"
property on their "owners." This latter is not a state wherein free
competition or freedom of contract are meaningful (153b.315-6). It is
neither a market society nor yet a welfare state. It is a community in
which "distribution" means forced redistribution of human productive
capital itself (a feature both of the Acts of Settlement and of

Bentham's Poor proposals) and in which government means comprehensive
control of every aspect of the subjects' lives.[58]

Bentham took it to be

> one of the corner stones of political science...
> [that]...the more strictly we are watched, the
> better we behave. (152b.332-3).

This could be the cornerstone, at any rate, of the politics of poverty,
of the "Pauper Kingdom." The only limitations, the reader will recall,
distinguishing a "general property" over human objects from the "integral" ownership of things had been a concern for "public detriment"
(which could mean for high poor-rates, idleness and drunkenness) and an
eye to the "interests" (pleasures and pains) of those subjected to the
property relationship. Now we can see that the poor, the powerless and
the propertyless, never having hoped, could not despair.[59] Having minimal expectations, they could not know the pain of disappointment.
Their "interest," their very capacity for pleasure and pain, was seen
as minimal, almost sub-human to the modern eye.

How then are we to resist the conclusion that "commodification"
was not only a fact in, but a product of, Bentham's "Pauper Kingdom"?
Bentham was unrepentant. "Democracy," he wrote, in reference to the
Friendly Societies,

> is no more of the essence of frugality than it
> is of prudence, tranquility or science.[60]

To the poor he offered only the mythology of capitalism, the vain vi-
sionary hope of becoming men of property through frugality. He offered
them "frugality banks" in their Panopticon prisons (152a.109). He offered his "Annuity Note" scheme to "attach the small saver to the government," observing that "where the treasure is, there will the heart
be also."[61] He spoke of the creation of a "little moneyed interest"
as attached to the status quo as ever the "great moneyed interest" had
been.[62] He offered to the absolute majority of the English populace a
secularized asceticism,[63] a rigid work ethic - and the prospect of continued poverty:

> Rank is relative: you cannot raise one of two
> contiguous ranks, but you depress the other...pover-
> ty you have at any rate. How do you like it best? -
> with or without industry - Take your choice. (152b.352).

The "security" which was the preeminent object of distributive law in
Bentham's system was the secure expectation that the "two nations"
would not become one.

Only by completely transforming one's view of the psychology of both wealth and poverty - perhaps by converting two psychologies into one - can one replace Bentham's two nations with a single "welfare state," his security with social security in its modern guise, his distaste for democracy with what we now know as liberal democracy, his notion of a double standard in contractual property rights with a social contract à la Harold Wilson.

In doing so, however, one introduces an ethical notion of social justice where none had been before. Bentham spoke little of justice and not always with approval when he did mention it. We have seen him distinguish its requirements from those of "humanity." However, his implicit idea of an optimum distribution of "goods" offers a bridge between the notions of property and justice found in David Hume's *Treatise* and that singularly influential modern construct, Professor Rawls' *Theory of Justice*.

Rawls deals explicitly, but not profoundly, with utilitarianism. He concentrates on the notion of aggregate social happiness, but formulates it in a way to which Bentham does not entirely conform. Rawls says that in the "strict classical doctrine" of utilitarianism,

> ...society is rightly ordered, and therefore just, when its major institutions are arranged so as to achieve the greatest net balance of satisfaction summed over all the individuals belonging to it.[64]

We may now ask, with Professor Lyons, "Was Bentham a Utilitarian?"[65] Rawls sees the utilitarian model as summing desires that are given. But the desires of the vast majority of Bentham's populace are more manufactured than given. The "summing" is rigged. Moreover, where Rawls emphasizes that utilitarianism seeks a sum, rather than employing a distinctive on-going apparatus for distributing increments, Bentham's essential distributive principles primarily confront change *per se*. Men of property are given "liberty, perfect liberty"[66] to augment their "opulence," while the poor are assuaged with the "INEQUALITY MINIMIZING PRINCIPLE," which asserts that

> As between individual and individual, the pleasure to the superior, to the power-holder, from the possession and exercise of the power, is not so great as the pain experienced by the party subject.[67]

A second distributive principle seems to offer a further mitigation of socio-economic inequalities:

> ...a given mass of wealth produces more happi-
> ness the greater the number of individuals among
> whom it is divided, so long as the parcels in which
> it is divided are not too minute to produce a sensa-
> tion in any individual... (153b.223).

But this principle operates only when subsistence is assumed as
"given." It appears, then, that it explains the distribution of increments in abundance only, thus implying a separate approach to the
quite different problem of subsistence.

Given the apparent complexity of Bentham's approaches to problems
of the distribution of social goods, it is puzzling to read in Rawls'
work that to utilitarians the distribution of a sum of satisfactions
"between persons" or "over time" "does not matter...except indirectly,"
and more than puzzling to read that "Utilitarianism does not take seriously the distinction between persons."[68] However our primary focus
here is not the mechanics of distributive mechanisms, but the relation
between theories of property and justice. For our purposes the most
illuminating comparisons between Bentham and Rawls centre on the notions of "primary goods" and the "original position."

> While the persons in the original position do
> not know their conception of the good, they do know,
> I assume, that they prefer more rather than less
> primary goods. And this information is sufficient
> for them to know how to advance their interests in
> the initial situation.[69]

The individuals in Rawls' "original position" have no particular interests or expectations. Distributive justice is a simple extrapolation
from their naturally shared rational view of the means and ends consonant with "the good" for man. The "goods" which are at stake are not
the external commodities whose instability and insecurity preoccupied
David Hume (and, in the end, Bentham), but the goods of mind and body
which Hume took to be untransferable and Bentham took to be manipul-
able. The theory of justice is, says Rawls, Socratic, and so is its
notion of goods of all sorts.[70] It is a branch of moral philosophy.
Bentham claimed to be a moral theorist as well, but was capable of reducing the idea of a moral principle to the most pragmatic and mundane
status:

> Pushpin is morality in as far as it keeps out
> drunkenness. (149.54).

Bentham and the Humanist Theory of Property

Property is the stuff of distributive justice. Corruptions of the notion of distributive justice derive not from a failure to link it to a concept of property but from the mistake of linking it too closely to an inadequate notion of property. Any comprehensive theory of property should be *ipso facto* a theory of distributive justice. Bentham seems to have grasped the closeness of this relationship, but at the same time he illustrates the "for better or worse" nature of the marriage of property and justice. The deficiencies of his notion of justice are essentially reflections of the (principally moral) deficiencies of his approach to property.

In one of its possible senses "property" refers to that over which one can exercise proprietorship, that to which one can acquire legal "entitlement." In another at least etymologically possible sense, however, surely property is what is "proper" to man - or are we to assume that property can and ought to have to do only with proprietorship, and not with propriety? The theory of property rightly concerns itself not simply with what man can possess through the appropriation of externalities, but also with what man's essential "properties" are - with what he "properly" is. On this definition of property the dimensions of entitlement are not determined by reference to concepts of occupation and possession (or in C. B. Macpherson's terms "extraction") but by a candid recognition of actual and potential human attributes. A humanist theory of property is neither incomprehensible nor self-evidently impracticable.

Those who disdain the idea of a distributive justice rooted directly in an analysis of human attributes must somehow evade the clear fact that no other basis for the concept has ever been suggested. What is entailed and implied by a humanist theory of property is not a shift from a hard, scientific, objective view of legal and social realities to a spiritual wish-fulfillment fantasy, but rather a switch from a view of man fast being rendered fundamentally untenable by changes both in relations between man and nature and in relations between man and man to a view of humanity as capable of a future not purchased at the cost of the exhaustion of nature and the alienation of humanity from itself. Even unintended contributions to the realization of such a notion of property are to be accepted with gratitude.

Our reaction to Bentham's various usages of and reflections on property is one of frustration rather than outright hostility. To see

Bentham as a simple enthusiastic proponent of unfettered individual
acquisition is to ignore both the paternalistic interventionism of his
actual social and governmental schemes and the substantial portion of
his theoretical reflections given over to the consideration of human
rights and powers as the basis, along with "corporeal objects," of
distributive justice. On the whole, however, as humanists from J. S.
Mill to Professor Macpherson have perceived, Bentham's hedonism was not
an adequate basis for a theory of human development.[71] His understanding of progress was limited, even in his own view, by his belief that
"the stock of sense...never can increase" and more importantly by his
very analyses of human "interest" and "expectations."[72]

By his own admission Bentham was a theorist not of human development but of social "technology."[73] His theory of property disappoints
not because, like Locke's, it is a class-based apology masquerading as
humanism, but because it assembles the methodological raw materials for
a full study of distributive justice as the essential prerequisite for
human development, only to reject genuine development in favour of mere
amelioration. "Abundance" *with* "equality" was for him out of the question: "security" on one hand, "subsistence" on the other, were the *de
facto* polarities of human existence in Bentham's England. To conclude
that in a utilitarian utopia

> ...toil even as now must be the prelude to
> subsistence. That the few may be wealthy, the many
> must be poor...and how much lighter so ever coercion
> may sit than it does now, coercion must be felt, that
> all may be secure. (142.200)

was to reject all genuine social change in favour of a gigantic ration-
alization of the status quo.

What Professor Rawls has done in our day Bentham did in his. Indeed Rawls accepts the utilitarian concept of distributive justice as
the norm which he must supersede. Bentham's theory of distributive
justice rests ultimately on a vulgarization of Hume's "moral sense"
theory and perhaps draws inspiration from other Scots as well.[74]
Rawls' is founded upon an alleged human "moral sense" derived from a
more remarkable hybrid: the "best" of Socrates, Kant and Rousseau.
Surely both Rawls and Bentham produce theories of the moral basis of
distributive justice which align comfortably with the fundamental social, political and economic institutional arrangements of their respective days. In each case the notion of a distribution of goods (as
process or as end-state) conducive to human development is

circumscribed by deference to notions of human motivation and productivity predominant in the author's immediate social context. Both
theories, then, may rightly be seen as contributions to the general
theory of property, but in neither is the fundamental character of property as an instrument of human development - of individuality as the
independent, rather than a dependent, variable in the theory - brought
to centre stage.

In Bentham's thought narrow ("real") and broad (human) conceptions
of property are juxtaposed, then conflated. The source of our theoretical frustration is that the development of a nascent broad theory,
humanist in intention, is rendered abortive by the dead hand of narrow
legalism. The science of man is in the end far more scientific than
humane. Bentham the neo-encyclopedist social scientist, heir to Hume
and Helvetius alike,[75] assembles the methodological raw materials for
a humanist theory of property simply by giving central attention in
his work to the effects of distributive law on human happiness. As far
as legal, social and economic arrangements are concerned this is a valuable insight. But thereafter Bentham reverses the correct priorities.
He allows the methodological structure of the legal system and of the
science of political economy to dictate the structure of happiness itself. His legislative theory overwhelms his moral theory. His humanism is perverted by his *esprit de système*. The result is an essay in
social engineering,[76] a crude behaviourism.[77] It is not man who develops, but rather utilitarian social planning itself. The stimuli
are comprehensively, even paternalistically organized. But man has become a respondent - a re-agent, not an agent. *Quis educavit educatores?*
It is the view of the human will itself, and of human sensibility, that
is impoverished here: not because it is explicitly capitalist, but because it is the foundation of a fundamentally circular and closed system, because it fails to be genuinely developmental at all. Insatiable
desire and incorrigible uneasiness, not creativity or self-expression,
must continue to provide the spur to the very pursuit of happiness itself:

> ...all must be tantalized more or less with the pros-
> pect of joys or supposed joys, which they are out
> of hopes of tasting...[78]

As Professor Wolin has observed, this is hardly a vision of human
history as an upward-bound escalator.[79] Rather it is an evocation of
a hedonistic treadmill. Is there not a glimpse here of the futility

of acquisitiveness? Of the depressing reality of the sense of scarcity
and uneasiness (insecurity) as the dynamics of productive activity? A
developmental theory of property takes abundance, equality and their
coexistence seriously. Indeed it gives their combination the highest
possible priority among social goals. Even Bentham himself seems to
have seen that the social system elaborated in his theory would per-
petuate (though it would perpetually deal with) both scarcity and inequality. A humanistic and developmental theory of property can accept
neither of these as a central instrument of human motivation.

Beginning as the most scathing of all critics of "everything as it
ought to be Blackstone," our subject ironically ends by being "everything as it ought to be Bentham." The radical critic of the legal profession and the legal system was incapable of applying equally radical
critical insight to the socio-economic system of his day. He goes to
the root of contemporary juridical usages of "property" and using his
notion of scientific method grasps the formal requirements for an adequate general theory. But just as his moral theory is vestigial, an
appendage of his understanding of legal rules and sanctions, so his
socio-economic theory of property never bears out in its substance the
promise offered by the form in which it was initially cast. The
"science of man," stripped of the idea of an intrinsically moral element in man's nature, shows us too much of eighteenth-century science
and too little of humanity.

FOOTNOTES

1 "Character of Jeremy Bentham as given on the 2nd of June, 1820, in and by the British House of Commons;" Jeremy Bentham Mss., University College, London, Box 60, pp. 12-13. Subsequent references to these Mss. consist of a parenthetical box and page number, e.g. (60, 12-13), inserted in the text of the article.

2 See J. H. Burns (ed.), *A Comment on the Commentaries* (London: Athlone U.P., 1977), esp. Chap. XV.

3 J. Bentham, *A Fragment on Government*, preface, para. 38.

4 Introduction, section 2. See also G. Jones (ed.), *The Sovereignty of the Law: Selections from Blackstone's Commentaries on the Laws of England* (Toronto: University of Toronto Press, 1973), chapter 2.

5 Jones, *Selections*, chapter 12, p. 118.

6 See. D. G. Long, *Bentham on Liberty: Jeremy Bentham's Idea of Liberty in Relation to His Utilitarianism* (Toronto: University of Toronto Press, 1977), p. 19.

7 For Bentham's projected "Digest of The Laws," see (79.1-137). For Utopias, see D. Long *Bentham on Liberty*, pp. 149 ff., and G. Himmelfarb, "Bentham's Utopia: The National Charity Company," *Journal of British Studies*, 10 (1970), 84-117.

8 Prof. Nozick's "entitlement" theory of distributive justice, particularly in its use of the idea of holdings (*ca*. pp. 150-151), shows interesting similarity to Bentham's, but Bentham was not consistently a minimal state theorist. See R. Nozick, *Anarchy, State and Utopia* (New York: Basic Books, 1974), esp. chapter 7.

9 J. Rawls, *A Theory of Justice* (Cambridge, Mass.: Belknap Press, 1971).

10 *Ibid.*, p. 22.

11 See Long, *op. cit.*, chapter 1.

12 *Ibid.*, pp. 30-34.

13 Jones, *Selections*, 123-4. See also II Comm., chap. 1.

14 Long, *Bentham on Liberty*, x, 25, 39-40.

15 W. Stark (ed.), *Jeremy Bentham's Economic Writings* (London: Allen and Unwin, 1952), 3 vols.; see vol. 3, p. 198.

16 He called it "a state of things...repugnant to the ordinary feel-
    ings and propensities of human nature" (29.2, headed "Civil Equali-
    zation").

17 *Supply Without Burthen: Or Escheat Vice Taxation*, in Stark, *Econo-
    mic Writings*, I, 304-5.

18 *Ibid.*, 318.

19 *Ibid.*, 328.

20 Jones, *Selections*, 73; see also I Comm., 171.

21 For my understanding of Bentham's Poor Plan and Panopticon schemes
    I am greatly indebted to Dr. C. F. Bahmueller, author of *The End
    of Contingency: Jeremy Bentham and English Poverty*, as yet unpub-
    lished, under consideration by the University of California Press.

22 Jones, *Selections*, 124; II Comm. 1.

23 Long, *op. cit.*, 148-9.

24 Jones, *Selections*, 62; I Comm. 1; cf. Bentham at (69.101, 145), and
    Long, *op. cit.*, XIV.

25 Jones, *Selections*, 124; II Comm. 1.

26 See Long, *Bentham on Liberty*, XI-XIV.

27 Jones, *Selections*, 124.

28 H. L. A. Hart (ed.), *Of Laws In General* (London: Athlone Press,
    Collected Works of Jeremy Bentham series, 1970), Appendix B, par's
    57-69, pp. 272-6.

29 Jones, *Selections*, 130; II Comm. 1.

30 See Long, *Bentham on Liberty*, chap. 9,

31 J. Bowring, *The Works of Jeremy Bentham* (Edinburgh: William Tait,
    1838-43, 11 Volumes), V, 389.

32 1959 Edition, vol. x, 250.

33 See Bowring, *Works*, v, 389-416.

34 *Ibid.*, 417-435.

35 "The question is not, can they reason? nor can they talk? but, can
    they suffer?"   J. H. Burns and H. L. A. Hart (eds.), *An Introduc-
    tion to the Principles of Morals and Legislation* (London: Athlone
    Press, 1970);   chapter 17, para. 4, fn.1.

36 W. Harrison (ed.) *A Fragment on Government* (Oxford: Blackwell,
    1948), chapter 1, para. 36.

37 Bowring, *Works*, XI, 240a (n).

38   L. A. Selby-Bigge (ed.), *A Treatise of Human Nature* (Oxford: Clarendon Press), Book III, p. 487.

39   *Ibid.*, pp. 487-8.

40   His arguments are briefly cited later in our discussion.

41   For a brief description, see G. Himmelfarb, "Bentham's Utopia: the National Charity Company," *Journal of British Studies*, 10, 1970, 84-117.   C. F. Bahmueller's *The End of Contingency* contains three excellent chapters on "The Company."

42   T. P. Peardon (ed.), *Second Treatise of Government* (New York: Bobbs-Merrill, 1852), chapter V, para. 27, p. 17.

43   Bowring, *Works*, V, 389.

44   Burns and Hart (eds.), *An Introduction to the Principles of Morals and Legislation*, chapter XVI, para. 26, p. 212.

45   *Ibid.*, p. 210.

46   See Hart, *Of Laws in General*, ed's. intro., XXXVII.

47   T. L. S. Sprigge (ed.), *The Correspondence of Jeremy Bentham* (London: Athlone Press, 1968), Vol. II, #372, p. 488.   (A volume in the *Collected Works* series).

48   Hart (ed.) *Of Laws in General*, Appendix B, Pt. 1, para. 1, p. 251.

49   *Ibid.*, p. 252; My emphasis.

50   *Ibid.*, p. 251-2.

51   Burns and Hart, *Introduction*, chapter 16, para. 26, p. 212 and n. 12.

52   See *Ibid.*, "preface", para's. 19-28.

53   Stark (ed.), *Economic Writings*, III, 257-8.

54   Bentham, J., *Equity Dispatch Court Proposal* (London: R. Heward, 1830), section IX, 43.

55   Stark, *Economic Writings*, III, p. 77.

56   *Ibid.*, p. 338.

57   Bowring, *Works*, VIII, 360 ff.

58   *Ibid.*, p. 374.

59   *Ibid.*, p. 388.

60   *Ibid.*, p. 416.

61   Stark, *Economic Writings*, III, p. 478.

62 *Ibid.*, II, p. 296.

63 On this point I am indebted to chapter VIII of C. F. Bahmueller's *The End of Contingency.*

64 Rawls, *A Theory of Justice*, p. 22.

65 D. Lyons, "Was Bentham a Utilitarian?", in *Reason and Reality*, the Royal Institute of Philosophy Lectures, 5, 1970-1 (London: St. Martin's Press, 1972).

66 See Long, *Bentham on Liberty*, p. 148.

67 Stark, *Eco. Writings*, I, p. 117.

68 Rawls, *Justice*, p. 26-7.

69 *Ibid.*, p. 93.

70 *Ibid.*, p. 49.

71 See Long, *Bentham on Liberty*, p. 9.

72 *Ibid.*, p. 148-9.

73 *Ibid.*, p. 216, 219, 261 n. 18.

74 Bentham was a neo-philosophe (see Long, *op. cit.*, chap. 1 *passim*) and there was, after all, a "Scottish Enlightenment."

75 See Long, *op. cit.*, chap. 1 *passim*.

76 See H. L. Beals, "Jeremy Bentham, Social Engineer," *The Listener*, 3 Aug. 1932, p. 148-50.

77 Long, *op. cit.*, p. 216-219.

78 *Ibid.*, p. 148-9.

79 S. S. Wolin, *Politics and Vision*, (p. 293).

It is commonly thought that John Stuart Mill's political thought
contains irreconcilable contradictions. John Gray challenges this view
by presenting a reinterpretation of Mill centering about his ideas on
property. He shows that Mill's view of *laissez-faire* and his theory of
property rights are compatible with his expanded utilitarianism. He
also demonstrates that Mill's property theory incorporates something
like Locke's labour theory of entitlement, which appears in Mill in the
guise of desert.

JOHN STUART MILL ON THE THEORY OF PROPERTY

Introduction

In this paper a received view of the character of John Stuart
Mill's social thought is contested. It is a commonplace of the intellectual history of nineteenth-century England that the younger Mill was
preeminently a transitional thinker whose writings on social and political questions disclose no settled or coherent doctrine, but only the
synthetic efforts of an ultimately unsuccessful eclecticism. In Mill's
work, we have long been told, rival commitments and sympathies are at
war: his commitment to utilitarianism competes with his affirmation of
values of self-development and originality, his democratic partisanship
is qualified by an elitist dread of majority tyranny, and his loyalty
to the principles of *laisser faire* is at odds with his concessionary
attitude to socialism. The burden of the argument that will be developed here is that this traditional interpretation of Mill's liberalism
fails to grasp the terms of Mill's eclectic method and caricatures his
relation to his utilitarian predecessors and to his liberal posterity.

More specifically, an examination of Mill's doctrine of the
grounds and limits of the institution of private property suggests that
his social thought occupies a middle ground between the more ambitious
systems of other, less discriminating nineteenth-century thinkers.
Mill's position on the land question, his strident neo-Malthusianism
and his radical proposals for the redistribution of inherited wealth
are wholly intelligible in terms of his Ricardian antecedents, and we
do not need to invoke the evil influence of Harriet Taylor to explain
his open-minded stance towards socialist experimentation. The crux of
the argument is the claim that Mill's doctrine of property has more in
common with Locke's labour theory of property acquisition than it has
with the wholly instrumental accounts of Hume and Bentham. It is the
independent weight he gives to considerations of desert that motivates
Mill's condemnation of the wealth inequalities of his day; and it is
his revised utilitarianism, which accommodates such considerations,
that supports an account of the purposes of private property whose
pluralism compares favourably with the more one-dimensional accounts
of such near-contemporaries as Spencer and Marx. (Attention will be

drawn to a somewhat neglected expressive dimension of Mill's doctrine
of property, however, which brings his thought much closer to that of
Marx than is generally allowed). We conclude by listing some of the
difficulties and limitations of Mill's doctrine of property, suggesting that the superannuation of Mill's thought by twentieth-century
realities is a fate it shares with other, rival intellectual traditions.

I

An indispensable preliminary move in any revisionary interpretation of Mill's doctrine of property is a demonstration that conventional accounts of the nature of Mill's utilitarianism are almost unrecog-
nisable caricatures of the complex and subtle theory of morality and
practical reasoning which is worked out in the *System of Logic*, *Utilitarianism*, *On Liberty* and in several of his important occasional essays. Along with much else that is unfortunate in contemporary philosophy, we have inherited from G. E. Moore a view of the place of the
principle of utility in Mill's thought, according to which it is a
moral principle that makes strong demands on action by requiring us to
maximise aggregate or average utility. It is this picture of the rôle
of the principle of utility in Mill's system which John Rawls adopts
and which he employs to elaborate a contrast between his own contrac-
tarian doctrine, in which he supposes considerations of justice to be
paramount, and forms of utilitarianism (such as Mill's) which (Rawls
assumes) can allow justice no independent weight.

More generally, intellectual historians and philosophers have until recently taken from Moore the belief that Mill's principle of utility must be an exclusively want-regarding principle whose application
leaves no room for values such as desert and self-perfection. Accordingly, the doctrine of the higher pleasures, which Mill develops in
Utilitarianism as part of a programme of salvage and reconstruction in
moral thought motivated by his awareness of the crudity of Benthamite
moral psychology and by his conviction of the crucial rôle of self-cul-
ture in the good society, is characterised as an incoherent half-way
house between a straightforward want-satisfying utilitarianism and a
more full-blooded perfectionist ideal of human flourishing. It is the
upshot of recent discussions,[1] however, that Mill's principle of utility is not a classical aggregative or average utility principle, that

its place in Mill's moral thought is not that of a substantive moral
principle, and that its demands on action cannot reasonably be assessed
outside the context of Mill's post-Benthamite theory of human nature.
Since it is a central feature of the view of man which Mill develops
against the claims of his Utilitarian predecessors that the components
of human happiness can never be exhaustively enumerated, but are liable
to indefinite multiplication and alteration in virtue of man's continuing experiments in living, it is not surprising that Mill's utility
principle should not be one that dictates bringing about maximum satisfaction of pre-existing wants.

As against the received view of his thought, Mill himself clearly
saw the principle of utility as a very abstract principle, governing
not just morality but the whole of the Art of Life. It is not a principle from which judgements about men's moral obligations can be derived in any very direct way; indeed, its subject-matter is not the
rightness and wrongness of actions at all. An axiological principle
specifying that happiness is the only thing desirable as an end rather
than a substantive moral principle, Mill's principle of utility is envisaged by him as "the test of all conduct." It applies as a critical
principle in all the areas of practical reasoning which Mill distinguishes when, in the account of the Art of Life given in the *System of
Logic*, he speaks of "its three departments, Morality, Prudence or Policy, and Aesthetics; the Right, the Expedient, and the Beautiful or
Noble, in human conduct or works."[2]

Several implications flow at once from this revisionary view of
Mill's utility principle. First, since it is not a moral principle
but the supreme principle of all practical reasoning, it makes rather
exiguous demands on action and does not condemn as a moral wrong any
failure to maximise utility. If this is right, it becomes intelligible
why Mill fails to see utility and justice as incapsulating incommensurable and competing considerations and regards distributive principles as supplements or corollaries of utility rather than rivals to it.
Second, though I think it demonstrably mistaken to suppose that Mill's
moral theory can be captured felicitously in later terminology of act
and rule utilitarianism, his constant emphasis on the importance of
secondary rules or *axiomata media* confirms that Mill never imagines
that policies can be deduced from the bare principle of utility. For,
though Mill often insists that we need a clear conception of the *summum
bonum* if we are to avoid appeal to intuition in the settlement of moral

disputes, he is in no doubt that practical reasoning typically has as
its province the secondary rules in whose absence he finds inconceiv-
able the formulation of a rational plan of life, or the coordination
of many such plans in social intercourse. Thirdly, it is plainly mistaken to think that Mill's overriding utilitarian commitment precludes
his according any independent weight to values such as desert and self-
perfection. Even the crudest hedonistic utilitarian may allow such
considerations to enter deliberation as tie-breakers, after all, providing pleasure is never sacrificed. Mill's Aristotelian conception
of happiness as sketched in *Utilitarianism* moves far enough away from
old-fashioned psychological hedonism towards a Coleridgean view of mind
and action to allow such considerations entry as constitutive ingred-
ients into the *summum bonum*. The nub of the theory of higher pleasures
is that the exercise of the human capacities of choice, reflective
thought and imagination is not just a means to human happiness, but a
vital ingredient of it. Further, if man's nature is such that it is
permanently liable to self-alteration, so that the content of human
happiness can never be authoritatively circumscribed, it can be seen
that Mill is not inconsistent in thinking that the pursuit of happiness may dictate discounting or overriding the claims of some existing
wants.

The vital centre of Mill's liberalism is not to be found in any
of the consequential arguments he adduces in *On Liberty* in support of
classical liberal freedoms of thought, expression and association, but
rather in a conception of human nature and self-development. It is a
conception whose centrality in Mill's thought is indicated by his epi-
graph to *On Liberty*, which is a quotation from Wilhelm von Humboldt em-
phasising "the absolute and essential importance of human development
in its richest diversity." According to this view, which Mill embraces
in *On Liberty* under the influence of such German writers as Schiller
and Novalis (who were in close touch with Humboldt when he was writing
Limits of State Action), and which he expounds more explicitly in the
seminal articles on *Bentham* and *Coleridge*, it is a complete mistake to
regard man as a natural object with fixed qualities and pre-determined
possibilities. Rather, man is to be conceived as a reflective and
self-critical agent who is actively engaged in the open-ended venture
of exploring his own powers and the world that he has created for himself. On this account, what distinguishes man from the inhabitants of
the animal kingdom and gives him a special moral relationship to

nature,[3] is only his capacity for reflective thought and deliberate
choice; but this is of capital importance. For the shape of man's
life, unlike that of an animal, is not ordained in advance by a reper-
toire of unalterable instincts, but is never more than the permanently
revisable product of his own past thought and action. Unlike the animals, man must be conceived as a progressive being; not, however, in
the sense that moral improvement or social progress is inevitable - a
view to which, even at the high water mark of his St. Simonian and Com-
tist sympathies, Mill never assented - but in the sense that he is to
be understood as having embarked on an interminable voyage of self-
transformation.

The idea - which derives ultimately from Hegel and which Mill imbibed from Hegel's British disciples - that with the exercise of capacities of critical thought an element of indeterminacy and openness enters into man's nature is, of course, quite incompatible with the mechanistic psychology of Mill's Utilitarian predecessors. It also severely restricts the scope and prospects of any science of society and human nature of the sort which Bentham, at least, envisaged. It is also
in apparent contrast with some of the claims Mill makes in his more
"official" writings on the nature of mind and action. Yet it is commonly recognised in recent Mill scholarship that at least in his writings on social and political questions, he broke with the idea of a
determinate, ascertainable human nature. Richard Wollheim declares
that "Mill denied the uniformity of human nature. In doing so he rejected a belief that, implicitly or explicitly, had been central to the
thought of the European Enlightenment, and thus, by descent to classical Utilitarianism."[4] In his recent study, R. J. Halliday asserts that
"Mill felt himself emancipated from simple psychological beliefs. Psychological hedonism, in particular, implied too neat and too narrow an
account of motivation; there was no permanent human nature, to be explained by universal and invariant laws... Mankind were not alike in
all times and places."[5] This is not to say that Mill ever decisively
relinquished the empiricist project of a science of society. It is to
say that Mill is not open to the Popperian charge of psychologism;
for, as Mill himself put it, "The phenomena of society do not depend,
in essentials, on some one agency or law of human nature, with only in-
considerable modifications from others."[6] It is to say, also, that
while he always retains a belief in the uniformity of human nature,
never abandoning the conviction that the way to render human actions

intelligible and to explain them is to subsume them under some few
law-like principles, he breaks with the Enlightment belief - enter-
tained as much by Bentham and by Mill's father as by Hume - in the
constancy of human nature. Though he affirms that a science of Ethology will one day identify the laws of formation of character, he does
not suppose, with Hume, that men are moved in all places and at all
times by the same invariant passions and impulses.

The most important implication for his social thought of Mill's
belief that human nature is open-ended is that his conception of happiness was bound to be at once highly abstract and no longer mainly
want-regarding. Mill's basic argument for a liberal society is thus
not that in such a society men's pre-existent wants will be most
effectively satisfied; for, if that were his argument, it would be open
to the crushing rejoinder that human wants might be satisfied more effectively in Huxley's *Brave New World*, in Skinner's *Walden Two* or in
Bentham's *Panopticon* than in any liberal society. In contrast with
Bentham, whose mechanistic psychology led him to view liberty solely as
a means to security, Mill's conviction that indeterminacy of nature was
partly constitutive of the human species enabled him to treat liberty
as part of the happiness it was his concern to promote.[7] His belief
in the alterability of human nature committed him to a belief which he
found wholly congenial - a belief in the indefinite diversity and cultural and historical variation of the forms of human happiness. Further, much of the argument of *On Liberty*, when taken in conjunction
with the repudiation of benevolent despotism in *Considerations on Representative Government*, with the disavowal of paternalism toward op-
pressed segments of mankind evident in *The Subjection of Women* and
with the chapter on the future of the working class in *The Principles
of Political Economy*, suggests that each man has a peculiar natural
endowment, a quiddity, the practical realisation of which is an indispensable condition of his happiness. In Mill's thought, then, men are
no longer conceived, as in Bentham, as natural places in which sensa-
tions of pain and pleasure have been found to occur, but as unique
sources of projects and possibilities whose achievement (and pursuit)
is constitutive of their happiness.

Thus when, in the introductory chapter in *On Liberty*, Mill eluci-
dates the claim that his defense of a liberal society will be a purely
utilitarian argument, he appeals to "utility in the largest sense,
grounded in the permanent interests of a man as a progressive being."

In making this appeal, Mill acknowledges as his main argument for liberalism the thesis that only an open society - a society whose central
institutions are regarded as alterable and improvable, in which "experiments in living" are tolerated, a diversity of lifestyles promoted
and no tradition is beyond criticism - only such a society can allow
man's possibilities to unfold and the diverse excellences of his nature to flourish "in innumerable divergent directions." Mill's central
argument for liberty, then, is in the claim that a liberal society is
the only kind of society in which men who see their lives leading out
into an open future, who are confident of their many possibilities but
critical of their powers and of each other, who aspire to the status
of autonomous agents and who conceive their individuality as consisting
largely in emancipation from uncritical conformity to custom, will consent to live.

II

What is the bearing of Mill's conception of happiness, and of the
view of human nature in which it is embedded, on his doctrine of property? It is, first of all, that, given his revised conception of
utility, we cannot expect Mill's theory of property to attach as much
weight to considerations of security of expectation and of the coordination of economic activities in a world of scarce resources as is the
case in the theories of Hume and Bentham. We must expect, rather,
that considerations of liberty and of self-development will be crucial
in Mill's assessment of rival institutions of property. Secondly,
granted Mill's conviction of the self-transformation of man and of the
mutability of all forms of social life, we are not puzzled when we find
him denying to some of the truths of classical (Ricardian) economics
the status of laws of nature. In response to Macaulay's famous attack
on his father's *Essay on Government*, Mill had, after all, abandoned his
father's "geometrical method" of deducing consequences from first principles about human nature as being too aprioristic to cope with the
complex realities of political life. Also in the essay "On the Definition and Method of Political Economy" he had affirmed that the assumptions of economic science were abstractions a long way removed from
concrete experience: "Political Economy presupposes an arbitrary definition of man, as a being who invariably does that by which he may obtain the greatest amount of necessaries, conveniences and luxuries,

with the smallest amount of labour and physical self-denial with which
they can be obtained in the existing state of knowledge."[8]

If, in this and similar assertions, Mill explicitly distances himself from that abstract creature, *homo economicus*, who is so often attributed to the classical economist, then we may anticipate his applying to property institutions the judgement that he applied to political institutions: namely, that questions of their desirability are
questions of "time, place and circumstance" and not of *a priori* deduc-
tion. Thus when in *Principles of Political Economy* (1848) Mill comes
to discuss the distribution of wealth, he begins by making his well-
known distinction between laws of production and laws of distribution:

> The laws and conditions of the production of wealth,
> partake of the character of physical truths. There
> is nothing optional or arbitrary in them... It is
> not so with the distribution of wealth. That is a
> matter of human institution solely. The things once
> there, mankind, individually or collectively, can do
> with them as they like.[9]

Thirdly, and following from the two points I have made, we may expect Mill to adopt a very open-minded attitude to socialist proposals
for the reform of existing property institutions. With several changes
of emphasis, this is just what he does. At no point does Mill invoke
the mechanical slogans of *laisser faire*; much of the time, indeed, he
is engaged in criticising them. It represents a fundamental misconception, then, to assert (as is still sometimes done) that Mill was
brought by the influence of Harriet Taylor from a standard *laisser
faire* position to something resembling what later became known as Fabian socialism. Mill was never a dogmatic exponent of *laisser faire* -
no Utilitarian of any description could be that, after all - and his
socialism is more a manifestation of his permanent commitment to social
experimentation than a doctrine of the public ownership of the means of
production. Since it differs in many fundamental respects from the
socialist tradition by which it was to be supplanted, Mill's socialism
needs scrupulously careful examination (which it will be given later in
this paper). At this point, however, by way of emphasizing the unity
of Mill's thought on social questions, it will be shown that his arguments about socialism and private property are of a piece with his arguments for liberty.

His notion of man as inherently a progressive being suggests to
Mill the necessity of defining the sphere of legitimate social control
in such a way as to protect and promote the development of men as

autonomous agents. This he does in *On Liberty* by proposing the famous principle of noninterference. In fact, this principle assumes
various forms at different stages in the argument of *On Liberty*, but
its main force is contained in the injunction that the liberty of the
individual should be invaded by society or the state only if his actions are (or may be) injurious to the interests of others - only
where, as Mill (echoing distinctions made by Bentham) might put it, a
man's actions are other-regarding rather than self-regarding. It is
worth noting that, though Mill stresses that it states a necessary and
not a sufficient condition of justified limitation of liberty (since
enforcement costs may make it wrong to limit liberty even where the
interests of others are clearly damaged by the conduct under consideration), he insists also that the noninterference principle is violated
whenever individuals enjoy a traditional freedom to act in ways injurious to others' interests. The example of a traditional right unjus-
tifiable by the noninterference principle which Mill cites most frequently is that of unrestricted procreation, which is injurious both
to the interests of the offspring of irresponsible parents and to the
interests of all who compete with them for scarce jobs and resources.
Further, it should not be thought that Mill's adamant opposition to
social coercion in respect of self-regarding conduct implies any support on his part for an attitude of indifference towards such conduct.
Repeatedly he goes out of his way to point out that recognition that
conduct is outside the domain of legal and social control in no way
commits us to refraining from comment on its prudence or nobility. In
fact one of the purposes of the noninterference principle is, drawing
on the account of the Art of Life set out in the *System of Logic*, to
distinguish between conduct which is properly subject to moral or legal
control and conduct in respect of which the appropriate appraisals are
prudential or aesthetic. In asserting that only actions which might
harm the interests of others could ever rightly be subject to coercion,
Mill did not intend to deprive society of the use of advice, exhorta-
tion and example; but, in proscribing coercion over a wide field of
personal conduct where assessments of its wisdom or its excellence
were salient, he staked a claim to a social space within which diversity and individuality might flourish.

   That the argument of *On Liberty* is continuous with Mill's discussion in the *Principles* of the limitations of the noninterference principle can be shown by considering the account he gives there of the

proper province of government. It is evident Mill thought that the
considerations which supported the noninterference principle of the
Liberty (1859) were the same considerations which supported granting to
the state a wide range of noncoercive functions in the *Principles*
(1848). In the latter volume Mill distinguished between "necessary"
and "optional" state functions, dividing the latter into two types,
"authoritative" and "nonauthoritative." Against dogmatic noninterven-
tionists, Mill argued for the complete inadequacy of restricting the
state to the prevention of force and fraud, concluding pragmatically
that the range of necessary government functions, though certainly
larger than supposed by many exponents of *laisser faire*, could not be
identified "by any universal rule, save the simple and vague one, that
it should never be admitted save when the case of expediency is
strong."[10] Against interventionists, however, Mill made a crucial distinction between two types of "optional" government interference, the
"authoritative" and the "non-authoritative." Since the former encompassed interventions by sanction and legal prohibition, there was a
strong presumption against it, deriving from utility in the larger
sense, whereas there was no such presumption against the latter, which
merely supplemented and did not replace successful private initiative.
Unlike the latter, which avoided all coercion beyond that involved in
the exercise of the state's taxing power, the former involved the state
as order-giver and tended to stultify the spirit of independence.

Thus it was Mill's belief that the larger utilitarian considerations supporting the noninterference principle justified granting the
state a wide range of functions where it was clear that private institutions could not provide the desirable things (public goods, as we
should say) in question. The state might in this way properly assume
a share of responsibility for poor relief, colonisation, scientific
research and the financing of education, among other things. Mill's
general view, in fact, was that the preservation of individuality in
the modern world could not be achieved by holding to any very fixed
rule, but demanded the maximum centralisation of information in the
state together with the maximum diffusion of power and initiative
throughout society.

If Mill was not at any time a dogmatic exponent of *laisser faire*,
it is no less important to mark the respects in which his criticism of
society differed from contemporary and subsequent socialist traditions.
The major targets of Mill's "new political economy"[11] were the

maldistribution of property and oppressive system of industrial organisation. Mill's views in the posthumously published "Chapters on
Socialism," which appeared in the *Fortnightly Review* in 1879, are in
no important respect different from these expressed in the *Principles*
of 1848, notwithstanding the warnings he gives in the *Review* against
catastrophist forms of socialism. Mill shows no signs of having modified the doctrine of the *Principles*, in which he had averred that, in
existing society, reward, instead of being proportioned to labour and
the abstinence of individuals, was almost in inverse ratio to it. One
of the primary causes of this inequitable distribution of rewards, according to Mill, was the concentration of fortunes through their unin-
terrupted accumulation across the generations. The remedy for this,
which Mill proposed in the first edition of his *Principles*, was the
institution, not of an estates duty, but of what we would nowadays call
an accessions duty or an inheritance tax, to be levied on the recipient
and not on the donor of the capital. For Mill the merit of such a tax
is that, unlike other arrangements, it need not transfer wealth from
private individuals to the state, since it is easily avoidable through
the eminently desirable expedient of dispersing one's wealth widely.
Importantly, Mill favoured a steeply progressive inheritance tax - one
which, though it would allow the transfer of a "modest competence,"
would bring down all great fortunes in a couple of generations.

Mill's support of progression in inheritance taxation contrasts
sharply with his strong opposition to it in the taxation of income. A
progressive income tax, he contended, was tantamount to "hanging a
weight upon the swift to diminish the distance between them and the
slow;" it would be to "impose a penalty on people for having worked
harder and saved more than their neighbours," which is the same as "re-
lieving the prodigal of the expenses of the prudent."[12] One explanation of this disparity lies in Mill's constant preoccupation with saving and his lifelong distaste for conspicuous consumption, motives
which led him to express his support in principle for an expenditure
tax before the Select Committee on Income and Property Tax of 1861.
Another, deeper reason for this contrast is a basic feature of his
thought, namely that, though he favoured a redistribution of property
and so of incomes, he was not a strict egalitarian. As he put it
himself:

> We hold with Bentham, that equality, though not
> the sole end, is one of the ends of good social
> arrangements; and that a system of institutions
> which does not make the scale turn in favour of
> equality, whenever this can be done without im-
> pairing the security of property which is the
> product and reward of personal exertion, is es-
> sentially a bad government - a government for
> the few, to the injury of many.[13]

This is an important quotation in that, as well as making clear
the subsidiary importance of equality in his doctrine, it also makes
clear that the instrumental value of the security of property derived
for Mill from its rôle in guaranteeing deserved rewards. The sense of
justice which animates his writings on property is, in general, a neo-
Lockean one which makes a straightforward appeal to thrift, industry
and risk-taking as grounds of just rewards. It is also true, of
course, that Mill opposed the inheritance of large fortunes because
huge concentrations of wealth might in his view become inimical to
liberty, whether they were held in public or in private hands. But the
independent weight of desert in his thought must not on this account be
neglected. One major contrast between Mill's thought on questions of
property and distribution and that found in socialist traditions is
that, though both draw on Ricardian ideas about the origins of economic
value in labour, Mill clearheadedly saw that such ideas (though they
had radical implications about the land question, which we shall consider presently) entailed no overriding commitment to equality.

A second point of contrast between Mill's critique of the emergent
industrial society of his day and that of any orthodox socialist tradition is found in his constant stress upon the virtues of competition.
It is true that Mill was a lifelong opponent of that mode of industrial
organisation in which enterprises are owned and managed by owners of
capital who stand in an authoritarian relationship with wage-earners -
a system which he thought became worse rather than better with the
growth of joint-stock companies. He opposed it because it institution-
alized a permanent conflict of interests between capital-owners and
wage-earners, and no productive system which rested on such a basis
could be expected to be either stable or efficient. The separation between wage-earners and owner-managers deprived workers of any real opportunity for personal initiative and precluded their becoming anything
like the responsible, self-reliant individuals celebrated in *On Liberty*. This is related to another point of contrast between Mill's

radicalism and the Fabian socialism by which it was to be largely supplanted in England. Mill insistently (and sometimes exaggeratedly)
disavowed all paternalism in regard to the working classes of his day.
So long as employers and employees continued in a master-servant relationship, hostility between the classes would not diminish significantly, and it would be foolish to expect much improvement in the mental and moral level of the working classes. The improvement Mill was
looking for, however, was not merely a greater prudence in want-satis-
faction, but the elevation of existing desires.

Mill's objections to the capitalist system of his day led him to
take a continuing interest in schemes for profit-sharing, industrial
partnership and producers' cooperation, but his boldest vision went far
beyond such proposals and (as Lionel Robbins has suggested) can best
be characterized as a form of nonrevolutionary competitive syndicalism.
As he put it,

> The form of association....which if mankind con-
> tinue to improve must be expected in the end to
> predominate is not that which can exist between
> a capitalist as Chief, and work-people without a
> voice in the management, but the association of
> labourers themselves on terms of equality, col-
> lectively owning the capital with which they
> carry on their operations and working under man-
> agers elected and removable by themselves.[14]

This vision of a non-state socialist society, unlike that of virtually all socialists, does not include the elimination of competition
and might (recalling Mill's support for piece-work) demand its intensi-
fication. If Mill was in any sense a socialist - and, apart from his
own avowals in the *Autobiography*, he certainly envisaged an economic
order which was no longer recognisably that of nineteenth-century
England, and which differs at least as much from our own capitalist
society - then his was decidedly a "market socialism" in which the core
capitalist institutions of private property in the instruments of production and commodity production for competitive markets were at no
point seriously compromised. In considering the relation between
Mill's *laisser faire* socialism and socialist orthodoxies, it is well
to remember that, despite his iconoclastic sympathies with trade union-
ism, he envisaged no real place for trade unions in the society of the
future; he looked forward to a time when the harmony of interests between all partners in production, facilitated by worker's ownership and
self-management, would allow "the true euthanasia of trades union-
ism."[15] Whereas Mill always criticised the narrowly acquisitive

aspects of his own society, his views on trade unions reveal no trace
of any solidaristic element in his opposition to the capitalist system
of his day.

A fourth and final point of contrast between Mill's thought and
socialist traditions is found in his opposition to productivist conceptions of the good life. Like the other classical economists, Mill
accepted that economic growth could only be temporary in a world of
scarce natural resources in which population constantly pressed on
land and food reserves. In contrast with all other economists in the
classical tradition and in its socialist aftermath, however, Mill did
not fear the arrival of a stationary economy, but rather welcomed it
as an opportunity for a large-scale transformation in social values.
It is no doubt true that a part of Mill's concern that society be re-
ordered to allow for a peaceful transition to a no-growth economy derives from his neo-Malthusian insistence on the finitude of the world's
resources and the ever-present danger of over-population. Yet the larger part of Mill's advocacy of a stationary-state economy is concerned,
not with considerations of resource-depletion, but with the damaging
effects on human character of the unremitting pursuit of possessions
and with the destructive consequences for the natural environment of
open-ended economic growth. In Mill's own emphatic words, in the chapter on "The Stationary State" in the *Principles*,

> I confess I am not charmed with the ideal of life
> held out by those who think that the normal state
> of human beings is that of struggling to get on;
> that the trampling, crushing, elbowing and tread-
> ing on each other's heels, which form the existing
> type of social life, are the most desirable lot of
> mankind, or anything but the disagreeable symptoms
> of one of the phases of industrial progress.[16]

In words which show him to have moved altogether outside the Benthamite
utilitarian tradition, Mill goes on to illustrate the harmful consequences for human development of an overcrowded world: "It is not good
for man to be kept perforce at all times in the presence of his species. A world from which solitude is extirpated, is a very poor ideal
...Nor is there much satisfaction in contemplating the world with nothing left to the spontaneous activity of nature." Concluding the chapter with the remark that "a stationary condition of capital and population implies no stationary state of human improvement," Mill effectively confirms his distance from the productivist central stream of classical economic thought and of its socialist posterity. It should be

clear of John Stuart Mill, at least, of the great liberals, how little
he owed to any culture of possessive individualism. It may be, as Professor Macpherson has himself argued, that Mill did not finally eman-
cipate himself from the heritage of James Mill and Jeremy Bentham; but
there can be no doubt that, as Professor Macpherson also emphasised,
the entire tendency of Mill's eclectic stance is to reduce the tradition of Bentham and his father to one partial aspect of a progressively
unfolding truth.

III

Having cleared the ground by dispelling some conventional misconceptions about Mill's relation to *laisser faire* and socialism, it is
now appropriate to undertake a more positive, systematic and extended
account of what we will characterize as his neo-Lockean doctrine of
property. An initial difficulty in any enterprise of comparing and
contrasting the accounts of the justifications of private property institutions advanced by Mill and Locke is that of interpreting Locke
himself. At the risk of seeming dogmatic, we shall claim without much
evidence that there are two currents of thought in Locke's writings
about government and property: one that is a sort of proto-utilitarian
deontology supported by Locke's theology, the other a theory of the
property-making relationship between men and things in which it is the
value that one's labour has added to a natural resource that gives one
a property right in it.[17]

A number of observations are in order at this point. The first is
that Locke plainly does not think that these strands of argument, taken
severally or collectively, support what we now ordinarily think of as
full liberal ownership (in Honoré's sense), which (as his account of
the rights and duties of children shows) he hedged about with several
important restrictions.[18] The second is that modern writers who see
themselves as revising a sort of Lockean entitlement theory of justice
in acquisition are plainly elaborating on an account very different
from Locke's. Nozick's account, for example, contains neither the
theologically reinforced utilitarianism nor the emphasis on a "value-
added" notion of desert which I have identified as the dominant motifs
in Locke's doctrine of property. Nozick's doctrine of property, its
Lockean proviso notwithstanding, has more in common with Kant's account of the acquisition of personal titles to property through positive acts of occupancy, or with Spencer's derivation of equal shares

in land from a natural right which accords to men an indefeasible
claim to equal freedom, than it has with anything in Locke. For labour
appears in the doctrines of Kant and Spencer, not as a ground of desert, but as the appropriative act which takes the area occupied or
homesteaded out of the commons. (Nozick's political thought, it would
seem, turns out to be a fusion, not of Locke with Hobbes, but - more
strangely - of Hobbes with Kant). Third, our claim regarding Mill is
that in his doctrine of property Lockean utilitarianism is secularised,
the element of desert as giving rise to a labour title in the full value of one's labour emphasised, and a wholly new expressivist aspect of
the doctrine of property added which derives from Coleridgean and
thereby Hegelian sources.

Mill's appropriation of Locke's desert theory is well illustrated
by the following quotation, which C. B. Macpherson describes as an extended definition of property according to Mill's doctrine:

> The institution of property, when limited to its
> essential elements, consists in the recognition,
> in each person, of a right to the exclusive dis-
> posal of what he or she have produced by their
> own exertions, or received either by gift or by
> fair agreement, without force or fraud, from
> those who produced it. The foundation of the
> whole is, the right of producers to what they
> themselves have produced.[19]

Given the basis in a theory of desert as the ground of private
property, we are now able to reconstruct rationally the doctrine of
property that supported Mill's opinions on trade unions, socialism and
laisser faire. Before writing the justly praised[20] review of W. T.
Thornton's book *On Labour and its Claims*, Mill had already come to dissent from the classical theory of the wages fund, asserting that

> The doctrine hitherto taught by all or most
> economists (including myself) which denied it
> to be possible that trade unions can raise
> wages, or which limited their operation in
> that respect to the somewhat earlier attain-
> ment of a rise which the competition of the
> market would have produced without them - the
> doctrine is deprived of its suitable founda-
> tion, and must be thrown aside.[21]

Mill's reaction to the classical wage-fund theory and his uncon-
ventional sympathy for all trade union activities of a non-restriction-
ist sort go far towards explaining his conviction that labourers were
rendered unfree by the capitalist system of his day as well as being
the victims of an injustice. As he put it in the *Principles*: "The

generality of labourers in this and most other countries have as little
choice of occupation or freedom of locomotion, are practically as dependent on fixed rules and on the will of others, as they could be on
any system short of actual slavery."[22]

When he compared communistic schemes with proposals for reform of
private property institutions, his sympathy for the former and his continued loyalty to the latter were as much the expression of his libertarian commitment as of the importance he attached to notions of desert:

> If, therefore, the choice were to be made between
> communism with all its chances, and the present
> state of society with all its suffering and in-
> justices; if the institution of private property
> necessarily carried with it as a consequence that
> the produce of labour should be apportioned as we
> now see it, almost in an inverse ratio to the
> labour..., if this, or Communism, were the alter-
> native, all the difficulties, great or small, of
> Communism would be but as dust in the balance.[23]

Mill's reservations about communistic schemes, as expressed in the
posthumous *Chapters on Socialism*, are not, as some have claimed,[24]
based on a negative libertarian insistence on unlimited contractual
freedom, but rather on his forebodings about the prospects of human
self-development in a regime from which private property inhibitions
had been extirpated. As Mill put it in the *Principles*: "The question
is whether there would be any asylum left for individuality of character; whether public opinion could not be a tyrannical yoke; whether the
absolute dependence of each on all, and surveillance of each by all,
would not grind all down into a tame uniformity of thoughts, feelings
and actions."[25]

Such reservations are wholly continuous with the concerns of
Mill's later writings and, above all, with the argument of *On Liberty*,
in which a strongly "positive" conception of freedom as autonomy figures centrally, notwithstanding that the subject matter of the book is
the classical liberal one of the grounds and limits of moral and political obligation. Thus it is Mill's distinctive synthesis of Lockean
desert theory with the Romantic concern for individuality and self-development that underlies both his criticism of the dogmas of *laisser
faire* and his ambivalence towards some of the wilder forms of socialist
thought. Mill's own *laisser faire* socialism, as I have termed his
prognostication about the future of the working class, represents an
attempt to work out radical reforms of the institution of private

property (which in Mill's view, had never had a fair trial anyway) that
yet preserved those possibilities of independence and self-reliance
which were its peculiar virtues.

Much of the argument so far has served to de-emphasize the classical utilitarian complexion of Mill on property, and to point up a contrast between his doctrine and that of Hume and Bentham. I have not
argued for an unbridgeable gulf between Mill and his utilitarian ances-
try, since it is obvious that they have common concerns. Hume, at any
rate, saw political liberty as among the justifying instrumental values
of property and Mill certainly did not dissent from Bentham in attaching great weight to security of property as an incentive to effort.
The gap is opened up between Mill and the school of Hume and Bentham in
part by Mill's absorption of a Lockean-Ricardian labour theory of value
from classical economic doctrine. It is this which explains why Mill
always treated the ownership of land as a special case in which the existence of permanent bequeathable property rights is least justifiable.
It also accounts for his sustained interest in schemes for peasant proprietorship and his unremitting hostility to landlords. It is a Lockean conviction that the marginal productivity of a man's labour is one
good test of his worth of which he should not be deprived, rather than
merely a concern for rational resource-allocation, which accounts for
his uncompromising defence of competition.[26]

An entirely new dimension of Mill on property, one that is wholly
absent from the utilitarian tradition, is what I have already referred
to as its expressive aspect - the dimension of property institutions
whereby they enhance or stunt the growth of personality. That Mill
should have gratefully imbibed expressivist doctrines from Coleridge's
writings on ecclesiastical property is readily intelligible when it is
remembered how far he had strayed from the abstractly individualist
picture of human nature which Maculay had attacked in James Mill's
Essay on Government. One general implication of a theory of the partial indeterminacy and substantial alterability of human nature and
of its intimate dependency on institutions and forms of social life
that are culturally and historically variable is to render incredible
and largely useless the picture of human society as a contractual association of rational egoists. And if human wants and purposes cannot
be conceived as if they were properties of an ahistorical, pre-social
essence, then the relation between men and social institutions can no
longer be conceptualised as a largely external and instrumental one.

It is clear from *Considerations on Representative Government*, for example, that Mill has broken with his father's economic model of political institutions as more or less effective contrivances for the satisfaction of pre-determined and largely private wants. Thus Mill saw the virtue of democratic institutions mainly in the disposition to active citizenship which only widespread opportunities for participation can inculcate. That participation in social institutions was internally related to the development of personality was, in any case, a truth Mill had learnt from his reading of Tocqueville on American democracy and one he never forgot in his treatment of distributive questions. It is Mill's recognition of the truth that men's experience of life in established social practices and institutions forms their wants and their concepts of the good life that, more than any other single development of his thought, separates him from the old want-regarding utilitarianism and pushes his inquiries into directions that were to be more thoroughly explored by English writers such as Bosanquet, Green and Hobhouse.

IV

How well does Mill on property stand a comparison with his near contemporaries, Spencer and Marx? And how much of Mill's doctrine retains relevance today? Certainly Mill's pluralistic account of the grounds and limitations of private property does not contain the internal contradictions of Spencer's (perhaps unjustly neglected) neo-Kantian theory. It is a fatal difficulty of Spencer's theory, as of Nozick's, that the universal entitlement to natural resources flowing from equal natural rights to freedom has the logical consequence of conferring part-ownership of one man's labour on all other men and so violates the original principle that each man is equally the owner of his person and his labour.[27] That neo-Kantian doctrines of property contain this insoluble dilemma emerges from the very obvious fact, with which both Spencer and Nozick try to grapple, that each generation's equal freedom to appropriate natural resources is substantially curtailed by its predecessor's exercise of the same right. It was in response to this fact that Spencer, holding that each man has an equal title to the land, at one time supported its nationalisation. Similarly Nozick has this fact in mind when he proposes that original appropriation must be conceived as generating an obligation to compensate

all those who have thereby suffered a net decrease in the well-being
they would otherwise have enjoyed. The difficulty in each case is that
remedying generational inequity involves conferring a partial title to
the labour of each man upon all the rest in virtue of the fact that
part of the value of the originally appropriated resource is now locked
into transformed objects.

Insofar as Mill faces a similar difficulty, it is far less pressing and one to which he may respond within the Lockean framework by
proposing that the means of production revert to something resembling
common ownership when the "enough and as good" proviso no longer operates. The difficulty is less central for Mill, in any case, in virtue
of his overall utilitarian commitment which, though revised so as to
accommodate values such as desert and individuality, contains much else
as well. For Mill there can be no question of deducing maxims about
property-distribution from first principles, and the judgement he makes
about rival schemes of property rights is always largely an empirical
(and conjectural) one. No less than Rawls, Mill sees the specific features of a society's productive and distributive system as being largely contingent matters of "time, place and circumstance," uniquely determined neither by historical laws nor by basic principles of right
and good. Like all social institutions, distributive arrangements are
institutions in respect of which an intelligent choice may be made.

Like Marx, Mill saw that the practical operation of private property institutions could defeat their purposes, and, like Marx, he saw
the continued existence of wage-labour as a fetter on working-class
development. Both writers perceived that property relations have an
important expressive and symbolic dimension and are closely related to
relations of power and authority in society. In each of them, moral
considerations deriving from a labour theory of the title to property
compete with the expressive conception of work. It is part of my argument that their respective posterities have grossly exaggerated the
fundamental difference in outlook between Marx and Mill, whose rival
conjectures regarding the future of society derive mainly from the divergent paradigms of economic thought they endorse rather than from
diametrically opposed metaphysical views of human nature. Where the
two writers differ in their doctrines of property, Marx plausibly comes
off worse, his refusal to speculate on the institutional framework of
post-capitalist society looking like historicist hybris rather than
anti-utopian modesty. Whereas both Marx and Mill were ineluctably

creatures of the nineteenth century and were writers almost wholly des-
titute of prophetic insight, it is Mill who approaches more closely to
our own concerns in an era in which the need for devolution of large
institutions and the stultifying effects of mass society are widely
acknowledged. Mill also seems to have been nearer the mark in pre-
dicting the stationary state rather than an ever-worsening trade cycle
as the occasion for a fundamental transition in political and economic
arrangements.

I do not want to conclude without indicating some of the limitations and difficulties of Mill's doctrine of property. At the level of
its underlying moral philosophy, there are good reasons to doubt the
coherence of Mill's version of utilitarianism - reasons which it is not
the purpose of this paper to explore, but whose force does not depend
upon common misconceptions of his moral thought. If they are valid,
such considerations count against any teleological theory, such as
Mill's, which seeks to incorporate values such as desert and individuality into a description of the *summum bonum*. This question about the
viability of Mill's moral theory becomes a question of practical and
political importance when it is recognised that individuality and justice may still in some circumstances be competitive values even in the
context of Mill's revisionary utilitarianism. At the methodological
level, we may well want to question the adequacy of Mill's sharp distinction between laws of production and laws of distribution, given
that something rather like the wages fund doctrine has surfaced under
other colours in modern growth theory. It is arguable, also, that Mill
was overly optimistic in supposing that men would respond to the arrival of the stationary state in a capitalist economy by a large-scale re-
valuation of values rather than by intensifying competition for a constant (and perhaps dwindling) quantity of goods and services. If such
a criticism has force, however, it bears against virtually the whole
body of modern social thought, which is exceptionally ill-equipped to
cope with the problems posed by the emergence of natural and social
constraints on further economic growth.

Finally, we may well question the practical cogency of Mill's
vision of a society of fraternal but competitive worker cooperatives.
When we read the *Principles*, we cannot help reflecting that it became
the standard economics textbook at a time when England was still only
semi-industrialised, when the statification of the economy was minimal
and the joint-stock revolution had only lately got under way. It is a

difficult, if profitable, task to try to envisage workable institutional vehicles for workers' ownership after a century in which the
cooperative movement has sunk into insignificance and the multinational
corporation has acquired a discretionary authority often exceeding that
of sovereign states. More specifically the history of labour-managed
economies (such as postwar Yugoslavia) suggests their liability to debilitating inefficiencies and apparently ineradicable inequalities.
The prospects for Mill's vision of a classless society in which core
capitalist institutions are yet preserved is plainly bleak. But, if it
is hard for us to share the cautious optimism with which he viewed the
future of society, perhaps the fault is not altogether Mill's. The
obsolescence of intellectual traditions is a fate that has overtaken,
not only Mill's liberalism, but also its socialist rivals. What is now
needed is a synoptic vision like Mill's, but allied to an originality
which his own thought lacked. We will do well, though, if we achieve
in our own social thought the synthesis of imaginative vigour, scrupulous clarity and reasoned partisanship which Mill displays in his reflections on property, its grounds, its limits and its bearing on the
human prospect.

FOOTNOTES

1   I have in mind particularly D. G. Brown's "Mill on Liberty and
    Morality," *Philosophical Review* LXXXI (1972), pp. 133-158; and
    David Lyons, "J. S. Mill's Theory of Morality," *Nomos*, 10,
    no. 2, May 1976.

2   *System of Logic*, VI, xiii, 6, *Collected Works*, vol. VIII, Toronto,
    1974.

3   See Mill's stimulating essay on "Nature," collected in volume 10 of
    his *Works* (Toronto, 1969).

4   Wollheim, Introduction to the World's Classics Edition of *On Liber-
    ty*, *Representative Government and the Subjection of Women*, London,
    1975, p xi.

5   R. J. Halliday, *John Stuart Mill* (London, 1976), pp. 55-56.

6   *System of Logic*, bk. VI, viii, p. 583.

7   I am indebted for this and several other points in my understanding
    of Bentham to D. G. Long's *Bentham on Liberty* (Toronto, 1977), a
    study no student of Utilitarianism or nineteenth-century English
    thought can afford to ignore.

8   *Collected Works*, IV, p. 326.

9   Principles of Political Economy, Book II, Chapter I, "Of Property,"
    first paragraph, *Collected Works*, vol. II, Toronto, 1965.

10 *Principles*, vol. III of *Collected Works*, p. 804.

11 I refer to the book by Pedro Schwartz, *J. S. Mill's New Political
    Economy* (London, 1968), from which I have learnt much.

12 See Mill's *Principles*, Penguin edition (London, 1970), p. 45.

13 See Mill's *Dissertations and Discussions* (London, 1839), p. 395.

14 *Principles*, Penguin ed., p. 133.

15 See Schwartz, op. cit., p. 103.

16 *Principles*, Penguin ed., p. 113 *et seq.*

17 I am indebted for my understanding of these aspects of Mill's
    thought, and so for several important points in my argument, to an
    unpublished (and untitled) paper by Alan Ryan, whose ongoing work
    on property promises to make a major contribution to our
    understanding of the subject. I have learnt much, also, from
    Lawrence C. Becker's discussion of Mill's doctrine in his recent
    important book, *Property Rights* (London, 1977).

18 See Honoré's classic paper, "Ownership," in A. G. Guest's *Oxford Essays in Jurisprudence I* (Oxford 1961).

19 See C. B. Macpherson, *The Life and Times of Liberal Democracy*, (London, 1977), p. 53, and his *Democratic Theory: Essays in Retrieval* (London, 1973), p. 99.

20 E.g. by George Stigler, cited in Schwartz, *op. cit.*, pp. 92, 274.

21 Cited by Schwartz, *op. cit.*, pp. 95-96.

22 Cited by Macpherson from *Principles*, Book II, chap. 1, sect. 3.

23 *Principles*, Penguin ed., p. 358.

24 E.g. Macpherson, *Democratic Theory*, p. 99 *et seq.*

25 *Principles*, Penguin ed., p. 361.

26 I owe this point to Alan Ryan's paper (cited *supra*, note 17). I do not claim that he will assent to my use of it in support of my overall reinterpretation of Mill on utility, liberty and property.

27 I am indebted for illumination on these points to Dr. Hillel Steiner's forthcoming paper "On Liberty, Liberalism and Justice," presented to the I.P.S.A. Conference in Edinburgh, August 16-21, 1976.

E. K. Hunt presents Karl Marx's theory of private property in the
broader context of his social thought. Extensive reference is made to
the process of production as described in the *Grundrisse* and in *Capi-*
tal as well as to the theme of alienation which appears in the *1844*
Manuscripts. Following Marx, Hunt claims that private property estranges man from his true identity as a social being. All production
is social in character, so that private appropriation destroys the
social base that makes man truly human.

MARX'S THEORY OF PROPERTY AND ALIENATION

Of the various theories of property examined in this symposium,
several posit property relations as a genre of social relations and
several furnish moral critiques of property relations. Marx's theory
fits into both of these categories. But Marx was the only theorist
that critically examined those aspects of property relations which are
general (i.e. common to all societies) and those which are specific
to capitalism. Consequently of the theories examined, Marx's is the
only social scientific and moral critique of capitalism as a socio-
economic system.

For Marx, human life is a social process in which man satisfies
human needs and develops human powers through social activities which
appropriate and transform nature. The relations between the individual and society and between the individual and nature are reciprocally
mediated, that is, the relation between an individual and nature is
mediated by that individual's relations in society, while most social
relations are mediated by the mode of people's appropriation of nature.

"Property", Marx writes, "originally means no more than a human
being's relation to his natural conditions of production as belonging
to him."[1] Thus, in its origins property merely involves the individual's recognition that the objects of nature with which he produces
are *natural presuppositions* of his self, which only form, so to speak,
his extended body."[2] But property is also always a social relation.
Thus property is the link connecting an individual with both nature
and society:

> An isolated individual could no more have pro-
> perty in land and soil than he could speak. He
> could, of course, live off it as substance, as do
> the animals. The relation to the earth as property
> is always mediated through the occupation of the
> land and soil...by the tribe, the commune, [or some
> other social formation] in some more or less natu-
> rally arisen or already historically developed form.
> The individual can never appear here in the dot-like
> isolation in which he appears as mere free worker.
> If the objective conditions of his labour are pre-
> supposed as belonging to him, then he himself is sub-
> jectively presupposed as a member of a commune,
> through which his relation to land and soil is medi-
> ated.[3]

In fact, property relations as relations to nature and relations
among members of a social group are necessary preconditions for human
life in all societies, in all times:

> [The] *natural conditions of existence*...[for
> any human being] are themselves double: (1) of a
> subjective and (2) of an objective nature. He
> finds himself a member of a family, clan, tribe
> etc....and, as such a member, he relates to a
> specific nature (say, here, still earth, land
> soil) as his own inorganic being, as a condition
> of his production and reproduction.[4]

In notebooks IV and V of the *Grundrisse* (pp. 373-554) Marx devotes
extensive discussion to precapitalist forms of property ownership. He
discusses primitive clan, Asiatic despotism, Roman, Germanic and feudal
forms of property. After a lengthy discussion of each of these modes
of ownership, Marx summarizes the features which appear more or less in
common in all precapitalist property relations:

> The main point is this: In all these forms -
> in which landed property and agriculture form the
> basis of the economic order, and where the economic
> aim is hence the production of use values, that is,
> the *reproduction of the individual* within the spe-
> cific relation to the commune in which he is its
> basis - there is to be found: (1) Appropriation not
> through labour, but presupposed to labour, appropria-
> tion of the natural conditions of labour, of the
> *earth* as the original instrument of labour as well as
> its workshop and repository of raw materials. The
> individual relates simply to the objective conditions
> of labour as being his; relates to them as the inor-
> ganic nature of his subjectivity, in which the latter
> realizes itself; the chief objective condition of
> labour does not itself appear as a *product* of labour,
> but is already there as *nature*; on one side of the
> living individual, on the other the earth, as the ob-
> jective condition of his reproduction; (2) but this
> *relation* to land and soil, to the earth, as the pro-
> perty of the labouring individual - who thus appears
> from the outset not merely as labouring individual,
> in this abstraction, but who has an *objective mode
> of existence* in his ownership of the land, an exis-
> tence *presupposed* to his activity, and not merely as
> a result of it, a presupposition of his activity
> just like his skin, his sense organs, which of course
> he also reproduces and develops etc. in the life pro-
> cess, but which are nevertheless presuppositions of
> this process of his reproduction - is instantly medi-
> ated by the naturally arisen, spontaneous, more or
> less historically developed and modified presence
> of the individual as *member of a commune* - his nat-
> urally arisen presence as a member of a tribe etc.[5]

Property relations, then, express both the manner in which people relate to nature and the manner in which they relate to each other. Both aspects of property relations are of central significance in the process that Marx labels "reproduction." The process of reproduction is, for Marx, a natural and social process containing numerous reciprocally interrelated aspects which form an organic whole. This concept is so important for Marx's critique of capitalism that we must examine it in greater detail.

For Marx human life is a continuous, interrelated social process. If the society is undergoing fundamental change, i.e. if it is in the process of transformation from one relatively stable mode of production to another, then the process will appear chaotic and unpredictable. But as long as a particular mode of production remains viable and relatively stable, the social process will have a certain observable, recurring, spiraling circularity.

Looked at from the standpoint of the social relations of production, the circularity can be seen in the fact that human activity always presupposes preexisting social relations by virtue of which individual actions are coordinated and integrated to make the process a social process. But the very social relations which were the prerequisites for individual social action are themselves the end products of the collective activities of the individuals involved in the process. Social relations do not have a mythical, metaphysical or ontological reality that exists independently of individuals; they are continuously created and recreated by the very actions of individuals. Thus, the preexisting social relations of production must always be recreated as the end result of productive activity or the mode of production will disintegrate. Therefore, in capitalism, for example, the various social classifications or categories of income are the *end results* of the productive process. In addition they correspond to the kinds of property relations characteristic of capitalism, but they are also the prerequisites for capitalist production. Thus prior capitalist production within capitalist property relations is always a prerequisite for current capitalist production. In Marx's words, in order for capitalist production to generate income as wages, interest, rent and profit, these income categories

> ...presuppose that the *general* character of reproduction will remain the same. And this is the case as long as the capitalist mode of production continues. Secondly, it is presupposed moreover that

the *specific relations* of this mode of production
remain the same during a certain period, and this
is in fact also more or less the case. Thus the
result of production crystallises into a *permanent* and *therefore prerequisite* condition of production.[6]

Similarly, in the continuous process of production and consumption
of material objects in which men satisfy their needs and develop their
human powers, there is a spiraling, circular aspect. Productive activity (and for Marx this includes virtually all end-oriented activity,
not simply that aspect of productive activity encompassed by capitalist
wage labor or working for hire) develops human powers. But productive
activity presupposes human needs which give the activity its teleological end in consumption or satisfaction of the needs. Moreover, productive activity or the development of human powers also presupposes prior
consumption or satisfaction of prior needs as a necessary precondition
for physical exertion to take place.

This process (which integrates what most economists would call
both production and consumption) is most generally what Marx refers to
as "production," or sometimes as "productive activity," or sometimes
simply as "life activity." It is the process by which man makes inorganic nature into the produce of his labor, and thereby the process by
which man creates himself physically, intellectually, aesthetically,
spiritually and emotionally both as an individual and as a social species-being. Both human relations with nature and social relations a-
mong human beings are prerequisites to, as well as results of, the production process. And since both sets of relations together constitute
property relations, it is clear that Marx defined property relations
very broadly and that property relations are at the core of his scheme
of human development. In Marx's words:

> The life of the species, both in man and in
> animals, consists physically in the fact that man
> (like the animal) lives on inorganic nature; and
> the more universal man (or the animal) is, the
> more universal is the sphere of inorganic nature
> on which he lives. Just as plants, animals,
> stones, air, light, etc., constitute theoretically
> a part of human consciousness, partly as objects
> of natural science, partly as art - his spiritual
> inorganic nature, spiritual nature, spiritual
> nourishment which he must first prepare to make
> palatable and digestible - so also in the realm
> of practice they constitute a part of human life
> and human activity. Physically man lives only
> on these products of nature, whether they appear

>in the form of food, heating, clothes, a dwelling,
>etc. The universality of man appears in practice
>precisely in the universality which makes all na-
>ture his inorganic body - both inasmuch as nature
>is (1) his direct means of life, and (2) the ma-
>terial, the object, and the instrument of his life
>activity. Nature is man's inorganic *body* - nature,
>that is, insofar as it is not itself human body.
>Man *lives* on nature - means that nature is his body,
>with which he must remain in continuous interchange
>if he is not to die. That man's physical and spiri-
>tual life is linked to nature means simply that na-
>ture is linked to itself, for man is a part of na-
>ture....
>   It is just in his work upon the objective
>world, therefore, that man really proves himself
>to be a *species-being*. This production is his ac-
>tive species-life. Through this production, nature
>appears as his work and his reality. The object of
>labour is, therefore, the *objectification of man's
>species-life:* for he duplicates himself not only
>as in consciousness, intellectually, but also ac-
>tively, in reality, and therefore he sees himself
>in a world that he has created.[7]

Thus man's labor (his entire sensuous activity) in transforming
nature is a process in which he creates himself. But throughout all of
his writings Marx continually insisted that human beings are a social
species. To be human is to be social:

>   The production (creation) of life, both of
>one's own in labour and of fresh life in procrea-
>tion, now appears as a twofold relation: on the
>one hand as a natural (i.e. a relation with nature),
>on the other hand as a social relation - social in
>the sense that it denotes the co-operation of sev-
>eral individuals, no matter under what conditions,
>in what manner and to what end.[8]

Man is, for Marx, both a natural biological being and a social
being. Man's nature has a biological foundation which consists of innate needs and potential powers. It is only through social activity
that these needs take on a specific form, that is become concrete, conscious desires. And it is only through social activity that these
needs can be satisfied. Furthermore the nature and extent of the particular means used to satisfy these needs are social. For example,
hunger has a biological foundation, but only in social intercourse does
hunger become the desire for a particular kind of food; and the means
for procuring this kind of food are social. Moreover, not all human
needs are satisfied by material substances. There are various social,
psychological, or spiritual needs which have some biological basis,
but which develop into conscious desires (for affection, approval,

belongingness, etc., in general and in particular for a husband, a
friend, membership in a club, etc.) only within a specific social context. Needless to say, the means of satisfying these needs are entirely social.

Needs are satisfied through social activities (through which they
are also concretized into actual conscious desires). The social activities are also the only means by which potential human powers - which
exist in original biological form as mere potentials - become actual
powers of an individual. The powers or faculties which an individual
develops are *social*. Only their potential is biological. The satisfaction of human (social) needs and the development of human (social)
powers are, in reality, only one interconnected process of social practice in which the individual creates himself as an individual. This
doctrine is so important (and so widely misunderstood) in Marx's writings that we shall quote him at length:

> Activity and enjoyment, both in their content and
> in their *mode of existence* are *social*: *social*
> activity and *social* enjoyment. The *human* aspect
> of nature exists only for *social* man; for only
> then does nature exist for him as a *bond* with *man* -
> as his existence for the other [human being] and
> the other's existence for him - and as the life-
> element in human reality. Only then does nature
> exist as the *foundation* of his own *human* experience.
> Only here has what is to him his *natural* existence
> become his *human* existence, and nature become man
> for him.[9]
>
> ...[The] *perceptible* appropriation for and by man
> of the human essence and of human life, of objec-
> tive man, of human *achievements*...should not be
> conceived merely in the sense of immediate one-
> sided enjoyment, merely in the sense of *possessing*
> or *having*. Man appropriates his comprehensive es-
> sence in a comprehensive manner, that is to say, as
> a whole man. Each of his *human* relations to the
> world - seeing, hearing, smelling, tasting, feeling,
> thinking, observing, experiencing, wanting, acting,
> loving - in short, all the organs of his individual
> being...are in their *objective* orientation, or in
> their *orientation to the object*,...the appropria-
> tion of *human* reality. Their orientation to their
> object is the *manifestation of the human reality*,
> it is human activity....[10]
>
> It is obvious that the *human* eye enjoys things
> in a way different from the crude, non human eye;
> the human ear different from the crude ear etc....
> On the one hand, therefore, it is only when
> the objective world becomes everywhere for man in
> society the world of man's essential powers - human

reality, and for that reason the reality of his
own essential powers - that all objects become
for him the *objectification* of himself, become
objects which confirm and realize his individuality, become *his* objects: that is, *man himself*
becomes the object. The *manner* in which they become *his* depends on the nature of the *objects* and
on the nature of the *essential power* corresponding
to it; for it is precisely the *determinate nature*
of this relationship which shapes the particular,
real mode of affirmation. To the eye an object
comes to be other than it is to the *ear*, and the
object of the eye *is* another object than the object
of the *ear*. The specific character of each essential power is precisely its *specific essence*, and
therefore also the specific mode of its objectification, of its *objectively actual*, living *being*. Thus
man is affirmed in the objective world not only in
the act of thinking, but with *all* his senses.
    On the other hand, let us look at this in its
subjective aspect. Just as only music awakens in
man the sense of music, and just as the most beautiful music has *no* sense for the unmusical ear - is
no object for it, because my object can only be the
confirmation of one of my essential powers - it can
therefore only exist for me insofar as my essential
power exists for itself as a subjective capacity;
because the meaning of an object for me goes only
so far as my *sense* goes (has only a meaning for a
sense corresponding to that object) - for this reason the *senses* of the social man *differ* from those
of the non-social man. Only through the objectively
unfolding richness of man's essential being is the
richness of subjective *human* sensibility (a musical
ear, an eye for beauty of form - in short, *senses*
capable of human gratification, senses affirming
themselves as essential powers of *man*) either cultivated or brought into being. For not only the
five senses but also so-called mental senses, the
practical senses (will, love, etc.), in a word,
human sense, the human nature of the senses, comes
to be by virtue of *its* object, by virtue of human-
ized nature.[11]

Thus, for Marx, human productive activity is virtually synonomous
with human purposive activity through which humans appropriate nature,
satisfy human needs and develop human powers. In this process, production and consumption are reciprocally interconnected and form a
unity. Similarly man's subjective self forms an interconnected unity
with man's objective self - both his organic body and his inorganic
body (nature). It is this total, interconnected unity that Marx calls
the production process.

The unity of this productive life process is of absolutely central
importance in understanding both Marx's critique of bourgeois theory

and his critique of capitalism. It is therefore necessary and important to quote his writing at length on this issue:

> *Production is at the same time also consumption.*
> Twofold consumption, subjective and objective. The
> individual who develops his faculties in production,
> is also expending them, consuming them in the act of
> production, just as procreation is in its way a con-
> sumption of vital powers. In the second place, pro-
> duction is consumption of the means of production
> which are used and used up and partly (as for example
> in burning) reduced to their natural elements. The
> same is true of the consumption of raw materials
> which do not remain in their natural form and state,
> being greatly absorbed in the process. The act of
> production is, therefore, in all its aspects an act
> of consumption as well....
>   Consumption is directly also production, just
> as in nature the consumption of the elements and of
> chemical matter constitutes production of plants.
> It is clear that in nutrition, for example, which is
> but one form of consumption, man produces his own
> body but it is equally true of every kind of con-
> sumption, which goes to produce the human being in
> one way or another.... Production furthers con-
> sumption by creating material for the latter which
> otherwise would lack its object. But consumption
> in its turn furthers production, by providing for
> the products the individual for whom they are pro-
> ducts.... Without production, no consumption; but,
> on the other hand without consumption, no production;
> since production would then be without a purpose.
> Consumption produces production in two ways.
>   In the first place, in that the product first
> becomes a real product in consumption; e.g. a gar-
> ment becomes a real garment only through the act
> of being worn; a dwelling which is not inhabited is
> really no dwelling; consequently, a product as dis-
> tinguished from a mere natural object, proves to be
> such, first *becomes* a product in consumption. Con-
> sumption gives the product its finishing touch by
> annihilating it, since a product is the result of
> production not merely as the material embodiment of
> activity, but also as a mere object for the active
> subject.
>   In the second place, consumption produces pro-
> duction by creating the necessity for new production,
> i.e. by providing the ideal [mental or spiritual],
> inward, impelling [teleological] cause which consti-
> tutes the prerequisite of production. Consumption
> furnishes the impulse for production as well as its
> object, which plays in production the part of its
> guiding aim. It is clear that while production fur-
> nishes the material object of consumption, consump-
> tion provides the ideal object of production, as its
> image, its want, its impulse and its purpose. It
> furnishes the object of production in its subjective
> form...

In its turn, production:
First, furnishes consumption with its material,
its object. Consumption without an object is no
consumption, hence production works in this direction by producing consumption.
Second. But it is not only the object that
production provides for consumption. It gives
consumption its definite outline, its character,
its finish.... For the object is not simply an
object in general, but a definite object, which
is consumed in a certain definite manner pre-
scribed in its turn by production. Hunger is
hunger; but the hunger that is satisfied with
cooked meat eaten with fork and knife is a different kind of hunger from the one that devours
raw meat with the aid of hands, nails, and teeth.
Not only the object of consumption, but the manner
of consumption is produced by production; that is
to say, consumption is created by production not
only objectively, but also subjectively. Production thus creates the consumers.
Third. Production not only supplies the want
with material but supplies the material with a want.
When consumption emerges from its first stage of
natural crudeness and directness...it is itself
furthered by its object as a moving spring. The
want of it which consumption experiences is created
by its appreciation of the product. The object of
art, as well as any other product, creates an artistic and beauty-enjoying public. Production thus
produces not only an object for the individual, but
also an individual for the object.[12]

The important point to be emphasized here is that
if production and consumption be considered as activities of one individual or of separate individuals, they appear at any rate as aspects of one
process in which production forms the actual starting point and is, therefore, the dominating factor.
Consumption, as a natural necessity, as a want,
constitutes an internal factor of productive activity, but the latter is the starting point of
realization and, therefore, its predominating factor, the act into which the entire process resolves
itself in the end.[13]

This quotation is well worth studying carefully. It (and innumerable passages that could be quoted) clearly refutes the notion that
Marx espoused a simplistic economic determinism in which "production"
(in the much narrower way in which the term production is used in the
orthodox social sciences and history) mechanically determines the mental, ideological and institutional "superstructure." Clearly the term
"production" was used by Marx as an abstract generalization denoting
the entire process of life-creating and life-affirming activities of
human beings, including the material aspects as well as the mental,

emotional and aesthetic aspects of that process. This is why, when
Marx expressed himself more clearly and more adequately, he abandoned
the crude first approximation of his theory (where he spoke as though
the mode of production mechanically determined the superstructure) and
used the metaphor (which more adequately captured the general nature
of his abstract notion) of production as "the universal light with
which all the other colours are tinged and are modified through its
peculiarity."[14]

Returning to our argument, we stated that Marx sees the human life
process as involving elements of a spiraling circularity. We saw first
that production presupposes existing social relations of production,
including property rights, but that these very social relations are
also the emergent results of the production process, as it continuously
reproduces the social relations. Second, we saw that the social life
process is one in which the satisfaction of needs presupposes human
powers but that the development of these human powers is the consequence of productive activity that satisfies needs. The development of
human powers presupposes needs but this development also creates needs
and wants. The interconnection of needs and powers results in the
life-creating process in which the individual, through the interconnected circular process of production and consumption, creates himself
both as an individual and as a species-being.

There is a third important vantage point from which the productive
process appears as a circularity. The production of finished goods requires as a prerequisite previously produced goods in the form of
tools, implements, partly processed raw materials and other produced
means of production. This means "that products of previous work serve
anew as means of production, as objects of labour, instruments of labour and means of subsistence for workers. The objective conditions
of labour do not face the worker...as mere natural objects,...but as
natural objects already transformed by human activity."[15] Hence, in
order for the production process to continue, a portion of what is
produced in any given time period must be created for use in future
production. Thus, at any time present production both depends upon
past production and provides for future production because the material
conditions of production must be continuously used up and continuously
reproduced for the future.

Therefore, in man's life activities both production and consumption are reciprocally interconnected, and both are involved in human

self-creation. Moreover, nature is, in Marx's words, "man's inorganic body" which makes this production possible. But not nature in isola-tion or apart from human consciousness and activities, but nature as it is known, molded and created in these activities. It follows that the previously produced material conditions of production are an inte-gral part of "man's inorganic body" as the self-created preconditions of productive activity and also as the material in which man objecti-fies both his conscious individual being and his species-being.

The foregoing discussion of the circular aspects of productive ac-tivity was concerned entirely with those aspects which Marx asserts (such assertions can be found in the *1844 Manuscripts, The Grundrisse, The Critique of Political Economy, Capital* and *Theories of Surplus Value*) are common to all modes of production. But they are effected and realized in varying degrees with varying consequences depending upon the property rights and the social relations of production that characterize a particular mode of production.

Nearly all of Marx's writings were primarily concerned with ana-lyzing the functioning and consequences of capitalist social relations of production. The most significant feature of capitalist relations of production is that the continuous, interconnected circular process of production (which is continuous in each of its three aspects we have just discussed) is fragmented and dissolved into discrete parts or as-pects. Each part comes to be conceived as separate and self-contained. Within this context, the production-consumption process takes place as if each integrally related aspect were in fact a separate, self-con-tained part. This reflects the fact that the process, at each point in its separation or fragmentation, is mediated by commodity exchange. This chopping up or fragmenting of the process through the mediating function of commodity exchange makes the process appear to be four separate, disconnected processes--production, distribution, commodity exchange and consumption. In capitalism Marx observes that "between the producer and the product distribution steps in, which determines by social laws his share of products; that is to say, distribution steps in between production and consumption."[16] But, as Marx takes pains to show, the laws of distribution are themselves the outcome of property rights and the social relations of production and hence dis-tribution is really an integral part of the production process. It appears to be separated from it because of the particular form of

capitalist production - the production of commodities for exchange.   In
capitalism commodities and money are constantly circulating through
the process of exchange:

> Circulation [of money and commodities] is but a certain
> aspect of exchange, or it may be defined as exchange
> considered as a whole. Since *exchange* is an inter-
> mediary factor between production and its dependent,
> distribution, on the one hand, and consumption, on
> the other, and since the latter [consumption] appears
> but as a constituent of production, exchange is mani-
> festly also a constituent part of production.[17]

The basis of Marx's criticism of the classical economists was that
they failed to see that exchange is but a subsidiary mechanism in the
capitalist system. Viewed from the social standpoint it does not
really separate the production process into the discrete self-contained
processes of production, distribution, exchange and consumption, even
though from the individual's standpoint exchange appears to make this
separation. Yet capitalism functions as though this separation not
only were real but also as though this separation had its basis in the
ontological nature of material things and people. The classical economists abstracted each of these elements out of the interconnected process within which each is an integral, inseparable part and treated
each in isolation from all of its essential connections to the whole
processes. In Marx's opinion, it was their belief in the autonomy of
these abstractions that led the classical economists to reify abstractions as things. This reification was the source of the obscurantist
elements in classical political economy. Marx always insisted that in
capitalism, as in all other modes of production, the production process
is an interrelated, unified, single process:

> The result we arrive at is not that production,
> distribution, exchange and consumption are identical,
> but that they are all members of one unit. Production
> [conceived of as the entire unitary process] pre-
> dominates not only over production itself...[as con-
> ceived in the narrower manner of orthodox social
> science], but over the other elements as well. With
> it the process constantly starts over again.[18]

But the error of the classical economists in abstracting and re-
ifying the separate conceptual aspects of the process is not simply
based on wrong thinking that could be easily set right by more persuasive, more correct thinking. Capitalism actually functions as
though certain abstractions were more real than the real people and

real material objects that are involved in the process. Therefore, for
Marx, a criticism of classical political economy had to be simultaneously a criticism of capitalism.

Capitalism, as a system of commodity exchange, systematically distorts the real nature of human wealth and of human existence. For
Marx, real human wealth is identical with the extent of the development
of human powers and the satisfaction of human needs.

> In fact, however, when the limited bourgeois
> form is stripped away, what is wealth other than
> the universality of individual needs, capacities,
> pleasures, productive forces, etc...? The full
> development of human mastery over the forces of
> nature, those of so-called nature as well as
> humanity's own nature? The absolute working-out
> of his creative potentialities, with no presup-
> position other than the previous historic develop-
> ment, i.e. the development of all human powers as
> such the end in itself, not as measured on a *pre-
> determined* yardstick?[19]

In capitalism commodity production and commodity exchange distort
the true nature of wealth: "The wealth in those societies in which the
capitalist mode of production prevails, presents itself as 'an immense
accumulation of commodities.'"[20] A central source of difficulty in
understanding the nature of commodities is the failure to clearly dif-
ferentiate between those aspects of a commodity which are the result of
it being a concrete, finite material thing with particular concrete
physical features and those abstractions, which are based on particular, historically specific, and transitory social relations including
property rights, that are symbolized by the commodity but have no inherent connection to the peculiar physical characteristics of the commodity as a finite, material object.

> A commodity is, in the first place, an object
> outside us, a thing that by its properties satisfies
> human wants of some sort or another....
> The utility of a thing makes it a use-value.
> But this utility is not a thing of air. Being
> limited by the physical properties of the com-
> modity, it has no existence apart from the com-
> modity. A commodity, such as iron, corn, or a
> diamond, is therefore, so far as it is a material
> thing, something useful.... Use-values become a
> reality only by use or consumption: They also
> constitute the [material] substance of all wealth,
> whatever may be the social form of that wealth.[21]

Since useful material objects exist in all societies, and represent the material substance of wealth in all societies, it is clear

that simply being a useful thing does not make an object a commodity.
"In the form of society [capitalism] we are about to consider, they
[commodities] are, in addition, the material depositories of exchange-
value."[22]

Exchange value, within the social context of a commodity producing
and commodity exchanging society, is what transforms a useful material
object (such as exists in every type of society) into a commodity. But
exchange value is *not* a physical characteristic of a material thing.
It is therefore merely a mental abstraction which reflects social relations among people and is not existentially or ontologically part of
the material thing. Exchange value, Marx writes, "cannot be either a
geometrical, a chemical, or any other natural property of commodities."[23] It can therefore be nothing but a mental abstraction. But it
is not an abstraction that was conjured up in the imagination or out of
thin air. It is an abstraction arising out of the social relations of
a commodity-producing society.

Products of human labor become commodities only when they are privately owned and are produced solely for exchange for money in a market, and not for the immediate use or enjoyment of the producers or
anyone directly associated with the producers. "The mode of production
in which the product takes the form of a commodity, or is produced directly for exchange," Marx wrote, "is the most general and most embry-
onic form of bourgeois production."[24] Commodity production is always
dominated by the single minded quest for exchange-value:

> Definite historical conditions are necessary that
> a product may become a commodity. It must not be
> produced as the immediate means of subsistence of
> the producer himself.... Production and circula-
> tion of commodities can take place, although the
> great mass of objects produced are intended for
> the immediate requirements of the producers, are
> not turned into commodities, and consequently
> social production is not yet by a long way domi-
> nated in its length and breadth by exchange-
> value.[25]

In order for a society to be "dominated in its length and breadth
by exchange-value," that is, in order for it to be *primarily* a commodity producing society, four historical prerequisites are necessary.
First, there has to evolve such a degree of productive specialization
that each individual producer produces and reproduces the same product
(or even portion of a product) in a monotonous never-ending repetition.
Second, such specialization necessarily requires the complete

"separation of use-value from exchange-value."[26] Because life is impossible without the consumption of innumerable use-values, a producer
can relate to his own produce only as an exchange-value and can only
acquire his necessary use-values from the products of others. Third,
a commodity producing society requires an extensive, well-developed
market, which requires the pervasive use of money as a universal value
equivalent, mediating every exchange. Fourth, whereas in most precapitalist societies some form of social ownership (with individuals
granted the rights of use by some form of social consent) predominates
over private ownership and reflects the social nature of production, in
a commodity-producing society private property ownership predominates.

In a commodity-producing society, any given producer works in isolation from all other producers. He is, of course, socially and economically connected, or related, to other producers: many of them cannot continue their ordinary daily patterns of consumption without the
performance of his labor in the creation of a commodity which they consume; and he cannot continue his pattern of consumption unless innumerable other producers continuously create the commodities which he
needs. Thus there is a definite, indispensable social relationship
among producers.

Each producer, however, produces only for sale in the market.
With the proceeds of his sale, he buys the commodities he needs. His
well-being appears to depend solely on the quantities of other commodities for which his commodity can exchange. "The quantities vary continually," Marx wrote, "independently of the will, foresight and action of the producers. To them their own social action takes the form
of the action of objects, which rule the producers, instead of being
ruled by them."[27] Thus, a social relationship among producers appears
to each producer to be simply a relationship between himself and an impersonal, immutable social institution - the market. And the market appears to involve simply a set of relationships among material things -
commodities. "Therefore, the relations connecting the labour of one
individual with that of the rest appear," Marx concluded, "not as direct social relations between individuals at work, but as...relations
between things."[28]

Thus, exchange values are abstractions which reflect the mutual
dependence of seemingly independent commodity producers. They are not
material qualities of things but mental reflections of social relations. But they are mental abstractions which are absolutely necessary

for a commodity-producing society to function. It is by acting as
though these abstractions were inherent qualities of the useful products of labor that individuals are able to engage in exchange. And
only by engaging in exchange can what erroneously appears to be private, individual production actually function as that which it truly
is - social production.

But capitalism is more than simply a commodity-producing society.
Capitalism comes into existence only when human productive activity
itself becomes a commodity to be bought and sold in the market. But
labor is not a thing like other commodities. It is an activity. The
only thing involved is the laborer's own body - his mental and physical
capacities as a living human organism. Now in a slave economy, human
bodies are treated as things to be owned by other humans. But capitalism is not a slave economy. Therefore, the only way in which human
productive activity can be sold as a commodity is through the recurring
sale of control over a worker's body for finite periods of time.

But this control over a worker's body can only mean control over
the worker's capacity to create. Marx called this capacity "labor
power" and differentiated this capacity from the actual expenditure of
labor or the realization of labor power. Labor power, then, is the
capacity to work, or potential labor. When labor power is sold as a
commodity, its use-value is simply the performance of work - the ac-
tualizing of the potential labor. When the work is performed it becomes embodied in a commodity. The commodity that is produced thus becomes the material objectification of the productive activity.

The existence of labor power as a commodity depends upon two essential conditions. First,

> labour-power can appear upon the market as a com-
> modity, only if, and so far as, its possessor, the
> individual whose labour-power it is, offers it for
> sale, or sells it, as a commodity. In order that
> he may be able to do this he...must be the untram-
> melled owner of his capacity for labour, i.e., of
> his person.... The owner of the labour-power...
> [must] sell it only for a definite period, for if
> he were to sell it rump and stump, once and for
> all, he would be selling himself, converting him-
> self from a free man into a slave, from an owner
> of a commodity into a commodity....
>
> The second essential condition...is...that
> the labourer instead of being in the position to
> sell commodities in which his labour is incorpor-
> ated, must be obliged to offer for sale as a

> commodity that very labour-power, which exists
> only in his living self.
>
> In order that man may be able to sell com-
> modities other than labour-power, he must of
> course have the means of production, such as raw
> materials, implements, etc. No boots can be made
> without leather. He requires also the means of
> subsistence....
>
> For the conversion of his money into capital,
> therefore, the owner of money must meet in the mar-
> ket with the free labourer, free in the double sense,
> that as a free man he can dispose of his labor-power
> as his own commodity, and that on the other hand he
> has no other commodity for sale, is short of every-
> thing necessary for the realization of his labour-
> power.[29]

This, then, is capitalism's defining feature, differentiating it
from a simple commodity-producing society. Capitalism exists when, in
a commodity-producing society, one small class of people - capitalists
- has monopolized the means of production through the laws of private
property, and where the great majority of the direct producers - workers - cannot produce independently because they own no means of production. Workers are "free" to make one of two choices: starve or sell
their labor power as a commodity.[30] Thus, capitalism is neither inevitable nor natural and eternal. It is a specific mode of production,
which has evolved under specific historical conditions, and which has a
ruling class that rules by virtue of its ability to expropriate surplus
labor from the producers of commodities through the laws of private
property and the processes of production and exchange:

> One thing...is clear - Nature does not produce on
> the one side owners of money or commodities, and
> on the other men possessing nothing but their own
> labour-power. This relation has no natural basis,
> neither is its social basis one that is common to
> all historical periods. It is clearly the result
> of a past historical development, the product of
> many economic revolutions, of the extinction of a
> whole series of older forms of social production.[31]

For Marx, the fact that labor is always a social process means
that there is in all societies at all times a division of labor and a
consequent interdependence of laborers. In no society can an individual laborer produce individually in isolation. Hence, any human being
is economically dependent upon other human beings. But in precapitalist society the "division of labour is...nothing but *coexisting labour*,
that is, the coexistence of *different* kinds of labour which are represented in *different kinds* of products"[32] which are necessary for pro-

productive individuals to sustain themselves. With capitalist private
property two things happen. First, with private property, a social interdependence caused by the division of labor becomes a private dependence of the worker in which a single individual controls the products
of the others upon whom the worker depends. Second, the division of
labor undergoes a qualitative change. We shall briefly consider each
of these.

In the period of transition from feudalism to capitalism the complex sets of obligations involved in feudal social property relations
were generally not well understood by the participants in that transitional process. What was clearly understood, however, was that a no-
bleman, by accident of birth, had the right to expropriate the produce
of others while playing no direct role in the production process. The
antithesis of this feudal expropriation seemed, to many of the most
radical thinkers of this period, to be a system of private property
rights which would give the producer property rights over the products
he created. All of the early defenses of private property, from Locke
to the classical liberals, repeated this rationale.

This classical rationale for private property completely ignored
the natural and social bases of human production. Nature, which furnishes the material that is creatively transformed in production, is
not the product of any individual's productive endeavor. Moreover,
the many products upon which any worker depends as means of consumption or tools and other means of production are the results of the labor of others. All of this is merely another way of saying that production is a social process in which individuals through definite social relations interact with and transform nature (and themselves).

The social historical process in which the natural and social
means of production were transformed into privately owned commodities
was referred to by Marx as the process of "primitive accumulation."
In primitive accumulation, the capitalist class acquired (by methods
which Marx recounted in vivid and lurid detail) ownership of the means
of production. It was in this way that the workers' social interdependence (which exists in all societies) was transformed into the individual dependence of each worker on capitalists. In capitalism the
natural and social prerequisites of productive endeavor confront the
worker as independent, hostile, alien forces personified by capitalists:

> Thus primitive accumulation...means nothing
> but the separation of labour and the worker from
> the conditions of labour, which confront him as
> independent forces.... Once capital exists, the
> capitalist mode of production itself evolves in
> such a way that it maintains and reproduces this
> separation on a constantly increasing scale.[33]

Thus, the classical liberal rationale for private property becomes
a rationale for a new expropriation of the products of labor that is
not unlike the feudal expropriation which classical liberalism attacked:

> At first the rights of property seemed to
> us to be based on a man's own labour. At least,
> some such assumption was necessary since only
> commodity-owners with equal rights confronted
> each other, and the sole means by which a man
> could become possessed of the commodities of
> others, was by alienating his own commodities;
> and these could be replaced by labour alone.
> Now, however, property turns out to be the
> right, on the part of the capitalist, to ap-
> propriate the unpaid labour of others or its
> product, and to be the impossibility, on the
> part of the labourer, of appropriating his own
> product. The separation of property from labour
> has become the necessary consequence of a law
> that originated in their identity.[34]

Once capitalist property relations dominate society the division
of labor undergoes a qualitative change. In precapitalist societies
individuals specialize in the production of one or a few products and,
hence, the division of labor is "outside the workshop, as a *separation
of occupations*.... The division of labor in the capitalist sense...
[is] the breaking down of the particular labour which produces a definite commodity into a series of simple and coordinated operations divided up amongst different workers."[35] This capitalist division of
labour "within the workshop" significantly increases the dependence of
the workers on the capitalists by reducing their productive skills and
"by differentiating and increasing the indirect preliminary work [of
other workers] that they require."[36] Thus, private ownership confers
on capitalists the power to render laborers helpless by denying them
the prerequisites of production.

Classical economists, at least from Nassau Senior onwards, constructed an ideology in which income from private property ownership
was defended on the basis of the supposed "productivity of capital".
Marx clearly saw that private property rights are simply a coercive social relation that has nothing to do with production:

> The utilization of the products of previous
> labour, of labour in general, as materials, tools,
> means of subsistence, is necessary if the worker
> wants to use his products for new production....
> But what on earth has this kind of utilization...
> of his product to do with the domination of his
> product over him, with its existence as capital,
> with the concentration in the hands of individual
> capitalists of the right to dispose of raw mater-
> ials and means of subsistence and the exclusion
> of the workers from ownership of their products?
> What has it to do with the fact that first of all
> they have to hand over their product gratis to a
> third party in order to buy it back again with
> their own labour and, what is more, they have to
> give him more labour than is contained in the pro-
> duct and thus they have to create surplus product
> for him?....
> As if the division of labour was not just as
> possible if its conditions belonged to the asso-
> ciated workers...and were regarded by the latter
> as their own products and the material elements
> of their own activity, which they are by their
> very nature.[37]

One of Marx's most central concerns was to analyze the effects of
this particular form of property rights and consequent form of social
relations of production as they affect individuals' abilities to develop their human powers and to satisfy their real human needs. In
other words, how do capitalist private property rights affect the individual's capacity to create himself as a fully developed individual and
as a human species-being (individual development and development as a
species-being are not, for Marx, separate developments, but rather two
sides of the same development)?

The effects of capitalism on individuals' development were discussed in nearly all of Marx's major writings. But they were discussed
most fully and adequately in the *1844 Manuscripts*. Here he described
the fragmentation of the production process through commodity exchange,
the transformation of the means of production as well as the products
of productive activity into commodities, and the transformation of human productive activity itself into a commodity, by a single term -
alienation.

Alienation reflects the fact that capitalist commodity production
fragments and dissociates the productive life processes of individuals.
The producers (workers) are separated or alienated from both the means
of physical subsistence and the previously produced means of production. In order to live and to produce they must sell their labor power

as a commodity. After the capitalist uses their labor power, i.e. after he forces them to produce, he owns the products of their labor. Of
course the capitalist accumulates wealth because the value of what
workers produce exceeds the value of the labor power that they expend
in production. The workers labor longer than is necessary for them to
produce the value equivalent of their wage. This extra labor, or surplus labor, is the source of surplus value which accrues to capitalists
in the forms of interest, rent and profit.

As we stated earlier, inorganic nature, in so far as it is understood and transformed by man, is an extension of man - it is man's "inorganic body." In particular, the previously created means of production which man uses in productive activity and the products in which
his mental and physical activities become embodied through the production process are the most essential inorganic extensions of man himself. They are the most important elements of man's "inorganic body."
Man's creative self-development depends upon his realization of himself in these inorganic extensions of himself. In capitalism the means
of production are commodities owned by capitalists, while the objects
created by labor also become commodities owned by capitalists.

Thus, in a commodity producing society, when the workers' means of
subsistence, means of production and productive output are alienated
from them in the form of commodities owned by nonworkers (capitalists),
these commodities become capital. Capital is not a characteristic of
these things as physical objects. It is a mental abstraction, which
is symbolized by physical objects but is really a mental reflection of
a coercive social relation:

> Capital is productive of value only as a
> [social] *relation*, in so far as it is a coer-
> cive force on wage-labour, compelling it to
> perform surplus-labour.... It only produces
> value as the power of labour's own material
> conditions over labour when these are alien-
> ated from labour.[38]

Under these circumstances, "the relationship of labour to the conditions of labour is turned upside-down, so that it is not the worker who
makes use of the conditions of labour, but the conditions of labour
which make use of the worker."[39]

This dissociation of the production process is at the same time a
coercive fragmenting of man's productive activity; it estranges him
from the objective, the subjective and the social aspects of his own
life activity; it is the alienation of labor. Marx viewed the

alienation of labor from four vantage points: (1) the relation of man
to the products he creates, (2) the relation of man to his own productive activity, (3) the relation of a man to his own "species-being,"
and (4) the relation of man to other men.

First, in capitalism, man's relation to the products he creates
is described in this way by Marx:

> The worker becomes all the poorer the more
> wealth he produces, the more his production in-
> creases in power and size.... The *devaluation*
> of the world of men is in direct proportion to
> the *increasing value* of things. Labour produces
> not only commodities: it produces itself and the
> worker as a *commodity*....
> This fact expresses merely that the object
> which labour produces - labour's product - confronts
> it as *something alien*, as a *power independent* of
> the producer. The produce of labour is labour
> which has been embodied in an object, which has be-
> come material: it is the *objectification* of labour.
> Labour's realization is its objectification. Under
> these economic conditions [capitalism] this realiza-
> tion of labour appears as *loss of realization* for
> the workers; objectification [appears] as *loss of
> object and bondage to it*; appropriation [appears] as
> *estrangement, as alienation*.... So much does the
> appropriation of the object appear as estrangement
> that the more objects the worker produces the less
> he can possess and the more he falls under the sway
> of his product, capital.
> All these consequences are implied in the state-
> ment that the worker is related to the *product of his
> labour* as to an *alien* object. For on this premise it
> is clear that the more the worker expends himself,
> the more powerful becomes the alien world of objects
> which he creates over and against himself, the poorer
> he himself - his inner world - becomes, the less be-
> longs to him as his own.[40]

Because of the pervasive misinterpretations of Marx's writings,
two points from this quotation need to be emphasized. The first point
to note is that even under capitalism, Marx continued to insist that
the objects produced still represent the material objectification of
man's subjective state. But because of private property rights, man
is coercively prevented from freely using the means of production, and
coercively prevented from personally (or collectively, in union with
other producers with whom the individual must cooperate in productive
activity) appropriating or using the objects he produces. The second
point to note is that Marx consistently used the verb "appear" rather
than "is" to describe alienation. This is because Marx's goal in
writing the *1844 Manuscripts* was to critically analyze the effects of

the fact that property rights are generally conceived of as "natural" and "eternal." They are taken for granted, or presupposed by most people. Thus the beginning sentences of Marx's discussion of "estranged labour" read: "We have proceeded from the premises of political economy. We have accepted its language and its laws. We have *presupposed private property.*"[41] Marx's point is that once private property is assumed, presupposed or taken for granted, then the material conditions of people's labor, which are themselves merely the product of their labor, appear to be objects which are alien, coercive, oppressive forces over the laborers. Marx's purpose in writing the *Manuscripts* (as well as most of his other writings) was to demonstrate analytically that this appearance is illusory. As long as workers hold these illusions to be true ideas they actively help to create their own oppression. The reality of the oppression is to be found in the forms of human coercion involved in the enforcement of property rights. Only because people take for granted or presuppose property rights does labor's realization appear as loss of realization, human objectification appear as loss of object and as bondage to object, and appropriation appear as estrangement. In reality, by the coercive enforcement of property rights, laborers' realization, their objectification, their appropriation, are forcefully and coercively separated from them, are stolen from them by other human beings.

This theft breaks the subjective-objective-subjective cycle of human self-production. Production begins with ideas and subjective powers within the individual. Through productive activity the subjective powers become objective powers as they are used to mold external material objects. And the subjective ideas become the model in the shape of which the material objects are molded. As the material objects become objectified ideas, the ideas are the teleological cause of which the objective product is the effect. Last, and very important, in seeing, hearing, touching, smelling, and using his products, the laborer converts his objectification back into a subjective appreciation of himself and his powers. Therefore, what began as a subjective state returns in the end as another subjective state, but in the latter subjective state the laborer mentally and emotionally realizes the development of his powers and the satisfaction of his needs through his own life-creating activities.

Capitalist private property as coercieve theft prevents this last stage in the cycle from occurring. Labor is objectified in objects.

But when the objects are coercively stolen and then used as the means
to coercively force labor to do more work, then the objects do not appear subjectively to the laborer as the development of his powers and
the satisfaction of his needs. The objects which he creates appear as
the means of his enslavement, the diminution of his powers, and the
denial of his needs.

Marx believed that in the early transition to capitalism, before
capitalist property laws were taken for granted, the real nature of
these property rights was much more closely seen. In *Theories of Surplus Value* he states that Martin Luther understood interest and profits better than most 19th century socialists. He quotes several long
passages from Luther's writings. Here are some parts of these quotations:

> Fifteen years ago I wrote against usury since
> it had already become so widespread that I could
> hope for no improvement. Since that time, it has
> exalted itself to such a degree that it *no longer
> wishes to be a vice, sin or infamy* but extols it-
> self as downright virtue and honour as if it con-
> ferred a great favour on and did a Christian ser-
> vice to the people....
> They also make a *usury out of buying and sel-
> ling*.... When we have put a stop to this (as on the
> Day of Judgment), then we will surely read the lesson
> with regard to *usurious trade*....
> Let whoever wants to do so extol himself, put on
> finery and adorn himself but pay no heed and keep
> firmly to the scripture...whoever takes more or better
> than he gives, that is usury and is *not a service, but
> a wrong* done to his neighbour, as when one steals and
> robs. All is not service and benefit to a neighbour
> that is called service and benefit.... A horseman
> does a great service to a robber by helping him to rob
> on the highway, and attack the people and the land.
> The papists do us a great service in that they do not
> drown, burn, murder all or let them rot in prison, but
> let some live and drive them out or take from them what
> they have.... The poets write about Cyclops Polyphemus,
> who said he would do Ulysses an act of friendship, name-
> ly, that he would eat his companions first and then
> Ulysses last. Such services and good deeds are per-
> formed nowadays most diligently by...[those] who buy
> goods up, pile up stocks, bring dear times, increase
> the price of corn, barley and of everything people
> need; they then wipe their mouths and say: Yes - one
> must have what one must have; I let my things out to
> help people although I might - and could - keep them
> to myself....
> But if this is the kind of service he does, then
> he does it for Satan himself; although a poor needy

man requires such a service and must accept it as
a service or a favour that he is not eaten up
completely....
 Therefore there is on this earth no greater
enemy of man, after the devil, than a miser and
a usurer, for *he wants to be God over all men*....
A usurer and money-grubber, such a one would have
the whole world perish of hunger and thirst, misery
and want, so far as in him lies [the power], so
that he may have all to himself and everyone *receive
from him as from a God and be his serf for evermore*....
 Therefore, a usurer and miser is, indeed, not
truly a human being, sins not in a human way and
must be looked upon as a werewolf, more than all
the tyrants, murderers and robbers, nearly as evil
as the devil himself, but one who sits in peace and
safety, not like an enemy, but like a friend and
citizen, yet robs and murders more horribly than
any enemy or incendiary.[42]

The capitalist "robs and murders more horribly than any enemy"
and is like an inhuman "werewolf" because he steals more than simply
some of the products of labor. He forcefully disrupts the life creating activities of human production and hence robs workers of some of
the essential elements of their very life creation - of their very hu-
manness. But once private property has become sacrosanct and is taken
for granted, this werewolf power of capitalists comes to appear as a
power exerted by the creations of laborers over the laborers themselves. Thus, the first vantage point from which Marx described alienation was that of the alienation of the product of labor from the
laborers themselves.

 Marx's second vantage point in analyzing alienation was to look
at the *activity* of producing in a capitalist society:

Estrangement is manifested...in the *act of production*, within the *producing activity* itself. How
could the worker come to face the product of his
activity as a stranger, were it not that in the
very act of production he was estranging himself
from himself? The product is after all but the
summary of the activity, of production. If then
the product of labour is alienation, production
itself must be active alienation, the alienation
of activity, the activity of alienation. In the
estrangement of the object of labour is merely
summarized the estrangement, the alienation, in
the activity of labour itself.
 What, then, constitutes the alienation of
labour?
 First, the fact that labour is *external* to
the worker, i.e. it does not belong to his intrinsic nature; that in his work, therefore, he
does not affirm himself but denies himself, does

not feel content but unhappy, does not develop
freely his physical and mental energy but morti-
fies his body and ruins his mind. The worker
therefore only feels himself outside his work,
and in his work feels outside himself. He feels
at home when he is not working, and when he is
working he does not feel at home. His labour is
therefore not voluntary, but coerced; it is
forced labour. It is therefore not the satisfaction of a need; it is merely a *means* to satisfy
needs external to it. Its alien character emerges
clearly in the fact that as soon as no physical or
other compulsion exists, labour is shunned like
the plague. External labour, labour in which man
alienates himself, is a labour of self-sacrifice,
of mortification. Lastly, the external character
of labour for the worker appears in the fact that
it is not his own, but someone else's, that it
does not belong to him, that in it he belongs not
to himself, but to another.... The worker's activity [is] not his spontaneous activity. It belongs to another; it is the loss of his self.

As a result, therefore man (the worker) only
feels himself freely active in his animal functions - eating, drinking, procreating, or at most
in his dwelling and in dressing-up, etc.; and in
his human functions he no longer feels himself to
be anything but an animal. What is animal becomes
human and what is human becomes animal.

Certainly eating, drinking, procreating, etc.,
are also genuinely human functions. But taken abstractly, separated from the sphere of all other
human activity and turned into sole and ultimate
ends, they are animal functions.[43]

The third vantage point from which alienation can be viewed is
the process by which man realizes himself as a species-being:

Man is a species-being, not only because in
practice and in theory he adopts the species (his
own as well as those of other things) as his object, but - and this is only another way of expressing it - also because he treats himself as the actual living species; because he treats himself as
a *universal* and therefore a free being....

In creating a *world of objects* by his practical activity, in his *work* upon inorganic nature,
man proves himself a conscious species-being, i.e.,
as a being that treats the species as its own essential being, or that treats itself as a species-
being.... An animal forms objects only in accordance with the standard and the need of the species
to which it belongs, whilst man knows how to produce in accordance with the standard of every
species, and knows how to apply everywhere the inherent standard to the object. Man therefore also
forms objects in accordance with the laws of beauty.

It is just in his work upon the objective
world, therefore, that man really proves himself
to be a *species-being*. This production is his
active species-life. Through this production,
nature appears as *his* work and his reality. The
object of labour is, therefore, the *objectification of man's species-life*: for he duplicates
himself not only, as in consciousness, intellectually, but also actively, in reality, and therefore he sees himself in a world that he has created. In tearing away from man the object of
production, therefore, estranged labour tears from
his *species-life*, his real objectivity as a member
of the species, and transforms his advantage over
animals into the disadvantage that his inorganic
body, nature, is taken away from him.
  Similarly, in degrading spontaneous, free activity to a means, estranged labour makes man's
species-life a means to his physical existence.
The consciousness which man has of his species is
thus transformed that species-life becomes for him
a means.
  Estranged labor thus turns man's species-being,
both nature and his spiritual species-property, into
a being *alien* to him, into a *means* for his *individual*
existence. It estranges from man his own body, as
well as external nature and his spiritual aspect,
his *human* aspect.[44]

Finally, the ultimate result of the previous three aspects of
alienation can be seen in the alienation of man from other human beings:

An immediate consequence of the fact that man
is estranged from the product of his labour, from
his life activity, from his species-being is the
estrangement of man from man.... The estrangement
of man, and in fact every relationship in which man
stands to himself, is realized only in the relationship in which a man stands to other men.
  Hence within the relationship of estranged labour each man views the other in accordance with the
standard and the relationship in which he finds himself as a worker.[45]

In this alienated state, of course, man's view of himself is that
he is a commodity. His life activity is a commodity to be bought and
sold. His life activity is therefore not an end, but merely a means
to continue living physically. And as we have seen, the feature that
distinguishes a useful physical object that is not a commodity from
one that is a commodity is merely that the latter is the symbol for a
social abstraction. Therefore, in capitalism, one individual sees
another as a commodity, as the physical symbol of an abstraction,
purely as means to be exchanged for the sake of continued existence.

The exchange value of a commodity is purely a mental abstraction symbolized by the actual, physically existing thing or person. And the higher-level abstraction of exchange value generally (as opposed to the exchange value of a particular thing) is money. It is an abstraction of abstractions.

Thus, when individuals are seen as commodities, all real human qualities come to appear as merely so many concrete aspects of exchange value generally, or of money. Other individuals appear to me only as so many commodities which I can buy if I have the money. And my own powers, i.e. my essential being, appear to be defined by the amount of money I possess:

> The extent of the power of [my] money is the extent of my power. Money's properties are my - the possessor's - properties and essential powers. Thus, what I *am* and *am capable of* is by no means determined by my individuality. I *am* ugly, but I can buy for myself the *most beautiful* of women. Therefore, I am not *ugly*, for the effect of *ugliness* - its deterrent power - is nullified by money. I, according to my individual characteristics, am *lame*, but money furnishes me with twenty-four feet. Therefore, I am not lame. I am bad, dishonest, unscrupulous, stupid; but money is honoured, and hence its possessor. Money is the supreme good, therefore its possessor is good. Money, besides, saves me the trouble of being dishonest: I am therefore presumed honest. I am *brainless*, but money is the *real brain* of all things and how then should its possessor be brainless? Besides he can buy clever people for himself, and is he who has power over the clever not more clever than the clever? Do not I, who thanks to money am capable of all that the human heart longs for, possess all human capacities? Does not my money, therefore, transform all my incapacities into their contrary?....
> The distorting and confounding of all human and natural qualities, the fraternisation of impossibilities - the *divine* power of money - lies in its *character* as men's estranged, alienating and self-disposing species-nature. Money is the alienated ability of mankind.[46]

Money is thus alienated human power and not truly human power. Ultimately its possessor (the capitalist) is privileged over the worker in a more limited way than appears in the illusion that money is real human power. The worker's very capacity to continue living, to continue to satisfy his animal needs of food, clothing and protection from the elements is always uncertain and precarious in capitalism. He must continuously find a buyer for his commodity labor power. And given the fact that a substantial proportion of the working class is always unemployed and that this proportion increases dramatically during the periodically recurring business crises of capitalism, the worker's ability to provide himself and his family with the means of mere physical existence must, for most workers, always remain precarious. Moreover, even when the worker successfully sells his labor power, his wage generally provides for only the most modest, socially defined subsistence.

The capitalist, however, always enjoys any quantity and quality that he desires of the physical amenities necessary for his animal functions. His money gives him all the powers he could desire for his animal existence. He can have any dwelling, any amount of food, of transportation, of clothing, of human objects from which to get sexual gratification.

But money is alienated human powers. The satisfaction of uniquely human needs (those needs which elevate the human above the animal) with the use of money is an illusory satisfaction because it does not involve the corresponding development of uniquely human powers within the individual. In Marx's words:

> Assume *man* to be *man* and his relation to the world to be a human one: then you can exchange love only for love, trust for trust, etc. If you want to enjoy art, you must be an artistically cultivated person; if you want to exercise influence over other people, you must be a person with a stimulating and encouraging effect on other people. Every one of your relations to man and to nature must be a *specific expression*, corresponding to the object of your will, of your *real individual life*. If you love without evoking love in return - that is, if your loving as loving does not produce reciprocal love, if through a *living expression* of yourself as a loving person you do not make yourself a *beloved one*, then your love is impotent - a misfortune.[47]

Marx's analysis of capitalist private property rights was a crucially important part of his general efforts to help to create a truly human society in which "you can exchange love only for love, trust for trust, etc." Only in such a society can human liberation and human development take place. Only when social and economic interdependences are freely and equally controlled by the interdependent producers can an individual be said to be free and independent. Dependence is personal and private - and results from private property rights. Human independence does not mean human isolation; it presupposes social interdependence but is incompatible with private dependence:

A *being* only considers himself independent
when he stands on his own feet; and he only stands
on his own feet when he owes his *existence* to himself. A man who lives by the grace of another regards himself as a dependent being. But I live completely by the grace of another if I owe him not
only the maintenance of my life, but if he has,
moreover, *created* my life. When it is not my own
creation, my life has necessarily a source of this
kind outside of it.[48]

Thus, the widespread "Marxist" notion that capitalist society de-
terministically creates the human being as an "alienated capitalist
man," while the task of a victorious Communist party or Communist government is to recreate man as a "socialist man" would have been repug-
nant to Marx. In the "Theses on Feuerbach" he wrote:

The materialist doctrine that men are products of circumstances and upbringing, and that,
therefore, changed men are products of other circumstances and changed upbringing, forgets that
it is men who change circumstances and that the
educator must himself be educated. Hence, this
doctrine is bound to divide society into two
parts, one of which is superior to society.[49]

This seems to be precisely how many Marxists view the relation between the "vanguard party" or the Communist government and the rest of
society. In addressing the question of whether man did not always
need a superior, higher being or person to create him, Marx answered:

Your question is itself a product of abstraction. Ask yourself how you arrived at that
question. Ask yourself whether your question
is not posed from a standpoint to which I cannot reply, because it is wrongly put.... When
you ask about the creation of nature and man,
you are abstracting, in so doing, from man and
nature. You postulate them as *non-existent*,
and yet you want me to prove them to you as
existing. Now I say to you: Give up your abstraction and you will also give up your question. Or if you want to hold on to your abstraction, then be consistent, and if you think
of men and nature as *non-existent*, then think
of yourself as non-existent, for you too are
surely nature and man. Don't think, don't ask
me, for as soon as you think and ask, your *abstraction* from the existence of nature and man
has no meaning. Or are you such an egotist
that you conceive everything as nothing, and
yet want yourself to exist?...
But since for the socialist man the *entire
so-called* history of the world is nothing but
the creation of man through human labour,...
since the *real existence* of man and nature has

> become evident in practice, through sense exper-
> ience, because man has thus become evident for
> man as the being of nature, and nature for man as
> the being of man, the question about an *alien*
> being, about a being above nature and man - a ques-
> tion which implies the admission of the unreality
> of nature and man - has become impossible in prac-
> tice.[50]

The relevance of this quotation to those "Marxist" notions of the Party or the Communist government as the creators of socialist man should be apparent. Marx was genuinely radical. He was the enemy of any coercive molding or making of man by other men in "higher posi-tions," whatever ideology they might espouse. He was a champion of the most fundamental human liberation. To him capitalism seemed to be the principal obstacle to human emancipation. While capitalism continues to play the same role it did in Marx's time, today it has competitors.

FOOTNOTES

1 Karl Marx, *Grundrisse* (London: Penguin Books, 1973), p. 491.

2 *Ibid.*

3 *Ibid.*, pp. 485-486.

4 *Ibid.*, p. 490.

5 *Ibid.*, p. 485.

6 Karl Marx, *Theories of Surplus Value* (Moscow: Progress Publishers, 1971), part III, p. 518.

7 Karl Marx, *Economic and Philosophic Manuscripts of 1844*, in *Karl Marx, Frederick Engels, Collected Works (MECW)* (New York: International Publishers, 1976), Vol. 3, pp. 275-277.

8 Karl Marx and F. Engels, *The German Ideology*, *MECW*, Vol. 5, p. 42.

9 Marx, *1844 Manuscripts*, *op. cit.*, p. 298.

10 *Ibid.*, pp. 299-300.

11 *Ibid.*, pp. 301-302.

12 Karl Marx, "Introduction to the Critique of Political Economy," in David Horowitz, ed., *Marx and Modern Economics* (New York: Monthly Review Press, 1968), pp. 28-31.

13 *Ibid.*, p. 32.

14 *Ibid.*, p. 46.

15 Marx, *Theories of Surplus Value*, *op. cit.*, part III, p. 264.

16 Marx, "Introduction to the Critique," *op. cit.*, p. 33.

17 *Ibid.*, pp. 37-38.

18 *Ibid.*, p. 38.

19 Marx, *Grundrisse*, *op. cit.*, p. 488.

20 Karl Marx, *Capital* (Moscow: Foreign Language Publishing House, 1961), Vol. I, p. 35.

21 *Ibid.*, pp. 35-36.

22 *Ibid.*, p. 36.

23 *Ibid.*, p. 37.

24 *Ibid.*, p. 82.

25 *Ibid.*, pp. 169-170.

26 *Ibid.*, p. 170.

27 *Ibid.*, p. 75.

28 *Ibid.*, p. 73.

29 *Ibid.*, pp. 168-169.

30 *Ibid.*, p. 170.

31 *Ibid.*, p. 169.

32 Marx, *Theories of Surplus Value*, *op. cit.*, part III, p. 268.

33 *Ibid.*, pp. 271-272.

34 Marx, *Capital*, *op. cit.*, Vol. I, pp. 583-584.

35 Marx, *Theories of Surplus Value*, *op. cit.*, part III, p. 268.

36 *Ibid.*, p. 269.

37 *Ibid.*, pp. 273-274.

38 *Ibid.*, part I, p. 93.

39 *Ibid.*, part III, p. 276.

40 Marx, *1844 Manuscripts*, *op. cit.*, pp. 271-272.

41 *Ibid.*, p. 270.

42 Taken from the quotations from Luther's writings that appear in *Theories of Surplus Value*, *op. cit.*, part III, pp. 532-537.

43 Marx, *1844 Manuscripts*, *op. cit.*, pp. 274-275.

44 *Ibid.*, pp. 275-277.

45 *Ibid.*, pp. 277-278.

46 *Ibid.*, pp. 324-325. Precisely the same point is made in the *Grundrisse*, *op. cit.*, pp. 221-222.

47 Marx, *1844 Manuscripts*, *op. cit.*, p. 326.

48 *Ibid.*, p. 304.

49 Karl Marx, "Theses on Feuerbach," *MECW*, *op. cit.*, Vol. 5, p. 7.

50 Marx, *1844 Manuscripts*, *op. cit.*, pp. 305-306.

Tom Settle begins by arguing that, while it would be desirable to
have an accepted ground of the rightness of property, as of morality in
general, no such ground has been convincingly demonstrated. Perhaps
the goal has been set too high; perhaps moral philosophers should follow the example of Karl Popper, who has tried to show that scientific
theory is never justified in any strict sense, but is accepted as long
as it is both useful and open to refutation or further precision.
Settle tries to indicate what such a tentative theory of property would
be like. He concludes that it would justify not full private ownership
in the capitalist sense, but only private use subject to provision for
the good of others and for the good of the property itself.

THE GROUND OF MORALS AND THE PROPRIETY OF PROPERTY

In my periodic bouts of despair over civilization, I consider it rather futile, even if interesting, to try to get theory right, and wonder what difference it will make if there are satisfactory solutions to the problems of the ground of morals, the legitimacy of this or that kind of government, the propriety of property, and so on. Most far-reaching decisions are made by people who will not know the solutions or, knowing, will not care. Worse, crucial decisions are probably - I say in these bouts - in the hands of self-serving people shrewd enough to suppress correct solutions if incorrect but specious theories serve them better. Occasionally, by contrast, I have hope that a bad decision here or there could be averted or modified if good arguments could be advanced for a better way. Even then, I feel a bit like the widow in Mark's story.[1] Despite being praised for giving all she had, she would know she would not affect the Temple's economy much. But if I did not offer the ideas I had, I would be as troublesome as the man in the plane who has done one of your crossword clues over your shoulder faster than you and is bursting to help you out.

The truth is, though, many disputes about who owns what or who may use what are settled by force. And this is true not only of wars or of frontier strife. It is true of expropriation for a new airport, a road widening or a hydro route. Let the man who lives on the land stand in the way of progress or lie down in front of the bulldozers and he will be carried away bodily. And he'll be locked up if he makes a nuisance of himself trying to regain possession. And what if such disputes are settled by force? Is not force necessary, even if we suppose that there may be pockets of society where custom rules without the threat of force? There may be primitive tribes, or early stages of modern civilization, when enforcement of custom was unknown; but a universal-izable theory of the good society has to reckon with the question how to deal with offenders or potential offenders, and I can see no way to escape the threat to use force as an ingredient in the recipe. The problem I want to deal with does not arise for a person who thinks that the use of force is fine and that one cannot improve on the out-come of a balance of forces, though perhaps even he could not quite silence the question of what was meant by "fine" and what criteria

were involved in valuing the outcome of a balance of forces more highly
than any other disposition of matters. But the problem arises very
acutely for those who, like me, not only do not acquiesce in just any
outcome of the use of force or of a balance of force - for not acquies-
cing might amount to no more than preferring an outcome we were powerless to achieve - but who, like me, also go further and hold that some
other outcome is sometimes somehow *owed* to people, that matters *ought*
sometimes to be differently disposed from how they are. For such people, it is not only an important question whom to permit to own what
property - that may be important also for people who think settling
ownership by force is fine - it is an important question what the
grounds are by which such a question is to be answered, even if the answer is to be assisted by force.

    This problem is, of course, touched on in a number of essays in
this volume, but here I want to make it central. I am going to take
for granted that it is worth probing to the propriety of property, that
it is legitimate to question settlements arrived at by force as to
their rightness, and I am going to press the question of grounds.
Pressing the question of grounds means going to a layer somewhat deeper
than the problem of the consistency of a right to real property with
the right of equality, or how the concept and institution of property
would need to change if property were to be consistent with a democratic society, or what the causes are that give rise to the rules societies adopt, or whether it is logically coherent to talk about a property in one's self, and so on.

    I shall have to press even deeper than the question whether my
having a right to a property implies my having social duties concerning
the use and disposal of the property. I am going to take for granted a
second sense in which rights and obligations imply each other: *my* having a certain right (for example, a right to the use of a piece of property) implies *your* having a certain obligation (in this case, not to
prevent my use of the property). And I am also going to take for
granted that when we ask for the grounds of decisions about the rightness of property, we are not asking for an explanation of the legitimacy of property within some system of law, but a deeper question which
challenges the rightness of what laws prescribe.

    But what is the problem about the grounds of rightness of proper-
ty? In short, this: there do not seem to be any such grounds, and yet
if there are none, there is no escape from force as the arbiter. But
let me explain more fully.

I have, on the one hand, to explain why I think there need to be objective grounds to escape the slide into force and, on the other, to explain why there seem not to be any objective grounds. Then, in an attempt to solve the problem, I should like to suggest how there could be objective grounds and what those grounds might be.

If you eschew objective grounds for morals in general and respect for property rights in particular, you must opt for either no grounds at all or subjective grounds. The effect is the same in both cases: you are left with no satisfactory argument against force as arbiter. Let me take first the case of a person who says there are no grounds for property rights beyond the grounds supplied in law. In a negotiation to change the laws affecting ownership or the right to own, such a person could not participate coherently as to why the laws should be changed, though there would be no hindrance to his stating what changes he would prefer. If his view is right that there are no grounds for property rights, then the allocation of property rights may take place peacefully, by negotiation between interested parties or their representatives, or violently, by seizure and physical defence. The latter has long precedent in history, which also supplies us with examples of treaties which result from negotiations to obviate violence. Please be clear: I think it inescapable that property allocation within a society reflects a balance of force. Sometimes the force to back up a property ownership dispute may seem so far removed from negotiations that we forget it. But the very choice of the expression "enforceable right" by which to pick out rights that are effective implies the existence of a back-up force, so that negotiations that replace force resemble the conventional displays of aggression and submission by which animals often manage to avoid the bloodshed their conflicting interests might otherwise trigger.

It is a very attractive viewpoint that human beings behave like animals with respect to property and that all talk about rights is so much conventional negotiation jargon by which human beings adopt postures of mixed agression-submission in an effort to get as much as they can of what they want without resort to violence, with the talk carrying hints as to the limits of tolerance before violence erupts. This point of view is attractive to biologists aiming for consistency in ethology and committed to the view that all adaptive behaviour is egotistical and advantage-maximizing. I shall return to this scientific question later, since I think much turns on it. The viewpoint is

attractive to many commentators on political affairs who think of politics as basically a power struggle with rules, much as boxing is a
fight with rules, though the referee in the political ring is clumsy
and inarticulate and keeps losing his whistle. And it is attractive to
people who accept the standard account of what drives the economy in
capitalist countries: the basic human motive of maximizing personal
gain. Students of psychology may find coherence between the view that
there are no grounds for property rights and various programs they have
for analysing human behaviour, in which, although offering alternatives
to mere gain as motivator, they nonetheless do not go beyond the assumption that human beings are driven by needs or desires. Such programs evacuate the idea that human beings sometimes act reasonably. It
almost seems as though there is a presumption in the scientific study
of man that giving reasons for actions does not suffice to explain them
and may even be superfluous. Actions are to be explained, it seems, by
causes, rather than by reasons.

There is an unholy alliance here which couples what I think is a
restricted view of science with what I think is a false view of man,
one which denies his autonomy and rationality. Still - not to argue
the full case against this position - despite its attractiveness, it
offers no brake on the slide to the use of force and no criterion on
which we might argue with a politician or a judge that he ought to act
in some particular manner - for example, in the public interest.

But in this last respect, the person is in no better case who believes that the grounds of morals in general, and of the moral rule to
respect property in particular, are subjective. For he, too, has no
basis to argue that a judge who acts from his own motives on criteria
that satisfy himself, but are not popularly agreed, ought to act otherwise.[2] Of course, a judge is at least legally obliged, if not morally
obliged, to act in the interests of justice, but if a legislator
changes the law to remove certain legal constraints upon his own cupid-
ity, what argument weighs against this, if moral grounds are subjective?

Let us posit a person whose moral values include respect for humanity and respect for property. If he thinks that grounds for morals
are subjective, a matter of personal choice, what argument could he
possibly adduce for someone else's sharing his values? He could, of
course, appeal to others to share his views[3] and his appeal might be
successful. He could perhaps show that a group of perfectly rational,

egoistic people, from a position of equal liberty and without knowing
what role they might have to play in life, would agree as to the rules
that should govern their behaviour, and that these rules would accord
very well with well-known moral maxims.[4] But this would not be the
same thing at all as providing any one of these people with a reason to
keep the rules (once he knows his own desires and his own situation)
beyond the extent dictated by prudence. If a person were not already
inclined to be moral past prudence, the one who thought the grounds of
morals subjective could hardly generate an argument for someone else's
being moral. The other person could always reasonably reply that he
was inclined to be self-serving in his actions but was pleased to find
the moral man more generously disposed. He could wish the moral man
well in his attempts to gain converts to morality, but claim that on
the moral man's own principles of respect and of the subjectivity of
morals he ought to be left free to follow his own inclinations.

  Would we fare any better if property rights were a communal value?
Would the slide to force as arbiter be arrested if morals were a matter
of mores and property rights were customary? I am afraid not. Of
course, if there were unanimity in a given community about what was
right, if there were no dispute about property (and there certainly
have been and even now still are small communities which enjoy such
unanimity), then I should see no reason to press in such cases the idea
that force lay behind agreements and property allocations. But only so
long as unanimity holds. The question what to do with the rebel cannot
be silenced. The rebel may come from within, born of the group but a
poor student of its mores, or from without, brought up well on other
values. Both these kinds of problems exist for nations or tribes or
villages which for long periods might enjoy unanimity on values. The
rebel who acts on his different values will need persuading one way or
another if his behaviour is to conform to custom. If he is rebellious
about tradition and argues that improvements in social conditions can
only come about when traditions are criticized and imaginatively improved upon, it will be a hard job to persuade him rationally, though
he may of course be persuaded by other means. If the rebel is insis-
tent in his criticism and in the alternative allocation he proposes,
custom can in the end be maintained only by force. As to whether resort to force is a near threat or a far one, I give my personal view
that violence lies very close to the surface in human society,

including Canadian. People are ready to fight over tennis courts,
seats at a ball game, who shall be employed in a firm, who shall enter
a works while the labour force is on strike, and so on.

But it is rational persuasion that interests us here, not the argument, "If you don't move, I'll punch you," or "If you do move, I'll
pay you handsomely." Animals are trained by punishment and reward, by
hitting and stroking, but the matter of grounds for property rights
raises the question of reasons for rights, not of how to train the
young to conform. This leads straight into the second thing to be explained: why there seem not to be any objective grounds.

The search for objective grounds is usually thought to comprise
finding premises for an argument which has property rights as its conclusion. And this is a very reasonable initial research program. The
problem of grounding property rights would certainly be solved if the
search were successful. But there are two obstacles that frustrate the
search. The first is that logic does not allow inferring an obligation
from premises that do not contain one. One cannot derive "ought" from
"is," as the jargon shorthand has it. This is admittedly an arguable
point, and there are thinkers who purport to have found a way to do
it.[5] I can't follow them. One can derive what I call "instrumental
'ought's'" from indicative statements, but this is because an instrumental "ought" is shorthand for a hypothesis about certain means
conducing to certain ends and not about owing or being obliged. Thus,
attempts to derive moral obligation from the natural propensities of
human beings to clamour for each other's attention, or to derive natural rights directly from the needs animals have for living- and grazing-
or hunting-space, will go awry.

If the first obstacle is the impossibility of deriving "ought"
from an "is" premise, the second obstacle is the lack of a convincing
premise of any kind from which to derive rights or obligations.[6] So
perhaps the shortest route would be simply to declare certain rights
self-evident. But the opposition any such declaration has aroused
among philosophers evinces the lack of self-evidence. Because philosophers have usually thought a view needed to be rationally justified
one way or another before it could be reasonably believed, attempts to
ground natural rights, including property rights, objectively, have not
been successful. This is, in my view, a very serious state of affairs,
since it leaves us quite without an answer - leave aside a convincing
answer - to the question of the criteria by which a business or

political decision-maker ought to make his decisions. It is cold comfort to suggest that the pressure from the electorate or from the consumer will drive him to correct decisions, cold for two reasons. These
pressures are so imprecise and the instrument of sanction so blunt that
a shrewd enough politician or wealthy enough businessman can ignore all
but the crudest of these "signals." And even if the will of the people
were coherent, it would not necessarily be morally right.

The story so far, then: there seem to be no objective grounds for
morals or for property rights because what seems required for grounds
to be objective cannot be satisfied. What shall we do? Give up the
crossword? Relapse into subjectivism (individualistic or conventional)
or into nihilism? Or pretend we have grounds, and thus engage in the
doubletalk common to politics and Chambers of Commerce? We could try
criticizing the usual philosophical demands and proposing an alternate
view of rational beliefs, one that might leave room for objective
grounds for rights and obligations. Not that one would want to strain
reason to propose an alternate just for the sake of answering the cynic
about morals and rights. For any theory of rational belief to deserve
lingering attention, it would have to do better than merely to solve
the problem of how regrettable force as arbiter is in property allocation disputes.

Mercifully, such a theory is to hand. It comes already somewhat
developed from philosophy of science. I refer to Karl Popper's theory
of rationality as openness to criticism, which is a generalization into
philosophy of his theory that knowledge grows in science by conjectures
aimed to solve problems, coupled with rigorous criticism both of how
the problem is formulated and of the rival solutions.[7]

Before Popper, the most important views about scientific knowledge
assumed it was justified, one way or another, and they ran thereby into
insuperable problems. Bacon's inductivism couldn't answer Hume's logical criticism that "all" cannot be inferred from "some," Descartes'
deductivism foundered for want of self-evident axioms, while positivism's distrust of theories undermined its ability to report on its
observations.[8] Popper broke clear from this tradition with his rejection of justification. Reading the message of the mind-boggling revo-
lutions in theoretical physics from 1895 to 1919, he proposed that the
distinguishing mark of physics was not the securing of its findings
but their being held open to criticism.[9] Given the examples of improvement in scientific theory, and the hope for still more

improvements, the point was not to argue how to establish a theory but rather how to replace it with a better one, and how to tell which of two rivals was the better. Of course, no theory would be given house room if it did not solve a problem. And those theories would be preferred which solved more problems than the ones that provoked their invention.

To return to our problem about rights, we may say immediately that political philosophers are not alone in being unable to justify their theories. Scientists are in their company. It should not, perhaps, come amiss to ape the scientists, who succeed in retaining intellectual integrity for their work and a sense of the objectivity of their knowledge, while at the same time lacking proof. The trick is to allow as knowledge what solves a problem and what, though it cannot be proved, can be held open to criticism, to comparison with rivals, to the demand of coherence with knowledge in other domains, and, moreover, I suggest shows some promise of solving other problems.

If we take seriously that rational integrity allows us to entertain and even to believe (tentatively) a theory we cannot prove, it is possible for us to allow as the premise, from which property rights might follow, a principle which is neither self-evident nor convincingly justified, providing it solves the problem the way scientific theories do. This is quite a radical departure in ethical theory. But then the state of that art has, for some time, seemed to cry out for a startling new approach.

In recent writings[10] I have proposed a theory of objective morality, the origin and content of which I shall briefly rehearse here before going on to more specific problems in the theory of property.

The puzzle that first led me to propose a theory of the grounds of morals was posed by inconsistencies within democratic theory in politics, and between popular theories of democracy on the one hand and theories of animal sociality on the other. It seemed to me theoretically impossible (as squaring the circle is) to have a peaceful, just society as a consequence of the popular assumption of the human being as a utility maximizer expected to be selfish. This assumption allows a person to have a dash of public-spiritedness or honour in his make-up, but it does not require it. If, and only if - accidentally in terms of this theory - public-spiritedness or honour or some such non-self-serving quality is present in key loci in the society, peace with justice becomes theoretically possible. It seemed a serious flaw in

popular democratic theory that what the theory was supposed to explain
- peaceful, just society - could come about only if people acted contrary to the expectations of the theory.

Even more trouble arises when the assumptions of this theory are
compared with theories in ethology needed to explain animal and insect
social behaviour. Here the weight of argument seems to favour the view
that some creatures act in a manner that goes against their own chances
to survive to reproduce, or even just to survive, to the benefit of
other creatures in their group.[11] It is not surprising that genes
should evolve which ensure the survival of groups of kin at the cost
of some members, given how disruptive of groups individual selfishness
is.[12] Of course, most animal behaviour most of the time is self-pre-
servative, but overlaying this is a pattern of group-preservative behaviour, the size and kinship integrity of the group varying somewhat.
All this gives rise to an expectation that one would find a basic self-
serving propensity in human beings overlaid with a light propensity to
aid the group to which an individual belongs. And in studies of human
behaviour by anthropologists, this is exactly what one does find. However, bare empirical studies of human behaviour do not quite get to the
point where they can serve political theory, since in politics the autonomy of the citizen is introduced. This is a property that may be
quite ignored by students of patterns of behaviour of groups and may
even be ignored in politics if all one cares for is how a prince should
exercise power who wishes to retain it. But with democratic theory, a
further assumption is introduced, namely, human rationality. This assumption is usually made to explain the behaviour of rulers, and then
has to be extended to that class of citizens from which the rulers come
if one is not to assume that being elected induces rationality.

By now, we have moved beyond ordinary ethology. We have proposed
properties of human beings that must be considered as emergent in evolution: autonomy and rationality. And the problem focuses itself
here: these properties are on a different level from the propensities
to self-serving or group-serving behaviour with which anthropology concerns itself. We are no longer considering genetic or cultural pressures to behave this way or that (though we are not denying these pressures). We are considering the human being as an autonomous animal
thinking out what to do next and choosing the next action at least
sometimes on the basis of weighed reasons for and against. What explains sociality at this level of analysis? Clearly, instinct or

social pressure or moral sentiment will not do, since these will all
come to undermine autonomy and bypass reason, important as moral sentiment and social pressure are in causing moral actions. What is needed is a property which constrains autonomy without compelling it, which
supplies a reason for socially useful action, and which, above all, is
relational in some way, as animal instincts towards social behaviour
are relational. I have proposed moral obligation as just such a property.

I made a more or less clean break with some old traditions in ethics in proposing to view obligation as a polyadic relation, with people
and actions as arguments. Thus, instead of trying to find out what
there is about an action that makes it right or analysing the word
"good" to see what fruit that yielded, I took my cue from "ought" being
part of the verb "to owe," which always requires a person as indirect
object. I also tried to remedy what I thought was a fundamental defect
of Biblical ethics, namely, that it was consistently about only two
persons. The result was the proposal that the basic structure of a
moral rule is: "A owes it to B to x C" where A, B and C are people and
"x-ing" is doing an action to or for C or having an attitude to or
about C. Two-person ethics is derived as a special case by making B =
C and duty to oneself is a further special case where A = B = C.

From this view of obligation come my proposals to solve the poli-
tical-ethological problem cluster. The human being who is, accurately
enough, described at the anthropological level as behaving mostly in a
self-serving way but sometimes in a social-serving way, may now be described at the level of emergent properties as autonomous, rational and
morally obliged. (I would fill out the content of obligation in part
in a traditional manner, stressing respect for the autonomy and rationality of others and attention to their needs.)

This theory of the human being is not, of course, complete. Without adding being curious and appreciative as common human characteristics, we can hardly explain science and art or answer the question of
the point of living - but my aim here is only to say enough to give a
handle to some problems in theory of property.

The problem in ethology, "How comes it such an adaptive property as
sociality disappears in man?" is answered. Sociality does not disappear. It is a logical corollary of moral obligation. And the problem
in political theory is answered: peaceful, just society is what would

be expected if people did what my biological theory declares they are
supposed, but not compelled, to do. Moreover, the clash is removed between the presuppositions of political theory and those of biology.
What is even more exciting for me is the discovery that my theory
solves the problem of the validity of law. Making laws to govern in-
terpersonal relations becomes an obligation in a complex society. Far
from having to seek a justification for government, the onus would be
to explain why laws were not being made to protect people from those
who flagrantly neglected their obligations. A series of interesting
problems arise, such as how obligations might be shared, or delegated,
and how social organizations such as business corporations or trades
unions or citizens' interest groups might have obligations. But I
shall resist the temptation to pursue these questions at length, con-
centrating rather on what light is shed on theory of property by my
claim about the human characteristic of being an obliged animal.

Assuming some logical reciprocity of rights and obligations, and
noticing that no theory of objectively valid natural rights has yet
passed muster, we can see a certain priority of obligations over
rights. Obligations confer rights, rather than rights implying obligations. This is a very interesting way of thinking about rights, and
reverses today's usual tendency to take rights as the starting point.
It is interesting because as one attempts to embed a particular right
in a field of universal obligation, obligations may be brought to light
which apply to the holder of the right. For example, if a person wants
to know whether he has the right to maintain a dangerous animal at his
home, or to experiment with dangerous chemicals, it may seem acceptable
for people to have an obligation, respecting his autonomy, to go some
way to allow him his whim, but it is difficult to see how they would
have an obligation to share the danger to the hilt. Hence he would
have no right to dump the danger on his neighbours. The right to dump
garbage where we please similarly can hardly get started without a general obligation to accept other people's garbage at their whim, which
is hard to warrant.

It needs to be noted that the content of the obligation people
have for their fellows will have great variety according to such accidental factors as climate and geography as well as social complexity
and population density. Even if it is agreed that human beings are
usually obliged animals, there is no straightforward way to derive the
precise nature of the obligation. Nonetheless, it entails an enormous

shift in the discussion about how to treat our fellows if the assumption is made that each has a moral obligation towards the others. This
move cuts off a very common retreat into completely self-centred behaviour, for while the obligation to respect one's fellows does not
pick out with precision what to do next, and even gives fuzzy boundar-
ies where it is hard to decide whether an act is morally permissible,
it does prohibit a whole range of possible actions incompatible with
respect. Its force is, like so many of the Old Testament's misleading-
ly termed "Commandments," proscriptive rather than prescriptive.

Now even though obligations imply rights and thus the theory of
obligation permits the development of a portfolio of rights, obligations are not replaceable by rights. It would be illicit to infer a
set of rights from some obligations and then detach those specific
rights from the background of obligation in general, considering them
in isolation. Thus, the change by which, under capitalism, property
became a right unconditional on the performance of any social function
seems to me wrong, a consequence of ignoring the field of obligation
against which the right to property should be set. It is not surprising, since capitalist theory is flawed at its core: it assumes that
the outcome of exchanges made by utility maximizers will be just, whatever it is. I would say no one has the right to own property, the way
ownership is construed within capitalist theory.

Respect for humanity and attention to people's needs suggests
everyone has some right of use of property to the extent human development needs it and the limited resources of the planet allow. This latter constraint explains why rights of use may vary over time with varying population density and why inheritance cannot be unconditional.
Human beings seem to need some measure of security in domestic property
and in property used for making a living (where these differ), so society needs rules that allow such security. This is consistent with
the abolition of ownership, since it is security in the right of use
rather than in title which is the primary psychological and social
need. It might avoid confusion if we dropped all talk of ownership
and talked piecemeal about the right to use property, the right to con-
strain the use of it, the right to the fruits of it, and the right to
dispose of it. But it is not merely to avoid confusion that I propose
replacing talk about ownership by talk about trusteeship. The concept
of trusteeship aptly captures the sense of rights constrained by obligations.

Now the crucial questions are, "Who may be entrusted with property?" and, from among this group, "Who ought to undertake the trust?" Whereas the squabble over ownership presupposed that owning was a means to self-aggrandizement, the switch to talk of trusteeship emphasizes that the management of property is an exercise of responsibility to society and to the property itself, whatever it be: a work of art, say, or a parcel of land, with its non-human inhabitants and users, vegetable and animal, its very rocks.

Property is too important to be left to those who covet it. The propriety appropriate to the grounds I have proposed is that it be entrusted to those who care for it, who cherish it, who take care. And "care" is a loaded word, it means both "love" and "toil," it is a sign of the covenant between the trustee and the trust; and the covenant of care, of right use, is the closest thing I would allow to title, but it is not title. It lends this world's goods into the hands of its Care Takers, and that is where, in the true sense of the word, they belong.

FOOTNOTES

1 *The Gospel according to St. Mark*, Chapter XII, 42-44.

2 Compare G. Tullock, "Public Decisions as Public Goods," *Journal of Political Economy* (July-August, 1971), 913-18.

3 D. A. J. Richards, *A Theory of Reasons for Action* (London: Oxford University Press, 1971).

4 Compare J. Rawls, *Theory of Justice* (London: Cambridge University Press, 1971).

5 For example, R. V. Hannaford, "You Ought to Derive 'Ought' from 'Is'," *Ethics* 82 (1972), 155-162.

6 Compare F. E. Oppenheim, *Moral Principles in Political Philosophy* (New York: Random House, 1968).

7 K. R. Popper, *The Open Society and Its Enemies* (London: Routledge and Kegan Paul, 4th edition 1962); *The Logic of Scientific Discovery* (London: Hutchinson, 1959); *Conjectures and Refutations* (London: Routledge and Kegan Paul, 1963); *Objective Knowledge* (London: Oxford University Press, 1972).

8 I have argued this more fully in my "Is Scientific Knowledge Rationally Justified?" in *Basic Issues in the Philosophy of Science*, W. R. Shea, (ed.) (New York: Science History Publications, 1976).

9 My disagreement with Popper over the success of his criterion of demarcation is expressed in my "Induction and Probability Unfused," *Philosophy of Karl R. Popper*, P. A. Schilpp (ed.), (Illinois: Library of Living Philosophers Open Court) 697-749.

10 Tom Settle, *In Search of a Third Way* (Toronto: McClelland and Stewart, 1976); "The Moral Dimension in Political Assessments of the Social Impact of Technology," *Philosophy of the Social Sciences* 6 (1976), 315-334.

11 See for example V. C. Wynne-Edwards, *Animal Dispersion in Relation to Social Behaviour* (New York: Hafner, 1962) and E. O. Wilson, *Sociobiology* (Cambridge, Mass.: Harvard University Press, 1975).

12 Richard Dawkins, *The Selfish Gene* (New York: Oxford University Press, 1976). The title of this book confuses the issue at stake. Selection of genes for their survival is perfectly consistent with selection of species for the trait of other-directed or socially advantageous behaviour. In short, a "selfish" gene could select for altruism in individual animals. The author also confuses the issue in the text, sliding covertly between "selfishness" in genes and individualistic adaptiveness in animals, as though they were the same thing.

Friedrich Hayek has produced what he calls a "restatement" of the principles of classical liberalism. This essay by Thomas Flanagan examines Hayek's central concept of "spontaneous order" and shows how private property is indispensable to such an order. Special attention is also given to the problem of justice. It is argued, following Hayek, that "social justice" in the current sense of state-enforced redistribution of wealth or income is not only inimical to true justice but will, if consistently implemented, destroy spontaneous order.

F. A. HAYEK ON PROPERTY AND JUSTICE

The Nobel Prize for economics was given in 1974 to Gunnar Myrdal and Friedrich Hayek. The award recognized both men's "pioneering work in the theory of money and economic fluctuations" and their "penetrating analysis of the interdependence of economic, social and institutional phenomena."[1] Little need be said here on the first point except to mention that Hayek was a product of the "Austrian school" of economists. His main contributions to technical economics came in the 1920's and 1930's, when he wrote extensively on monetary theory, the business cycle, the theory of capital, and socialist planning. He left a mark on each of these subjects which would have guaranteed his professional reputation, even if he had done nothing more.[2]

In the 1940's he became increasingly interested in the general question of a free society, including but transcending the economist's marketplace. An early result was his most famous book, *The Road to Serfdom* (1944), which argued that the then fashionable ideas of economic planning would, if consistently implemented, lead to a totalitarian regime, similar to Nazi Germany.

Hayek's interest in political theory continued to grow after this beginning. He undertook numerous historical studies which can be found in *The Counter-Revolution of Science* (1952) and three volumes of collected essays.[3] He produced a systematic statement of his views in *The Constitution of Liberty* (1960), and is now in process of publishing a revised and final formulation of his theory in the three volumes of *Law, Legislation, and Liberty*. Volume I, entitled *Rules and Order*, appeared in 1973, followed by *The Mirage of Social Justice* in 1976. Volume III, *The Political Order of a Free Society*, exists in manuscript form and has been promised for publication "as soon as the advance of old age permits."[4]

Since Hayek's contribution has not yet received the attention it deserves, this paper is written with the intention of helping to make his ideas more widely known.[5] It presents his views on property and justice as they appear in the mature formulation of his latest works.

Hayek has said that he would like to be able to call himself a liberal, but does not do so for two reasons. First, the term has been appropriated in North America by left-wing reformers who are

really democratic socialists; and second, there is a "great gulf" between Hayek's position and the rationalistic, utilitarian liberalism
of the nineteenth century.[6] Liberalism has been chiefly associated
with the utilitarian tradition of Bentham and J. S. Mill, or with the
contractarianism of Locke and Jefferson. But Hayek sees both contractarianism and utilitarianism as examples of the "constructivist"
error in political thought. His own intellectual mentors are David
Hume and Adam Smith, Adam Ferguson and Edmund Burke, Alexis de Tocqueville and Lord Acton. His central concepts are neither social contract nor utility, but spontaneous order and evolutionary growth.
Perhaps this is why his contribution is not widely appreciated. It
meshes as poorly with the utilitarianism of most economists as with
the revised contractarianism of philosophers like John Rawls.

    As with any thinker of rank, Hayek's views about particular ques-
tions like property are based on a broader understanding of man and
society. His foundation is not a transcendental or metaphysical philosophy of human nature, but an instrumental theory of social order as
the means by which man increases his chances for survival, comfort,
and happiness. This theory is explored in the next section of the
paper.

Two Kinds of Order

    Hayek distinguishes two fundamentally different types of human
order.[7] One, which he calls "organization," "made order," or *taxis*,
is a deliberate arrangement of elements according to the conscious intention of some person or group, expressed in the form of commands and
subsidiary rules. Examples of organizations are business firms, government agencies, churches, and voluntary associations or, at a different level, legal structures like the Criminal Code or artificial
languages like Esperanto. All have been deliberately created to serve
some conscious human purpose.

    The second kind of order, called "spontaneous order," "grown or-
der," or *cosmos*, emerges from the mutual interaction of elements. It
is not imposed by command nor created by design. It is the "result of
human action but not the execution of any human design," to cite a
phrase of Adam Ferguson which Hayek often quotes.[8] A perfect example
of spontaneous order is human language. No single intelligence has
created our languages; they are products of evolutionary growth from
beginnings which are now only conjectural. Other examples of

spontaneous order are the common law and the marketplace. Society itself is an all-inclusive spontaneous order, composed of subordinate
organizations and spontaneous orders which mutually adjust to each
other.

Both kinds of order depend upon man's propensity to follow rules.
Indeed, the very essence of a human order, system, or structure is
that behaviour limited by rules produces patterns of intelligibility,
regularity, and predictability. But the rules are different in the
two cases. An organization depends upon commands which are consciously given and consciously obeyed. The epitome of the made order is its
rule book, administrative manual, or by-laws. In contrast, a spontaneous order demands only that individuals follow rules, not that
they be able to state them or even be aware of them.

Hayek uses the Greek work *thesis* to describe the rules of an organization. *Thesis* is defined as "any rule which is applicable only
to particular people or in the service of the ends of rulers." In
contrast, a rule of a spontaneous order is called *nomos*, defined as
"a universal rule of just conduct applying to an unknown number of
future instances and equally to all persons in the objective circumstances described by the rule, irrespective of the effects which observance of the rule will produce in a particular situation."[9]

Nomoi allow an overall order to emerge which no one designed,
intended, or foresaw. This is what Adam Smith meant to say for the
special case of the marketplace with his famous metaphor of the "invisible hand." In pursuing their self-interest under certain rules
of honesty, justice, and respect for agreements, men create a spontaneous order in which scarce resources are optimally distributed to
diverse enterprises.

The rules of existing spontaneous orders such as language, common
law, and the market have themselves evolved spontaneously. But as men
gradually begin to understand these rules through philosophy and social science, it becomes possible to think of improving them through
deliberate alteration and experimentation. Such improvement is possible, as long as it is done in harmony with the immanent principles
of an order, and not to replace them.

The word "spontaneous" does not mean there is no need for enforcement of the rules of order. Language may not need enforcement,
but common law and the market certainly do. It is often in our short-
term interest to violate rules on the assumption that others will obey

them, thus giving us a special advantage. E.g., most thieves do not
want to abolish the institution of private property, they just want
to appropriate the property of others. In the jargon of contemporary
economics, they are "free riders." Enforcement against free-riders
is acceptable and indeed essential to many spontaneous orders.

There are three major differences between spontaneous and made
orders, which can be tabulated as follows:[10]

	Organization	Spontaneous Order
tends to	simplicity	complexity
tends to	concreteness	abstractness
serves	purpose of the maker	no single purpose

Organization tends to simple structures, divisions, and hier-
archies because it is a product of the limited powers of one or a
few conscious minds. But since spontaneous order is not bound by the
need of a superintending intelligence, it can become as complex as
circumstances demand. Bertrand de Jouvenel has cleverly illustrated
this point with his "problem of the orchard."[11] Tell a group of
schoolboys that a hundred thousand apples are to be harvested, and ask
how they should be piled. The answer will usually be a thousand piles
of a hundred apples or a hundred piles of a thousand, symmetrically
spaces throughout the orchard. Now ask the boys to actually harvest
and heap up the apples, without direct supervision. A complex and un-
symmetrical assortment of heaps will result, reflecting the skills,
strength, and industry of the different pickers, as well as peculiar-
ities of the individual trees.

Organizations also tend to concreteness, which is to say that
particular people are put in particular places and told to do specified things. "Go to this office, do this job, file this report, hire
this person." But a spontaneous order is abstract, in that the positions of individuals are not specified. A market demands buyers and
sellers, but it does not matter who nor how many play these roles.

Abstractness, of course, is a matter of degree. Hayek interprets human progress as an increase in the abstractness of social relations. Rules of conduct become less specific in the obligations
they impose upon men. Obligations of fair dealing are generalized
from family, relatives, and friends to apply to all with whom one

comes in contact. Hayek uses the terms "Great Society" and "Open Society," borrowed from Adam Smith and Karl Popper respectively, to denote the highly abstract Western society of recent centuries.[12]

An organization serves the purpose of its makers. Government enforces the law, a corporation makes money, and a church unites people to worship. More than one purpose might be pursued (governments also deliver mail and pave roads), but this does not affect the principle that purpose is consciously imposed from above. A spontaneous order, in comparison, cannot be said to have a purpose. It is a milieu or matrix which helps individuals to pursue their own goals in infinite profusion. It provides means but not ends, as is clearly true of language, common law, or the market. Society as a whole, which is a spontaneous order, has no purpose beyond facilitating the various ends of its participants.

Both forms of order are useful to mankind, and each has its special strength. Organization is particularly efficient where one purpose is to be pursued to the exclusion of others. But the deficiency of organization is that it must be designed, and so can only receive the benefit of a limited amount of intelligence. Spontaneous order, on the other hand, allows for the continuing contribution of many minds over time. Thus arise structures like language, which no one could ever have created or even envisioned.

This last point is particularly important because all intelligences are severely limited in one crucial way. Even the most brilliant mind has little knowledge of the particular circumstances of others' lives.[13] I may be an architect who knows all about housebuilding, but I know little of the particular needs, desires, and financial resources of those who want homes. A spontaneous order allows these quanta of particular knowledge to be adjusted to one another. The very fact that spontaneous order is unplanned and undesigned makes it superior to organization in using the plenitude of information which is available in the separated minds of men.

Society as a whole is a spontaneous order, though many organizations act within it. The remarkable progress of civilization, and particularly of the West in modern times, bears testimony to the power of spontaneous order. The absence of imposed purpose allows free play to creative initiative, while maintaining an effective filtering system to sort out beneficial innovations. Ego proposes, but Other disposes. The individual's freedom to initiate is matched by others'

freedom to reject, accept, or imitate. In this way words are coined,
ideas accepted, marriages concluded, and commodities sold.

Similarly, spontaneous order itself is always changing because
its rules are modified through the pressure of initiative and acceptance. There is an evolutionary process of "survival of the fittest"
- not of men, but of rules.[14] Those groups which follow rules of,
say, kinship or property which strengthen them will prevail over
groups whose innovations are less constructive. Historical progress
is not an accident but a logical result of the power of spontaneous
order to solve problems by experimentation.

It is sometimes maintained that society has become so complex
that it must be planned; but the very opposite, says Hayek, is true.
Spontaneous order becomes more indispensable as progress puts civilization further beyond the comprehension of a single intelligence or
committee, no matter how talented. Men may use their growing knowledge to improve rules of order in certain respects, but conscious
overall direction is an illusion.

Private Property

Hayek quotes with approval the remarks of Acton that "a people
averse to the institution of private property is without the first
element of freedom," and of Maine that "nobody is at liberty to attack several property and to say at the same time that he values civilization."[15] But he has never written a lengthy disquisition on property, perhaps because it is conceptually subordinate to spontaneous
order and can readily be related to it.

The general line of thought is strictly utilitarian. Hayek takes
it for granted that men wish to have wealth at their disposal in order
to pursue more effectively whatever goals they may have. The important question, then, is what set of rules to follow in order to maximize available wealth. The answer will inevitably be some form of
spontaneous order, since we are dealing with the whole of society,
which is too complex to be organized and directed from above.

Spontaneous social order means freedom to plan our lives within
abstract rules. This implies a private sphere within which we are
protected from external coercion, subject to the protection of others'
spheres. As Hayek has said:

> We are rarely in a position to carry out a co-
> herent plan of action unless we are certain of
> our exclusive control of some material objects;
> and where we do not control them, it is neces-
> sary that we know who does if we are to collab-
> orate with others. The recognition of property
> is clearly the first step in the delimitation
> of the private sphere which protects us against
> coercion....[16]

Thus property is useful to the owner because it allows him freedom of choice; but it is equally useful to others because it creates a
predictable situation within which they may plan. Of course, predictability might be conferred in other ways, as by a system of public or
community property administered under law. But this would diminish
the field for private initiative which through spontaneous order works
for the potential benefit of all. Thus it is difficult to conceive of
spontaneous order without private property.

This is not to deny that there is a place for common property.
The community as a whole may wish to retain or acquire the rights of
ownership to certain things, especially where they are the focus of
strong neighborhood effects.[17] Spontaneous order could adjust to any
given situation of common property, as long as there were clear rules
about its use. But a vast extension of common property would jeopar-
dize spontaneous order because the common property would have to be
under public control, which would inhibit the experimentation possible
under private ownership.

The primary argument for private property is not the logical
proof that it is indispensable to spontaneous order but the historical
experience that property develops *pari passu* with the advance of civilization. Property, like freedom, is natural only in Hume's special
sense. Arguments like Locke's famous labour theory are constructivist
misinterpretations. The complex of rules which defines property
rights in our society is a "result of human action but not of human
design," although it has been reinforced with positive law.

Property is an evolving institution which must continually adapt
to unforeseen circumstances. Hertzian waves give rise to novel problems of radio, television, and telecommunications. The growth of in-
surance and pension schemes poses difficulties of its own, as does the
contemporary trend of condominium home ownership. "Property" is an
abstraction for the bundle of rights pertaining to possession, control, and disposition of such things. No intelligence could lay down

a priori rules to cover all contingencies. Rules evolve as needed in
the form of habit, custom, common law, legislation, and judicial decisions. Throughout this process, the criterion and justification is
the utility of rules, as evaluated by experience in the great labora-
tory of spontaneous order.

This evolutionary view agrees with the words of J. S. Mill:

> The idea of property is not some one thing,
> identical throughout history and incapable
> of alteration, but is variable like all other
> creations of the human mind; at any given time
> it is a brief expression denoting the rights
> over things conferred by the law or custom of
> some given society at that time; but neither
> on this point nor on any other has the law and
> custom of a given time and place a claim to be
> stereotyped for ever.[18]

Mill wrote these sentences to justify social reform through alterations in the laws of property. He wished to show that property,
since it was a humanly created and evolving institution, could not resist change by invoking the "rights of property." This is correct as
far as it goes, but it raises a further question about which Mill was
not altogether clear: What sort of changes may we make in the rules
of property without losing the creative benefits of spontaneous order?

The answer must be that we are not free to superimpose whatever
institutions of property we please upon a functioning spontaneous order. Its interconnected rules may not be arbitrarily altered without
engendering all sorts of unexpected and undesirable consequences.
What is possible is more subtle. We can do our best to comprehend the
immanent principles of spontaneous order. With this knowledge, we may
essay piecemeal amendment of rules designed to enhance the operations
of that order. In practice, this will often mean removing obstacles
to progress which have been unintentionally or unwisely established by
previous generations. But we are not free to start *ex nihilo*. As
Hayek has said of rules of conduct in general:

> ...although we can endeavour to find out what
> function a particular rule performs within a
> given system of rules, and to judge how well
> it has performed that function, and may as a
> result try to improve it, we can do so always
> only against the background of the whole sys-
> tem of other rules which together determine
> the order of action in that society. But we
> can never rationally reconstruct in the same
> manner the whole system of rules, because we
> lack the knowledge of all the experiences that
> entered into its formation.[19]

Hayek himself has given us an example of this approach to social reform. His essay on "The Corporation in a Democratic Society" contains two suggestions about property rights which would entail rather substantial changes in the corporate world. First, he would give each stockholder a "legally enforceable claim to his share in the whole profits of the corporation."[20] At present, a majority of stockholders, advised by management, may decide for all what proportion of profits will be paid out and what proportion retained. Second, Hayek would prohibit corporations from exercising voting rights pertaining to shares they might hold in other corporations.[21]

These suggestions were made in the context of discussing A. A. Berle's famous thesis about the role of management in the modern corporation. Hayek's point is that the limited-liability corporation is a highly artificial construct, the result partly of spontaneous growth and partly of legislative and judicial decisions in the nineteenth century. Management's emancipation from stockholder control may be "not a fact which we must accept as inevitable, but largely the result of special conditions which the law has created and the law can change."[22] Adoption of Hayek's two suggestions, by restraining management's freedom to dispose of corporate assets, would give shareholders more control over corporate business.

Further reflection also shows that Hayek's suggestions are compatible with the immanent principles of the market. Constructs such as firms or corporations are not ends in themselves, like people, but are tools for human use. Their purpose is to allow people to pool property for projects which are too large for individual resources. If rules have been adopted which unintentionally enlarge the powers of management, this is an obstacle to private property, not an intrinsic part of property rights. Thus remedial legislation may be necessary. (Of course, the remedy will in turn create unforeseen difficulties, which will also have to be corrected in the light of experience.) There is thus a great role for conscious intelligence in accelerating the progress of spontaneous order, on one overriding condition: that reforms are done in a spirit of humility to enhance the order, not in the vain conceit that human design can achieve whatever it desires.

It is on this point that Mill's legacy is ambiguous. His famous distinction between production and distribution created the impression that the state is at liberty to "distribute" or "redistribute"

property once it is produced. "The laws and conditions of the production of wealth," wrote Mill, "partake of the character of physical
truths.... It is not so with the Distribution of Wealth. This is a
matter of human institution solely."[23] The words suggest unlimited
vistas of egalitarian reform.

Now Mill himself cautioned against drawing rash conclusions from
his premises. He warned that distribution has its own laws, which
"are as little arbitrary...as the laws of production." Society may
create "whatever rules it thinks best,"[24] but practical consequences
will flow which cannot be disregarded.

In spite of this warning, Mill was fascinated with the reform of
property laws. He seriously examined socialism and communism, and
discussed profound changes in the laws of inheritance. His intellectual heirs have moved even further in this direction under the slogans
of "distributive" or "social justice." Hayek's critique of these elusive terms is one of his greatest contributions to contemporary political debate. However, before proceeding to the contentious subject
of social justice, we must glance at Hayek's views on the more basic
question of justice as such.

Justice

Probably everyone accepts the famous formula of Ulpian, that
justice "is a firm and unceasing will to give each man his due" (*jus
suum cuique tribuere*).[25] However problems quickly arise because *suum
cuique* is a formal phrase which does not in itself explain how its
content is to be determined. What determines that which is "one's
own?" Clearly, some further criterion is called for, which Aristotle
realized when he said that justice is proportionality.[26] In the modern terms of Bertrand de Jouvenel, justice is a share-out of something
among men in proportion to their standing on some relevant criterion.[27] Since it is not obvious which of many possible criteria is
relevant to a particular case, disputes are bound to arise. It is at
this point that conceptions of justice begin to diverge.

Hayek nowhere offers a capsule definition of justice, but he obviously stands in the Whig-liberal tradition, whose view could be formulated approximately as follows: "one's own" is that which one acquires without violation of equal rules of conduct which leave it open
to others to do likewise. This seems broad enough to include various
liberal theories of justice from Locke to Robert Nozick's recent

"entitlement theory." Justice in the liberal tradition does not demand that a particular outcome result from action in the spontaneous
order of society; it merely stipulates that certain rules be followed.
The purpose of justice is "to tell each what he can count upon,"[28] to
promote the stability of expectations upon which spontaneous order depends. Equalization of holdings is not unjust if it happens to arise
from impartial enforcement of rules; but it cannot be itself a part of
justice, because it would involve "correcting" the result of following
rules. To do this consistently or even frequently would destroy the
stability of expectations which justice aims at.

Hayek's conception of justice is not novel, but his theory of
spontaneous order has enabled him to elaborate several aspects of
justice in a distinctive way. Let us look at three of his special
contributions to the understanding of justice:

1. Of what or whom can justice be predicated? In the first instance,
justice is a virtue of individual human beings. It is a habit, a virtue, or as Ulpian said, "a firm and unceasing will" (*constans et
perpetua voluntas*). It is a property of men's intentions toward other
men. Derived from this, we may also speak of "just actions," which
are acts performed under rules tending to preserve or restore *jus suum
cuique*. This could apply to actions either of individuals or of organizations, such as the government, as long as the actions are deliberate.

It is also customary to speak of rules themselves as just or unjust, a usage which is bound to give rise to confusion. Hayek allows
us to speak of rules as just or unjust only if we are clear about what
is meant. A rule is unjust if it is not congruent with the overall
system of rules which establishes justice in a particular society.
There are no absolutely just or unjust rules, apart from the bizarre
examples constructed by social philosophers. In reality every society
has its own tradition of just behaviour which furnishes the background
for discussion of individual rules.

It is not meaningful to predicate justice of the results of any
spontaneous order, and certainly not of society as a whole. For no
one has intended the outcomes of a spontaneous order. They have occurred as a result of human action, but not of human design.

In short, one may enquire into the justice of persons, actions
or rules, but not of outcomes. If the persons, actions, and rules
are not unjust, there is no more to be said. The outcomes may not

agree with our subjective preferences, but it makes no sense to cri-
ticize them as unjust. Such criticism is an anthropomorphic fallacy,
based on confusion of spontaneous order with an acting person.[29]
2. Another way of expressing the same idea is to say that justice is
"abstract." It refers only to selected aspects of person or actions,
namely their conformity to rules of just conduct. In contrast, outcomes of social processes are concrete facts of existence. Justice
does not mean arranging the particulars of reality to achieve a desired outcome. We could pursue such a goal only if we were endowed
with the omniscient intelligence demanded by consistent Benthamite
act-utilitarianism, which calls upon us to calculate all the consequences of our actions. But since we are not so endowed, we must rely
upon the general tendency of rules as applied over a multitude of
cases.[30] As Hume pointed out in a famous simile, justice is like an
arch which can stand only if all its stones remain in place.[31] A
rule is useful only in as much as it is consistently enforced. If exceptions are made, the point of having a rule is lost, and we are left
in the impossible situation of judging each case on its merits.

It is always tempting to deviate from enforcing rules in particular cases because we think we can see a superior outcome (e.g. "I
won't fail *this* student for plagiarism because he has already learned
his lesson.") But such manipulation of rules would be logical only if
we could foresee the outcome not only of this case but of all future
cases which may be affected by it. Since we cannot, we must fall back
upon abstract rules as the safest guide for our limited intellects.
It is a policy of humility, whose modest aim is to stabilize our environment through regulation of conduct, so that individuals can plan
their lives with greater confidence.
3. Justice is negative, in two senses. First, justice tells us with
very few exceptions not what to do but what not to do - not to steal,
lie, slander, and so on. At least this is the general character of
relations of autonomous adults to one another. Exceptions chiefly
arise with children or other dependents, or in unusual circumstances
where men are thrown together (e.g. shipwreck, where English common
law recognizes a duty of assistance). But by and large, "we shall not
go far wrong if for our purposes we treat all rules of just conduct as
negative in character."[32]

Second, the test of justice is negative. That is, we can determine what is unjust, but we cannot specify what is just. After the

unjust is eliminated, there always remains an infinity of just possibilities. The test of injustice is the universalization principle of
the Golden Rule or of Kant's categorical imperative, always to act as
if you were legislating for all mankind. This criterion allows us to
reject actions which, if they were generalized, would tend to destroy
the whole system of rules of just conduct. It is not possible for
everyone to steal all the time, for there would be no property to
steal, and both private property and theft would cease to be meaningful terms. Hence theft can only be performed by a few and does not
meet the test of generalization. This familiar line of reasoning allows us to call theft unjust, but it says nothing about the precise
character of property laws. Their actual composition will be determined by historical evolution, and will differ widely from one society
to another.

In an interesting aside, Hayek points out that this negative test
of justice resembles Karl Popper's well-known theory that scientific
error can be demonstrated, but not scientific truth. Truth is really
a short word for "not yet falsified." Similarly, just really means
"not unjust." This is not just a word game but an important insight
into the nature of justice, linking it up with the limited character
of human intelligence. Man cannot demonstrate truth beyond all doubt,
but he can eliminate errors. Likewise, man cannot create and impose
a single pattern of justice, but he can recognize and eliminate injustice. What is left is in both cases indeterminate. The liberal
outlook yields parallel results both in social theory and in scientific methodology.[33]

Social Justice

The term "social justice" and its equivalents "economic justice"
and "distributive justice" are widely used today. Yet although such
terms are current, it is by no means easy to say what they mean. A
brief look at the contemporary literature reveals numerous possibilities. Some authors use "social justice" simply as a variant for
"justice" without attaching an additional meaning to the longer
term.[34] Such usage is pleonastic, for justice is intrinsically social; but it seems to be establishing itself. R. W. Baldwin, fully
aware that the adjective is unnecessary, nonetheless entitled his
book *Social Justice* "to conform to the current vogue."[35] Other authors have tried to attribute some substantive meaning to social or

distributive justice. Rawls sees distributive justice in an idealized
democratic welfare state which keeps close control over a market economy to ensure that inequalities do not get too large.[36] Runciman
speaks even more strongly of "a continuous transfer of wealth, from
richest to poorest" unless "special claims" intervene.[37] Honoré has
stated approvingly that social justice is such an egalitarian concept
that "many sober citizens will be startled" when they recognize its
full implications.[38] And a recent book from Sweden asserts that distributive justice means "substantive equality," that is, the equalization of economic welfare. This is not quite strict equality of
holdings, but proportionality according to need.[39]

    Social justice can thus in practice mean anything from the demo-
cratic liberalism of Rawls to the pure communism of "....to each according to his needs." Fortunately we do not need to explore these
differences further, for we are concerned with the appropriateness of
the term in the first place. Hayek's critique does not concern this
or that theory of social justice, but the coherence of the very idea.

    What all contemporary theorists of social justice have in common
is that they talk not about rules of conduct but about arrangements
which result from social processes. This is least evident in the
case of Rawls, who claims to be concerned with "pure procedural justice."[40] Indeed Hayek, taking Rawls at his word, speculates that he
and Rawls may be saying much the same thing.[41] However, Robert Nozick
has demonstrated that Rawls' theory is concerned more with "end-state
principles of distribution" than with "historical-entitlement" principles.[42] This is much more obvious in other writers, such as
Frankena, who says: "I propose to take social justice, not as a property of individuals and their actions, but as a predicate of societies...," or Ericsson, who announces that he will study "nothing but
the states of affairs which constitute the internal distributive effects of society."[43]

    Now the concept of distributive justice has been understood ever
since Aristotle. However, the traditional concept referred to the
way in which things were distributed within some made order (*taxis*).
The example given by Aristotle - distribution of awards by government -
made this clear.[44] The modern concept of social or distributive justice is different in that it calls upon the state not to distribute
its own resources within a particular organization but to "correct"
the outcome of spontaneous social order whose results do not meet some

a priori ideal of equality, by appropriating the property of some
citizens to give to others. This notion has gained such wide support
that objections to it are usually made only on grounds of economic efficiency. It is claimed that, since incentives are necessary in an
economy, too much redistribution will interfere with efficiency, and
might even make poorer those whom it is intended to help. Or in other
words, do not kill the goose that lays the golden eggs. Practically
all the philosophers who have written on social justice acknowledge
this point. Some do it by asserting that social justice is only one
value among many, and may have to be balanced against efficiency.[45]
Others, like Rawls, bring efficiency into their definition of social
justice. Rawls would elevate the minimum standard of living until
economic effects were so severe that "the expectations of the lowest
class...no longer improve but begin to decline."[46] The goose is kept
alive on minimum rations.

Hayek's view is sharply different. He is not concerned about
the conflict of social justice with efficiency, but with the validity
of social justice as such. He holds that any attempt to implement
social justice through correcting the outcome of spontaneous order is
immoral because it is a violation of justice *per se*. It means that
some men must surrender part of their property, not because it was il-
licitly acquired, but simply because others have not acquired as much.

Social justice is an empty term. It is self-contradictory to
speak of correcting the results of a spontaneous order. We can accept
such an order and work within it, or we can reject it and attempt to
destroy it; but we cannot accept it while simultaneously altering its
results. For by definition spontaneous order means self-determining
outcomes occurring under abstract rules. Thus Hayek writes of social
justice:

> ...The greatest service I can still render to
> my fellow men would be if it were in my power
> to make them ashamed of ever again using that
> hollow incantation. I felt it my duty at
> least to try and free them of that incubus
> which today makes fine sentiments the instru-
> ments for the destruction of all values of a
> free civilization.[47]

The incompatibility of social justice with spontaneous order can
be seen by returning to the three aspects of authentic justice discussed in the previous section: that it cannot be predicated of an
impersonal process, that it is abstract, and that it is negative. Social justice proves to be the opposite on all three counts.

1) Social justice by definition has to mean the evaluation of the results of impersonal processes as if they were the results of intentional actions. This is not a subcategory of justice but the opposite of justice. Social justice would make sense only if society were an organization with a directing will.[48] But since society is the milieu or spontaneous order in which such organizations interact, to speak of social justice or a just society is an anthropomorphic fallacy.

Anthropomorphism runs throughout the vocabulary of social justice. For example, "redistribution" suggests that one is only correcting an earlier "distribution" of property. But in fact impersonal market processes give rise to a distribution only in the statistical sense of a set of data. There is no original distribution according to an act of human will; hence redistribution is a euphemism for imposing a distribution upon an impersonal allocation.

What Hayek has written of socialism would also apply to social justice, that it "is not based merely on a different system of ultimate values from that of liberalism, which one would have to respect even if one disagreed; it is based on an intellectual error which makes its adherents blind to its consequences."[49] The error is the constructivist fallacy that society acts like an organization under the direction of someone's will.

2) True justice is concerned with conformity to abstract rules, but social justice has to be concrete. It is the deliberate distribution of resources to specified individuals or groups of people because of their relative holdings. It is not an abstract rule of conduct but a transfer to selected people. "Claims to social justice are claims on behalf of a group," as Runciman has put it.[50] But such claims of particular groups are incompatible with rules of just conduct. Groups must take what they get if the rules are just.

3) Social justice is positive in opposition to Hayek's two aspects of negativity. Justice tells us to leave others' property alone (negative), whereas social justice commands the specific action of taking it away (positive). More profoundly, social justice cannot pass the test of universalization. If we generalized the practice of taking from those who have to give to those who have not, we would destroy the institution of private property. Yet social justice, as usually understood today in the Western world, is meant to be a corrective supplement to private property, not its destruction. Of

course, if there were only "a little bit" of social justice, it would not completely destroy private property. But the whole point of the test of universalization is to detect such spurious rules which cannot be consistently implemented without destroying their basis. In contrast, there is no such problem with justice. Private holdings acquired under just rules can be universally protected without any logical contradiction.

Social justice is at bottom a rejection of the Great Society in favour of a "made order." If implemented consistently, it would transform society into a great *taxis* in which a central authority distributes all property proportionally to its own criteria of merit.[51] Social justice is a "Trojan Horse" for totalitarianism.[52] Which is not to say that advocates of social justice perceive this totalitarian future or would favour it if they did. As in Hayek's most famous book, *The Road to Serfdom*, the argument is simply that principles which have demonstrably bad consequences if pushed to their logical conclusion should be unmasked for what they are.

Why should there be such widespread revulsion against the Great Society which has brought us the tremendous benefits of the last two centuries? One answer is that success and failure under this system are not related in any simple and obvious way to merit or desert. People accumulate property for all sorts of reasons--industriousness, innate ability, inherited wealth, education, inventiveness, unscrupulousness, or pure luck. Conversely, men often fail in spite of hard work and honest effort.

Throughout the literature on social justice there is an attempt to make the rewards of life proportionate to merit or desert. Underserved rewards are attacked as unjust. Let one example from Rawls - the most important writer in this vein - suffice. In explaining his "difference principle," which holds that inequalities are justified if they benefit the least-advantaged, Rawls discards two possible versions of that principle, which he calls "natural liberty" and "liberal equality." The first is rejected because it allows social inequalities like inherited wealth to reap a reward. The second is also rejected because, although it equalizes social advantages, it does nothing about the effect of natural talents. Compensation for this form of inequality must also be introduced, says Rawls, because natural talents are no more deserved than social advantages.[53]

This approach assumes that it is the business of society to reward merit. Distributive justice in its valid sense of apportionment
of rewards within an organization is extended in an invalid way to
cover the whole of society. But for Aristotle justice was not solely
distributive justice; there was also "diorthotic" justice, or justice
in exchange, which applied to the situation of mutual dealing between
consenting parties. Modernizing the distinction between the two types
of justice, Hayek argues that the Great Society cannot possibly hope
to reward merit, for this would require some directing intelligence to
play the distributive role. Merit may be observed within particular
organizations, but for society as a whole the principle of allocation
is "value," subjectively defined as what others are willing to offer
in exchange for one's products or services.[54] Nozick has expressed
the same idea: "From each as they [sic] choose, to each as they [sic]
are chosen."[55] It is what economists refer to as the determination of
earnings by marginal product.

An example may make this more clear. It is not the fault of a
Newfoundland fisherman that he was born to a harsh and unremunerative
life. His low marginal product is determined by a network of economic
relationships for which he cannot possibly be blamed. Nonetheless,
his marginal product is a signal representing other men's desire for
fish, given prevailing supplies not only of fish but of competing commodities. He may have to leave his trade and even his native province
to find a situation where he can earn more. That is a hard lot, which
would be unjust if any person or organization had deliberately willed
it upon him. But within the Great Society, it is his free response
to the facts of other people's preferences, as cumulated and represented in market signals. It is part of the general submission to
abstract rules which, as a system, work for the benefit of all, even
if certain individuals have to suffer undeserved hardship.

This illustration in fact represents one of the most common situations in which the claim of social justice is made. Men who have become accustomed to a certain mode of life naturally think that its
rewards are deserved. A threat to the *status quo* consequently seems
unjust. In practice the cry for social justice is usually a conserva-
tive force, an effort to shelter particular groups from the effects of
technological innovation or shifts in taste.[56] The cry is intuitively
appealing, but governmental response tends to destroy the creative
capacity of spontaneous order.

The desire to see property apportioned according to desert, important as it is, is only a special aspect of a wider revulsion from spontaneous order. As Hayek points out, the Open Society is a relatively recent invention. Men are not yet comfortable with its ethical rules, which are difficult in a number of ways.[57] They require humility, because they teach us to realize that our actions are not fully controlled by our designs. They command submission to impersonal and spontaneous processes in place of conscious direction. Social morality is reduced to abstract and negative rules, so that justice replaces loyalty as the central social virtue. A sense of common purpose is lost, as men pursue their individual goals. Hayek has captured the essence of the Open Society by describing it as one in which there is agreement about means but not ends. Society becomes a milieu which enhances the ability of all to pursue their own ends because all, in limited ways, become means to those ends.[58] When the talents of others are made available to purchasers in the market place, the result is provision of an amazing variety of means to my ends, for which I must pay by becoming a means to the ends of others.

The ethics of the Great Society are a powerful engine of progress, but they are emotionally unsatisfying. Men still desire the unity, loyalty, and common purpose of the closed society. Both socialism and nationalism, like other constructivist ideologies, are expressions of nostalgia for the closed society. They propose a "tribal" ethics of preferential treatment toward the group to which one belongs, whereas the Great Society demands conduct according to universal norms of fair dealing. The demand for social justice is part of the same emotional reaction. The state is called upon to guarantee the position of particular groups - farmers, fishermen, labour, racial minorities, or whatever - who are felt to be especially deserving. It is still an open question whether the Great Society will be able to resist this tide of emotionalism and reestablish the integrity of the intellectual ethics on which its survival ultimately must depend.[59]

Evaluation

Hayek has made two important contributions to the discussion of private property. First, his theory of spontaneous order provides a powerful defense of private property and the market system. The principles of his theory are not new, having already been enunciated by

the social philosophers of the Scottish Enlightenment; but they are a
novel and refreshing alternative to the constructivist ideologies
which have dominated political thought in this century. Hayek's emphasis on the tacit following of rules as opposed to the conscious
design of institutions is a theoretical achievement that will have to
be taken into account even by those who do not accept his political
position.

Second, Hayek has offered a fundamental challenge to the current
debate about social justice. The last two decades have seen an astonishing amount of discussion on this subject, much of it focused on the
work of John Rawls. Now Hayek has shown that this discussion rests on
the misconception that society, which is a spontaneous order, can be
just or unjust as a whole. This again is not a new idea, but Hayek
has stated it in a compelling way. Henceforth, any spokesman for social justice who ignores this challenge will not be intellectually
credible.

Academic and intellectual trends are correlated with broader social processes. The prolonged discussion of social justice has taken
place in a period when government control of economic and social life
has become very much more pervasive in most countries of the Western
World. Only time will tell whether Hayek's critique of social justice is an isolated protest or part of a wider movement away from
governmental regulation and towards spontaneous order.

FOOTNOTES

1   Official Announcement of the Royal Academy of Sciences, quoted in
    Fritz Machlup (ed.), *Essays on Hayek* (New York, 1976), p. xv.

2   Fritz Machlup, "Hayek's Contribution to Economics," *ibid.*, pp. 13-
    51.

3   *Individualism and Economic Order* (London and Chicago, 1948); *Stud-
    ies in Philosophy, Politics and Economics* (London and Chicago,
    1967); *New Studies in Philosophy, Politics, and Economics and the
    History of Ideas* (Chicago, 1978). This last volume was received
    after this paper was completed so references to it have not been
    incorporated into the text.

4   Hayek, *The Mirage of Social Justice* (Chicago, 1976), p. xiii.
    There is a bibliography of Hayek's works, complete through 1975,
    in Machlup, *op. cit.*, pp. 51-59.

5   The academic literature on Hayek's social philosophy is not ex-
    tensive. See Herman Finer's famous attack, *Road to Reaction*
    (Boston, 1945); Arthur Seldon (ed.), *Agenda for a Free Society*
    (London, 1961); Erich Streissler (ed.), *Roads to Freedom* (London,
    1969); Machlup, *op. cit.*; Christian Bay, "Hayek's Liberalism:
    The Constitution of Perpetual Privilege," *Political Science Re-
    viewer*, 1 (1971), pp. 93-124; M. M. Wilhelm, "The Political
    Thought of Friedrich A. Hayek," *Political Studies*, 20 (1972), pp.
    169-184; A. Shenfield, "The New Thought of F. A. Hayek," *Modern
    Age*, 20 (1976), pp. 54-61.

6   Hayek, *The Constitution of Liberty* (Chicago, 1960), p. 407.

7   Hayek's theory of order was presented for the special case of the
    marketplace in "The Use of Knowledge in Society," *American Econom-
    ic Review*, 35 (1945). It is best formulated in *Rules and Order*
    (Chicago, 1973), Ch. 2. My presentation is based on this chapter
    except where noted.

8   Adam Ferguson, *An Essay on the History of Civil Society* (London,
    1767) p. 187, cited in *Rules and Order*, p. 150.

9   Hayek, "The Confusion of Language in Political Thought," Institute
    for Economic Analysis, *Occasional Paper*, No. 20, 1968.

10 *Rules and Order*, pp. 38-39.

11 Bertrand de Jouvenel, "Order vs. Organization," in Mary Sennholz
    (ed.), *On Freedom and Free Enterprise: Essays in Honour of Ludwig
    Von Mises* (Princeton, N. J., 1956), pp. 41-51.

12 *Rules and Order*, pp. 2, 154-55; Adam Smith, *Theory of the Moral
    Sentiments*, Part 6, Ch. 2; Karl Popper, *The Open Society and Its
    Enemies* (New York, 1963; 4th ed.), Vol. I, pp. 202-3.

13 Hayek, "The Use of Knowledge in Society," reprinted by the Institute for Humane Studies, 1977, p. 8.

14 *Constitution of Liberty*, p. 59.

15 *Constitution of Liberty*, p. 140.

16 *Ibid.*

17 *Ibid.*, p. 141.

18 J. S. Mill, "Chapters on Socialism," in *Collected Works* (Toronto, 1963), Vol. 5, p. 753.

19 *Mirage of Social Justice*, p. 5; cf. also pp. 24-27.

20 *Studies in Philosophy, Politics and Economics*, p. 307.

21 *Ibid.*, pp. 309-310.

22 *Ibid.*, p. 311.

23 J. S. Mill, *Principles of Political Economy*, ed. D. Winch (Harmondsworth, 1970) Book II, Ch. 1, pp. 349-50.

24 *Ibid.*

25 Ulpian, *Digest*, I, 1.

26 *Nicomachean Ethics*, V, 3.

27 Bertrand de Jouvenel, *Sovereignty*, (Chicago, 1957), Ch. 9.

28 *Mirage of Social Justice*, p. 37.

29 *Ibid.*, pp. 31-33; cf. *Sovereignty*, pp. 139-141, 164-65.

30 *Mirage of Social Justice*, p. 20.

31 James Moore, "Hume's Theory of Justice and Property," *Political Studies*, 24 (1976), p. 109.

32 *Mirage of Social Justice*, p. 36.

33 *Ibid.*, p. 43.

34 E.g. Gregory Vlastos, "Justice and Equality," in R. B. Brandt (ed.), *Social Justice* (Englewood Cliffs, N. J.; 1962), pp. 31-74.

35 R. W. Baldwin, *Social Justice* (Oxford, 1966), p. 1.

36 John Rawls, *A Theory of Justice* (Cambridge, Mass.; 1971).

37 W. G. Runciman, *Relative Deprivation and Social Justice* (London, 1966), p. 316.

38 A. M. Honoré, "Social Justice," in R. S. Summers, *Essays in Legal Philosophy* (Berkeley and Los Angeles, 1968), p. 92.

39 Lars O. Ericsson, *Justice in the Distribution of Economic Re-sources* (Stockholm, 1976), pp. 124-127.

40 Rawls, *op. cit.*, pp. 85 ff.

41 *Mirage of Social Justice*, p. 100.

42 Robert Nozick, *Anarchy, State, and Utopia* (New York, 1974), pp. 198-204.

43 William Frankena, "The Concept of Social Justice," in Brandt, *op. cit.*, p. 1.; Ericsson, op. cit., p. 13.

44 *Nicomachean Ethics*, V. 3.

45 E.g. Nicholas Rescher, *Distributive Justice* (Indianapolis, 1966); also Ericsson.

46 Rawls, "Distributive Justice," in E. S. Phelps (ed.), *Economic Justice* (Harmondsworth, 1973), p. 352.

47 *Mirage of Social Justice*, p. 97.

48 *Ibid.*, pp. 69, 81.

49 *Ibid.*, p. 136.

50 Runciman, *op. cit.*, p. 323.

51 *Mirage of Social Justice*, p. 142.

52 *Ibid.*, p. 136.

53 *A Theory of Justice*, pp. 73-74.

54 *Constitution of Liberty*, ch. 6; *Mirage of Social Justice*, p. 120.

55 Nozick, *op. cit.*, p. 160.

56 *Mirage of Social Justice*, p. 141.

57 *Ibid.*, p. 146,; cf. Jouvenel, *Sovereignty*, p. 134.

58 *Mirage of Social Justice*, p. 113.

59 *Ibid.*, pp. 144-152.

Shadia Drury examines Robert Nozick's theory of property based on natural rights. She finds that Nozick, although he claims to base his theory on Locke, is more extreme than Locke. The author attempts to demonstrate that Nozick's elevation of property rights over any general rights, such as the right to life, is logically unfounded. Property rights must be limited by other rights, as has always been done in the natural law tradition.

ROBERT NOZICK AND THE RIGHT TO PROPERTY

Robert Nozick's widely noted book purports to provide us with a theory of property founded on the venerated concept of natural right.[1] Nozick does not defend private property on utilitarian grounds. He does not argue that a system of private property is desirable in view of its effects - for example, that it increases the social product by putting the means of production in the hands of those who can use them most efficiently or profitably, or that it encourages experimentation, or that it protects future persons by leading some to hold back current consumption. Presumably he believes it to have all these good effects, but that is not for him the reason to defend it. Instead, Nozick defends the right to private property strictly on moral grounds.

The purpose of this essay is to examine the moral principles that make up the foundation of the Nozickian theory of property. It is my contention that, even if we go along with Nozick in rejecting consequentialism and endorsing a moral theory grounded in the absolute and inviolable rights of individuals, we need not accept the unlimited scope that Nozick bestows on the right to property. Indeed, giving precedence to property rights over other rights makes a mockery of the natural right tradition in which Nozick likes to situate himself.

Moral Principles

Before asking how the state should be organized, political philosophers should, according to Nozick, examine whether the state is necessary and whether any state can exist without the violation of individual rights. Nozick sets out to provide a moral justification of the "minimal state" against the objections of the "individualist anarchist." The minimal state is basically the night-watchman state of classical liberalism whose function is to enforce contracts, protect its citizens against violence, theft, fraud, etc. It is characterized (as is any state) by having a monopoly over force within its territory and by protecting all its citizens, even those who cannot pay for its services.[2] The "individualist anarchist" objects that the very existence of the state violates the rights of individuals since it (1) monopolizes the use of force and punishes those who would use force to enforce their rights, and (2) forces some to purchase protection for

others by means of coercive taxation.[3] I suspect that the "individualist anarchist" is Nozick's own ghost, and it is one he never succeeds
in dispelling.

Nozick begins his political philosophizing from the best anarchic
situation that can reasonably be expected--the Lockian state of nature.
Although this is a non-political starting point, it is far from being
a non-moral one. For Nozick, a moral starting point is a necessary
background in the attempt to justify the political.[4] What then are the
pre-political moral constraints that the state must satisfy? Nozick
does not pretend to give a satisfactory account of the fundamental moral data; instead, he seeks comfort in the "respectable tradition of
Locke."[5]

Nozick thinks his moral assumptions are borrowed from Locke and
Kant. Following Locke, he maintains that there is a line that circum-
scribes an area in moral space around an individual. This line is determined by an individual's natural rights and sets the limits on the
actions of others.[6] Others are forbidden to perform actions that
transgress the boundary or encroach upon the circumscribed area, except by the consent of the one whose boundary is to be crossed. Nozick
is aware that Locke would not fully accept this interpretation of his
moral theory. He knows that for Locke there are things people cannot
do to you even by your own permission - namely, those things you have
no right to do to yourself. For example, giving your permission cannot
make it morally permissible to kill you, since you have no right to
kill yourself.[7] Nozick chooses to ignore this aspect of Locke's philosophy as an old vestige of "paternalism." After all, why should God
tell you what to do with your rights? According to Nozick, one may
"choose (or permit another) to do to himself *anything*."[8] These Lockian
ideas are, according to Nozick, compatible with the Kantian principle
that "individuals are ends and not merely means, they are not to be
sacrificed or used for the achieving of other's ends without their consent. Individuals are inviolable."[9] These are the principles on which
Nozick proposes to erect his philosophy.

Lockian rights, coupled with the Kantian moral imperative, lead
Nozick to conclude that morality consists in refraining from "boundary
crossings" (his metaphor for the violation of rights) and from treating individuals as means for the benefit of others without their consent. The inviolability of the individual means that he can never be
sacrificed for the greater good of society, no matter how great the

benefits to the latter or how small the disadvantages to the individual. Nozick launches an attack on utilitarian consequentialism in ethics. He argues that his moral assumptions provide politics not so much with "moral goals" as with "moral constraints."[10] A moral goal is "an end state for some activities to achieve as their result."[11] Utilitarianism is a moral theory of this kind. In its concern with the "end-state," utilitarianism fails (1) to take rights and their violation into account and (2) to take the separateness of individuals seriously. First, utilitarianism fails to take rights into account since it does not find it objectionable to "punish an innocent man to save a neighborhood from a vengeful rampage."[12] Secondly, it does not treat the separateness of individuals seriously because it applies to society a model acceptable only for individuals: "Individually, we each sometimes choose to undergo some pain or sacrifice for a greater benefit or to avoid a greater harm..."[13] When this model is applied to society, some persons are made to bear some costs for the overall social good. Such a theory fails according to Nozick to recognize moral restraints on actions - even actions that may bring about a desired end-state. Simply put, it makes any means permissible as long as they contribute to the realization of the desired end. On Nozick's view, "there is no *social entity*,"[14] there are only different individual people: "Using one of these people to benefit others, uses him and benefits others. Nothing more... Talk of an overall social good covers this up."[15]

Contrary to "moral goal" or "end-state" theories, a theory based on the inviolability of individuals and their rights recognizes "side constraints" on actions. This does not mean that it favours a society that minimizes the violation of rights. It refuses to consider the non-violation of rights as "a desirable end-state to be achieved."[16] A position of this sort would simply be a "utilitarianism of rights," replacing the "maximization of happiness" in classical utilitarianism with the "non-violation of rights." A utilitarianism of rights would allow one to violate rights in order to lessen their total violation in society.

The question arises: "Can the rights of an individual be overridden to avoid a greater evil to others?" For Nozick, the answer is clearly NO. But he is aware that this answer becomes barbarous in cases where the inconvenience to the individual is minute and the benefit to others enormous. In a footnote, Nozick writes:

The question of whether these side constraints are
absolute, or whether they may be violated to avoid
catastrophic moral horror, and if the latter, what
the resulting structure might look like, is one I
hope largely to avoid.[17]

In order to overcome the problem of "catastrophic moral horror," some
philosophers have suggested that rights should be considered *prima
facie*, rather than absolute and inviolable.[18] In this way, rights
could be overridden whenever higher moral considerations or weightier
interests were involved. But those who take rights seriously reject
this notion on the ground that it makes a sham of rights.[19] *Prima
facie* rights are nothing solid for a man to stand on; they come and go
with changing circumstances. Furthermore, *prima facie* rights have the
effect of discouraging "the spirit of reluctance, apology and respect
that should attend even justified or necessary injustice." Indeed,
they tend to blur the distinction between "sorrowful infringement or
suspensions of right" and the "authoritative redefining of right boun-
daries."[20] The notion of *prima facie* rights has the disadvantage of
leaving too much discretionary power in the hands of the authorities.
In so doing, it frustrates the very idea of limited government which
is the *raison d'être* of a theory of rights. Nozick would therefore
rather leave the problem of "catastrophic moral horror" unsolved than
adopt the notion of *prima facie* rights.

One more thing needs to be said about *prima facie* rights. As Nozick makes clear, a theory of rights differs very significantly from a
utilitarian moral theory. This however is not the case with a theory
of *prima facie* rights. The latter is designed to suit the requirements of a utilitarian theory. In characteristic utilitarian style,
determining the existence or non-existence of *prima facie* rights in
any given situation is but an act of balancing, meant to determine
where the greatest "weight" lies. But for Nozick, morality does not
consist of interest-balancing procedures. Individual rights have an
absolute weight, they do not come and go with the circumstances.

Leaving aside the problem of catastrophic moral horror, a theory
that considers inviolable rights as the fundamental moral phenomena
must provide directives for resolving the inevitable clash of different but equally "inviolable" rights. For example, someone's right to
life may conflict with another's right to property, in the case of a
famine. Or, one may hold that the right to life makes it incumbent on
the community to provide for the helpless, the crippled and old

through some sort of redistributive mechanism. In such clashes of
"rights," Nozick clearly gives the right to property precedence over
general rights. Indeed, Nozick objects to Ayn Rand's contention that
the right to life provides a foundation for the right to property, and
maintains that "one *first* needs a theory of property rights before one
can apply any supposed right to life."[21] What then is Nozick's theory
of property rights? And why is a theory of property rights fundamental for a rights-based moral theory?

The Entitlement Theory of Justice
       Nozick refers to his theory of property rights as the entitlement
theory of justice in holdings. This theory of distributive justice
has three aspects: (1) the "principle of justice in acquisition" that
determines the justice of original acquisition or "the appropriation
of unheld things," (2) the "principle of justice in transfer" that
determines "the transfer of holdings from one person to another"
(i.e., exchange, gifts, inheritance) and (3) the principle of "rectification of injustice in holdings," intended to rectify violations of
the first two principles.[22] According to the entitlement theory, a
distribution is just if it is the result of the just application of
the first two principles (justice in acquisition and justice in transfer). Needless to say, a thief is not entitled to his holdings. Nozick contends that his theory differs from other theories of distributive justice because it is historical.[23] According to Nozick theories
of distributive justice tend to rely on "end-result" or "end-state"
principles. Such theories are completely ahistorical - they judge any
given distribution by its profile, and not by how that distribution
came about.[24] Welfare economics, is on Nozick's view, a "current
time-slice" theory concerned primarily with the "resulting pattern" of
distribution, rather than with the underlying principle responsible
for the distribution that emerges. For Nozick, a utilitarian theory
of distributive justice would necessarily be an end-state theory,
since it would favour a distribution that maximizes utility, regardless of how it came about. Nozick dismisses such theories as unjust
for the following reasons:

              If some persons are in prison for murder or war
              crimes, we do not say that to assess the justice
              of the distribution in the society we must look
              only at what this person has, and that person

has,.... We think it relevant to ask whether
someone did something so that he *deserved* to be
punished, deserved to have a lower share.[25]

Nozick is anxious to distinguish his entitlement theory not only
from "current time-slice" and "end-state" theories, but also from
other historical theories which are "patterned." A patterned theory
of distributive justice "specifies that a distribution is to vary a-
long some natural dimension, weighted sum of natural dimensions, or
lexicographic ordering of natural dimensions."[26] Examples of "natural
dimensions" include, moral merit, usefulness to society, need, effort
etc... Almost every suggested principle of distributive justice according to Nozick is patterned. Most principles of distributive justice try to fill in the blank in the statement, "to each according to
his ----." For example, Nozick considers Hayek's theory to be patterned, even though Hayek maintains that he is opposed to impressing
on society any patterns of distribution. Nevertheless, Hayek argues
that since we cannot know enough about each person's situation in order to distribute to each according to his moral merit,[27] we should
allow the operation of a "free society" to determine the distribution
in accordance with the perceived value of a person's actions and services to others.[28] Nozick agrees with Hayek that in a free capitalist
society the value others place on our services will exhibit a major
patterned strand in distribution. But he adds that it is only a
strand and does not constitute the whole pattern of a system of en-
titlements since inheritance, gifts and charity influence the final
pattern of distribution. The problem with putting too much emphasis
on the pattern is that, given *any* pattern considered just, deviations
from that pattern are inevitable as a result of the actions of free
individuals (i.e., gifts to loved ones, bequests to children, charity,
etc...).[29] Furthermore, if the pattern is considered just, deviations
from it will not likely be tolerated. Yet any given pattern cannot be
maintained without constant interference with the free actions of individuals. For example, in a socialist society where everyone's needs
are satisfied and where the means of production are publicly owned,
private ownership of the means of production and private factories
will inevitably spring up unless "capitalist acts among consenting
adults" are strictly forbidden.[30] There will always be people who
want more than they need, and people who may be able to fare better
in the private sector. Nozick assumes that freedom will inevitably

upset the socialist pattern. He therefore concludes that only a non-patterned theory can meet the demands of justice and avoid the violation of rights.

In contrast to patterned theories, the entitlement view does not treat production and distribution as separate or independent matters.[31] On Nozick's view, whoever makes something is entitled to it. Unlike patterned principles of distribution, the entitlement theory of justice in holdings requires no *redistribution*. This is the mark of its superiority; for Nozick, redistribution *per se* violates the rights of individuals. Taxation is a form of redistribution - it involves taking from some what they are entitled to and giving it to others (in order to realize some desired pattern of distribution). Nozick denounces it as on a par with forced labour.

Let us assume we accept the entitlement theory's stand against redistribution. How do we know people have acquired their holdings justly and owe no compensation to others? Such knowledge, on Nozick's account, is historical and so presents problems that he is reluctant to deal with. But let us grant that such knowledge can be had; then how do persons justly acquire unheld property?

At the heart of the entitlement theory is the Lockian theory of initial appropriation of previously unheld things. For Nozick as for Locke, property rights in an unheld thing originate with labour. It is not simply that mixing one's labour with things gives one title to these things. As Nozick points out, the idea is rather that "laboring on something improves it and makes it more valuable; and anyone is entitled to own a thing whose value he has created."[32] However, the Lockian theory includes a proviso that is a source of complications for the entitlement theory. Locke insists that there should be no waste - no one has a right to appropriate more than he can use before it spoils. On Nozick's view this is meant to insure that others are not made worse off by the appropriation in question. What is important is that there be "enough and as good left in common for others."[33] Nozick proposes two possible interpretations of what would constitute making others worse off. It could mean (1) losing the opportunity to improve one's situation by appropriation, or (2) being unable to use freely what one previously could. A strong proviso would insist that *both* of these conditions be satisfied. A weak

proviso would insist only that the second condition be satisfied -
namely that people are not made worse off by being unable to use what
they previously could.

Even though Locke may not have made his meaning perfectly clear,
Nozick argues that only the weaker interpretation of the proviso is
plausible. The strong interpretation of the proviso makes *any* appropriation of property illegitimate. His argument is as follows:

> Consider the first person Z for whom there is not
> enough and as good left to appropriate. The last
> person Y to appropriate left Z without his previous
> liberty to act on an object, and so worsened Z's
> situation. So Y's appropriation is not allowed un-
> der Locke's proviso. Therefore the next to last
> person X to appropriate left Y in a worse position,
> for X's act ended permissible appropriation. There-
> fore X's appropriation wasn't permissible... And so
> on back to the first person A to appropriate a per-
> manent property right.[34]

Nozick therefore concludes that the strict interpretation of the proviso is untenable if *any* right to property is to be established. The
weaker proviso (i.e., that no one is made worse off by not being able
to use things) is the only tenable one. All a theory of property has
to show is that the weaker proviso is indeed satisfied.

Nozick proceeds to argue that the situation of persons who are unable to appropriate (there being no useful unheld objects) is not wor-
sened by a system that allows appropriation and permanent property. In
many cases, appropriation improves the condition of others. If it
fails to do so, it must compensate others to the extent that it makes
them worse off.[35] For example, those who own and profit from airports
should compensate those whose property is devalued and whose nerves are
jangled by noise pollution.

It would seem that the weak proviso, coupled with the principle of
compensation, does not set any limit on appropriation. But Nozick adds
that "a person may not appropriate the only water hole in the desert
and charge what he will."[36] Even if he owned one, and all the others
dried up, the Lockian proviso would come into play and limit his property right. I will ignore the difficulty involved in mixing one's
labour with a water hole in order to appropriate it. Notice that
Nozick does *not* say that rights are overridden to avoid a catastro-
phe.[37] The right is not overridden, it is limited for reasons internal
to the theory of property itself. The proviso comes into play to insure that the person who, for example, has appropriated the total

supply of drinkable water in the world does not "charge what he will."
But the proviso does *not* prevent anyone from appropriating the total
supply of things necessary for life - e.g., drinkable water. It simply prevents that person from charging "certain prices" for his supply.
Hopefully we can infer that those who cannot pay would be compensated
by being allowed to *use* (not appropriate) what they could have prior
to the appropriation in question. But on the whole, Nozick is convinced that "the free operation of a market system will not actually
run afoul of the Lockian proviso."[38] But the latter cannot be understood to include making people worse off for lack of opportunity to
appropriate, but only for lack of opportunity to use.[39] If appropriation violates this weak proviso, it is illegitimate unless it compen-
sates those thereby made worse off up to some determinable "base
line."[40] To compensate someone is not to give him what he would have
had, given the opportunity to appropriate the thing in question, but
only to give him what he would have had, had he had the opportunity to
use the thing in question. In a footnote, Nozick notes that

> Fourier held that since the process of civilization
> had deprived the members of society of certain liber-
> ties (to gather, pasture, engage in the chase), a
> socially guaranteed minimum provision for persons was
> justified as compensation for the loss.... But this
> puts the point too strongly. This compensation would
> be due those persons, if any, for whom the process of
> civilization was a *net loss*, for whom the benefits of
> civilization did not counterbalance being deprived of
> these particular liberties.[41]

Needless to say, it is a point of contention whether civilization,
especially one along Nozickian lines, can be said to benefit those it
excludes from any possibility of appropriation, there being no useful
unheld objects left to appropriate. In any case, the above note makes
it clear that Nozick's principle of compensation is not simply a disguised form of redistribution. Nozick does not give back with one
hand what he has taken with the other. He is not suggesting a form of
welfare. On the principle of compensation, the community owes nothing
to the helpless, the crippled, or old, as long as it has not directly
contributed to their condition - if, in other words, they would have
been no better off in the state of nature.

Nozick makes it clear that under certain conditions appropriating
the total supply of something necessary for life and refusing to share
it with others does not run afoul of the proviso. For example:

> A medical researcher who synthesizes a new sub-
> stance that effectively treats a certain disease
> and who refuses to sell except on his terms does
> not worsen the situation of others by depriving
> them of whatever he has appropriated.[42]

On Nozick's view, the right of the medical researcher over his product is unlimited, since his appropriation of the total supply does
not put people in a "situation worse than the baseline one." On Nozick's view, no one can have a complaint on the ground of justice a-
gainst the medical researcher. Justice consists merely in the non-
violation of rights, and no one but the medical researcher had any
rightful claim to the life-sustaining substance. He can be made to
part with it only on his own terms. Surely, it is not difficult to
imagine what kind of agreements would be made between those in desper-
ate need for something to continue living and one who holds the trump
card of life. The medical researcher may refuse to part with his property unless those in need agreed to become his life-long devoted
slaves. But we need not resort to such extreme conditions to see the
effects of giving particular property rights such unlimited scope.

"Market conditions" alone may force some to sell themselves in
order to survive. But does that mean that those in a position to buy
do so justly? Nozick's account of consent is at best superficial;
and it has the effect of making a mockery of the dignity of individuals possessed with "inviolable rights." One may hold that agreeing
to be enslaved does not constitute a valid contract since it conflicts
with the natural right to liberty that each man has. But for Nozick,
rights are not inalienable. All rights on Nozick's view can be for-
feited, or even sold. Nozick rejects what he considers the vestiges
of paternalism in the Lockian theory of rights which forbids men from
forfeiting their rights to life or liberty by their own consent, on
the ground that these are God's property, with which men cannot do as
they please. For Locke, what we do with our rights is subject to
God's law, the law of nature, whose content, contrary to Nozick's
claims, is far more extensive than the non-violation of the rights of
others. We need not accept the whole of the Lockian philosophy of
natural law in order to recognize that our obligations transcend the
existence of rights. It is often said that rights and obligations
are correlative, which is true. But not all obligations need have
correlative rights. There are obligations even where there are no

rights. In so far as rights are among other things moral claims, children, animals and the mentally defective can have no rights. But this need not mean that we owe them no obligations.

There is a far greater difference between the Nozickian and the traditional Lockian conception of natural rights than what Nozick refers to as the vestige of paternalism in the Lockian philosophy. I am referring to Nozick's rejection of *general* rights.

In the seventeenth century, the idea that all men had certain God-given rights gained popularity. This was a revolutionary idea that stood in marked contrast with the earlier conception of the rights of men as emanating from their status in the community. These were often referred to as "birthrights."[43] In a hierarchically ordered society, rights increased with increasing status. What is novel in the idea of natural rights is that, unlike specific birthrights, these rights belong to men simply in virtue of being human. The implications of this doctrine were politically explosive since it paid little heed to inherited wealth and status, insisting that the powers of the rich and mighty were limited in view of the rights all men have in virtue of being human. Paradoxically, this politically radical doctrine becomes in Nozick's hands the basis of a political philosophy that exalts original title and correct transferal.[44] Nozick does this by giving specific property rights absolute weight and going so far as to deny the existence of most *general* rights.

Philosophers tend to divide general rights into two categories-- "positive" and "negative" rights.[45] Negative rights are those that forbid others from interfering with your liberty to do or forebear from doing something. The rights not to be tortured or enslaved, for example, are "negative" rights since they are correlative with other people's not doing certain things to the right holder. Nozick seems to accept the existence of such general negative rights since he advocates a minimal state that would protect its citizens against violence, theft or fraud - in other words, it would protect their negative rights and so insure non-interference on the part of others. Positive general rights, unlike negative rights, impose on others positive duties. For example, the right to work, the right to education or the right to life require more than the duty of non-interference. They impose a positive duty (usually on the state) to provide its citizens with these amenities. It is these "positive" rights whose existence Nozick totally denies.

One may hold that the right to life places a duty on the community to provide for the helpless, the crippled and the old through some
sort of redistributive mechanism like taxation. Nozick, however, objects that this involves using some individuals as a means to benefit
others by unjustly forcing some to contribute to the welfare of others. As he puts it,

> being *forced* to contribute to another's welfare
> violates your rights, whereas someone else's not
> providing you with the things you need greatly,
> including things essential to the protection of
> your rights, does not *itself* violate your
> rights... [46]

On this view, the "right to life" has no weight against the right to
property. Nozick denies the existence of the right to life in any
meaningful sense. At most, the right to life is a "right to have or
strive for whatever one needs to live, provided that having it does
not violate any rights of others."[47] Nozick would not agree with St.
Thomas Aquinas that a person in immediate danger of physical privation
may take what is necessary from the surplus of another; nor is this
"strictly speaking, fraud or robbery."[48] Nor would Nozick say with
Locke that "*Charity* gives every Man a Title to so much out of another's Plenty, as will keep him from extreme want."[49] Nozick does not
acknowledge the right to life apart from the right to property. He
argues that general rights of this sort,

> require a substructure of things and materials
> and actions; and *other* people may have rights
> and entitlements over these... No rights exist
> in conflict with this substructure of particular
> rights. Since no neatly contoured right to a-
> chieve a goal will avoid incompatibility with
> this substructure, no such rights exist. The par-
> ticular rights over things fill the space of rights,
> leaving no room for general rights...[50]

It is clear that for Nozick the right to property always has precedence over the right to life and other general rights of this sort.
What reason could one have for giving precedence to the right to property over the right to life? Is it more than a simple prejudice?

Clearly, respecting the right to life is contingent on the adequacy of supply. Conditions of extreme scarcity like famines present
difficulties. This is true of all "positive" general rights. They
can never be absolutely guaranteed to individuals unconditionally.
But surely, this is not a reason to refuse to acknowledge these rights
under conditions of abundance. This is precisely the condition in

which Nozick wishes to enforce the right to property, and he does this only by totally denying the existence of a right to life that may under certain circumstances place limits on the right to property. This need not make the latter merely a *prima facie* right that can be overridden whenever weightier interests are involved. The right to property could still remain inviolable and absolute within its own proper domain. A right need not be unlimited in order to be absolute and inviolable within its domain. But Nozick's conception of the right to property is virtually unlimited except by a weak proviso.

I am not maintaining that the state is obligated to supply *all* its citizens with enough food whenever the supply is plentiful. We have no obligation to provide for those who are able but unwilling to work, on the ground that they too have a right to life. General human rights need not be totally divorced from human merit.[51] One need not be a radical egalitarian in order to acknowledge the existence of general human rights. Locke for example, did not maintain that criminal offenders, unfit for civilized life, have an equal right to life with others. Men can forfeit their rights by their actions.

Nozick's rejection of the right to life has the effect of extending the scope of the right to property. And his preference of that right over other rights is just that, a preference. Nozick of course would have us believe that if we reject the entitlement theory, we would inevitably fall prey to consequentialism. But this is not so. One may go along with Nozick in rejecting consequentialism without embracing the entitlement theory of justice.

Political Implications

The political implications of Nozick's entitlement theory of property are clear. The only legitimate function of the state is to protect the rights and property of individuals from the invasion of others. Nozick's truly fanciful account of how such a state could legitimately emerge is well known. A brief account of it is as follows. In order to remedy the inconveniences of the state of nature, Nozick imagines the emergence of "protective associations" or groups who would lend each other mutual protection against those who would transgress the rights of any member of the group. The disadvantages of this system become quickly apparent as everyone finds himself at the beck and call of the cantankerous and paranoid members. Division of labour is the obvious solution. Some people are "hired" to perform

protective functions. Entrepreneurs enter the business of selling
protective services, and an array of protective policies can be purchased in the market place. Needless to say, different policies will
have different prices depending on the extent of protection one desires. Those who have a great deal to protect will tend to buy the
most expensive policies. Initially there is a great deal of competition among protective agencies. But finally, one agency emerges as
the dominant one since it has proved to be victorious when doing bat-
tle with other agencies on behalf of its clients. Correspondingly,
agencies that tend to lose battles will also lose customers. The dominant protective agency in any given territory cannot qualify as a
minimal state until it (1) succeeds in protecting all those within its
domain, and (2) acquires a monopoly over force in its territory. The
dominant protective agency can only protect those who buy its policies, since no self-respecting business can force some of its clients
to pay the cost of providing its services to others. By the same tok-
en, the dominant protective agency cannot monopolize force in a territory without violating the rights of the "independents" who refuse
to buy its policies and insist on self-help enforcement of their
rights. To qualify as a minimal state, the dominant protective agency
designs an exquisite policy meant to protect clients against the un-
reliable methods used by the "independents" to enforce their rights.
This is the most extensive coverage imaginable and is readily bought
by all those who can afford it. However, the dominant protective a-
gency cannot prevent the independents from enforcing their rights
since this itself involves the violation of the rights of the independents. But on Nozick's principles it can do so as long as it compen-
sates them for the disadvantages involved. This it can do very simply
by providing them with its minimum policies. This is Nozick's account
of how the dominant protective agency emerges as a minimal state without violating anyone's rights. Moreover, Nozick insists that any
state more extensive involves gross violations of rights. The only
legitimate way a state more extensive can emerge is if people begin
to sell each other shares in themselves. Only in so doing can others
acquire rights over them and thus do with them and their property what
they please (depending on the extent of their shareholdings). If
eventually every one buys a share in everyone else so that everyone is
owned by others to the extent he owns all those others, we would have
a state that is more extensive (not to mention more democratic). All

the owners of the "Great Corporation Shares" would assemble and make
collective decisions mutually affecting one another. In such a state
people will probably believe that "when everybody owns everybody, nobody owns anybody."[52] This is Nozick's delightful parody of the democratic state (particularly one designed along Rousseauian lines). For
Nozick this way of bringing about a more extensive state would be morally legitimate, given the assumption that one has a right over oneself and so can do anything to oneself (including selling oneself into slavery) and so can consent to give others a right to do anything
to oneself. But who would want to sell himself? Of course Nozick is
suggesting that we have all chosen to do just that.

    Need we go so far as selling ourselves to the "Great Corporation"
before we can acknowledge any obligations to our fellow citizens? Nozick rejects the notion that there is such a thing as a "social entity" which should figure in our moral reasoning. He denies that "social co-operation" makes any difference to the obligations we owe to
others. For Nozick, the claims that two men living on two separate
desert islands can make on one another differ hardly at all from the
claims individuals living in society can make on one another. This
issue makes up part of Nozick's well-known debate with John Rawls. On
Rawls' view, social co-operation is mutually beneficial since it makes
possible a "better life for all than any would have if each were to
live solely by his own efforts."[53] A theory of justice is therefore
needed to determine how the joint product of social co-operation is
to be equitably divided. Nozick objects to this argument on the
ground that working together jointly to produce something does not
make it impossible to disentangle people's respective contributions.
The truth of the matter, according to Nozick, is that Rawls wishes to
alleviate the effects of the natural lottery (i.e. differential natural talents and abilities) upon the resulting distribution of shares.
Rawls had argued that such chance contingencies as accident and good
fortune are arbitrary from a moral point of view, and so should not
have an unrestrained role in the explanation and justification of distributive shares.[54] Since our natural talents and abilities are "undeserved," redistributing their products is, on Rawls' view, justified. Nozick's rebuttal is as follows:

    1. People are entitled to their natural assets.

2. If people are entitled to something, they are entitled to whatever flows from it (via specific types of processes).

3. People's holdings flow from their natural assets.

Therefore,

4. People are entitled to their holdings.

5. If people are entitled to something, then they ought to have it (and this overrides any presumption of equality there may be about holdings).[55]

Nozick replaces talk of "deserving" our natural assets with the claim that we are simply entitled to them and therefore to whatever flows from them. For Nozick, talk of redistributing natural assets is absurd; we may as well talk of redistributing bodily parts. None of us has done anything to deserve our eyes...why should we have two while others have none?[56] At this point, Nozick sounds positively hysterical. Of course, Rawls' argument (i.e. that we do not "deserve" our natural assets and abilities, which, being arbitrary from a moral point of view, should be regarded as collective assets, and their products redistributed) is unfortunate. Perhaps there are better reasons why distributive shares should not be governed by the unrestrained effects of the natural lottery. Perhaps the real reason those who are well endowed by the natural lottery owe society some part of what flows from their natural endowment is that talents and abilities, unlike eyes and ears, are not simply given but must be developed within a social context. It is social co-operation that makes the development of God-given talents possible. Without social co-operation, the greatest musical, artistic and philosophical talents come to naught.

In conclusion, Nozick's claim that the existence of inviolable individual rights necessitates the inordinate respect for property advocated by his entitlement theory is vacuous. Rights may be inviolable without being unlimited in scope. The right to property must be qualified and its domain defined by the existence of other rights which Nozick wishes to ignore. But even apart from the existence of rights, we should acknowledge our obligations to others, especially those whose co-operation makes it possible for us to live a fully human life.

FOOTNOTES

1   *Anarchy, State and Utopia* (New York: Basic Books, 1974). No-
    zick's book won the National Book Award, in Religion and Philoso-
    phy, 1974.

2   Nozick, *op. cit.*, p. 26.

3   *Ibid.*, p. 51.

4   *Ibid.*, p. 6.

5   *Ibid.*, p. 9.

6   *Ibid.*, p. 57.

7   *Ibid.*, p. 58.

8   *Loc. cit.*

9   *Ibid.*, p. 31.

10 *Ibid.*, pp. 28ff.

11 *Ibid.*, p. 28.

12 *Ibid.*, p. 28.

13 *Ibid.*, p. 32.

14 *Ibid.*, p. 32.

15 *Loc. cit.*

16 *Ibid.*, p. 28.

17 *Ibid.*, p. 30, footnote.

18 This idea was suggested to me by Professor Kai Nielsen. For a
    similar modification of Nozickian rights see T. C. Grey, "Property
    and Need: The Welfare State and Theories of Distributive Justice,"
    Stanford Law Review, Vol. 28, No. 5, May 1976, pp. 877-902. For a
    good discussion of *prima facie* rights, see R. B. Brandt, *Ethical
    Theory* (Englewood Cliffs, N. J.: Prentice Hall, Inc., 1959), p.
    437.

19 See Joel Feinberg, *Social Philosophy* (Englewood Cliffs, N. J.:
    Prentice-Hall, Inc., 1973), pp. 73-75. See also Herbert Morris,
    "Persons and Punishment," *The Monist* (October 1968), also re-
    printed in A. I. Melden (ed.), *Human Rights* (Belmont, California:
    Wadsworth Publishing Co., Inc., 1970).

20 Joel Feinberg, *Social Philosophy*, p. 82.

21 Nozick, *op. cit.*, p. 179, footnote.

22 *Ibid.*, pp. 150-152.

23 *Ibid.*, p. 152.

24 *Ibid.*, p. 154.

25 *Ibid.*, p. 155.

26 *Ibid.*, p. 156.

27 Nozick doubts that justice demands that we should do this if we had this knowledge.

28 Nozick claims that a more accurate rendition of Hayek's principle is as follows: "To each according to how much he benefits others who have the resources for benefiting those who benefit them." Nozick, *op. cit.*, p. 158.

29 I really doubt that people's charity or their giving each other gifts constitutes a problem for distributive justice. Perhaps Nozick would like us to think it does, so he can proceed to argue that his entitlement theory is alone compatible with family life, indeed with love in general. See his comments on the astounding similarities between love and entitlement, pp. 166-170.

30 Nozick, *op. cit.*, p. 163.

31 *Ibid.*, p. 160.

32 *Ibid.*, p. 175.

33 Locke, *Second Treatise*, sec. 27.

34 Nozick, *op. cit.*, p. 176.

35 *Ibid.*, p. 178.

36 *Ibid.*, p. 180.

37 *Loc. cit.* See also Nozick's "Moral Complications and Moral Structures," *Natural Law Forum*, 1968, pp. 1-50.

38 *Ibid.*, p. 182.

39 *Ibid.*, p. 178.

40 *Ibid.*, p. 177. Needless to say, the "base line" is difficult to determine and Nozick does not attempt to do so.

41 *Ibid.*, pp. 178-179.

42 *Ibid.*, p. 181.

43 S. I. Benn, "Rights," *The Encyclopedia of Philosophy*, ed. Paul Edwards (New York: Macmillan Publishing Co., 1967), 8 vols., vol. 7, pp. 195-199.

44 Virginia Held, "John Locke on Robert Nozick," *Social Research*, Vol. 43, 1976, pp. 169-195. Held argues that Nozick is not entitled to wrap himself in the mantle of Locke, since it was Filmer, not Locke, who insisted on the importance of original title (God gave the earth to Adam) and correct transferal from Adam, through the patriarchs, to the kings of nations.

45 Joel Feinberg, *Social Philosophy*, pp. 94-95.

46 Nozick, *op. cit.*, p. 30.

47 *Ibid.*, p. 179, footnote.

48 *Summa theologiae*, II-II, 66, 9, 7.

49 Locke, *First Treatise*, sec. 42.

50 Nozick, *op. cit.*, p. 238.

51 The idea that men have rights in virtue of being human has been criticized on the ground that it does not take into account that men are not of equal merit. See Gregory Vlastos, "Justice and Equality," in *Social Justice*, ed. Richard B. Brandt (Englewood Cliffs, N. J.: Prentice-Hall, Inc., 1962), pp. 31-72. This criticism may be valid against the naiveté of political documents like the Declaration of the Rights of Man and Citizen (1789) but is less true of more sophisticated accounts like Locke's. On the latter's view, rights belong to *persons*--that is, to moral agents and not simply to creatures resembling human beings in their biological characteristics.

52 Nozick, *op. cit.*, p. 286.

53 J. Rawls, *A Theory of Justice* (Cambridge, Massachusetts: Harvard University Press, 1971), p. 4.

54 *Ibid*, p. 72.

55 Nozick, *op. cit.*, pp. 225-226.

56 *Ibid.*, p. 206.

BIBLIOGRAPHY

The following is not intended as an exhaustive bibliography of the literature on property, but it is hoped that it may be of some value as a list of readings for students. No attempt has been made to list obvious titles by the masters of political thought such as Aristotle, Locke, Rousseau, etc. Only English titles are included.

Agar, H. "Private Property or Capitalism." *American Scholar*, 3 (1934), 396-403.

Baldwin, R. W. *Social Justice*. Oxford: Pergamon Press, 1966.

Barry, Brian. *The Liberal Theory of Justice*. Oxford: Clarendon Press, 1973.

Beaglehole, Ernest. *Property: A Study in Social Psychology*. New York: Macmillan, 1932.

Becker, Lawrence C. *Property Rights, Philosophic Foundations*. London: Routledge and Kegan Paul, 1977.

Benn, S. "Property." In *The Encyclopedia of Philosophy*, edited by P. Edwards. Vol. 5. New York: MacMillan and The Free Press, 1967.

Berle, A. A. and Means, G. C. *The Modern Corporation and Private Property*. New York: Macmillan, 1939.

Berle, A. A. "Property, Production and Revolution." *Columbia Law Review*, 65 (1965) 1-20.

Blume, F. H. "Human Rights and Property Rights." *United States Law Review*, 64 (1930), 581-94.

Blumenfeld, S. L. (ed.) *Property in a Humane Economy: A Selection of Essays*. LaSalle, Ill.: Open Court, 1974.

Boderick, A. "The Radical Middle: The Natural Right of Property in Aquinas and the Popes." *The Solicitor Quarterly*, 3 (1964), 127 ff.

Bond, H. "Possession in the Roman Law." *Law Quarterly Review*, 6 (1890), 259 ff.

Bosanquet, Bernard. "The Principle of Private Property." In *Aspects of the Social Problem*. London: Macmillan, 1895.

Brandt, R. B. (ed.) *Social Justice*. Englewood Cliffs, N. J.: Prentice-Hall, 1962.

Chaudhuri, J. "Toward a Democratic Theory of Property and the Modern Corporation." *Ethics*, 81 (1971), 271-286.

Chubb, Thomas. *Two Enquiries, one of them Concerning Property...* London: J. Roberts, 1717.

Clark, E. H. G. *Man's Birthright: or, The Higher Law of Property*. London: G. P. Putnam's Sons, 1885.

Cohen, M. R. "Property and Sovereignty." In *Law and the Social Order*. New York: Harcourt, Brace and Co., 1933.

Cohen, M. R. and Cohen, F. S. *Readings in Jurisprudence and Legal Philosophy*. New York: Prentice-Hall, 1951.

Coker, F. W. "American Traditions Concerning Property and Liberty." *American Political Science Review*, 30 (1936), 1-23.

Coker, Francis W. (ed.) *Democracy, Liberty and Property; Readings in the American Political Tradition*. New York: Macmillan, 1942.

Cropsey, Joseph. *Polity and Economy: An Interpretation of the Principles of Adam Smith*. The Hague: M. Nijhoff, 1957.

Cropsey, Joseph. "On the Relation of Political Science and Economics." *American Political Science Review*, 54 (1960) 3-14.

Cunliffe, Marcus. *The Right to Property: A Theme in American History*. Leicester: Leicester University Press, 1974.

Curtis, T. D. "Marshall and Weber on Wealth and Property: A Comparative Appraisal." *American Journal of Economics*, 27 (1968), 89-98.

Cutler, A. C. "Some Concepts of Human Rights and Obligations in Classical Protestantism." In *Natural Law and Natural Rights*, edited by A. L. Harding. Dallas: Southern Methodist University Press, 1955.

Czajkowski, C. J. *The Theory of Private Property in John Locke's Political Philosophy*. Notre Dame, Ind.: Dissertation, Notre Dame University, 1941.

Davis, Jerome. *Capitalism and its Culture*. New York: Farrar & Rinehart, 1935.

Day, J. P. "Locke on Property." *Philosophical Quarterly*, 16 (1966), 207-221.

Demsetz, H. "Toward a Theory of Property Rights." *American Economic Review; Papers and Proceedings*, 57 (1967), 347-59.

Denman, D. R. *Origins of Ownership*. London: Allen and Unwin, 1958.

Derrick, Paul. *Lost Property; Proposals for the Distribution of Property in an Industrial Age*. London: D. Dobson, 1947.

Dietze, Gottfried. *In Defence of Property*. Chicago: Henry Regnery, 1963.

Ely, R. T. *Property and Contract in their Relation to the Distribution of Wealth*. New York: Macmillan, 1914.

Ely, Richard T. *Studies in the Evolution of Industrial Society*. London: Macmillan, 1903.

Engels, Friedrich. *The Origin of the Family, Private Property and the State, in the Light of the Researches of Lewis H. Morgan*. New York: International, 1972.

Ericsson, L. O. *Justice in the Distribution of Economic Resources*. Stockholm: Almquist and Wiksell, 1976.

Field, O. P. "Property and Authority: The Modification of Property Rights under American Law." *Journal of Politics*, 3 (1941), 253-75.

Finley, M. I. *Studies in Roman Property*. Cambridge: Cambridge University Press, 1976.

Friedman, M. *Capitalism and Freedom*. Chicago: University of Chicago Press, 1962.

Friedman, W. *Law in a Changing Society*. London: Stevens and Sons, 1959 (Chapter 3.)

Friedman, W. "Property, Freedom, Security and the Supreme Court of the United States." *Modern Law Review*, 19 (1956), 461-477.

Furubotn, F. G. and Pejovich, S. *The Economics of Property Rights*. Cambridge, Mass.: Ballinger, 1974.

Gambs, John S. *Beyond Supply and Demand*. New York: Columbia University Press, 1946.

George, Henry. *Progress and Poverty*. New York: Doubleday and McClure, 1899.

George, Henry. *Social Problems*. New York: Doubleday and McClure, 1900.

Goodwin, William. *Political Justice*. (A Reprint of The Essay on Property.) Edited by H. S. Salt. London: George Allen and Unwin, 1890.

Gore, C., Hobhouse, L. T., Bortlett, V. and others. *Property, its Duties and Rights, Historically, Philosophically and Religiously Regarded*. New York: Macmillan, 1922.

Grace, Frank. *The Concept of Property in Modern Christian Thought*. Urbana, Ill.: University of Illinois Press, 1953.

Grey, T. C. "Property and Need: The Welfare State and Theories of Distributive Justice." *Stanford Law Review* 28 (1976), 877-902.

Hall, J. S. "Possession, Custody, and Ownership: a Philosophical Approach." *The Solicitor*, 27 (1960), 85 ff.

Hall, J. *Theft, Law and Society*. Indianapolis: Bobbs-Merrill, 1952.

Hallowell, A. I. "The Nature and Function of Property as a Social Institution." *Journal of Legal and Political Sociology*. 1 (1943), 115 ff.

Harding, R. W. "The Evolution of Roman Catholic Views of Private Property as a Natural Right." *The Solicitor Quarterly*, 2 (1963), 124 ff.

Harris, D. R. "The Concept of Possession in English Law." *Oxford Essays in Jurisprudence*. Edited by A. G. Guest. London: Oxford University Press, 1961 (Ch. 4.)

Haslam, C. J. *The Evils of Private Property*. London: Netherington; Hulme, W. Chadwick, etc., 1838.

Hayek, F. A. *The Constitution of Liberty*. Chicago: University of Chicago Press, 1960.

Hayek, F. A. *Law, Legislation and Liberty*. Vol. 1, *Rules and Order*. Vol. 2, *The Mirage of Social Justice*. Chicago: University of Chicago Press, 1973.

Hayek, F. A. *Individualism and Economic Order*. Chicago: University of Chicago Press, 1948.

Hayek, F. A. *The Road to Serfdom*. Chicago: The University of Chicago Press, 1944.

Hearne, W. E. *The Theory of Legal Duties and Rights*. London: Trubner and Co., 1883.

Helleiner, K. "Moral Conditions of Economic Growth." *Journal of Economic History*, 11 (1951) 97-116.

Herbert, A. and Levy, J. H. *Taxation and Anarchism*. London: The Personal Rights Association, 1912.

Hilton, John. *Rich Man, Poor Man*. London: George Allen and Unwin, 1944.

Hirschman, A. O. *The Passions and the Interests*. Princeton, N. J.: Princeton University Press, 1967.

Hobhouse, L. T. *The Elements of Social Justice*. London: G. Allen and Unwin, 1922.

Hobhouse, L. T., Wheeler, G. C., and Ginsberg, M. *The Material Culture and Social Institutions of the Simpler Peoples: An Essay in Correlation*. London: Routledge & Kegan Paul, 1915.

Hobson, J. A. *The Science of Wealth*. London: Oxford University Press, 1950.

Hobson, J. A. *Wealth and Life: A Study in Values*. London: Macmillan, 1929.

Hobson, J. A. *Work and Wealth: A Human Valuation*. New York: Macmillan, 1914.

Hodgskin, Thomas. "The Natural and Artificial Right of Property Contrasted. A Series of Letters..." *Labourer*, (1832.)

Hollis, C. *Christianity and Economics*. New York: Hawthorn Books, 1961.

Holmes, O. W. "Possession." *American Law Review*, 12 (1877-78), 688 ff.

Honoré, A. M. "Ownership." In *Oxford Essays in Jurisprudence*. (first series), edited by A. G. Guest. Oxford: Oxford University Press, 1968.

Honoré, A. M. "Social Justice." In R. S. Summers (ed.), *Essays in Legal Philosophy*. Berkeley and Los Angeles: University of California Press, 1968.

Hoselitz, B. F. *Sociological Aspects of Economic Growth*. Glencoe, Ill.: Free Press, 1960.

Hunt, E. K. *Property and Prophets; the Evolution of Economic Institutions and Ideologies*. New York: Harper and Row, 1975.

Jackson, John Hampden. *Marx, Proudhon and European Socialism*. London, English Universities Press, 1957.

Jenks, E. "Property and the Courts of Justice." *Sociological Review*, 27 (1935), 56-74.

Jones, Alfred Winslow. *Life, Liberty, and Property; a Story of Conflict and a Measurement of Conflicting Rights*. New York: Octagon, 1964.

Jones, J. W. "Forms of Ownership." *Tulane Law Review*, 22 (1947-48), 82 ff.

Jouvenel, Bertrand de. *The Ethics of Redistribution*. Cambridge: Cambridge University Press, 1952.

Kamenka, E. and Neale, R. S. (Editors) *Feudalism, Capitalism and Beyond*. London: Edward Arnold, 1975.

Kardiner, Abram. *The Individual and His Society, the Psychodynamics of Primitive Social Organization*. New York: Columbia University Press, 1939.

Kelsen, H. "Foundations of Democracy." *Ethics*, 66 (1955), 86-94.

Kinnear, J. B. *Principles of Property*. London: Smith, Elder and Co., 1914.

Kitch, M. J. *Capitalism and the Reformation*. London: Longman, 1967.

Knight, F. H., and Merrian, T. W. *The Economic Order and Religion*. London: Paul, Trench, Trubner, 1948.

Kohak, E. "Possessing, Owning, Belonging." *Dissent*, 21 (1974), 344-53.

Kruse, L. F. V. *The Right of Property*. London: Oxford University Press, 1939.

Lacy, E. W. "Relation of Property and Dominion to the Law of Nature." *Speculum*, 24 (1949), 407-9.

Lafargue, Paul. *The Evolution of Property from Savagery to Civilization*. London: S. Sonnenschein, 1905.

Larkin, P. *Property in the Eighteenth Century with Special Preference to England and Locke*. London: Longmans, Green and Co., 1930.

Laski, Harold. *The Rise of Liberalism: The Philosophy of a Business Civilization*. New York: Harper and Brothers, 1936.

Laveleye, E. L. V. *Primitive Property*. Translated by G. R. L. Marriot. London: Macmillan, 1878.

Lawson, F. H. *Introduction to the Law of Property*. Oxford: Clarendon Press, 1958.

Lefebvre, Marcus. "'Private Property' According to St. Thomas and Recent Papal Encyclicals." In the Blackfriars Translation of *Summa Theologiae*, Vol. 38. London: Eyre and Spottiswode, 1975.

Lester, W. R. *Poverty and Plenty: The True National Dividend; The Pros and Cons of Social Credit*. London: Hogarth Press, 1935.

Letourneau, C. *Property: Its Origin and Development*. London: W. Scott, 1892.

Lewinski, J. S. *The Origin of Property*. London: Constable and Sons, 1913.

Lewis, Thomas J. "Adam Smith: The Labour Market as the Basis of Natural Right." *Journal of Economic Issues*, 11 (1977), 21-50.

Lewis, Thomas. "Acquisition and Anxiety: Aristotle's Case Against the Market." *Canadian Journal of Economics*, 11 (1978), 69-90.

Lightwood, J. M. "Possession in Roman Law." *Law Quarterly Review*, 3 (1887), 32 ff.

Lindbeck, Assar. *The Political Economy of the New Left: An Outsider's View*. New York: Harper and Row, 1977.

Little, I. M. D. *A Critique of Welfare Economics*. Oxford: Clarendon Press, 1950.

Long, D. G. *Bentham on Liberty*. Toronto: University of Toronto Press, 1977.

Lowie, R. H. "Incorporeal Property in Primitive Society." *Yale Law Journal*, 37 (1927-28), 551 ff.

McKeon, R. "Development of the Concept of Property in Political Philosophy: A Study of the Background of the Constitution." *Ethics*, 48 (1938), 297-366.

Macpherson, C. B. *Democratic Theory; Essays in Retrieval*. Oxford: Clarendon Press, 1973.

Macpherson, C. B. "Human Rights and Property Rights." *Dissent*, 24 (1977), 72-7.

Macpherson, C. B. *The Political Theory of Possessive Individualism: Hobbes to Locke*. Oxford: Clarendon Press, 1962.

Macpherson, C. B. (editor.) *Property: Mainstream and Critical Positions*. Toronto: University of Toronto Press, 1978.

Maine, H. G. *The Economics of Legal Relationships: Readings in the Theory of Property Rights*. St. Paul: West Pub. Co., 1975.

Maritain, Jacques. *The Rights of Man and Natural Law*. New York: C. Scribner's Sons, 1943.

Meade, J. E. *Efficiency, Equality, and the Ownership of Property*. Cambridge, Mass.: Harvard University Press, 1965.

Meislin, B. J., and Cohen, M. L., "Background of the Biblical Law Against Usury." *Comparative Studies in Society and History*, 6 (1963-64), 250-67.

Merino, D. B. *Natural Justice and Private Property*. St. Louis: B. Herder, 1923.

Mises, Ludwig von. *Human Action*. New Haven: Yale University Press, 1949.

Moore, James. "Hume's Theory of Justice and Property." *Political Studies*, 24 (1976), 103-19.

Moulds, H. "Private Property in John Locke's State of Nature." *American Journal of Economics*, 23 (1964), 179-88.

Mulsow, Thomas A. *Allodialism: The Ownership of an Estate: The Pure Philosophy of Economy: The Case for a Non-Reciprocal System*. Hicksville, N. Y.: Exposition Press, 1974.

Myrdal, G. *The Political Element in the Development of Economic Theory*. Cambridge, Mass.: Harvard University Press, 1954.

Nelson, B. N. *The Idea of Usury*. Princeton: Princeton University Press, 1949.

Noonan, J. T. *The Scholastic Analysis of Usury*. Cambridge, Mass.: Harvard University Press, 1957.

Noyes, C. Reinold. *The Institution of Property*. New York: Longmans, Green and Co., 1936.

Nozick, R. *Anarchy, State and Utopia*. New York: Basic Books, 1974.

O'Brien, G. A. T. *An Essay on Mediaeval Economic Teaching*. London: Longmans, Green, and Co., 1920.

Ogilvie, William. *Birthright in Land: An Essay on the Right of Property in Land.* London: Kegan Paul, Trench Trubner, 1891.

Oliver, H. M. *A Critique of Socioeconomic Goals.* Bloomington, Ind.: Indiana University Press, 1954.

Parel, A. J. "The Thomistic Theory of Property, Regime, and the Good Life." In *Calgary Aquinas Studies*, edited by A. J. Parel, pp. 77-104. Toronto: Pontifical Institute of Mediaeval Studies, 1978.

Paton, G. W. "Possession." *Res Judicata*, 1 (1935), 187 ff.

Patton, Charles. *The Effects of Property upon Society and Government Investigated...* London, 1797.

Petre, M. D. "Property-Possession-Usufruct." *Hibbert Journal*, 41 (1942), 60-7.

Philbrick, F. S. "Changing Conceptions of Property in Law." *University of Pennsylvania Law Review*, 86 (1938), 691 ff.

Poirot, Paul L. "Property Rights and Human Rights," *Essays on Liberty*. (Vol. 2). Irvington-on-Hudson, N. Y.: Foundation for Economic Education, 1954.

Proudhon, Pierre Joseph. *What is Property; An Inquiry Into the Principle of Right and of Government.* Translated by B. R. Tucker. London: William Reeves, 1902.

Pryor, F. L. *Property and Industrial Organization in Communist and Capitalist Nations.* Bloomington, Ind.: Indiana University Press, 1973.

Rawls, John. *A Theory of Justice.* Cambridge, Mass.: Harvard University Press, 1971.

Read, Samuel. *Political Economy: An Inquiry into the Natural Grounds of Right to Vendible Property or Wealth.* Clifton, N. J.: A. M. Kelly, 1976.

Rescher, Nicholas. *Distributive Justice.* Indianapolis: Bobbs-Merrill, 1966.

Robertson, H. M. *Aspects of the Rise of Economic Individualism.* New York: Kelly and Millman, 1959.

Roche, A. "Classics and Property." *Dublin Review*, 205 (1939), 390-403.

Rodger, Alan. *Owners and Neighbors in Roman Law.* Oxford: Clarendon Press, 1972.

Ross, Alf. *On Law and Justice.* London: Stevens, 1958.

Rothbard, Murray N. "Human Rights are Property Rights." *Essays on Liberty*. (Vol. 6). Irvington-on-Hudson, N. Y.: Foundation for Economic Education, 1954.

Rothbard, M. *Man, Economy, and State.* 2 vols. Princeton: D. van Nostrand, 1962.

Rothbard, Murray N. "On Freedom and the Law." *New Individualist Review*, (1962.)

Rothbard, Murray N. *Power and Market; Government and the Economy.* Menlo Park, California: Institute for Humane Studies, 1970.

Runciman, W. G. *Relative Deprivation and Social Justice*. London: Routledge and Kegan Paul, 1966.

Ryan, A. "Locke and the Dictatorship of the Bourgeoisie." *Political Studies*, 13 (1965), 219-30.

Samuels, W. J. "Physiocratic Theory of Property and State." *Quarterly Journal of Economics*, 75 (1961), 96-111.

Schlatter, R. *Private Property, The History of an Idea*. London: Allen and Unwin, 1951.

Schumpeter, J. A. *The Theory of Economic Development*. Cambridge: Harvard University Press, 1934.

Seckler, David William. *Thorstein Veblen and the Institutionalists: A Study in the Social Philosophy of Economics*. Boulder: Colorado Associated University Press, 1975.

Sennholz, Mary H. (ed.) *On Freedom and Free Enterprise*. Princeton, N. J.: D. Van Nostrand, 1972.

Serra, W. G. *Property, its Substance and Value*. Translated by T. V. Holmes. London: Figurehead, 1935.

Shatzman, I. *Senatorial Wealth and Roman Politics*. Brussels: Latomus, 1975.

Simpson, A. W. B. "The Analysis of Legal Concepts." *Law Quarterly Review*, 80 (1964), 535-558.

Skelton, N. "Private Property: a Unionist Ideal." *Spectator*, 132 (1924), 702-3.

Skidmore, Thomas. *The Rights of Man to Property*. New York: A. Ming, Jr., 1829.

Smith, David R. *Ownership and Sovereignty; an Outline of the True Republic*. Cohoes, N. Y.: Clark and Foster, 1883.

Sombart, W. *The Quintessence of Capitalism: A Study of the History and Psychology of the Modern Businessman*. London: T. F. Unwin, 1915.

Spengler, J. J. and Allen, W. (editors) *Essays in Economic Thought: Aristotle to Marshall*. Chicago: Rand McNally, 1960.

Stark, Werner. *The Contained Economy: An Interpretation of Medieval Economic Thought*. Aquinas Society of London, Papers, 26. London: Blackfriars, 1956.

Stone, J. *Social Dimensions of Law and Justice*. London: Stevens and Sons, 1966.

Strahan, J. A. *A General View of the Law of Property*. (7th. ed.) London: Stevens and Sons, 1926.

Tawney, R. H. *The Acquisitive Society*. London: G. Bell, 1922.

Tawney, R. H. *Religion and the Rise of Capitalism: An Historical Study*. New York: Harcourt, Brace, 1926.

Tawney, R. H. *The Sickness of an Acquisitive Society*. London: The Fabian Society and George Allen & Unwin, 1920.

Temple, John. *What is Property? Observations on Property; addressed to the King, the Lords and the Commons*. London, 1837.

Thayer, A. S. "Possession and Ownership." *Law Quarterly Review*, 23 (1907), 175-314.

Trever, A. A. *A History of Greek Economic Thought.* Chicago: University of Chicago Press, 1916.

Tucker, Benjamin R. *Individual Liberty.* New York: Vanguard Press, 1926.

Veblen, Thorstein. *Absentee Ownership and Business Enterprise in Recent Times: The Case of America.* New York: A. M. Kelly, bookseller, 1964. (first ed. 1923)

Veblen, Thorstein. "The Beginnings of Ownership." *American Journal of Sociology*, (1898), 352-365.

Veblen, Thorstein. *The Theory of the Leisure Class.* (Introduction by J. K. Galbraith.) Boston: Houghton Mifflin, 1973.

Viner, Jacob. "Adam Smith and Laissez-Faire." *Journal of Political Economy*, 35 (1927), 198-232.

Wallas, G. *The Great Society: A Psychological Analysis.* New York: Macmillan, 1914.

Wallas, G. "Property Under Socialism." *Fabian Essays in Socialism.* London: Fabian Society, 1931.

Warbasse, J. P. "Private Ownership of Property." *Co-operation*, 14 (1928), 204-6.

Watt, Lewis. *Capitalism and Morality.* London: Cassell and Co., 1929.

Weber, Max. *The Protestant Ethic and the Spirit of Capitalism.* Translated by T. Parsons, Foreword by R. H. Tawney. London: George Allen and Unwin, 1930.

Weber, Max. *The Theory of Social and Economic Organization.* Translated by A. M. Henderson and T. Parsons. Glencoe, Ill.: Free Press, 1947.

Weisskoph, W. A. *The Psychology of Economics.* Chicago: University of Chicago Press, 1955.

Wells, H. G. "Anatomy of Frustration: the Frustration of Abundance." *Spectator*, 156 (1936), 608-10.

Wilken, F. *New Forms of Ownership in Industry.* Varanasi: Sarva Seva Sangh Prakashan, 1962.

Winch, Donald. *Adam Smith's Politics: An Essay in Historiographic Revision.* Cambridge: Cambridge University Press, 1978.

INDEX

Acton, J. E. (Lord), 336, 340
Adam, 122, 126-127, 130
Addison, Joseph, 149, 152-153
Aelians, 76
Agrippa, Julius, 72
Agrippa, Marcus, 71
Albertario, A., 47
Althusser, Louis, 116, 196-197
Ambrose, 98
Ammianus, 65
Anne I, 152
Antony, Mark, 64
Apollinaris, Sidonius, 64
Appleby, Joyce, 151, 163
Arescusa, 71
Aquinas, Thomas, 4-5, 88-111, 114, 120, 122-123, 129, 132, 141-143,
    372
Aristotle, 3-5, 8, 12-32, 42, 99-101, 103, 141-142, 145, 182, 223,
    260, 344, 348, 352
Atticus, 62-63, 66, 73
Augustine, 5, 172
Augustus, 68-69, 71, 76
Austen, Jane, 58-59
Austin, John, 230
Bacon, Francis, 325
Baldwin, R. W., 347
Barbeyrac, Jean, 125-127, 130, 175
Barker, Ernest, 17, 19
Barrington, Daines, 224
Becker, L., 194
Becker, Marvin, 154
Bentham, Jeremiah, 221
Bentham, Jeremy, 4-8, 140, 143, 164, 195, 220-254, 257-263, 265, 268,
    270-271, 274, 336, 346
Berle, A. A., 343
Beseler, G. V., 44, 46-47
Blackstone, William, 124, 221-222, 224-229, 233, 239, 250
Boethius, 103
Bolingbroke, Henry, 147, 171
Bosanquet, Bernard, 275
Brady, Robert, 173
Britannicus, 69
Brutus, 63
Buckland, W. W., 36, 44, 46
Buffon, G. L., 158, 183, 188
Burdett, Francis, 230
Burke, Edmund, 336
Burlamaqui, J.-J., 224
Burlington, Earl of (Richard), 61
Bynkershoek, Cornelius, 175

Cabet, Etienne, 115
Caesar, Julius, 60, 63-64
Carmichael, Gerschom, 174-175
Catullus, 60
Cellini, Benevuto, 40
Celsus, 65
Charles II, 118
Cicero, 42, 54-68, 73, 98, 124
Cicero, Marcus, 58, 66-69
Cicero, Tullia, 66-67
Cicero, Quintus, 62, 68-69
Claudius, 69
Coke, Edward, 224
Coleridge, S. T., 260, 272, 274
Comte, Auguste, 90, 261
Copleston, Frederick, 128
Crook, J. A., 68-69
Cropsey, Joseph, 144
Cumberland, Richard, 175
Daphnis, 64
D'Arms, John, 66
Davenant, Charles, 171
David, 130
Day, J. P., 131
Defoe, Daniel, 149-150, 152, 156
Dellius, 72
Delolme, Jean-Louis, 224
Descartes, René, 90, 325
Devonshire, Duke of (William Cavendish), 61
Diderot, Denis, 190
Diogenes, 53
Disraeli, Bengamin, 242
Dobb, Maurice, 116
Domna, Julia, 72
Driver, Charles, 115
Dunn, John, 116, 173
Dupin, P.-C.-F., 170
Dutot, 170
Ericsson, L. O., 348
Eros, 71
Fairfax, B., 61
Fairfax, Thomas (Lord), 61
Ferguson, Adam, 163, 172, 336
Feuerbach, Ludwig, 312
Filmer, Robert, 118-119, 122, 124, 126-128, 130, 132, 146, 148, 175
Forbes, Duncan, 144
Foucault, Michel, 116
Fourier, F. M., 369
Frankena, William, 348
Friedman, Milton, 3, 8
Gadamer, H. G., 116
Gerson, Jean, 120
Gibbon, Edward, 156-159, 162
Girard, P. F., 36
Gray, Thomas, 56
Green, T. H., 3-4, 6, 275
Grotius, Hugo, 119-120, 123-126, 128-131, 155, 175, 224
Grün, Karl, 115

Hale, Matthew, 224
Halliday, R. J., 261
Hammurabi, 43
Harrington, James, 144-148, 163, 169, 175
Hayek, Friedrich, 334-357, 366
Hegel, G. W. F., 3-4, 6, 8, 186, 261, 272
Helvétius, C. A., 249
Hirschman, Albert, 152-153
Hobbes, Thomas, 5-6, 144-145, 163-164, 167, 181-182, 190, 196, 272
Hobhouse, L. T., 275
Home, Henry, 175
Honoré, A. M., 271, 348
Horace, 53-54, 63-65, 67, 72
Houseman, A. E., 73
Humboldt, Wilhelm von, 260
Hume, David, 140, 144, 159, 161, 163, 169-172, 175, 190, 233-235, 240-
    241, 245-246, 248-249, 257, 262-263, 274, 325, 336, 341, 346
Humphreys, James, 230-231, 236
Hundert, E. J., 116
Hunt, E. K., 141
Hutcheson, Francis, 174-175
Huxley, Aldous, 262
Irnerius, 46
James (Duke of York), 118
Javolenus, 76
Jefferson, Thomas, 3, 336
Jesus, 38
Jones, A. M. H., 68
Jouvenel, Bertrand de, 338, 344
Julian, 42, 47
Justinian, 36, 39-41, 44, 46
Kames, H. H. (Lord), 174
Kant, Immanuel, 89, 248, 271-272, 275, 347, 362
Kantorowicz, Hermann, 46
Kelly, John, 37
Keohane, N. O., 180
Kipling, Rudyard, 55-56
Kunkel, Wolfgang, 44
Laslett, Peter, 118, 125
Law, John, 170
Lecky, William, 171
Lenel, O., 45-47
Littleton, A. C., 224
Locke, John, 4, 17, 114-138, 140, 142-144, 146-151, 155-156, 160, 163,
    167, 173-175, 189, 194, 196, 204-206, 208, 211, 224-226, 235,
    248, 256-257, 271-274, 276, 300, 336, 341, 344, 360, 362, 367-
    373
Luther, Martin, 141, 306
Lycurgus, 154
Lyons, D., 245
MacAdam, James, 203-217
Macaulay, Thomas, 263, 274
McCulloch, John, 164
Machiavelli, Niccolo, 142, 152, 156, 224
MacIntosh, James, 230
Macpherson, C. B., 2-9, 115, 143, 145, 247-248, 271-272
McNair, A. D., 44

Maevius, 70
Maine, Henry, 340
Malthus, Thomas, 257
Mandeville, Bernard, 153, 163, 172-173, 190, 194, 196
Mark, 319
Marx, Karl, 4, 90, 115, 141-142, 145, 163, 187, 257-258, 275-276,
    282-315
Melania (the Younger), 53
Melon, J.-F., 170
Midas, 23
Mill, James, 164, 263, 271, 274-275
Mill, J. S., 7-8, 141, 248, 256-280, 336, 342-344
Mingay, G. E., 60
Molina, Louis de, 120
Montesquieu, Charles, 152, 154, 157-158, 163, 170, 172
Moore, G. E., 258
Moore, James, 140
More, Thomas, 4
Myrdal, Gunnar, 335
Namier, Lewis, 171
Neale, R. S., 116
Nero, 69
Newcastle, Duke of (T. P. Holles), 61
Noah, 130
Nörr, D., 42
Novalis (Hardenberg, F. L.), 260
Noyes, Alfred, 64
Nozick, Robert, 131, 271-272, 275, 344, 348, 352, 360-379
Octavian, 64
Odysseus, 62-63, 306
Pandora, 153
Papinian, 75
Parel, A. J., 141
Partsch, Joseph, 46
Paul, 45, 74-75
Pedius, Sextus, 74
Pinianus, 53
Pitt, William (the Elder), 171
Pitt, William (the Younger), 60
Pius XI, 41
Plato, 12, 14, 23, 25-27, 154, 194
Plautus, 41
Pliny, (the Younger) 55, 64, 67
Pocock, J. G. A., 116, 132, 167-177
Polanyi, Karl, 132
Pompey, 64, 66
Popper, Karl, 173, 261, 318, 325, 339, 347
Postumus, 54, 72
Proculians, 39-40
Prometheus, 153
Pufendorf, Samuel, 119, 125-126, 129, 131, 155, 174-175, 224
Rand, Ayn, 365
Rawls, John, 8, 224, 245-246, 248, 258, 276, 336, 348-349, 351, 354,
    375-376
Rawson, Elizabeth, 56-58, 60-61, 63, 65-68, 73
Reid, Thomas, 174
Ricardo, David, 164, 257, 263, 268, 274
Robbins, Lionel, 269

Robertson, William, 158-159
Rodger, Alan, 38
Rousseau, J.-J., 3-4, 158, 160, 163, 180-217, 221, 248, 375
Rufus, 59
Runciman, W. G., 348, 350
Sabinians, 39-40
Saint-Simon, Henri, 261
Schiller, Friedrich, 260
Seia, 70
Seneca, 53, 65, 67
Senior, Nassau, 301
Sentians, 76
Shaftesbury, Earl of (A. A. Cooper), 172, 174-175
Shakespeare, William, 39
Skinner, B. F., 262
Skinner, Quentin, 116
Smith, Adam, 150, 162-164, 170-172, 174-175, 241-243, 336-337, 339
Socrates, 25-27, 182, 246, 248
Somersett, Duke of (Seymour), 61
Soto, Domingo de, 120
Spencer, Herbert, 257, 271-272, 275
Stichus, 71
Strauss, Leo, 115
Suarez, Francisco, 120-125, 127, 130, 143
Suetonius, 67
Sulla, 64
Swift, Jonathan, 147
Tacitus, 67, 156-157
Taylor, Charles, 116
Taylor, Harriet, 257, 264
Temple, Sir William, 145, 161
Thornton, W. T., 272
Titius, 70
Titus, 69
Tocqueville, Alexis de, 275, 336
Tooke, John Horne, 230
Tribe, Keith, 116, 132
Tucker, Josiah, 154, 159-161
Tully, James, 143-144, 146, 173, 175
Tyrrell, James, 174
Ulpian, 44-45, 75-76, 344-345
Varro, 35
Viehweg, T., 42
Virgil, 55, 64, 67
Vitoria, Francisco de, 120
Voltaire, François, 190
Watson, Alan, 36, 43
Wilson, Harold, 245
Winch, Donald, 164
Winstanley, Gerrard, 4
Wolin, Sheldon, 249
Wollheim, Richard, 261
Yolton, J. W., 131